# Through a Glass Darkly

## The Social Sciences Look at the Neoliberal University

# Through a Glass Darkly

The Social Sciences Look at the Neoliberal University

Edited by Margaret Thornton

Australian
National
University

PRESS

*In memory of Scott*

**ANU PRESS**

Published by ANU Press
The Australian National University
Acton ACT 2601, Australia
Email: anupress@anu.edu.au
This title is also available online at press.anu.edu.au

National Library of Australia Cataloguing-in-Publication entry

| | |
|---|---|
| Creator: | Thornton, Margaret, author. |
| Title: | Through a glass darkly : The social sciences look at the neoliberal university / Margaret Thornton. |
| ISBN: | 9781925022131 (paperback) 9781925022148 (ebook) |
| Subjects: | Education, Higher--Australia--Evaluation. Higher education and state--Australia. Education, Higher--Economic aspects--Australia. Social sciences--Study and teaching (Higher)--Australia. Educational change--Australia. |
| Dewey Number: | 378.94 |

Cover image: *Three Figures*, 1971. Carlos Merida (1891-1984)/SOMAAP. Licensed by Viscopy, 2014. Credit: Private CollectionPhoto @ Christie's Images/Bridgeman Images

Cover design and layout by ANU Press

ACADEMY OF
THE SOCIAL SCIENCES
IN AUSTRALIA

# Contents

## Part I: Theorising the Modern University

## Part II: Markets, Managers and Mandarins

## Part III: Education for the 'Real World'

## Part IV: Conditions of Knowledge Production

## Part V: Telling It How It Is

## Part VI: University Futures?

# Acknowledgements

This collection emerged from a workshop entitled 'Markets and the Modern University', which Glenn Withers AO and I jointly convened in Canberra in 2013. The aim of the workshop was to explore the impact of the market on the contemporary academy from the perspective of the social sciences. I thank Glenn warmly for his support in organising and running the workshop.

The workshop was funded by the Academy of Social Sciences in Australia (ASSA) in its Workshop Program for 2012–13 and I am grateful to ASSA for financial support and to Dr John Beaton, ASSA's Executive Director, for agreeing to consider our application at a late stage. Funding allowed us to bring leading social scientists together with several early-career researchers from a range of disciplines to Canberra for the workshop.

I appreciate the support of the ANU College of Law and its Dean, Professor Stephen Bottomley, in hosting the workshop. (The round-table format of the Moot Court was conducive to discussion and did not prove to be the ordeal that some participants feared!) I thank members of the College Outreach and Administrative Support Team (COAST) — Christine de Bono, Wendy Mohring and Kristian Drexel and Sarah Hull — for administering the workshop with their customary professionalism.

I am grateful to Professor Don Anton and the ANU College of Law Press Advisory Committee for processing the book proposal and arranging for the refereeing of the manuscript. I also acknowledge the role of the referees in their assiduous reading of the text and for making helpful suggestions to improve it. With no tickable box for refereeing in the audit culture, this task may no longer be valued by management, but it remains integral to the scholarly enterprise and is appreciated by authors.

I thank John Owen for his careful work in copy-editing and styling the manuscript, as well as David Gardiner and the ANU Press team for skilfully turning this manuscript into a book, which is enhanced by Carlos Merida's *Three Figures* (1971) on the cover.

I thank Nick James and the *Legal Education Review* for permission to reproduce '"Selling the Dream": Law School Branding and the Illusion of Choice' in a different form from that which appeared in (2013) 23 *Legal Education Review* 249–71.

Finally, I thank the contributors for their fine essays, each of which assisted in confirming the essential but sometimes discomfiting role of the social sciences as critique and conscience of society.

Margaret Thornton
ANU College of Law
The Australian National University
Canberra
October 2014

# Contributors

**Tony Aspromourgos** is Professor of Economics in the University of Sydney. He has published extensively on the history of economic thought in particular, in all the major field journals, and is the author of *The Science of Wealth: Adam Smith and the Framing of Political Economy* (Routledge 2009). Tony Aspromourgos is a founding and continuing member of the Editorial Board of the *European Journal of the History of Economic Thought*, and is Co-editor of *History of Economics Review*.

**Peter Beilharz** is Professor of Sociology at La Trobe University. He has taught and researched in Australian and American universities for 35 years. He is author or editor of 24 books and 200 articles. He has edited the international journal of social theory, *Thesis Eleven*, since 1980.

**Judith Bessant** is a professor at RMIT University in Melbourne. Her areas of research include political theory, sociology, new media, justice studies, youth studies, education and social policy. Judith has been active as a policy adviser to local and international NGOs and governments, and has developed curriculum for the state government and within the university. She also loves teaching.

**Jill Blackmore** is Alfred Deakin Professor in the Faculty of Arts and Education, Deakin University, Director of the Centre for Research in Educational Futures and Innovation, and Fellow of the Academy of Social Sciences. Her research interests include, from a feminist perspective, globalisation, education policy and governance across education in universities, TAFE, schools and community; local/global articulations of internationalisation; educational restructuring, organisational change and innovation; educational leadership and spatial redesign; teachers' and academics' work and equity policy. Publications include *Educational Leadership and Nancy Fraser*, Routledge (forthcoming); *Performing and Reforming Leaders: gender, educational restructuring and organisational change*, (with J. Sachs (2007)) SUNY Press.

**Rebecca Boden** is Professor of Critical Management at the University of Roehampton, London. Her primary research focus is on how regimes of management and accounting control affect sites of knowledge creation, with a particular emphasis on universities. She is widely published in both management and education journals, where she espouses imaginative solutions to the travails of higher education globally. She is currently a full partner in UNIKE, a major European Union-funded project investigating universities in the knowledge economy.

**Geoffrey Brennan** is an economist who works at the intersection of economics and moral and political philosophy. He holds positions in the Philosophy Program at The Australian National University (ANU), and jointly in Philosophy at UNC-Chapel Hill and Political Science at Duke University where he is Director of the joint Duke/UNC PPE Program. His most recent book is *Explaining Norms* (CUP 2013) written jointly with Robert Goodin, Lena Ericsson and Nicholas Southwood.

**Professor Jennifer Corbett** is Pro Vice-chancellor (Research and Research Training) at ANU. She was previously Executive Director, Australia-Japan Research Centre, Crawford School of Public Policy at ANU. She also holds an appointment as Reader on the Economy of Japan at the University of Oxford. Her research interests are the economic performance and economic policy of Japan, the operation of financial systems and financial integration in the Asian region. Details of her current research may be found at https://researchers.anu.edu.au/researchers/corbett-jm.

**Dr Johannah Fahey** is Senior Research Fellow in the Faculty of Education at Monash University. Her research interests focus on education and global studies, and are informed by her expertise in cultural studies. Her most recent jointly edited book is *Globalising the Research Imagination*, published by Routledge in 2009. She is currently working on a jointly edited book called *In the Realm of the Senses: the Sensory Dynamics of Privilege*. She is currently a Senior Research Fellow on the ARC team project called 'Elite independent schools in globalising circumstances: a multi-sited global ethnography'.

**Hannah Forsyth** is Lecturer in Australian History at the Australian Catholic University in Sydney. Hannah is currently writing a book, *Knowing Australia: a history of the modern university* for UNSW Press, based on her PhD, which was completed at the University of Sydney in 2012. Hannah's current research includes the history of universities, historical knowledge and citizenship in Australia and the history of Australian professions.

**Kanishka Jayasuriya** is currently Director of the Indo-Pacific Governance Research Centre (IPGRC) and Professor of Politics and International studies at the University of Adelaide. He has held teaching and research appointments in several Australian and overseas universities including ANU, the University of Sydney, Murdoch University, National University of Singapore, and City University of Hong Kong. He has published extensively and is author or editor of nine books and over 100 articles.

**Fiona Jenkins** is a Senior Lecturer in Philosophy at the Research School of Social Sciences, ANU, and Convenor of ANU Gender Institute. Her current research covers two projects, one which focuses on Judith Butler's contribution to questions of political legitimacy, violence and non-violence, in post-national frameworks; the other on gender equity in academic disciplines. She has published widely in journals and is the joint editor of *Women in Philosophy; What Needs to Change?* (OUP 2013); *Allegiance and Identity in a Globalising World* (CUP 2014), as well as special issues of *Angelaki* and *Australian Feminist Studies*.

**Jane Kenway** is an Australian Professorial Fellow of the Australian Research Council, member of the Australian Academy of Social Sciences and Professor, Education Faculty at Monash. Her research expertise is in the sociology of education and focuses on the politics of educational change in the context of wider social, cultural and political change. Her more recent jointly authored books are *Haunting the Knowledge Economy (*Routledge 2006),and *Masculinity Beyond the Metropolis* (Palgrave, 2006). Her most recent jointly edited book is *Globalising the Research Imagination* (Routledge, 2008). She currently leads the ARC international team project called 'Elite independent schools in globalising circumstances: a multi-sited global ethnography'.

**Diane Kirkby** FAAH, FASSA, is Professor of History at La Trobe University, Melbourne. She has now written several books exploring the cultural and political history of work, for women, for barmaids, for seafarers and including a prize-winning biography of feminist labour journalist Alice Henry. She has a continuing research interest in the cultural and social importance of work and workplaces and in the intersection of labour, law and history.

**Bruce Lindsay** completed his PhD at ANU College of Law in 2010 with a study of decision-making and administrative law standards in the university setting. He presently works as a researcher and project officer with the Environment Defenders Office in Melbourne and with Trust for Nature.

**Professor Andrew Macintyre** is Deputy Vice-Chancellor International & Vice President at RMIT. He was previously Dean of the College of Asia & the Pacific at ANU. His primary research interests currently centre on enhancing universities, international affairs and Southeast Asian political economy. His most recent scholarly publication is *Integrating Regions: Asia in Comparative Context*, Stanford University Press, 2013 (co-edited with Miles Kahler).

**Inger Mewburn** has been a research educator since 2005, following a 10-year career as an architect. She is the founder and managing editor of the 'Thesis Whisperer' blog and is currently the Director of Research Training at ANU, where she co-ordinates, measures and evaluates cross-disciplinary research training. She writes scholarly papers, books and book chapters about research students and their experiences.

**Nigel Palmer** is a doctoral candidate with ANU. He was formerly a Research Fellow with the University of Melbourne's Centre for the Study of Higher Education, and prior to that was National President of the Council of Australian Postgraduate Associations from 2007–2009, and CAPA's National Policy and Research Advisor in 2010. His research interests include graduate mobility, higher education quality assurance, management and research, and research training policy and practice.

**Dr Kerreen Reiger** is an Australian historical sociologist who has published widely on family relationships, advocacy, organisational change and its impact on professional work in health care and university settings. She is presently a Chief Investigator on the Australian Generations oral history project, and is working on a biography of Professor Murray Enkin, a founder then a critic of the use of evidence-based medicine. Her concern about the deteriorating conditions of higher education reflects not only experience, but fears about the implications for future generations, including her grandchildren, of the demise of critical thinking they portend.

**Lucinda Shannon** graduated with a Bachelor in Arts and Laws from ANU in 2010, majoring in Gender Studies. Her law degree left her with the feeling that she was not so much interested in the black letter law, but in the people and systems that make the laws and those that have to live under them. She currently works in LGBTIQ rights and education in Tasmania, in a role that gives her time to pursue creative endeavours.

**Margaret Thornton** is Professor of Law and ANU Public Policy Fellow at ANU. Her research interests span feminist legal theory, discrimination law and policy, legal education and the corporatisation of universities. Her most recent book is *Privatising the Public University: The Case of Law*, Routledge, 2012. She is a Fellow of the Academy of Social Sciences in Australia, a Foundation Fellow of the Australian Academy of Law and a former President of the Association for the Public University.

**Glenn Withers** is an Honorary Professor of Economics at ANU. He has held previous appointments at ANU, Cambridge, Harvard, Macquarie and La Trobe universities. He helped to establish Universities Australia, the Crawford School of Public Policy, the Productivity Commission, and the Australia and New Zealand School of Government, and has advised government, business and community organisations in Australia and overseas. Glenn researches and teaches in the applied economics and policy areas. He has a Harvard PhD and was awarded an AO in 1991 for development of the Australian immigration points system.

# Acronyms and Abbreviations

| | |
|---|---|
| AARNET | Australian Academic and Research Network |
| ACDE | Australian Council of Deans of Education |
| ACOLA | Australian Council of Learned Academies |
| All ER | All England Reports |
| ALTC | Australian Learning and Teaching Council |
| ANU | The Australian National University |
| AQFC | Australian Qualifications Framework Council |
| ARC | Australian Research Council |
| ASQA | Australian Skills Quality Authority |
| BURF | Better Universities Renewal Fund |
| CSIRO | Commonwealth Scientific and Industrial Research Organisation |
| CTEC | Commonwealth Tertiary Education Commission |
| Cth | Commonwealth |
| CV | Curriculum Vitae |
| DfL | Design for Learning |
| DSTO | Defence Science and Technology Organisation |
| DVC | Deputy Vice-chancellor |
| EBA | Enterprise Bargaining Agreement |
| EFTSU | Equivalent Full Time Student Unit |
| EIF | Education Investment Fund |
| ELR | Education Law Reports |
| EOWW | Equal Opportunity for Women in the Workplace |

| ERA | Excellence in Research for Australia |
| ESOS | Education Services for Overseas Students |
| FCA | Federal Court of Australia |
| FHUSS | Faculty of Humanities and Social Sciences |
| FWA | Fair Work Australia |
| FOI | Freedom of Information |
| GDP | Gross Domestic Product |
| GFC | Global Financial Crisis |
| Go8 | Group of Eight |
| GSDS | Gender Sexuality and Diversity Studies |
| HASS | Humanities and Social Sciences |
| HE | Higher Education |
| HECS | Higher Education Contribution Scheme |
| HEEF | Higher Education Endowment Fund |
| HEI | Higher Education Institution (UK) |
| HES | Higher Education Supplement |
| HR | Human Resources |
| HREOC | Human Rights and Equal Opportunity Commission |
| HUSS | Humanities and Social Sciences |
| IDP | International Development Program |
| KPI | Key Performance Indicator |
| LERU | League of European Research Universities |
| LGBTIQ | Lesbian, Gay, Bisexual, Transgender, Intersex, Queer |
| LTU | La Trobe University |
| MOOC | Massive Open Online Course |
| NHMRC | National Health and Medical Research Council |
| NSWLR | New South Wales Law Reports |
| NSWSC | New South Wales Supreme Court |
| NTEU | National Tertiary Education Union |
| NZHC | New Zealand High Court |

| | |
|---|---|
| OCIS | Organisational Implementation Strategy |
| OECD | Organisation for Economic Cooperation and Development |
| PBRF | Performance-based Research Fund |
| PET | Private Education and Training |
| PVC | Pro Vice-chancellor |
| RAE | Research Assessment Exercise |
| RMIT | Royal Melbourne Institute of Technology |
| RRC | Redundancy Review Committee |
| SES | Socio-economic Status |
| STEM | Science, Technology, Engineering and Mathematics |
| TAFE | Technical and Further Education |
| TEQSA | Tertiary Education Quality and Standards Agency |
| TLCF | Teaching and Learning Capital Fund |
| UA | Universities Australia |
| UCLA | University of California, Los Angeles |
| UCU | University and College Union (UK) |
| UKBA | United Kingdom Border Authority |
| UNESCO | United Nations Educational, Scientific and Cultural Organisation |
| UNIKE | Universities in the Knowledge Economy |
| VC | Vice-chancellor |
| VET | Vocational Education and Training |
| VSC | Victorian Supreme Court |
| WLR | Weekly Law Reports |

# Introduction: The Retreat from the Critical

Margaret Thornton

This collection of essays, representing a range of social science perspectives, arose from a concern about the way Australian universities are being affected by a single-minded focus on economic rationality. This has involved the transformation of higher education from a predominantly public to a predominantly private good, which has profound ramifications not only for the future of the public university, but also for the working of democracy. While numerous studies have focused on the deleterious impact of the neoliberal turn on the humanities (e.g Small 2013; Nussbaum 2010; Donoghue 2008), the social sciences have attracted comparatively little attention, although the effect may be no less harmful. It is not only that social science departments are being closed down – although redundancies are an everyday occurrence – but that the social sciences are being constrained in the exercise of their critical role.

State disinvestment in higher education has caused the university's primary role to become more overtly instrumental, for it is now deployed by the state specifically to serve the new knowledge economy. This is not to deny the ideological role played by the university in the service of the state in the past, such as the inculcation of nationalism or the transmission of culture (Readings 1996). However, such a role did not entail the wholesale targeting, recruiting and training of students that is in evidence today. The pressure on public universities is now directed towards producing large numbers of job-ready graduates cheaply in minimum time to serve the needs of industry. The private benefits of higher education are also invariably conceived in economic terms, emphasising vocationalism and wealth accumulation in order to justify a user-pays regime.

The privatising aspect of the new regime, together with the dramatic increase in the number of students, or so-called 'massification', has induced a pronounced shift in terms of both what is taught and how it is taught. In particular, theory and critique are likely to be downplayed, if not discarded altogether, in favour of applied knowledge, which better suits the instrumental aims now in vogue.

The pressure on academics to perform productively and reinvent the self, according to the dictates of the moment, has also profoundly affected academic careers, causing them to become less fulfilling than they once were. The focus is on producing 'world-class research' to enable universities to enhance their prestige and compete on the world stage. At the same time, academics are required to teach more and more students, while collegiality and academic freedom have been eroded in the face of increasing managerialism, a highly gendered phenomenon on which several contributors elaborate.

I set the scene for the collection by overviewing the trajectory of change in higher education policy in Australia over the last quarter of a century that has led to this state of affairs and by briefly addressing its significance for the social sciences. But, first, a word about the neoliberal turn.

## The neoliberal embrace

Neoliberalism lacks a precise denotation but encompasses a constellation of values emphasising market freedom – competition, free trade and entrepreneurialism – in conjunction with profit-making and private good. The social acceptance of the 'market metanarrative' (Roberts 1998) is such that liberal democracies are no longer prepared to sustain public goods as was once the norm. Instead, and despite the ostensible moves in favour of deregulation, the state is playing a key role in creating and preserving an institutional framework to facilitate market rationality (cf. Harvey 2005, 3).

From the early 1980s and 1990s, neoliberalism began to impact on Australian public policy under Labor prime ministers Bob Hawke and Paul Keating. A key initiative that laid the foundation for emergence of the free market was the Hilmer Report (1993), which advocated privatising public goods and restructuring the economy around competition, a concept that might be regarded as the leitmotif of neoliberalism. The market began to play a much more significant role with the support of the state, an imperative that was ratcheted up by Liberal prime minister John Howard. He was encouraged by the leading world policy institutions – namely, the OECD (1996), the World Bank (1998) and the International Monetary Fund (IMF) (1998). What was occurring in Australia, then, was by no means unique, although Australia's embrace of neoliberalism, particularly so far as higher education policy is concerned, has been particularly ardent.

Public universities were not instantaneously privatised as a result of the neoliberal turn, as commonly occurred with other formerly public goods, such as utilities and public transport. Instead, the process has been an incremental one, involving the increasing application of business practices to them as if they were for-profit corporations. In other words, they have been 'corporatised'. While the federal government has sloughed off a significant proportion of the financial responsibility for higher education, universities have considerably less autonomy than for-profit corporations. They are still nominally public institutions but decisions to lift the cap on student enrolments or to deregulate fees, for example, are made by government in the first instance, not universities themselves. Thus, the application of neoliberal policies to universities has been artfully effected through what might be described as a combination of free-market rhetoric and intense bureaucratic control (Lorenz 2012, 600; cf. Corden 2005).

As a result of the key role now played by the market, the pursuit of knowledge for its own sake à la Newman no longer has the status it once had, for the concepts of efficiency, productivity and usefulness now dominate the managerial discourse that resounds throughout the higher education sector. However, while the extent of the phenomenon is unprecedented in the Anglo-Australian tradition of free, or virtually free, higher education, the potentially negative impact of corporatist and managerial values on the pursuit of learning and independent thought was acknowledged at least a century ago (e.g. Veblen 1957 [1918], 198).

The study of society and culture, which is central to both the humanities and the social sciences, has not disappeared altogether, but there has been a marked turning away from such studies in favour of the functional and the 'relevant', a voguish concept that has come to mean business-related. Humanistic, critical and theoretical knowledge has been dismissed as 'useless' (Small 2013, 4) in an environment where the labour market is primarily interested in skills, applied knowledge and 'know-how'. Indeed, 'skills' have supplanted traditional forms of knowledge in the public imagination as to what is deemed to be most desirable in a university education, as they have come to be associated with modernisation, success and productivity (Urciuoli 2010). Universities are therefore expected to demonstrate their 'usefulness' by training large numbers of productive workers to support the new knowledge economy and by generating academic capitalism through research.

# Universities upside down

The transformation of the Australian university sector began in 1988 when minister John Dawkins incorporated all colleges of advanced education (CAEs) – teaching institutions that did not conduct research – into a uniform higher education system (Dawkins 1988). This resulted in the creation of 16 new universities, forced up school retention rates and 'convinced a new generation of adolescents that university was the logical course for a post-school commitment' (Marginson and Considine 2000, 29). Lyotard (1984) had observed only a few years before that knowledge had replaced land, raw materials and cheap labour in the struggle between nation-states. As Australia's economic performance, long reliant on agriculture and manufacturing, had slipped in OECD rankings (Brett 2003; Casey 2006), the idea of a knowledge-based economy was appealing as it would augment the production of wealth and enable Australia to be more competitive on the world stage. 'New knowledge', of the kind Lyotard had in mind, is not synonymous with Newman's idea of universal knowledge (1966 [1852]), but is a more fluid concept, shaped by informatics, postmodern scepticism and the variability of market needs.

Despite the orchestrated transition from an élite to a mass higher-education system, there was not a commensurate increase in public funding. Instead, the neoliberal imperative induced a shift from free higher education to a user-pays system. Influenced by the gurus of neoliberalism, Hayek (1976) and Friedman (1962), it was accepted that students should assume at least partial responsibility for the cost of their education themselves as a degree would boost their future earnings. A user-pays system inevitably encourages the teaching of applied knowledge and more vocationally oriented courses as student-consumers are necessarily concerned about the return on their investment. Consumerism has therefore been a crucial factor in inducing the education pendulum to swing away from theory and critique towards applied knowledge, or from 'know what' to 'know how'.

To maximise the utility of the user-pays philosophy, a loan scheme was implemented by the Australian federal government based on an idea of Friedman (1962, 105) and developed by Bruce Chapman, an economist at The Australian National University (ANU). The Higher Education Contribution Scheme (HECS), subsequently known as FEE-HELP, is an income-contingency loan scheme that does not require graduates to begin repayment until they earn a certain level of income (Australian Government, Study Assist). While there were widespread demonstrations from Australian students initially, the language of 'contributions' rather than 'fees', a moderate A$1,800 per annum across all disciplines and the deferred repayment scheme served to quell dissent. Also notable is the fact that a large proportion of private school students in Australia pay much higher fees, despite the fact that such schools are heavily subsidised by the state. Accordingly, the normalisation of the user-pays philosophy in conjunction with a deferred repayment scheme enabled not only an incremental increase in fees but also the imposition of disciplinary-based differences.

In the UK, there were widespread student demonstrations when implementation of the radical recommendations of the Browne Report (2010) was announced for commencement in 2013. Not only did these reforms triple tuition fees but it was determined that no public money at all would be available for the support of undergraduate teaching other than science, technology, engineering and mathematics (STEM) subjects, underscoring the prevailing view that the social sciences and the humanities are of lesser value based on their relative income-earning potential through knowledge transfer. While Australia had not gone so far at the time of writing (2014), the UK example does not portend well for the future funding of the social sciences and the humanities in Australia, given the similarities in higher education policy. Indeed, it is already the case that some social science disciplines receive a very low rate of support from the Australian government. Law, for example, receives approximately 15 per cent of the cost of a government-funded place.

It is apparent, therefore, that the user-pays philosophy has paved the way for the ultimate full-scale privatisation of higher education (Thornton 2012). Commodification has not only enabled the state to slough off responsibility for a significant proportion of the cost of higher education and make rapid progress towards realising its goal of becoming a new knowledge economy, but it has also enabled public coffers to be significantly augmented. For example, by 2004, the proportion of full fee-paying international students had increased from four per cent (pre-Dawkins) to 24 per cent of all university students in Australia (Corden 2005, 8). As a result, higher education quickly became the third-largest export 'industry', worth billions of dollars per year. Australia now vies with the UK, the US and France for the lion's share of the international market in educational services. However, to sustain the new 'industry' and to ensure that it remained profitable, it needed to be closely regulated, despite the prevalence of free-market discourse.

'Moscow on the Molonglo' is the witty sub-title of an article by economist Max Corden (2005), which captures a sense of the higher education scheme in Australia, with Moscow signifying the scheme's high degree of regulation and Molonglo, the small river in Canberra, signifying the key role played by the federal government in determining what leeways, if any, might be allowed to universities. Universities were encouraged to accept prevailing policies and pursue specified courses of action, not so much as a result of punitive Kremlin-like edicts but through positive inducements (Corden 2005, 12). While there has been a laissez-faire approach towards course offerings, determined largely by consumer demand (with the exception of medicine), higher education policy is marked by increasing government regulation. The Tertiary Education Qualifications and Standards Agency (TEQSA), for example, is designed to exercise a homogenising effect on all degree courses. In addition, a plethora of auditing regimes has been established at the national level to guard against risk, all of which demand transparency and accountability. Thus, it is somewhat ironic that as government funding has decreased, universities have been subjected to increasing oversight and control – hence, more Moscow than Molonglo.

The new forms of governance have also changed the relationship between individual academics and the university. These forms of governmentality (Foucault 1991 [1978]; Rose 1999) have been implemented to ensure that academics and students are not only managed – but are also expected to manage themselves – in order to pursue state ends in terms of productivity, efficiency and relevance. The more pronounced the degree of disinvestment in higher education, the more insistent is the pressure on institutions – and individual academics – to pursue an entrepreneurial path. Indeed, enterprise, or entrepreneurialism, has been described as the 'third mission' or 'third stream' activity of the neoliberal university, along with teaching and research (Shore and McLauchlan 2012). A close liaison between academic researchers and industry has been effected through government funding initiatives, such as Australian Research Council (ARC) Linkage Grants, in order to encourage applied and 'relevant' research, but the pressure from industry partners to shape outcomes can be problematic. The veneer of equal treatment between 'pure research' and applied funding regimes occludes the way applied research has contributed to a dilution of independent, critical and theoretical research (Tombs and Whyte 2003, 207).

Perhaps of even more significance is the way such research policies have subtly contributed to the inversion of the meanings of public and private to reflect the ideology of the market turn. This is illustrated by an insightful ethnographic study of the discourse of entrepreneurialism and commercialism at the University of Auckland conducted by Cris Shore and Laura McLauchlan (2012). They show how profit arising from private investment and knowledge transfer has come to signify public good in relation to knowledge production within the university community. The changed discourse has effectively silenced dissent and normalised commodification. The fostering of innovators and entrepreneurs also suggests a preference for 'scientists, technicians and business people rather than social scientists or those trained in the humanities' (Shore and McLauchlan 2012, 281). More insidiously, it shows how neoliberalism has been able to assert itself as the common sense view of the world (Harvey 2005, 3), thereby resisting critique.

Corporatisation and competition have inevitably brought in their wake a more distinct hierarchisation of universities. Rarely encountered prior to the turn of the century, league tables and rankings now animate vice-chancellors and university managers everywhere in the worldwide 'battle for excellence' (Hazelkorn 2011, 4). While undergraduate students are regarded as the major source of regular income for most universities, research is what counts for the Go8 (Group of Eight) research-intensive universities and those aspiring to join their ranks. On its face, the paradox to be confronted is that while excellence in social science and humanities research is lauded, overall funding has been reduced in favour of areas perceived to have greater use value in the market, such as technoscience, thereby entrenching the historic divisions and tensions between the 'two cultures'.

## Wrestling with the social

Given the diffidence about the social sciences, one might then ask, what is distinctive about this cluster of disciplines vis-à-vis the humanities and the sciences? Whether 'social science' appears in the singular or the plural, it is an amorphous concept encompassing the study of society, culture and the state. Although such studies may be conducted from the perspective of a single discipline, it is thought that they generally function better in combination than separately (Brewer 2013, 10). The boundaries between disciplines are nevertheless often impermeable because of traditional claims to distinctiveness, university structures and the competition for resources, as well as government funding and reporting requirements. The current research assessment exercise, Excellence in Research for Australia (ERA), for example, is primarily discipline-based, which inhibits interdisciplinary research, despite the rhetoric.

There is nevertheless continuing ambivalence about the status of the social sciences. The 'two cultures' model of the university, famously articulated by CP Snow (1964), illustrates the science/humanities dualism that discounts the social sciences. After being trenchantly attacked, however, Snow (1964, 71) conceded that a third culture would eventually come about. Jerome Kagan (2009) was one who took up the challenge, arguing that the premises, analytic tools and concepts of the three cultures represent 'language communities that impose distinct meaning networks' (2009, 6). Despite attempts of this kind to establish the uniqueness of the social sciences, there nevertheless seems to have been something of a reversion to the two-cultures model, possibly boosted by conservative reactions to postmodernism, which was embraced by academics in both the humanities and the social sciences, but not the sciences. Whether such factors contributed to a conflation between the humanities and the social sciences in the popular imagination or not is impossible to say, but it is apparent that the distinction between the humanities and the social sciences is weakening (Macintyre 2010, 298).

In any case, it is difficult to categorise entire disciplines schematically, as they all rely on a range of techniques and theories. The scholarly shift away from positivism, empiricism and behaviourism in favour of the subjectivity and ambiguity of epistemological standpoints has further blurred the distinction. Furthermore, disciplines such as history and philosophy are included in the cluster of disciplines recognised by both the Academy of the Humanities and the Academy of the Social Sciences in Australia. Similarly, disciplines such as law are sometimes grouped with the humanities, sometimes with the social sciences, sometimes in a separate category with 'the professions' and sometimes as a discrete discipline altogether, a point that highlights the futility of attempts to develop a precise taxonomy.

It is apparent that the social sciences thrived under social liberalism in the Australia of the 1960s and 1970s. Their fortunes received a boost with the establishment of the 'gumtree universities', viz. Flinders, Griffith, La Trobe, Macquarie and Murdoch (Marginson and Considine 2000), which accorded special attention to the study of society and culture, often through a multidisciplinary lens. Like the humanities, however, they suffered a decline in status with the neoliberal turn and were subjected to faculty closures and mergers.

Macintyre suggests that it was the funding formula for research policy under the Howard government that entrenched the status of the social sciences as 'the poor relation' (2010, 330), when large sums were injected into science and technology as the primary sources of innovation. As suggested, the social sciences, like the humanities, do not engage in techno-scientific research and there is little expectation of patents and commercialisation. Furthermore, the methodologies of audit, such as bibliometrics, which are designed to render 'excellence' calculable, favour the physical, life and medical sciences (Hazelkorn 2011, 71).

Nevertheless, it would seem to be the political rather than the methodological role of the social sciences that is primarily responsible for the change of status in the contemporary climate. The shift from a focus on civil society and citizenship to the market, entrepreneurialism and consumerism marks the transition from social liberalism to neoliberalism. The transition has been such that Rose (1999, 100) and other theorists refer to the 'death of the social'. Indeed, it would appear that it is the social in the social sciences that is not only resistant to containment within a classificatory box, it is a cause of distrust. Positivist and technocratic methodologies are therefore preferred as they suppress both the social and the critical and are less likely to expose the dark underside of wealth maximisation policies, including those emanating from the corporatisation of the university. Attempts to excise the socio-legal from the teaching of law aptly illustrates the point (Baron 2013; Thornton 2006). Thus, the nub of the explanation as to why some social science research has fallen out of favour is because of its critical role, particularly in regard to government policy (Sawer 2004; Sawer and Hindess 2004; cf. Brewer 2013, 9), just as the fear of the humanities has caused them to be attacked (Nussbaum 2010, 23).

One of the traditional aims of the public university has been to carry out the role of 'critic and conscience of society', a role that is distinctively associated with the social sciences and the humanities (cf. Small 2013, 137). Although none of the Australian university Acts of Incorporation advert to this crucial role of critic and conscience, it is explicit in the New Zealand legislation (Education Act 1989 (NZ), s 4(a)(v)). The nearest any of the Australian Acts come to articulating such an aim is a provision included in an amendment to the Victorian Acts in 2003 (University Acts (Amendment) Act 2003 (Vic), s 3(b) et seq), which specifies that universities should promote 'critical enquiry within the university and in the general community'. Somewhat ironically, this provision was added only after universities had been thoroughly corporatised (Thornton 2012, 194). Nevertheless, it needs to be kept in mind that 'critical enquiry' is an express legislative aim; it is not merely a Newmanite ideal.

The critic and conscience role of the social sciences is comparable to that of the gadfly invoked by Socrates (Plato 30d–31a). The allusion captures the crucial but sometimes discomfiting role of one who critiques prevailing values thought to be contrary to the best interests of society. Unsurprisingly, the critic and conscience role has become increasingly unpopular in a neoliberal climate in the context of the corporatised university and beyond, where managerial deference rather than academic freedom is the order of the day, despite a renewed focus on freedom-of-speech rhetoric in public discourse.[1]

A notorious example of an attempt by government to inhibit the critic and conscience role occurred in 2004–05 when the then Higher Education Minister, Dr Brendan Nelson, vetoed a number of ARC grants in the humanities and social science that involved research on gender, sexuality and green politics. Dr Nelson set up a scrutiny committee of 'supremely unqualified people' (Peter Doherty, Nobel Prize winner, quoted in Bonnell 2014, 21) to determine whether

---

1  Attorney-General's Department (Australian Government, *Right to Freedom of Opinion and Expression*. Retrieved 2 October 2014, from www.ag.gov.au/RightsAndProtections/HumanRights/PublicSectorGuidanceSheets/Pages/Righttofreedomofopinionandexpression.aspx). A 'Freedom Commissioner' was appointed to the Australian Human Rights Commission in 2014. Retrieved 2 October 2014, from www.humanrights.gov.au/about/commissioners/human-rights-commissioner-mr-tim-wilson.

a list of humanities and social science projects would deliver 'national benefit'. The academic community was incensed with this overt interference as the projects had already been subjected to peer review.

Interventions of the Nelson kind are nevertheless so overt that they are quickly exposed. More invidious is the routine policing of critical research and teaching under the now familiar rubrics of excellence, competitiveness and standardisation. It is these practices, normalised within the ostensibly rational auditing processes of the neoliberal university, which are rapidly eroding academic freedom.

It would therefore appear that the critic and conscience role has become more vexed and elusive at the very moment society is most in need of it. While there is undoubtedly an absence of unanimity as to the diagnosis of the malaise within the contemporary university, let alone the way forward, the social sciences can bring their critical skills to bear in theorising and critiquing the challenge to the public good in order to inform public debate, as the contributors to this collection set out to do.

# The collection

The wide range of disciplines represented in this collection, viz. economics, education, history, law, philosophy, political science, sociology and cultural studies, encompass a range of perspectives that conveys something of the rich tapestry of the social sciences. The essays reflect a range of methodologies and standpoints, drawing on the experiences of both managers and the managed in the neoliberal university. The contributors bring their disciplinary insights to bear in placing the corporatised university under the microscope, as well as reflexively examining the impact of the market and competition policy on the student experience and academic life.

A focus on the changing nature of academics as new knowledge workers, students as citizen-consumers and the academy itself as a commodified space has far-reaching ramifications for the nature of society, including the future of democracy. While all the contributors may not imagine themselves as Socratic gadflies, they have relentlessly pursued the critic and conscience role in the best tradition of the social sciences.

## Part I: Theorising the modern university

1. *Hannah Forsyth* sets the scene by historicising the university with particular regard to the Australian context. She presents a view that does not mythologise the pre-Dawkins era as a 'golden age', a tendency that

may emerge or appear to emerge as a corollary of focusing on the harsh post-1988 reforms. With careful regard to archival material, Forsyth shows how academics had in fact moved away from the notion of the idealised 'disinterested scholar' much earlier in the 20th century. Forsyth argues that academics had already become self-confessed interested parties, which has had significant consequences for the characterisation of the public interest.

2.   In developing a critical theory of the modern university, *Peter Beilharz* problematises the twin issues of time and technology, partly to transcend the culture of complaint presently besetting academia. The conjunction of time and technology not only encourages a propensity in favour of the 'hurried life' for which there is no 'off-switch', but it encourages the pursuit of a particular kind of knowledge. The preference is for facts and information instantaneously available at the press of a button, a phenomenon that has captivated students and impacted on teaching. The 'hurried life' and the pace of technological change pose hard questions for what universities might look like in the coming decades. However, instead of taking them for granted, their conjunction must be the focus of a critical theory of the university.

3.   Philosophy has been central to the traditional 'idea of the university' and, on its face, is at odds with the prevailing culture of market rationality as it has no obvious use value but, as *Fiona Jenkins* points out, the discipline of philosophy is highly rated in terms of 'research excellence'. Nevertheless, women in philosophy fare less well than their male peers, with a dearth of women occupying senior positions, particularly in élite institutions, a gendered hierarchisation that is mapped onto philosophical scholarship. Hence, the 'hard' areas, such as epistemology and metaphysics, in which men predominate, fare significantly better than the 'soft' areas of critique and feminist theory. Jenkins argues that it is the right to judge that gives rise to status affirmation in the audit culture, which succeeds in maintaining a masculinist ordering. Seeing and hearing what one wants to is then secured by relations of power and the partiality of the social sciences within an 'excellence' paradigm. Jenkins exhorts a questioning of the mismatch between experience and theory to establish a practice of transformative criticism that contests the prevailing epistemic hegemony.

## Part II: Markets, managers and mandarins

4.   *Geoffrey Brennan* takes quite a different approach to those who aver that knowledge is changing as a result of marketisation, suggesting that both the focus of the 2013 workshop and this collection of essays, is misplaced. While he does not deny the incidence of change, he suggests that it has emanated from government, not the workings of the market, although the market rhetoric is undeniably present. Brennan attributes the material

changes that have occurred within universities largely to a matter of scale. It is inevitable, he suggests, that the shift to a mass system would produce a greater incidence of vocationalism. Furthermore, he avers that the 'good old days' were not necessarily so good after all, especially in view of what he claims was its tolerance of 'freeloaders'. In his conclusion, he endorses the basic Newmanite idealisation of the university as the pursuit of knowledge for its own sake which, he believes, continues to motivate academics.

5.  The argument put forward in *Tony Aspromourgos'* chapter is complementary to that of Geoffrey Brennan in so far as he argues that a genuinely competitive market is not possible in the case of universities. Aspromourgos suggests that this is because universities possess information not available to consumers. Information asymmetry can have distorting effects, such as the likelihood of low-quality education driving out high-quality. Like many of the contributors to the collection, Aspromourgos is nevertheless critical of the managerialist predilections of the contemporary university, particularly its tendency to erode a civic sensibility. For example, the key-performance indicator (KPI) approach adopted by some universities leads them to compete for 'star performers' and pay salary supplements, which cause academics to be beholden to managers. Aspromourgos identifies the global university rankings as the most pernicious KPI of all.

6.  In problematising the 'public university', *Kanishka Jayasuriya* observes how the concept of 'public' changes according to time and circumstance. Massification, constraints on funding, the growing role of rankings, especially in research, and the demands of the post-industrial service-based economy have all played a role in inducing changes to higher education. Jayasuriya endeavours to make sense of the way the public university relates to governance changes in the state. He argues that market citizenship has not hollowed out the public university, but has reconstituted it through new patterns of regulatory governance that underline different notions of 'publicness'.

7.  In presenting an overview of reforms that have occurred in the 21st century in sometimes less-than-propitious circumstances, *Glenn Withers* shows that higher education, like many endeavours, comprises a mixture of public and private variables. He argues that the reforms, emanating from both Liberal and Labor government policy, have maintained 'the market, mandarin and management momentum' at the expense of collegiality. In looking to the future, Withers cautions against overuse of the word 'university', as it is a concept that should be restricted to institutions with a public benefit role. He believes that this should include private institutions, but not those of a for-profit nature.

## Part III: Education for the 'real world'

8.  Like the authors in Part II, *Nigel Palmer* problematises the idea of the marketisation of the modern university but focuses specifically on what he terms the 'university–student transaction'. The role played by governments in reshaping higher education with the use of market-like mechanisms produces ambiguous and contradictory responses, particularly on the part of university managers. Students are savvy consumers who are getting more than knowledge in exchange for fees. While they are attracted by the academic reputation of a university, the branding of a university is likely to stress other aspects of the student experience for marketing purposes. Despite the current enthusiasm for measuring academic activity, the precise nature of the student experience is becoming obscure. Palmer nevertheless suggests that students are becoming more sophisticated, which requires universities to pay attention as to how they engage with the market.

9.  *Bruce Lindsay* argues that as students have become consumers or bearers of cognitive capital, they are key figures in the economic optimisation of knowledge. Accordingly, the management of students has become a central plank of the governance of the university. Misconduct and unsatisfactory progress are the examples that Lindsay highlights as these are both areas in which new forms of governance have been formalised and standardised according to legal models. The technologies involved represent not only a break with the informal and paternalistic approaches of the past, but they also facilitate a greater degree of surveillance over students who are being prepared for strategic roles in the contemporary labour market. The possibility of effectively taking issue with this new reality poses an acute challenge in a neoliberal climate.

10. *Margaret Thornton* and *Lucinda Shannon*, through a study of law school websites, show how the market is exercising a negative effect on legal education. They argue that the new marketised framework positions students as customers who are encouraged to choose the most attractive educational 'product'. Thornton and Shannon show how choice is constructed with the aid of 'branding'. While sameness could be said to be a characteristic of legal education, choice requires an element of difference. In presenting themselves to fickle customers as the means of realising a bright future filled with excitement and glamour, law schools play down the civic role of legal education. Rather than promoting a commitment to critical thinking and social justice, Thornton and Shannon argue, law school marketing encourages consumerism as the ultimate realisation of the good life.

## Part IV: Conditions of knowledge production

11. *Jill Blackmore* is concerned to show how the corporatised university is essentially a gendered phenomenon. Its characteristics of managerialism, marketisation and privatisation have moved to a new phase with globalisation. She argues that the increasing number of women in the academy obscures the gender imperative associated with managerialism. The hard sciences are viewed as more productive than the humanities and the social sciences, the disciplines where women predominate, but it is from the masculinised hard sciences that university research leaders tend to be selected. In addition, factors such as the tendency to unbundle research and teaching through the creation of increasing numbers of teaching-only and casualised positions are exerting a disproportionately gendered impact. The result is leading not only to a de-professionalisation of academic work but to a re-masculinisation of the academy.

12. *Jenny Corbett*, *Andrew MacIntyre* and *Inger Mewburn* are not convinced of the negative effects of managerialism upon research. They suggest that critics of the contemporary university tend to compare it with an imaginary golden age, although universities have always been subject to the prescripts of the state or church that funded them. They also suggest that critics are unlikely to have had experience of management themselves. More fundamentally, they evince a scepticism about the role of critique itself, particularly as it appears to have had little discernible effect. In contrast, Corbett et al. seek to put a positive spin on the new modes of academic practice and point to the plethora of new opportunities arising from multiple funding sources. They suggest that new initiatives, such as crowd-funding, could overcome the possibility of improper influence by a funder. While casualisation is challenging for those not in full-time employment, Corbett et al. argue that developments in technology can be used productively.

## Part V: Telling it how it is

13. *Diane Kirkby* and *Kerreen Reiger* argue that trust and relational networking are central to productive academic workplaces and reveal what happens when these values are absent in the context of a case study of organisational change involving a faculty of humanities and social sciences. The authors elaborate upon the new culture of managerialism that has emerged from the corporatised top-down university in which collegiality has declined and academics are treated not only disrespectfully but are regarded as 'the problem'. Kirkby and Reiger report how they conducted interviews and engaged in other forms of interaction with approximately 50 members of staff at La Trobe University to highlight the 'dark side' of managerialism, revealing

how the proposed changes and their implementation induced trauma, grief and depression. The authors also show how the new managerialism privileges masculinity, for the process of change disproportionately impacted on female staff, as well as feminised areas of the curriculum. The La Trobe experience graphically highlights the contemporary challenge for the social sciences, underscoring the way social science scholars are deemed not to have use-value in the corporatised academy.

14. Continuing the critique of managerialism in the contemporary academy, *Judith Bessant* recounts her own gruelling experience as an academic who challenged not only the bullying and harassment of her immediate supervisor but that of senior university managers, which led to her dismissal on spurious grounds. With the support of the National Tertiary Education Union (NTEU), the matter was pursued and successfully resolved in the Federal Court where Bessant's reinstatement was ordered. She draws attention not only to the failings of management in 'dark times', but the self-silencing by colleagues that such times induce. Bessant argues that while 'speaking truth to power' is essential for academic integrity, effective challenge is possible only with collective support. As the evisceration of collegiality is a marked characteristic of the managerialist university, reclaiming it poses a major challenge.

## Part VI: University futures?

15. *Jane Kenway*, *Rebecca Boden* and *Johannah Fahey* acknowledge the injurious impact of neoliberalism on academic life but, rather than dwell on the despair it induces, they set out to seek a more positive message to make 'hope possible'. They argue that hope can be a subversive force and consider some resources that enable universities to be reconceptualised in other than neoliberal terms. Kenway, Boden and Fahey recount several notable examples of insurgent intellectuals creating spaces of hope through imaginative teaching and research. They also recount several instances of collective activism, involving both staff and students who have campaigned against restructuring and job cuts. As activism may provoke violent reprisals, the participants' bravery must be regarded as a source of inspiration and optimism.

# Part I: Theorising the Modern University

# 1. Disinterested Scholars or Interested Parties? The Public's Investment in Self-interested Universities

Hannah Forsyth

## Introduction

The university's authority over knowledge is more tenuous than we think. The basis of university authority has been grounded, over the long history of higher education, in nothing more than ideas and values. Such ideas, however have taken institutions quite a long way. Other institutions – religious and political authorities, for example – have vied for a say over knowledge and yet the university has prevailed as the institution, arguably, that we trust the most. In the 20th century the university grew to enormous proportions and has gained significant influence. And yet it has arguably also faced more threats to both its standing and integrity than ever before.

Since the 1980s as universities became more overtly commercial, anxieties about the integrity of university knowledge have been raised. It is a worldwide concern. In 2011 the head of the London School of Economics resigned over a scandal that suggested funding from Libya's Gaddafi regime influenced that institution in academic ways. In Australia in 2013, Marcia Langton was criticised for her support of mining of Indigenous land in her 2012 Boyer lecture without disclosing the hundreds of thousands of dollars of research funding that her institute received from interested mining parties (Woolf 2011; Crook 2013). This chapter considers the growth of the entrepreneurial university in the context of academic freedom, for it is not only mining companies and political regimes that have an interest in knowledge. As universities became commercial entities themselves, they have developed a financial stake of their own in knowledge. What does this self-interest do to their credibility and their value to the public – and how does it relate to older ideas that universities ought to be 'disinterested' scholars, able to pursue knowledge objectively? It was a question that came to the fore in 2008 and 2009 when medical researcher Robert Gray made a claim for personal ownership of the wealth that resulted from the knowledge he produced, now reconceived by both Gray and his university as 'intellectual property' (*UWA v Gray* 2008).

Understanding university history is more difficult, in some respects, than other institutions, for longstanding traditions often infuse the way scholars speak about academic principles, as if scholarly values are universal and eternal. From the morally superior position such universal values provide, universities often seem connected to a theological-like theory of their place in society. Typically these values are attributed to Cardinal John Newman who, in the mid-19th century, wrote a series of lectures whose title alone helps in this quest – *The Idea of the University* – as if there was only ever one idea and it should stand for all time (Newman 1852. For critique, see Collini 2012, 39–60). Historicising the university more carefully allows us to consider instead what is at stake as university values have changed. This is particularly pertinent in the current political environment, where Coalition Education Minister Christopher Pyne seeks to deregulate university fees, propelling universities still further into the land of commercial values.

I will approach this particular history of universities from two perspectives, each derived from the issues central to what now seems to be at stake. The first is academic freedom, an ideal that has its own, and in fact quite troubled, history. The second perspective is the public interest. It is obvious to scholars that the public interest is compromised when academic freedom is undermined, but it is by a more thorough understanding of the history of universities that the importance of this link between academic freedom and the public interest can be more firmly established – refuting oft-voiced suspicions that academic freedom is merely an expression of self-interest by an already over-privileged scholarly élite.

Like academic freedom, the public interest is also a historically contingent concept. It is important that we understand it, however, for it is the reason our universities are maintained as they are. In the 20th century, the public interest (and investment) in knowledge grew considerably. Knowledge defined and regulated labour supply and social capital; it underpinned economic growth with technological development and research; and it increasingly legitimised parliamentary decision-making. Indeed, by the end of the 20th century, knowledge was a key element of national life, with universities its primary guardian. Universities were to educate the nation and make our labour market competitive; with new research, industries too would be able to compete internationally; they were guardians of ideas and values in art, music, history and philosophy, underpinning the disciplines that make us more than merely function; and they promoted and supported the health of the population, the security of food and the ethics and professionalism of Australian occupations. Since the mid-20th century, universities grew enormously, paralleling this growing public need.

Knowledge is so important that the public, its political representatives keep telling us, require universities to account to government bodies, reassuring them in constant, painstaking ways that universities working for the national interest. Why don't they trust us? We can gesture to a few things – rational choice theories that declare academics to be more likely to indulge in our hobbies than research, if we can get away with it; 'neoliberal' values that insist on a tangible return on public investment (see Redden 2008). But while such diagnoses are fair, such catch-all concepts deflect responsibility away from ourselves as scholars and, by pointing only to a past that we cannot recover, fail to show us a pathway by which we, within the scholarly community, might help to rebuild the public's trust.

# Academic freedom and the idea of the university

Over the past two centuries, university academics have argued that certain scholarly freedoms are necessary to assure the integrity of knowledge. The grounds for their claims to intellectual and institutional autonomy have shifted, historically, as the idea of the university has adjusted to changing public need.

This long history of academic freedom is a bumpy one, continually negotiated under changing conditions (see Russell 1993). There was, of course, no original idea of the university. Medieval universities emerged in a messy, fragmented way, with no fundamental rules and principles. Universities across Europe were not separated from the church and the beliefs it espoused (Daly 1961). Medievalists tell us that university links to the church inhibited some scholarly freedoms, especially in philosophy and theology, but that the church also helped secure their autonomy. Ecclesiastical governance, characterised by autonomy from the state, gave universities a foundation on which to claim academic freedom in subsequent centuries (Haskins 1957, 50–7). German enlightenment values took the church's conventions of autonomy further, insisting on principles of academic freedom for their universities as a way of assuring the reliability of the research that was their hallmark (Fuller 2009).

It was Wilhelm von Humboldt who formalised academic freedom in Germany in 1810, linking it not only to freedom from interference by other claimants to knowledge but also connecting it to what Newman would later describe as 'knowledge for its own sake', or curiosity-based inquiry, sometimes (but not always) historically associated with 'pure', rather than 'applied' research (McLelland 1980, 101–61).

As universities were established in the United States, they initially adopted this German, research-focused, model (Flexner 1930). With this model came ideas. *Lehrfreiheit* suggested that academics and their institutions needed a degree of autonomy to be able to do their job: *Lernfreiheit* was the freedom of students to choose their study and regulate the space in which they lived and worked (Macintyre 2010). But there was something different about American universities: they were not all conceived as state-run institutions. Because of this, there was a particular potentiality for being controlled by the private interests who funded them. By the late 19th century, progressivist educationalists like John Dewey argued that structural mechanisms must be put in place to protect knowledge from control by university trustees (Scott 2009). This was how, in American universities, academic tenure became so closely bound to the concept of scholarly freedom. The argument was that when private interests controlled the universities, only scholars secure in their employment could really pursue unbiased work. Because of the risk associated with private interests, American academic freedom was codified more extensively than in most other nations, by university professors themselves, not by the state or by institutional leaders.

American academic freedom had a dark side, however, argues Joan Wallach Scott (2009). She maintains that its proclamation in 1915 by the American Association of University Professors (AAUP) also functioned to enact the myth that knowledge (as truth) was separable from power. In so de-politicising scholarship, Scott suggests, the AAUP was complicit in the assertion of certain *types* of truths that themselves, as Michel Foucault famously argued, asserted a sometimes-insidious power (Foucault 1972).

In Britain, the interests at stake were quite different. As a result, there the key turning point in the development of academic freedom was when Cambridge and Oxford relinquished their religious test (requiring acceptance of the 39 Articles of the Church of England as a condition of enrolment) in 1871. This secularisation of universities freed scholars from some of the constraints experienced by thinkers of past generations. Nevertheless, such academic freedom did not assure a wholly independent scholarship since, throughout the 19th century, Oxford and Cambridge maintained strong links to British administrative and political power (Drever 1953, 17–24).

Scholars seem to have felt, however, that far from being influenced by government they in fact did the influencing. It was not until government funding became central to the running of higher education in Britain early in the 20th century that university members became concerned. In the end, the autonomy of the universities was (at least theoretically) protected by the Universities Grants Committee, established in 1919 with the explicit aim of providing a 'buffer' between political interests and university spending – and thus scholarly priorities (Gallagher 1982; Shattock 1994).

Other systems intended to protect the integrity and quality of scholarship were also adapted from ecclesiastical conventions (Fuller 2009). Convocation, an assembly of members (usually alumni) who share responsibility for governance, evolved into the collegial systems of decision-making, legitimisation, course approval (or disapproval) and general academic authority that, prior to the 1970s, characterised our Australian universities and which were seen as key to academic freedom (Rowe 1960; Serle 1963). Such collegiality has not entirely disappeared: most public universities in Australia are still legally defined by their academic membership, even if this structure seems now to be rarely actualised.[1] There is one recent exception. In 2014 an attempt was made to invoke an assembly of convocation at the University of Sydney to compel the vice-chancellor to represent staff views on fee deregulation in the public sphere. The University Senate quashed this attempt, in part arguing that convocation was unrepresentative of the relevant constituents and that, with hundreds of thousands of university graduates it is now too large to plausibly assemble (Gilmore 2014).

In the mid-20th century, academic freedom became central to debates about the university (especially research) worldwide. The asylum granted to German scientists and scholars fleeing Nazi Germany was perceived as much a mechanism to protect knowledge as it was to protect the scholars under attack (Ash and Sollner 1996). Let us not be too idealistic about this – it was a war of science and accumulating German scientists also deprived the Nazi regime of a key military tool. But it did prompt a new way of thinking about the political and economic value of knowledge that included philosophical reflections about the problem of allying ideas to political regimes. This marks a new phase in the history of academic freedom.

---

1    Of Australia's 39 universities, 36 are public institutions, 25 of which (or 67 per cent) are membership-based. Membership-based institutions are organisations that are defined by their members, normally the academic staff, students and graduates. No university in Queensland is membership-based: seven of the nine public universities that are not membership-based are located in Queensland. The other two are the University of Canberra and the University of South Australia. (The various university Acts of Incorporation are found under the name of each university at Australasian Legal Information Institute: www.austlii.edu.au/.)

German-Swiss author Herman Hesse captured the nuances of the 20th-century problem in his novel *The Glass Bead Game*, published in 1943. In this, he described Castalia, an idealised scholarly community (with its own flaws, not least a problem of legitimacy) that was created in contrast to an earlier era, which had 'insisted that Mind itself must serve politics or the military' (p. 338). Then, not only had scholarship been *deployed* for propagandistic purposes, it was also *controlled* so that 'not the faculty but His Excellency the General can properly determine the sum of two and two' (p. 334). It was a world of persecution or compliance for academics, where there was 'truly no pleasure and no honor in being a scholar or a writer' (p. 334).

There were, in fact, greater things at stake, Hesse's narrator shows, than the health and wellbeing of scholars. Compliant scholars did terrible damage:

> The scholar who knowingly speaks, writes, or teaches falsehood, who knowingly supports lies and deceptions, not only violates organic principles. He also, no matter how things may seem at the given moment, does his people a grave disservice. He corrupts its air and soil, its food and drink; he poisons its thinking and its laws, and he gives aid and comfort to all the hostile, evil forces that threaten the nation with annihilation (Hesse 1970, 339).

It was *this* kind of public good that demanded academic freedom, protecting the nation from ideas (like fascism) that would undermine their civility. Public leaders such as Labor politician Kim Beazley (Senior) and CSIRO chair Ian Clunies Ross were concerned about the quality of research in postwar Australia because they believed the integrity of scholarly thinking was foundational to the integrity of the nation (e.g. CPD, 28 November 1958). Especially in postwar Australia, the public needed to be able to trust in the knowledge they needed and paid for. Hesse (1970, 338) put it this way:

> We are specialists in examining, analysing and measuring. We are the guardians and constant verifiers of all alphabets, multiplication tables and methods. We are the bureaus of standards for cultural weights and measures. Granted, we are other things also. In some circumstances we can also be innovators, adventurers, conquerors and reintepreters. But our first and most important function, the reason the people need and keep us, is to preserve the purity of all sources of knowledge.

Joan Scott (or Michel Foucault for that matter) would undoubtedly not approve of the sense of universal knowledge or truth that this suggests, but it would have resonated at the time, not only with the international protection of German scholars but also with the lesson democratic governments believed they learned as a result of the Lysenko affair in Soviet Russia.

In the 1930s, Soviet geneticist Trofim Lysenko proposed a theory of genetics that aligned to political sentiment, promoting collective farming. Agreement with Lysenko's theory was enforced and scientific genetics was inhibited – even *prohibited* – for decades. This not only repressed the development and application of genetics, however, it also had an immediate impact on an agricultural system already prone to failure and famine. Scientists knew that Lysenko's theory was never going to produce the agricultural yields needed to support the new industrial society, but they were not permitted to say so. Nor could they offer the solutions that would enable the regime to feed its population (Soyfer 1989). Western nations, thus alerted to the dangers of aligning scholarship to political goals, adopted the ideal that democratic states, by contrast to the Soviet and Nazi regimes, would protect academic freedom in their universities.

Nevertheless, despite inheriting centuries of tradition and new pressing reasons to protect academic freedom, in Australia in 1944, influential British scholar Eric Ashby observed that universities here were under more threat from political and sectarian influence than in other Commonwealth countries (Ashby 1946). Due to regular external pressures on the nation's universities, Australian vice-chancellors were notoriously wary of government interference. Indeed, this was a key frustration for CSIRO chair Ian Clunies Ross, who expended considerable energy in the late 1940s and early 1950s encouraging vice-chancellors to petition the Commonwealth government for ongoing financial support of the State-funded universities, finding that (despite working in quite impoverished conditions) vice-chancellors feared the government influence associated with funding (1955).

Eventually Clunies Ross was successful in persuading both the universities and the Prime Minister, Robert Menzies, to conduct a review. In 1957, the Murray Review of Australian Universities established a national framework for funding and conceptualising the university for the national good. It recommended that the Commonwealth invest considerable sums in higher education and that a buffer body like the British Universities Grants Committee be established to administer this funding (Murray et al. 1957).

From within the universities, the government was being watched closely. In this period, scholars were particularly anxious about their freedoms. News of ASIO surveillance in the universities and of reports of the loss of academic freedom in the United States under Senator Joseph McCarthy's anti-communist policies, led academics to scrutinise the Murray report meticulously (Buckley and Wheelwright 1958). All seemed to be well, at least as far as the Murray report was concerned. Even though there was plenty of evidence of ASIO surveillance in universities, Menzies was generally accepted as a 'university man'

(Forsyth 2014). For the most part, historians have since acclaimed his habit of protecting university autonomy from interference by other, less sympathetic, politicians (Martin and Hardy 1999; Bessant 1977).

Confidential cabinet documents held in the Australian National Archives, however, tell a different story. Much as Menzies was sympathetic to the universities, he was also compelled to ensure that federal funding resulted in national benefits. While scholars considered the Australian Universities Commission to be a buffer body like its UK counterpart, Menzies instead saw it as the vehicle for assuring fulfilment of government goals. To Cabinet, he argued that 'Money is the weapon by which oversight of universities will be secured' (Menzies 1959). He went on to describe the kind of details that he hoped government would be able to influence, a hope also reflected in his assessment of the Mills report, which he submitted to parliament some years earlier (Forsyth 2012). While the kinds of things Menzies sought to control were fairly modest – buildings, equipment and so on – it did open the universities to more government control than they were led to believe. Historians Peter Tannock (1975) and AP Gallagher (1982) both showed the ways that Menzies' legislation gave latent potential; for government control. Moreover, there is plenty of evidence that this worked, though slowly: the Australian Universities Commission mediated gradual but steady increases in government involvement in university business (Gallagher 1982).

When Gallagher published his book, the most significant threat to university autonomy was still five years away. The 1987 Dawkins reforms not only removed the buffer between government and higher education, government also clawed back recurrent university funding and redistributed it competitively, with the Commonwealth's economic goals a priority criterion for funding allocations (Aitkin 2000). Closer government involvement in the minutiae of university affairs was led by, among other things, a belief among Australian politicians that, left to their own devices, universities were unlikely to work towards the public benefit (Redden 2008).

This is a well-known story. Labor Minister John Dawkins retains a kind of 'bogeyman' status in the narrative of Australian universities. It is time, I argue, for us to complicate this narrative – for if we fail to do so, we may well never get past our tendency to recall a mythical pre-Dawkins 'golden age', allowing nostalgia, or a desire to return to a past irrevocably lost, to hold us back from solving the problems higher education now faces. A key reason that history is important is that it shows how things have changed – this can help us to do more than understand what went wrong in the past. By identifying changes in context and need, it can help us know what to do now.

# The public interest and the idea of the university

Accountability by universities for the public interest was always in tension with university autonomy. This is in fact a structural tension, inherent to publicly funded universities, and must be continually negotiated (Russell 1993). In 1944, for example, University of Sydney Vice-Chancellor Sir Robert Wallace argues that the Chair of the Universities Commission, Richard Charles Mills, had the 'wrong attitude' when he wanted the university to run building plans past the government that funded them (Universities Commission 1946).

Perhaps it says something of the place of universities in society that Sir Robert was confident enough to be so blunt – though of course he also knew Mills well; they had been colleagues at Sydney University for years. Nevertheless, it was, in fact, a wholly different scholarly world, which we would now struggle to recognise – or indeed condone. Before the Second World War there were only six universities, educating less than 0.2 per cent of the population, a vast majority of those the children of the top 10 per cent of the nation's earners. They were public universities but served very narrow public functions.

Not all of the founders of these six public universities intended for higher education to manufacture and sustain social and financial privilege. Indeed, as Julia Horne and Geoffrey Sherington argue, merit was a key colonial value that infused the establishment of the University of Sydney in particular, with the result that a wider demographic than is often imagined attended university from early days (Horne and Sherington 2012, 48–51). Despite this, when it came to universities the public interest was imagined rather narrowly (and so, in fact, was merit). Universities should educate the best, believed William Charles Wentworth (1853), in order to establish an Antipodean aristocracy, forging society's leaders.

Academics, too, were not what they are now. Professors were figures of public importance whose arrival, normally from Great Britain, was announced in the newspapers, as was their attendance at official functions, where their wives' outfits were documented as items of public interest (*SMH*, 2 August 1938). The public's interest, it seems, was also quite narrowly conceived.

This world of privilege was not wholly self-serving. Their high social standing enabled academic staff to promote the university and their disciplines in the public sphere and many did so to great effect, including in offering public lectures. Within their institutions, scholars protected and imparted knowledge by reading, teaching and setting examinations (including matriculation examinations at the end of secondary school) that would test and assure the accuracy of their students' learning. This was indeed a public service, though their conceptions of merit were also aligned to class-based attributes, so that they tended to benefit the children of Australia's elite (Forsyth 2014).

What pre-war academics rarely did was research. There was some research, especially in medicine and agriculture, but the research culture that we now consider to be core to the idea of the university did not emerge in Australia until the postwar period, when research and innovation became key to Australian defence strategy and economic growth as well as to our standing as a democratic and civilised nation on the international stage. The Humboldtian tradition that infused the German research universities had little impact on the British tradition – and thus limited influence in Australia – until the experience of war demonstrated to government and the public that investment in research carried with it a significant and sustained public good (Flexner 1930, 56–61).

The change was rapid, but not universal. An American Carnegie Foundation visitor in the 1940s found that most professors considered their central role to be the protection of 'standards' in the universities, not research or innovation (Conant 1951). The PhD had no real place in Australian universities until the 1940s. Even in the 1950s, many remained against it, arguing that scholarship – the kind of 'mastery' of a discipline that defined the British MA tradition – was the longer, harder and more important route to expertise than the 'horribly American' PhD, which privileged mere discovery of something new (Connell 1995, 204–8).

But the postwar era required research and lots of it. This emerged from wartime and quite a lot of the research conducted both within the universities and the CSIRO had military application. More importantly, the 'mobilising' mentality of war, which had contributed to everything from optical munitions to malaria treatments, from psychological testing of combatants to social scientific studies of morale, extended into the peace. The awareness of the value of research that came from the war effort slipped into an ongoing necessity of research for the national good (Hobbins and Forsyth 2013).

The new era of nation-focused research was launched, though not without some effort from government researchers, especially Ian Clunies Ross, and university researchers, such as Marcus Oliphant. Atomic energy, diplomacy in Asia and the Pacific, technological innovation to support agricultural and manufacturing industries and engineering advances to facilitate mining and energy production were all key priorities. Medical research and population health management were also emphasised. This was not just a scientific revolution. Research supporting wartime 'morale' developed into a robust system of social scientific inquiry (Pomeroy 1995; Macintyre 2010). The research culture that often dominates contemporary expressions of the 'idea of the university' emerged not from 'pure' inquiry by groups of cloistered academics, but from a sustained and (often) Commonwealth-funded period of conscious nation building, with research that aligned to government strategy.

This link to government did not go unnoticed. When they were not gossiping over the salacious Orr case involving a seduced student at the University of Tasmania, *the* debate in university corridors in the 1950s was whether universities should be 'ivory towers' or 'service stations' to government and the public interest. By the mid-1960s, most scholars conceded that the service station side had won out. Political philosopher Perce Partridge (1965) argued: 'It is no longer a wry jest: universities *are* now, in considerable part, public utilities or instrumentalities. They are being increasingly supported by governments from public funds because they carry out public functions, as hospitals and public transport systems do.'

The key cause of this shift was the significant injection of funding to the universities by the federal government after the 1957 Murray Review. Just as educators in America noticed the connection between money and ideas as their trustees asserted their influence, so also Menzies' monetary 'weapon' had a significant effect on the universities. From one perspective, it gave the government the tool with which they could control universities in the public interest.

The public's interests and the government's, however, were not necessarily the same thing. This is the other story that could be told — and which *was* told by the student radicals who occupied university campuses from the late 1960s to the mid-1970s. Democracy and the public good might also be served by dissent, by offering divergent ideas to the public sphere. The 'truths' that government-sanctioned research inculcated also oppressed, failing in particular the more vulnerable of society by perpetuating ideas about economics, race, gender and sexuality as 'truths' that in fact benefited the already-powerful (Giroux and McLaren 1989). They argued that although government had an important role in funding knowledge for the public good, universities must also remain independent from government, enabling a questioning and expansion of the idea of the public good itself.

Despite these critiques, however, the government's postwar investment in research was indisputably beneficial to the public. As a result of that investment, we inherit, in universities, a spectacular record of research. Despite the large literature on the decline and fall of the university, in Australia and internationally, everything from snake anti-venom, public health, food safety, addressing climate change, safer mining, revival of Indigenous languages, better power sources and more productive international relations have emerged (and continue to emerge) from university research culture.

# The evolution of self-interested universities

And yet, on the other hand, everywhere we look we see symptoms of a sickness so ingrained it is tempting to despair. Universities have become focused on their own commercial self-interest, the symptoms of which are in the growing managerialism, neoliberalism, audit-culture, casualisation and student consumerism (see Shore and Wright 2008, 57–89; Hil 2012). These broad concepts, however, do not give us the specific causal history that properly explains the contemporary university – and without understanding these causalities, our responses to the problems we face are limited.

While the 1987 Dawkins reforms were revolutionary, there is plenty of evidence to suggest that many of the issues were already emerging in the universities without much help from government at all. For an explanation, we need to look back to the 1970s where, even though going to university was finally free of tuition fees, students were not enrolling at the rates universities had come to expect. There were, it seems, several reasons for the decline in growth. One was that the growth experienced before this was propped up by the baby boom – by the mid to late 1970s that population bubble was almost all through university.

The completion of tertiary education for the baby boomers did not fully explain the shift in the pattern of student demand, for there was also a significant shift in the *percentage* of young people choosing university. This was due, from all contemporary analyses, to a perception that a university education no longer assured a 'university type' job on completion, a result of a shifting economy that had not quite shifted yet to accommodate recent graduates and a government policy framework that could no longer support full employment (Gross and Western 1981). Widespread inclusion of university graduates in a changing labour market was impeded by the effect of the oil shocks, which contributed to rising unemployment. This interrupted development of the 'knowledge economy', sought by the likes of prominent American educational leader Clark Kerr. This relocation of competitive advantage to creative, flexible and innovative ideas (rather than the efficiency of production) was in part a symptom of an economy that had been shifting for some decades away from a predominance of unskilled or semi-skilled labour towards white-collar professions, including the growth of a managerial class, service professions and the finance sector. Some of this shift was to be fuelled, according to Kerr, by the larger number of university-educated youth graduating in the 1960s and 1970s (Kerr 1972).

The sudden shortage of public money in the second half of the 1970s under the conditions of 'stagflation' had a more immediate and pressing effect as the Fraser government began to seek cost savings from a university sector that had become accustomed to more substantial growth. Experts in higher education called it the 'end of the golden age' and indeed they were right (Gross and Western 1981). At the OECD in 1980, higher education leaders collectively declared an international crisis in the perceived value of higher education. There was a 'real danger', they agreed (OECD 1983, 8), that if the current crisis in public confidence in higher education continued, the university 'could be seriously and perhaps irretrievably compromised'.

It was also in 1980 that Rupert Murdoch's *The Australian* newspaper launched its 'Higher Education Supplement'. Between coverage of the successful opposition by staff and student unions to Malcolm Fraser's 'razor gang' cuts to higher education, the Supplement began to profile a new type of academic ideal. A modern, American-style entrepreneurial academic who did not whinge about declining sources of income, who sought his own industry-based research funding, taking a commercial stance to his work, began to be held up, in the Supplement, as the academic who would meet the challenges of the 1980s. He (sadly, still mostly males were represented, even though feminism was now important in the universities) was contrasted to the bumbling ineptitude of the grotesquely caricatured British 'layabout don' (e.g. Bremer 1982; Hamilton 1980; Johnson 1982; Anon 1980a, 1980b, 1983; Ford 1983, 1984; Howard 1983; Trinca 1984).

With a shortage of students to keep government income flowing, by around 1980, Sydney University began to advertise. Initially shocked and betrayed, accusing Sydney of 'selling themselves like soap powder', by 1982, the other universities joined in.[2] Nevertheless, growth slowed to its lowest point since the withdrawal of the Commonwealth Reconstruction Training Scheme in the 1950s (DETYA 2000). Salary and other costs, of course, were not slowing in the same way, causing problems (Macintyre 2013).

Vice-chancellors and others deployed the 1980s catch-phrase 'more scholar for the dollar', as they sought cost savings (Ferguson 1981). The division between the vice-chancellors and their staff, growing since the 1950s, widened still further, threatening the collegial culture of university governance (Ferguson 1981). Shortly after the Hawke Labor government was elected, universities were establishing research commercialisation offices to seek additional sources of income (Dawson 1984; Morris 1984; Anon 1984, 1985; Stanton 1984; Simmonds 1985).

Many vocal scholars within the university were in favour of complete de-regulation. Students did not value higher education, argued the most vocal of these neoliberal voices, Don Watts from Western Australia Institute of

---

2 'Problems of Campus Promotion', HES, 16 April 1980; 'Competing for Student Advantage', HES, 27 January 1982.

Technology, because it did not cost anything (Watts 1987, 35). The relationship between price and value, which sat lightly on course fees from the beginning,[3] now began to infuse the debate about the real value of free education, which remained, for the time being, policy for both Labor and the staff and student unions (Marginson 1993, 180–2).

By the mid-1980s, a compromise proposal was taken seriously. Higher education, ANU economist Helen Hughes (among others) argued, could be turned from a liability into an asset by charging fees to international students, establishing an educational 'export market'. With the low price of Australia's key commodities causing significant problems for the balance of trade, a new export market was an attractive proposition. For universities, the opportunity to charge international student fees was a lifeline many felt they could not ignore (Hughes 1988, 217–46).

Within a year of that initial reform, the Dawkins green paper was released (Dawkins 1987a). The key reforms intended to facilitate a shift in Australia's economic foundations towards 'human resources and labour force skills' and to make universities and workplaces more responsive to shifts in the global market (Dawkins 1987b). Reforms led to the inclusion of many more students from wider social backgrounds in a mass system, which also extended the benefits of higher education to more members of the community (Robinson and Rodan 1990, 22; James et al. 2013, 126–45). The result, Labor hoped, would be a 'clever country', an aspiration that Dawkins claimed he fed to Prime Minister Bob Hawke (Cain and Hewitt 2004, 41).

The stain of 'layabout dons' still did not go away. The Liberal 'waste-watch' committee began to ridicule the titles of publicly-funded research projects and government began to crack down on 'hobby' research – one element of the reasoning behind a claw-back of recurrent university funds, re-allocated competitively through the Australian Research Council (Baume 1987).

For similar reasons, vice-chancellors were under increasing pressure to manage the performance of their scholars. 'Managerial' changes were implemented, sometimes with government backing, sometimes on university leaders' own initiative. Not all of the criticisms of academic performance were unearned. Since I began researching the history of Australian universities in 2008, many scholars have shared stories from the 1970s and 1980s, telling of long scholarly morning teas, which indeed sometimes (though not often enough to justify them)

---

3   When the NSW University of Technology (later renamed University of NSW) was setting its first course fees, they wished to be more accessible to working-class students but nevertheless did not pitch course fees much lower than Sydney University so as not to 'devalue' the degree. This is quite different from the market signals associated with higher fees: whereas the latter are concerned with attracting students in a market, the former was about the value of the UNSW credential for graduates in the labour market (NSW University of Technology, 1947).

resulted in some interesting research collaborations and collegial discoveries. The expectation to publish and to do so extensively was not yet widespread so failure to do so cannot be measured in the same terms that might be applied today. But then, as now, while we wish all scholars behaved with integrity, some did not. The downside to collegiality, as Herman Hesse's novel pointed out, was a self-serving legitimacy (Hesse 1970, 324–43). It offered governance structures that could and often did function as an exclusive 'boys' club', as many women academics will testify and also fostered some lax work patterns (Marginson and Considine 2000,116). In some ways, in audit culture, academics got the external scrutiny they deserved.[4]

But in unravelling collegial structures and (in attempting to keep them more honest) re-focusing the universities and their scholars to monetary gain, there were unintended effects. The shift in emphasis to commercial entrepreneurialism had an ontological impact. The economists now dominating Canberra's corridors preferred the phrase 'positive externalities' to what Ian Clunies Ross and others would once have called 'civilisation' (Stanford 1986). The 'real' value of knowledge was in its exchange, defined by the money commodity, not by any contribution to civilisation, which itself seemed an outdated concept. As a result, in widespread public discussions about academic freedom, many expressed bewilderment over what academic freedom was *for*. When knowledge had mere monetary value, academic freedom became a 'tradition', as antiquated as 'civilisation' but more damaging: offering unearned license to the intellectual elite (Biggins 1984, 6–9).

As these discussions grew louder and universities shifted towards a more entrepreneurial stance, the language used to describe knowledge changed. A key term, which helps to identify the change, was 'intellectual property'. Intellectual property became important partly because, as research commercialisation increased, legal protection of inventions became a significant legal concern. The language of property, however, spread far further than its legal necessity (Monotti and Ricketson 2003; McKeough and Stewart 2004, 19). While knowledge is not in fact the same as intellectual property, the application of the concept of property to knowledge resonated with the cultural and structural changes the universities were experiencing. Afterwards it became possible to say this (ANU Research Office 2013): 'Intellectual property lies at the heart of all basic, strategic and applied research conducted across all Colleges and disciplines at the ANU. Put simply, IP is the ANU's core business: it's what we produce.'

---

4   While scrutiny seems to have led to increased productivity, it has not done much for scholarly integrity. Indeed, if the gossip among research assistants is anything to go by, it seems likely that the decline of collegial scrutiny, replaced by more bureaucratic structures, has led to a sense of entitlement, perhaps in fact caused by audit culture. This has prompted the use of ARC and other university funds in ways that more closely resemble the travel habits of Chrysler CEOs than publicly funded scholars seeking knowledge for the public good.

Knowledge was no longer something the universities protected (or guarded or imparted) as an intrinsically valuable substance. It became the commodity commercial universities produced and traded for money.

In the 2008–09 case of *UWA v Gray*, it became evident, at least to the presiding judge, French J., that this restructure of university motives refocused them away from the public interest and towards their own. In fact, everyone's self-interest was at play in this case, as medical researcher Robert Gray sought the approximately $75 million value on his research as his own, while the university wanted it for the institution. In this case, however, UWA argued that *as a trading corporation*, its academic staff had a responsibility to protect its financial interests. The Federal Court disagreed. Examining the UWA Act, the Court maintained that an academic was responsible for producing and protecting knowledge for the *public* interest. Moreover, it was impossible for academics to do so if they must prioritise the university's commercial interests, even though no one wished for Gray to profit as he did. Unless the university was structured in a way that provided the academic freedom that enabled academic staff to put knowledge before profit, the university was unable to perform its task or fulfil its public responsibility in accordance with its Act.

Australia's higher education sector was shocked when the court found against UWA. In particular, the sector's intellectual property lawyers (who had the most to lose from the decision) were profoundly concerned (Lane 2010). Outraged, members of the legal profession argued that the finding reflected an outdated conception of the university. Justice French, they claimed, failed to notice that in recent years the modern university has a *commercial* purpose (*Lawyers Weekly*, 9 July 2009; Bushby 2009).

This was why patent lawyers, like all of us in the universities, need history. Without understanding why the Court (which had a better grounding in history than UWA's lawyers) considered it to be important that the university protect knowledge first, patent lawyers across Australia were unable to see that there was more than money at stake. This made them blind to the real issues, leading the sector to encourage UWA to appeal. The Court's mistake seemed so obvious, they were sure that they would succeed before the Full Bench of the Federal Court. In 2009, UWA appealed and failed. UWA only strengthened its argument that the responsibilities of university staff should be the same as any other employee of a profit-making organisation. In response, the Court only strengthened its position that if academics were subject to the commercial interests of their employer that would give the universities the right to suppress research evidence, edit research findings or limit the release of research to the public if that would benefit the university from a financial perspective. The Court could see that structuring academic priorities to the university's self-interest was not in the *public* interest. It was academic freedom, structured into institutions, that helped ensure the public could access and trust university knowledge.

Financial interests, however, were not necessarily the primary motivation for university leaders throughout the many changes that built entrepreneurship into higher education. The shift in language and priorities as value began to be measured in dollars did not wholly shift university attention to money for its own sake. Rather, universities sought money as an indicator of esteem. Esteem sat close to longstanding university traditions, for it measured the relative value of what academics did. The extent to which a scholar's work – their teaching, research, scholarship and scholarly character – was valued by other academics contributed to their authority and voice in the public sphere. When esteem was increasingly attached to income, universities sought it vociferously. You can see it on a smaller scale when humanities scholars mention they need a grant – but that they need it to meet esteem measures, not because they need the money to actually perform the research tasks (Forsyth 2014; see also Brennan and Petit 2004).

## Conclusions

University claims to a right to academic freedom are based on the need for institutions to protect the integrity of research and scholarship if they are to be of much value. The belief that such things can be protected through academic freedom rests on an assumption that separating scholarly inquiry from political, sectarian and financial interests will assure quality work. It is not really a very complex idea, akin to the need, common in several spheres, to avoid conflicts of interest. Historically, universities had this structured into their institutional frameworks in order to assure that their priorities were focused to the public interest, rather than their own.

This is not to suggest that their own interests were ever absent: I am not making the case that academics were once objective and now are not. In the 1980s and 1990s – in fact even into the 2000s – postmodern sensibilities rightly required us to acknowledge that the university and its scholars were never in fact as 'disinterested' as they claimed. They were not only aligned to sets of knowledges and values that regulated social interaction, as Foucault demonstrated, they were also often directly aligned with the interests of the state (Foucault 1972). Sins of omission can be included in this, since, as Raewyn Connell has demonstrated, the exclusion of certain sources of knowledge in the university means the institution has gone beyond legitimising nations to also prop up Western global dominance (Connell 2007). For Indigenous knowledge in

Australia, the consequences have been lasting and tragic, but will hopefully not remain so forever. But while we must have this discussion, the suggestion that universities should be structured to protect knowledge from their own financial self-interest does imply that I also argue for an 'objective' scholarship. There has always been an element of self-interest in academic work, but this does not excuse structuring financial self-interest into the pursuit of knowledge. Placing academics in a system of obligation so that the knowledge they produce and protect is measured against *more than whether it earns money* is what makes the university different from commercial research and development, applied government science and private schools of tuition.

Several realities intersect at this point. Do university leaders *really* care about money – or is that money just a signifier while institutional structures compel motives that are *really* about esteem, which forms the basis of much scholarly authority? From the perspective of the integrity of knowledge it does not matter a lot, for both have clearly required institutions to sacrifice their dedication to autonomy and academic freedom on the altar of commercialisation, even if the money has primarily symbolic power.

Certainly by the 1990s universities were reconceptualised as an industry, shaped by their competition with one another for government support, student fee income and industry backing. No longer really the public institutions they had been formed to be, the institutions themselves sit at odds with the academics they house. Compelled from one historical angle to put knowledge first, institutional leaders re-imagined their fiduciary obligation to the institution in ways that sometimes contradicted its older mission to protect knowledge, as the case of *UWA v Gray* demonstrated, transferring their allegiance instead to their (also very real) responsibility for institutions' financial sustainability.

This seems, when we consider the long history of universities, short sighted and irresponsible. The university is a historical phenomenon, albeit a remarkably resilient one, but there is no reason it should last forever. Its ongoing existence is dependent on the maintenance of that which gives the university its special authority and indeed its reason for being – an authority over knowledge derived from public trust in its special, independent integrity.

# 2. Critical Theory and the New University: Reflections on Time and Technology

Peter Beilharz

What does critical theory bring to the discussion about universities, the institutions to which many of us have given our lives? Perhaps not a great deal, directly: we shall see. But at a broader societal level, I suspect that one of our collective shortcomings as university workers has been to fail to look for possible dots to connect between our everyday lives, our institutions, and our theoretical traditions. So this series of reflections is, in a sense, an attempt to bring critical theory back home, to connect up the personal and the societal in our lives as university workers, all this in the context of dramatic and apparently irreversible change.

Twenty years ago I published a book called *Transforming Labor* (Beilharz 1994). What I wanted to argue there was that the Australian Labor Party (ALP) was both the subject and the object of the transformation begun under Hawke and Keating: Labor was both the transformer and the transformed. My colleagues Mark Considine and Simon Marginson made this case for tertiary education: the process of change which began under Dawkins has cascaded on ever since. What they called the Enterprise University became a new model for Australian development (Marginson and Considine 2000). This process of transformation of the universities has continued on since, compounded by Federal intervention coupled with decreased funding, increased national competition, and increased emphasis on product standardisation coupled with claims to vocational accessibility.

My sense is that we face a dual task and responsibility in seeking to make sense of our universities today. The first is immanent, or internal, and I defer here to the wisdom of others who know better than I the empirical conditions of the

39 universities in Australia. The only emphasis to which I would add my voice here is that the *range* of experience, across the Group of Eight (Go8) and the rest, and from case to case, university to university, will reinforce the importance of path dependency: there are certain common determinants, but an enormous array of local factors forming these different experiences. Some universities may move more slowly, but those more trade-exposed are compelled to seek advantage, especially via marketing and claims to novelty. Those outside the Go8 need especially to compete for students and other scarce resources such as outside funding: they commonly compete by distinction of mission, as well as by claiming Ivy-League research excellence. The second is contextual. As we seek better to make sense of universities in Australia, we should also retain the insights pioneered by Marx and Freud, that to understand any phenomenon we may need to look outside, or elsewhere. My claim here is that the transformation of everyday life in what Hartmut Rosa calls 'accelerated modernity' (Rosa 2013) means that broader trends, caught up with time and technology, will necessarily frame and form the life of the campus as we historically think of it.

This means looking, in the first instance, elsewhere, beyond the universities to the societal imperatives or logics of modernity which frame and constrain universities in the institutional sense. If we need to look closely inside the institutions, immanently, and draw due attention to universities, rather than 'the University', then we might need also to look outside the boxes, if you like, at the logics of the social system which drive and direct its subsystems (health, education, crime, housing, and so on). But there will also be more abstract logics at work here. Two of the most important themes that present themselves are *time* and *technology*. For the transformation in university life is framed and driven by trends elsewhere, from which universities cannot apparently escape (there is nothing outside society).

There is a throwaway line in Marx's *Grundrisse* (Marx 1857–58, 173) that could be the *leitmotif* here: 'Economy of time, to this all economy ultimately reduces itself.' The acceleration of time which underlies 'flexibilisation' is a major social trend which deserves our scrutiny. For there is not enough time, and too much information, 'too much civilization', as Marx puts it in the *Communist Manifesto*. As Zygmunt Bauman puts it, more recently, in various places in his work, the irony of overdevelopment is that where in the 19th century we (educators, people like us) believed that we could solve problems such as poverty if only we had the information, we now have so much information that we can no longer see the problem (try it – Google 'poverty' – 104 million entries in 11 seconds – there's progress for you!). To state the obvious, we still need the critical culture which enables us to *filter* this mess of stuff; and this is what universities used to do and I think still need to do: to cultivate knowledge and interpretation rather than just gather and accumulate information.

Flexibilisation is deeply problematical. Some academics used to joke, a way back, that the perfect university would have no students. The new joke is that it may have no teachers, just a few stragglers at help-desks in libraries that have been transformed into lounges. If we need still to use the language of rationalisation and commodification, say, after Lukács, it seems to me we also need to be looking to make sense of *informationalisation*, the reduction of knowledge/thinking to bite-size bits. Make it easy! Make it quick!

Tara Brabazon takes a turn at making sense of this new academic culture in *Digital Hemlock* (2002) and *The University of Google* (2007). The first book is angry, as she admits; but the issues evoked are painfully familiar: the student who asks, in dismay, 'Do I really have to go to the library?' or the essay extension request five hours before deadline from 'Miss Last Minute'. The students who take no notes, because their expectations have been socialised into powerpoint karaoke. 'I don't have any notes and I can't find anything on the web!' Or the survey responses for net-based courses – 'What are the advantages of net-based courses?' Some data from Tara Brabazon (2007, 89):

'I have gained more practical knowledge of computers and how to use them in the workforce.'

'Flexibility – can work from home; can fill in breaks; effectively can overload on units.'

'More freedom to do other things. It doesn't seem as time consuming.'

All this echoes, powerfully, with our teaching lives today; but it also issues out of a culture of complaint, and raises the spectre of nostalgia. Nostalgia, as David Lowenthal (1985, 8) suggested, is something like memory with the pain cut out; though our problem, generationally, might also be characterised as mourning and melancholy. We need to recognise the power of these ways of seeing, but also to be clear-eyed about the transformations that are upon us.

We all know that our students have been professionally socialised into different worlds than us, as senior academics, children of a different time and academic culture, when university experience was more like immersion (Murphy 2013). For some of us, at least, from the seventies on, universities were little communities; they offered a way of life. That may well have been a moment of privilege, a moment of exception. Whatever the case, times have changed. Some odd data from the present; today:

61 per cent of fulltime Australian students work more than they study.

University of California, Berkeley students spend 12 hours a week socialising, 11 hours using PCs for fun, 13 hours to study, six to watch TV, six to exercise, five hours for hobbies (Murphy 2013: 50).

Per contra, according to Zimbardo (of whom more later) Stanford students are so future-oriented, rather than hedonistic, that they don't even have time to fuck, so future-oriented are they: too busy working to score, according to *The Score on Scoring: The Guidebook*, (Zimbardo and Boyd 2008, 250).

As German sociologist of technology Gernot Böhme observes, the point here is not to complain about our children, but rather to face the issue of the changing forms of sociability that technologies bring. What we face here is a process of cultural transformation which also sweeps university life along with it. For example, as Böhme (2012, 6) observes, mobile phones bring about profound changes in habits and time sensibilities, especially among young people: for fixed appointments are practically obsolete in a world in which it is always possible to make new arrangements at the last minute. So this is less an individualised issue of 'Miss Last Minute' and more a matter of a last-minute culture which, by the way, is also how some large institutions such as universities themselves work, constantly reinventing. We might call it *nowism*.

So much by way of introduction. Let us shift to the more apparent question, if you come from where I come: what might a critical theory of the university look like?

There are some obvious echoes. If we were thinking of the Frankfurt School in general, Habermas would come to mind: the idea of the public sphere, the coffee shops of the 18th century, the small presses, the pre-academic informal institutionalisation of intellectual culture; another world, before state and capital transform the university, before we come to *identify* the university and intellectual activity, occluding the rich series of traditions associated with social movements, churches, workers and women's movements, clubs and societies that made up the strength of civil society into the 20th century.

Habermas might come to mind again, later: *The Theory of Communicative Action*, perhaps – a perverse thought on my part. A different spin rather on Marx – too much civilisation – too much information – too much communication! The world of the sorcerer's apprentice – a world without an 'off' switch? Is that the world we inhabit? ('I emailed 5 minutes ago and you still haven't responded!')

In back of this, the first question: Adorno and Horkheimer, in *Dialectic of Enlightenment*. Have we arrived in the totally administered society? Well, never quite. The will to rational mastery of the world, as Cornelius Castoriadis (1985) puts it, is ahead of us but clear as a will to power; earlier, the critique of instrumental reason, the critique of positivism or positive knowledge which *is* information and informationalisation.

So there are some possible connections between critical theory and the critique of universities, but let's turn elsewhere, momentarily, away from German critical theory, to East European critical theory: the now solitary figure of Zygmunt Bauman.

Bauman's most important work here is *Modernity and Ambivalence* (1991). ('You expect us to read a book from back then?') It is a critique of classificatory reason. This is not a new idea: not, A is not B, as we are often told; but A is B, or at least that all the phenomena of the lifeworld are open to multiple meanings or classifications. This in contrast to the reduction of knowledge to information, bite-size pieces, knowledge made easy. Teaching, especially at undergraduate levels, becomes automated, subsumed to the popular powerpoint karaoke. A is A, four dotpoints per slide, all of which can be memorised without being deeply understood; no ambiguity. Yet there is ambiguity all around. Bauman's critical sociology has more to offer than this. In various texts, including 'Tourists and Vagabonds', Bauman problematises the way in which 'liquid modernity' establishes a sense of the 'continuous present' (Bauman 1997; and see Beilharz 2001). Bauman suggests that we are guilty of 'cutting off time at both ends', absolutising the present and its promise of gratification at the expense of a decent grounding in the past and a sufficient orientation to the future. We are running on short time. 'To keep the game short means to beware long term commitments … To forbid the past to bear on the present … to cut the present off at both ends' (Bauman 2001, 89). For Bauman, liquid modern times generate 'nowism' as well as 'newism'; it could be that we are less postmodern than pushmodern.

Like much else in Bauman's work, this is not a strikingly original position; it draws on arguments and sensibilities given to us by the past. Bauman's concerns can also be found in, for example, Richard Sennett's *Corrosion of Character*, where it takes the form of the practice and culture of discontinuous reinvention. By this Sennett refers to reinventing the wheel or, in other words, eliminating the traditional stock of in-house (say) workplace knowledge that is conferred on younger workers by older workers, those possessed of more experience, so that not every challenge or issue has to be taken on as new. For Bauman, the key ambit image or enabling metaphor is that of liquid modernity. Not because our lives are actually liquid, or mercurial, but because the repertoires traditionally passed on to us hitherto are now presumed in advance to be automatically useless, obsolete, or ineffective. Bauman's approach is also sympathetic with an old marxian one, that the management of the firm would do well to recognise that capital is past, or accumulated labour: the skills and practical wisdom of the primary producers of knowledge, those on the factory floor, or coalface, or doing the teaching are themselves constitutive of value. Every time an established professional or general university worker is made redundant, there is an institutional and cultural loss of some proportion, a loss, to use an old term, of the kind of wisdom that hitherto-existing societies have drawn and depended on for very many years.

Bauman summons Sennett, on occasion, to argue this case, but he also returns to the insight of Christopher Lasch. According to Lasch, the disposable society now extends also to disposable identities. Identities can also now be adopted and discarded like a change of costume (Bauman 1997, 88). The rules of the game keep changing for Bauman, even in the playing. Determination to live one day at a time, and depicting daily life as a series of minor emergencies become the guiding principles of all rational life. And this is, in this way of thinking, a new rationality.

Is it really all so bad? How could these kinds of claims be empirically established? Sociologists like Bauman and Sennett and critics like Lasch take the risk of seeking to name emergent trends and possibilities. They can each be criticised, but also I think celebrated, as sociological impressionists. Claims like theirs will resonate for some of us and not for others. The baseline, for thinkers like Bauman, is that Marx was onto something fundamental with the idea of space–time compression. As Bauman (2000, 112) puts it: 'Modernity was born under the stars of acceleration and land conquest, and these stars form the constellation which contains all the information about its character, conduct, and fate.' These are exactly the same issues that in a different approach concern Zimbardo, as we shall see, both in personal and in social and sociological registers.

Our students demand that what they learn should be reducible to a series of analytic propositions, correct or incorrect, tick the box. In bite-size pieces, like McNuggets. A contrast to the first course I taught in Politics at Monash, 1978, 'Revolutionary Theories' with Alastair Davidson, where the subject guide indicated that students were expected to 'read and inwardly digest'! This was only a generation ago: it feels like a world away. For it was still connected, then, to the German Enlightenment image of *Bildung*. (This doesn't mean that we don't have good and smart students: we do. But theirs is the world of the quick fix, Wikipedia, and multiskilling. A culture which is instrumentalised in this way cannot but have a long-term effect on the habits and sensibilities of its carriers.)

The impact of Bauman's thinking is the subject of some new work by younger minds working at Leeds in the Bauman Institute. The interest here is what Mark Davis, following Bauman, calls *hurried life*, for which *time* is the central variable (Davis 2013). We know the general themes: efficiency, individualism, want-it-all-want-it-now, the avoidance of commitment, 'you mean I need to go to the library?' The broader curiosity, which necessarily remains tentative, is indicated by the shift from analogue to digital time; and to anticipate, this should at least be enough to make us wonder (in terms of the history of culture and technology) whether analogue to digital is a revolution of similar proportions to that indicated by the arrival of clock-time and clock-culture. Perhaps what we need now is the contemporary version of EP Thompson's essay on 'Time-Work Discipline and Industrial Capitalism', new today.

Now Davis, working on the theme of 'hurried life' performs a neat pirouette on Bauman by reintroducing into discussion the more recent work of Philip Zimbardo. Zimbardo's, you will recall, was the famous/infamous Stanford 1971 project, parallel to the Milgram experiments, involving the use of Stanford students role-playing as prisoners and jailers, with toxic results. Zimbardo is alive and well, and centrally concerned with the issue of time. Why is time now so important? As Davis puts it, we are at risk now of losing the capacity to process information at 'less-than-internet' speeds. 'We are no longer knowledge seekers, but information data processors … roaming from one fact to another' (Davis 2013, 15) – perhaps, contra to what we need of a new EP Thompson, we are back with Gradgrind after all. Is all we need really facts, or information? Wikipedia? Whatever the case, the trend seems to be against 'deep reading', 'deep thinking', *because we lack the time*. There are simply too many other competing demands and possibilities.

But of course, if we are back with Bauman, and we have too much intelligence regarding, say, poverty, then we still need the frames or paradigms or theories or theoretical culture to interpret this world, however compromising these frames or theories might be.

Davis (2013, 15) quotes educationalist Mark Fisher: "'Ask students to read for more than a couple of sentences and many [at A level] will protest that they can't do it. The most frequent complaint teachers hear is that it's boring.'"

Boring – it's a complaint that always makes me mindful of the German equivalent – *langweilig*. Understanding takes a while, it takes some time, it might take a long time. Against the popular current of speed, you need to engage, to slow down. Take a leaf from the Slow Food movement. But as Davis continues, 'to be bored is to be momentarily forced out of the flow of communication that has become the lifeblood of lives assimilated into the virtual world that new technologies have made possible' (ibid). Being connected has become fundamental to Western patterns of identity formation.

Zimbardo's work on time is available in book form, as *The Time Paradox*, or on the net for those in a rush as *The Secret Powers of Time*. His work suggests that time perspectives are now notionalised by the second. The average limit in time-duration response to a computer boot up is around 60 seconds; this is the brief interval available before subjects begin to exhibit advanced states of anger. *Waiting*, in other words, is now understood as a *waste of time*, a 'waste of valuable seconds' (Davis 2013, 13). As part of his research, Zimbardo proposed to his subjects the hypothetical possibility of an eighth day in the week, asking respondents what they would do with it. Walk? Sleep? Read? Make love? Recover? Just be? *All* respondents replied that this would be a great initiative, *because with an eighth day they could work harder, get more done at work and so get further ahead of their colleagues and peers.* This is scary, but it is also symptomatic: for it implies the spread of that culture of individualism, in which subjects could imagine the offer to be individual, to them alone, to facilitate their own advantage rather than being collective or social in nature. To invoke the name of EP Thompson again, it is interesting to remember that there *was* (so to say) an eighth day before the industrial revolution – Saint Monday – and it was both collective or shared and lazy, given to recovery or inactivity.

Both Zimbardo and Bauman are in their advanced years, likely watching the clock. Their reunion here, twenty years after Bauman set the Stanford Zimbardo project to work in his 1989 classic, *Modernity and the Holocaust*, is timely. If, as Marx put it in 1857, 'economy of time, to this all economy ultimately reduces itself', then Zimbardo's spin would be that all life ultimately reduces itself to a matter of time. Given the absence of appropriate institutions in the public sphere for us as citizens together to discuss these matters, the logic of individualism puts us in a place where we are compelled to seek personal solutions to social problems. Senior academics, for example, exit, having given up on the prospects of voice or dreams of loyalty, or else they seek to save themselves, so to speak, through time-management schemes and individual counselling. We personalise responsibility and response to this culture which has no off-switch.

But all of this seems so immediate, so urgent, so pressing. We need also, perhaps, to slow our analysis and response down.

Let me add two more frames of reference for thinking towards the frames of time and technology, in this necessarily speculative set of reflections which is the best, at the moment, I can offer you. The first is historical, the second more properly sociological. If we are to transcend the 'culture of complaint' then we need to be open to the question of precedents in the history of technology.

Along with the work of EP Thompson, there is some good social history or history of technology and culture which might be useful here. Stephen Kern, for example, in *The Culture of Time and Space 1880–1918* (1983) deploys the usual kind of images: in 1870 a traveller from Washington to San Francisco would have to reset their watch more than 200 times (Kern 1983: 12). The cult of fixed time and punctuality which we in sociology associate with Weber, *The Protestant Ethic*, with Baxter and Franklin – 'time is money!' – all of this is stunningly new and arbitrary, viewed from the long term or *longue durée* of civilisations and their histories.

This is inherently interesting, but especially so because it comes to permeate ordinary culture and everyday life. Some alarmism, including medical alarmism, results, as in George Beard's *fin-de-siècle* book *American Nervousness* (Kern 1983, 15). Beard blamed the perfection of clocks and the invention of watches for causing nervousness wherein 'a delay of a few moments might destroy hopes of a lifetime'. Every glance at a watch for these nervous types affects the pulse and puts a strain on the nerves. Kern does not make the connection, but this sensibility echoes that of Georg Simmel in the 1903 classic 'The Metropolis and Mental Life'. As Simmel puts it, the metropolis is of significance precisely because of its effect on culture or what he here calls mental life (*Geistesleben*). Its basis is in the *intensification of nervous stimuli*, which as he famously says has as its secondary effect the blasé attitude. Speed, discontinuity, fragmentation become normalised. Money, calculation and time schedules become central. 'If all clocks and watches in Berlin would suddenly go wrong in different ways, even if only by one hour, all economic life and communication of the city would be disrupted for a long time' (Simmel 1950, 413).

All economy reduces to a matter of time – Marx; but this is also a fundamental premise for Ford, and a central premise of Fordism, which remains an active factor in the culture of the new university: the pressure toward standardisation of curriculum, delivery and staff and student expectations. Is this not a new culture of conformism? Or is it just a new version of second nature?

The culture of time is central to this process, and not only in terms of flexibilisation. But the broader effects of technological revolution are cultural: they change our common sense and expectations. Kern (1983: 91) quotes the historian Herbert Casson, writing in 1910 on the cultural impact of an earlier technological concern, that associated with the telephone. Casson noted: '... with the use of the telephone has come a new habit of mind. The slow and sluggish mood has been sloughed off ... life has become more tense, alert, vivid. It receives its reply at once and is set free to consider other matters.'

Similar issues are addressed for Europe by the German social historian Wolfgang Schivelbusch in his book *The Railway Journey. The Industrialization of Time and Space in the Nineteenth Century* (1977). Schivelbusch is interested in the locomotive revolution, in its preconditions and its effects. Its preconditions – and its effects, actually – include a revolution in time – in timetables, and the standardisation of time, as well as a revolution in etiquette, culture and manners. Similar local patterns are tracked by Graeme Davison in his history of time-effects in Australia (Davison 1993). So my general point here is that if we are to take on some of these big or bigger issues, then the history of technology or technology studies may be one major source or optic in the attempt to make sense of what is happening in universities today. Universities are formed by the cultures that surround them, however exactly we choose to characterise these. We need closer analyses of what is happening inside universities, but we are also in need of optics that are wider, and look to connecting up micro- and macro-processes of transformation.

Some of these macro-processes are likely to be opaque, or to make sense at a high level of abstraction or generality. Social change is by definition opaque, and often will make sense only after the fact. Yet we need to seek to make sense of the transformation now, midstream.

Marx was, famously, one of the first I think to articulate the idea of space/time compression. *The Grundrisse* (1857–58, 538), again: 'While capital … must strive to tear down every barrier … to exchange and conquer the whole earth for its markets, it strives on the other side to annihilate this space with time.'

Everyday life is more and more dominated by speed (Beilharz 2011). This brings us to the sociological supplement, provided here in timely manner by Hartmut Rosa in his study just to hand –*Social Acceleration: A New Theory of Modernity* (2013).

Rosa's book seeks to respond to the quotidian sense of accelerated life, but also to problematise it. After all, it is in principle possible that we – people like us – have an exaggerated sense of the hurried life. Rosa begins from the Marxian sensibility, that capitalism is indeed characterised by an acceleration of time. This he refracts through the work of Peter Conrad in *Modern Times, Modern Places*: 'Modernity is about the acceleration of time' (Rosa 2013, 14). Rosa wants to push this further, as it remains possible that this is a projection, that we project or universalise our personal sense of the hurried life onto social trends. In order to avoid too much confusion when we look at a present that seems, in some settings, to be characterised by the discontinuous reinvention of permanent reform, Rosa sets out to differentiate between the technical (or technological) compression of time (enhancements of performance in sport, transportation or computer technology) and increased *social* rates of change (accelerated changeovers in jobs, party preferences, intimate partners). He also draws attention to a third level of change, where the heightening of the pace of life results from an increase in episodes of action and experience per unit of time (ibid). For Rosa these trends are analytically separable: what is interesting is how they might connect. The point is not simply that everything is 'faster', but that even despite certain forms of time-gain in the last hundred years, the pace of life nevertheless seems ruthlessly to accelerate. Like Böhme, Rosa observes that time arrangements are now negotiated *on the move* (Rosa 2013, 127). We fear missing out, and we feel compelled to adapt. The pursuit of the full and good life leads to the hurried life (p. 134). The more means of experience (TV programs, clothes, vacations, partners) we appropriate, and the more we concentrate them in time, the richer our lives will be – the social norm indicates an increase in being through an increase in having (p.182). To use an older language, there is an absence of a sense of limits or hubris, as sense reminiscent of early romanticism that 'I can be everything', indeed, perhaps, serially (p. 184).

Where does all this leave us? As I indicated in the beginning, as social scientists we have our work cut out. For the immanent challenges of explaining what is happening in universities remain. But so, too, do the tasks of seeking to connect, to place these institutions socially, and to frame them with themes like those of technology and time. Universities have become paradigm cases of the kind of commodified-bureaucratic 'irrationality of rationality' that Weber feared and Kafka had nightmares about. Yet this is only a first response: they can still be subjected to clearer processes of understanding, criticism, reform and transformation.

What will universities look like in twenty years? The logic of my approach here is to suggest that we might benefit from opening the analytical optic, in order to subject universities to the same kind of critique that we would apply to other aspects of everyday life as they are transformed before us. The processes which Rosa wants us to disaggregate analytically do seem to me actually to historically coincide. Everyday life does seem to be subject to a process of accelerating change, which is accompanied in the case of the universities by powerful trends to standardisation, heightened levels of product or marketing differentiation and increasingly stringent external regulation via Canberra. Teachers, in this new world, may well be less the inspirational figures who contributed to a process of *Bildungsprozess* in the past, so much as instructors in a self-educative program that is increasingly DIY. In this context Australian universities struggle to position themselves for market position, seeking advantage through promotion and branding rather than through the older, now apparently redundant, model of cultivating culture or simply seeking to do good work. It is not good enough, now, to be good; everything needs to be justified, which is to say measured.

The most significant limit for academics, here, is in the diminution of our own autonomy or capacity to influence or inform future planning. This does not mean that good work will grind to a halt in the universities, but it does seem to suggest that room for manoeuvre is restricted. Analytically speaking, both the logics of state and market can be faulted here; perhaps it is their toxic combination that is most potentially destructive of what universities earlier used to be. Yet there are even larger dynamics or forces at work too, not least those of technology and its own vicissitudes. The idea of technological progress has become taken for granted, a matter of second nature for us moderns. The residual issue is what losses go together with these gains. Are the universities now self-steering systems, or are their rationalities more mixed, vexed and complicated? Truly, these would be opportune times to move forward on the critical theory of universities.

# 3. Gendered Hierarchies of Knowledge and the Prestige Factor: How Philosophy Survives Market Rationality

Fiona Jenkins

Neoliberalism – a term now used only by critics – evokes the absorption of the erstwhile social state into a corporate culture. The purported minimisation of the scope of political power corresponds to the ascendency of economic man, characterised by entrepreneurial spirit, individualism, flexibility, and adaptability. Appeals to economic rationality and practical constraints, and the use of words like 'performance', 'efficiency', 'mobility', 'competitiveness' and 'evaluation', cast mockery at institutions modelled on solidarity, social security, justice or the substantive values of democracy. What lacks market value also lacks the right to exist. The university, to survive, must engage in benchmarking, marketing; seek public-private partnerships; generate profits; incentivise its employees; and offer up its technocratic expert knowledge, as evidence of its co-operative participation in presumptively necessary processes of change.

Given that this shapes the framework of evaluation of all aspects of intellectual endeavour, how does it impact a discipline like philosophy? My interest here is first in how, given a core conception of its nature and value, institutional philosophy might survive within this market framework; and second, at what price, in terms of its ongoing commitment to the correspondingly devalued realms of merely 'social' concern. In particular, I would like to try to track some inter-relations between the following points: (a) how certain defining but also competing 'internal' conceptions of the discipline might be regarded as adapting themselves to the spirit of the times (involving answering in a particular way key problems endemic to the discipline; for instance, about how philosophy orientates itself to truth, or the nature of reason that it properly embodies); (b) how the dominance of one or other such conception carries with it implications for gender relations within the discipline; and thus (c) how the particular sorts of social ends marked by feminism fare within the terms provided by the project of disciplinary survival in the neoliberal academy. If I speak of 'survival', it is because philosophy on the face of it lacks the market-defined right to exist; and yet one could also remark that at least some parts of institutional philosophy have in fact flourished under the competitive systems introduced in the university sector to mimic market-driven rationality – notably via the discourse of 'excellence' and the logic of rankings.

Again, my question about these terms of flourishing will be: at what price for feminist projects, both in intellectual terms and in terms of seeking equality? The adaptations contemporary feminism has made to market conditions also need to be considered here. It is important to note that much of the current push to redress overwhelming male dominance in all areas of university leadership and the severe underrepresentation of women in certain areas (notably the Science, Technology, Engineering and Mathematics (STEM) disciplines) frames itself as an appeal to economic and performance-based concerns. Thus contemporary arguments for gender equality have to a significant extent ceased to be framed as arguments for social justice and have instead become framed as arguments for economic efficiency. Again, the aspect of this I will be interested in is how this way of framing equality intersects with conceptions of disciplinary integrity, and the relation between the pursuit of knowledge and the pursuit of social justice. The case of philosophy is interesting because the levels of underrepresentation of women are like STEM disciplines, yet it is unclear what kind of parallel arguments could be made about the economic importance of including women, given the non-self-evident economic value of the discipline itself.

No doubt there is a very complex story to be told about how market rationality and the means of taking advantage of it, has impacted and fostered the gendering of knowledge and the status of epistemic agents. Here I try to sketch what just a few aspects of that story might look like in one discipline and to use it as a lens for asking from a feminist perspective how to evaluate the kinds of change we are seeing in universities.

## Philosophy and the market

The question of what is 'proper' to philosophy is repeatedly staged at its very inception. If Socrates taught in the marketplace or *agora*, he as surely defined the practice and orientation of philosophy in terms that defied market values. Mere Sophists sold their intellectual wares to the highest bidder, and taught skills in rhetoric and argumentation that would serve a man in the business of politics or in the courts. But Socrates sought to teach a virtue or 'excellence' of knowledge that would transcend such instrumental ends. Without participating in practical affairs, Socrates aimed at politics in the highest sense, as institutional arrangements based in justice and truth; and his gadfly provocations to authority come down to us in history as the emblem of all that academic freedom should mean. Plato's opposition to the Sophistic mode of education resting on what we would now call 'consumer demand' forms a background to many of the dialogues, including the *Theaetetus*, which in concerning itself with the question 'what is knowledge?' specifies philosophy's difference from any other discipline. These are engaged with object-oriented types of knowledge, while philosophy examines knowledge as such. Philosophy is this way receives a definition as the mode of inquiry that transcends all others and could be used by Kant to define the very meaning of the modern university, over which philosophy presided as the 'Queen of the Sciences' (Readings 1986, 56). Although such pretensions have surely been humbled, and much in philosophy today has diversified, we still have undeniably core areas that stand for this task, and wrestle with the broad questions Socrates raised. Epistemology, for instance, still asks whether knowledge can be defined as justified true belief, or how to mark the difference between believing correctly and really knowing; and defending the objectivity of knowledge against an array of threatening relativisms, remains a defining philosophical motif or manifesto for its defence.[1]

The ideals expressed in the Socratic paradigm might in this way form a tempting object of nostalgia in times when universities find themselves squeezed into the frameworks of market rationality, and disciplines like philosophy seem doomed to fit their wares to the servicing of ethics committees, or to delivering the vaguely rendered marketability of 'critical skills' to employers. Yet although one aspect of the survival of such venerable ancient disciplines may indeed involve these kinds of adaptation to the spirit of the times, philosophy might also exemplify the capacity to play the system in another way, by occupying the 'elite' status connoted precisely by the pursuit of disinterested, abstract and non-instrumental thought. Perhaps, indeed, such extra-economic sites remain a key component in neoliberalism, securing the vital relationship between raw

---

1   Here is Todd Edwin Jones (2011), for instance, responding to the closure of the Nevada philosophy department by defending philosophy from the ignorance of those hostile to it, just as Plato sought to do, and claiming the role of first discipline: 'People think of philosophy as a luxury only if they don't really understand what philosophy departments do. I teach one of the core areas of philosophy, epistemology: what knowledge is and how we obtain it. People from all walks of life – physicists, physicians, detectives, politicians – can only come to good conclusions on the basis of thoroughly examining the appropriate evidence. And the whole idea of what constitutes good evidence and how certain kinds of evidence can and can't justify certain conclusions is a central part of what philosophers study. Philosophers look at what can and can't be inferred from prior claims. They examine what makes analogies strong or weak, the conditions under which we should and shouldn't defer to experts, and what kinds of things (e.g. inflammatory rhetoric, wishful thinking, inadequate sample size) lead us to reason poorly.'

market values – what one can buy and sell – and the privileged and authoritative status of elite universities, the 'top 100' whose economy of *judgments* must wield the prestige to structure scales of value that flow downstream into the academic 'market' in the form of journal rankings, esteem ratings, etc.[2]

Here another take on what the implementation of neoliberal policies has meant within universities, and in particular ways at disciplinary level, may be necessary. Part of the violence at work in introducing neoliberal reforms stems from how they re-negotiate, displace or reverse relations of ends and means, or of what serves whom, in ways that re-articulate the proper names of the parties involved and the nature of their transactions. For instance, the university which was once supported by the state to serve the ends of society, is now a site of state investment, offering returns by way of outputs contributory to growing the economy; if students once came to learn subjects like philosophy for the intrinsic benefits of doing so, they now are encouraged to study at tertiary level primarily in order to buy a training that puts them individually at competitive advantage in the graduate job market, making them into paying customers for the university's goods. But within what might seem the simple imposition of market values lurk fundamentally political relations. In this context who serves whom, and thus what constitutes a means and what an end, are questions inseparable from relations of dominance and subordination, and indeed the rights of judgment. Who is answerable to whom? Who or what is judged to be of value and by what right? One characteristic of this field of power as it impacts the university is that to gain the upper hand in determining the subordination of the end of 'pure knowledge' to economic instrumentation, forms of generalised judgment (most often the discourse of 'excellence') are instituted that at once incorporate and transcend, distort and preserve academic judgment. These terms of 'excellence' thus provide scope, paradoxically, to lay claims within the 'market-driven' rationale to occupy the position of the idealised and neutral judge, able to survey a field that is given under a certain definition (for instance, via a disciplinary name) as if all contestation over what constitutes that field can be dealt with by hierarchically ranking 'core' and 'sub-disciplinary' concerns. Certain epistemic convictions, or put differently, the symbolic status afforded to certain epistemic convictions will prove more conducive to occupying this position than others. Thus for instance, if as is the case for many feminist philosophers, one is persuaded by one form or another of argument for a standpoint-based epistemology, one will be less well-

---

2   As noted by Corbett et al. (this volume): 'Prospective funding agencies are drawn not just to the reality of independent analysis, but also the perception and prestige of independent analysis, for the powerful legitimating benefits this can bring to their intramural policy battles within the government sector as well as their efforts to lead public thinking on particular issues.' My argument is that this may be of broader importance within the trajectories of disciplines themselves.

suited to occupy the position of neutral judge than someone who believes in – and publishes extensively in the 'top' journals about – an epistemic position supportive of abstract ideals of objectivity.

As purveyors of academic judgment, as well as individual practitioners of career entrepreneurship, academics contribute to generating the hierarchies of institutions, faculties and journals that secure investment for some, and dis-investment for many. It would be wrong to suppose that the academic politics of defining values plays no part in this production of 'excellence', but this is always intertwined with negotiation and dispute over values intrinsic to disciplinary character: there is thus competition between the ideals and values held by diverse disciplinary practitioners, together with the struggle to secure disciplinary status, within long historical traditions that can be invoked to legitimate self-conceptions that are nonetheless also highly adapted to the spirit of the times. To be able to lay claim to practise a discipline of exemplary epistemic integrity, one that concerns itself with 'knowledge as such' may seem suicidal in a market-defined context; yet insofar as this is a quality-defining value, the prestige it carries may be worth far more than anything that is merely available for exchange.

It is broadly within these terms that I would explain how it is that philosophy – or at least, as I shall come to, the right type of philosophy – has not done nearly as badly as one might expect. Under prevailing models of the 'purpose' of universities, and of the public and private goods they should serve, philosophy readily looks to be fairly useless;[3] and despite there being stories to be told about how philosophy contributes to society, and particularly in contexts where it is 'applied' in various ways,[4] when asked to specify the 'national importance' of a conventional philosophical project on an ARC application, or to weigh one's 'impact' outside the academy, it is possible – I can testify – to feel some despair. Yet for some, this despair would be misplaced. In certain incarnations, philosophy seems to be much better able to survive market pressures than any simple picture

---

3   In the last days of the 2013 Australian Federal election, the then Leader of the Opposition Tony Abbott undertook an assault on the futility of three named research projects, two of which were in the field of continental philosophy. It is significant for my argument that these projects were in an area of research in philosophy that is not mainstream in Anglophone philosophy, and is therefore perhaps particularly vulnerable (Benson 2013).

4   See Peter Bowden responding to department closures by exhorting philosophers to meet the imperative to both educate and train by offering their skills in ethics throughout the university. 'Philosophy has failed dismally to train teachers, as it has failed to develop researchers in moral practices across the other academic disciplines. The educational literature from each of these professions demonstrates the great variety of ethics courses that has resulted from this DIY approach. The diversity is truly amazing, ranging from courses that have no moral educational content at all, to courses that are a little more than an adaptation of a history of ethics course from a department of philosophy. The blame lies with philosophers. There are virtually no training programs in the schools of philosophy for people who want to teach ethics in other disciplines. More worrying, there are very few training courses for people who have to resolve ethical issues and establish ethical practices in the workforce. As the mother discipline, this need can only be satisfied by a school of philosophy.'

of how its 'value' could be reduced to market formulae might lead one to suppose. The discipline has done very well under models of 'research excellence', since 'excellence' constitutes its own special market, bridging between disciplinary and global forms of competition. In New Zealand, Philosophy has been ranked as the highest performing discipline under ERA-type ratings Performance-Based Research Fund (PBRF) and it does exceptionally well in Australia and the UK too. This in part reflects such factors as a well-developed system of peer review, equally well-developed international networks, with collegial patterns of mutual citation especially strong in certain fields. It transpires that the way to address the question of 'national importance' is most likely to be in terms of one's project's claims to enhancing Australia's academic prestige, by contributing to a field in which one may claim international recognition. But supporting this capacity to deliver a solid validation regime there is also, as I shall go on to argue, an increasingly well-established hierarchy in the kinds of questions philosophy properly addresses, organised by a gendered distinction between 'hard' and 'soft' ends of the discipline.

Before coming to this point, however, I should place it in the context that interests me here; namely, that women do not on the whole do well in philosophy (Hutchison and Jenkins 2013). To give an indicative sample of data, in Australia, according to data collected by the Australasian Association of Philosophy (AAP), women held only 28 per cent of continuing positions in philosophy in 2009, and there is extreme vertical segregation, with around 10 per cent female professors (only two of these few at Go8 universities) (Bishop 2013). There has been little change in the gender composition of the discipline since the early 1990s. From the USA, which has a similar picture, Haslanger shows that women generally are disproportionately underrepresented at elite institutions, and that publishing patterns can be analysed to show that what are deemed the 'top' 20 journals publish articles by women at rates significantly lower than even the levels of women who have made it into tenure at elite universities (Haslanger 2008). And to give another sort of indicator, it is worth noting that during the period of the rise of PBRF, between July 2005 and April 2013, New Zealand departments appointed 20 men and just one woman to positions in philosophy. The one woman was appointed to a 0.5 position, while just four of the 20 men were also appointed to fractional positions. Although this clearly constitutes a very small sample, it invites speculation on how exercises like the PBRF or ARC measure excellence, potential, productivity and employability, in ways that are not merely entrenching but badly exacerbating gender differentials (Rini 2013).

The gendering of knowledge as 'hard' versus 'soft' finds ample expression in philosophy as an element in composing rankings of excellence, facilitating the way that certain fields of inquiry – both those practised in the majority by men, and associated, for wider reasons, with masculinity – are coded as being more worthy than others. Thus the 'hard' end of philosophy (logic, epistemology, metaphysics, as well as specific fields of ethical and socio-political inquiry that can be classed as engaged in suitably 'meta'-level theoretical activity) successfully poses as more estimable in its achievements in part because of the way in which it seems able to stand for a particular pure, rigorous and quasi-scientific inquiry, unsullied even by deference to the practical outcomes of science. Meanwhile applied aspects of philosophy, feminist theory, anything non Anglo-centric, as well as most historical interests or anything we might class as 'critique', in disciplinary terms all occupy lower tiers.[5] If the gendered dimensions of this hierarchical ordering to some degree correspond to actual distributions of men and women across the fields of philosophy (there do seem to be far fewer women in the field of logic, say, than in ethics),[6] clearly they also correspond to a normative distribution (Knights and Richards 2003, 222–3). This is further reflected in the hierarchy established by journal rankings, as well as the rankings of departments that such assessments of quality inform. One part of philosophy today *succeeds* by renewing its claims on the 'hard' values of truth and rationality. It aligns itself with scientific forms of rationality; it models a kind of neutrality that eschews values of plurality, and radical practices of critique. Thus the discipline in neoliberal times – or those who are the discipline's elite partisans – might be said to engage in a process of re-masculinisation or what Haslanger (2008) calls the 'hyper-masculine' coding of its forms of knowledge. These are aspects of contemporary disciplinary survival that lay claim to the 'objective' all too neatly; and I would wager that they conveniently coincide with employment practices which secure and re-secure male lineage, all the while under a gender-blind signage.

## Market mechanisms and global values

One way to ask how the nexus of market rationality and prestige-value has impacted on gender relations within disciplinary philosophy in recent times might be to examine the question of a particularly *intellectual* kind of relation of domination and subordination – *Who judges whom? By what right?* Bill Readings

---

5   This claim would require further work to substantiate it than I have room for here, but compare my longer discussion in Jenkins (2013). Analysis of the now defunct ERA journal rankings in Australia would provide further evidence; for instance, Hypatia is the only feminist philosophy journal ranked A* – a fact that might seem justified by the thought that this is a specialised area of study, until one also discovers that the top 'general journals' fail to publish work by women at appropriate rates, and likewise publish little or no feminist philosophy. Indeed the majority of what they publish is predominantly by male philosophers and on the 'hard' end of the discipline. Compare the list Haslanger (2008) gives of the 'top 20 journals' with the journal rankings produced in Australia under the ERA.
6   Survey data of American Philosophical Association membership supplies evidence here (Haslanger 2009).

(1996, 193) tells us that the discourse of 'excellence' arises in a nihilistic vacuum, where we prove unable to answer questions about what the university is for, as the unifying idea of 'culture' comes undone with the waning of the nation-state:

> An order of knowledge and an institutional structure are now breaking down, and in their place comes the discourse of excellence that tells teachers and students simply not to worry about how things fit together, since that is not their problem. All they have to do is get on with doing what they always have done, and the general question of integration will be resolved by the administration with the help of grids that chart the achievement of goals and tabulate efficiency.

The sign of this nihilism is extreme tolerance – you may believe what you like in the University of Excellence, 'all is simply fodder for evaluation in terms of excellence itself' (Readings 1996: 192). Yet Readings' view may be overly sanguine about how the power of 'hard' judgment fades in the wake of neoliberal reforms, overlooking the ways in which it continues to be evoked to legitimate relations of power. Certainly there is what he calls a 'de-referentialisation' at work in the discourse of excellence – that is, the inability to say what anything is excellent for, which facilitates the 'use' of excellence to trump all concrete questions of value. But the hypostatising of the idea of 'excellence' can also be achieved by presenting the appearance of neutrality attaching to objectivity, or the situationless integrity of knowledge claims (Kennedy 1990). Readings suggests that if rankings can be produced through a hybrid and arbitrary set of norms, it is primarily because there is no real 'object' – no real university – to apply them to; whereas, I would suggest that the authority of the rankings incorporates both epistemic symbols and established 'benchmark' norms in ways that function to translate contestation into hierarchical compliance (subordination) across multiple dimensions. If 'excellence' is what must be referenced in every interaction and rewarded, it is not only by way of an administrative rationality, but it also feeds off intellectual and epistemic demands for hierarchy. This constellation of university administration, academic hierarchy, and 'hard' judgment vindicates politically subordinating all that can be deemed to make merely *relative* claims to truth.

The hard/soft distinction can also be read in terms of the dominance of certain kinds of epistemic claim over others; it operates to gender disciplinary areas in alignment with ready-made perceptions of the epistemic credibility or status of disciplinary participants, but also to re-secure entitlements within the field of judgment. The wider audience for such a staging of value as hard or soft belong not just in philosophy but also in the wider institutional context of the neoliberal academy. Where journals are ranked as most significant in the field, and as belonging to the 'hard' not the 'soft' end of the discipline, what is being privileged is the aspect of the discipline more able to establish its 'excellent' credentials under particular and difficult conditions – for instance, to inflect its achievements with a quasi-scientific status that has done much to ensure philosophy's success in an academic world which very often values science over the humanities. This corresponds to a devaluing of all sorts of epistemic claims that incorporate a social dimension, including those of feminist theory, readily regarded in the prevailing neoliberal atmosphere as advancing only 'special interests' (Connell 2014). In such a context it is perhaps unsurprising that the important development of feminist critiques of the masculine hegemony lying concealed within ideals of 'pure, disinterested knowledge' has had little impact on the mainstream discipline of philosophy, or indeed that the mainstream has in many areas in fact strengthened the claims to 'objectivity' that feminist critique contested.

Ranking exercises may thus serve to reinforce established status at multiple levels. If global university rankings are to be intuitively plausible they must preserve the hierarchy with which we are already familiar – if Oxford, Cambridge, Harvard, Yale or Princeton were not in the top 10, we would most likely assume something had gone terribly wrong.[7] Likewise the micro-hierarchies composed of esteem, reputation, respect and so forth, composing some of the key mechanisms and indices of these modes of measurement, will not challenge existing conceptions. Just as the UN produces maps of the world which show, say, the distribution of respect for human rights in the world, these colour-coded schemas of excellence will reveal a world no different from the political contours established in the long history of empire. In these figurations of virtue we will find nothing that differs from visions of enduring hegemony (Davis et al. 2012). Existing patterns of dominance here reaffirm their legitimacy rather than being called into question by the inquiry. To the objective of affirming global hierarchy as such, the technical difficulties of obtaining internationally comparable data, the plurality of standards that might apply, even the highly questionable assumption that English is the only valid language of research, matter little. The globalisation of higher education becomes framed in these rankings as a competition for status and resources between players which will reaffirm the advantages of placing the vast bulk of funding into the hands of the few who are already the richest and best networked. The faculty and students who flow to such highly-ranked institutions may expect to benefit from the prestige accruing to membership in these illustrious institutions. Their movement reconfirms the high value of these centres, even as they may rightly anticipate accruing greater individual advantages to themselves.

---

7  'The fact is that essentially all of the measures used to assess quality and construct rankings enhance the stature of the large universities in the major English-speaking centres of science and scholarship and especially the United States and the United Kingdom' (Altbach 2006, 3).

Simon Marginson and Marijk van der Wende (2007: 326) comment that it remains an open question as to 'the extent to which the prestige fostered by rankings is grounded in real differences in HEI quality or merely recycles the status order'. But it is undoubtedly the case that this notion of 'quality' cannot get going without incorporating generous doses of status affirmation concerning the *right to judge* – and this perhaps in direct proportion to the need to counteract potential scepticism about the *capacity to measure* what is being 'produced' across a wide range of needs and differences. Thus it is that:

> Most systems of rankings tend to emphasise vertical differences between institutions and between nations, differences of power and authority. At the same time, they obscure horizontal differences, differences of purpose and type. Despite the attractions of horizontal diversity in higher education, league tables have a compelling popularity, regardless of questions of validity, of the uses to which the data are put, and of the effects in system organisation. Rankings are easily recalled, as league tables, and have quickly become part of commonsense knowledge of the sector (Marginson and Van de Wende 2007, 326).

There is a pattern here of self-aggrandisement corresponding to the persistent undervaluing and marginalisation of difference. This should remind us of all that feminists have long contended against. What has been their response to these phenomena?

## Gender equality in the orbit of 'excellence'

A recent manifesto demanding equality of opportunity and pay for female academics calls for institutions to declare how many of their professors, top researchers and students are female, and for this gender profiling to enter into the global rankings of quality. This call to arms cites a report from UNESCO detailing how in 2010, just 29 per cent of researchers worldwide were female (Matthews 2012). The aim of getting global rankings to incorporate measures such as the pay gap between men and women and the gender make-up of senior management is in line with the trend of equity activism in the academic sector to advocate to a high degree within the terms offered by the neoliberal framing of the university sector.

Most discussion of gender equality in academia is now driven by the vocabulary and rationale of the market. It evokes the vocabulary of excellence in order to make a range of claims that link economic benefits to gender parity. In this genre, the fact that women leave academia at much higher rates than men, despite rough parity of numbers on average at PhD level – this reflecting amongst other things, generally unsupportive working conditions and a large gender pay gap – is taken up in the mainstream advocacy literature as cause for concern primarily on the grounds that this leakage clearly reduces the pool of talent on which employers might draw. The League of European Research Universities (LERU) report *Women, Research and Universities: Excellence without Gender Bias* (LERU 2012), can be taken as exemplary of the argument presently being put in many quarters:

> more women than men drop out of research careers, resulting in an underrepresentation of women in leading positions, a loss of talent for society and a lack of diversity in the workplace, each of which presents a potential threat to the search for excellence in research (LERU 2012, 3).

As an aspect of its concern to specify the 'good economic as well as value-based arguments' (p. 5) that should underpin universities' gender policies, the report cites 'the lack of an appropriate gender dimension in research design, implementation and organisation' as resulting in 'serious flaws with potentially harmful effects, e.g. in medical research, thus limiting scientific excellence, creativity and benefits to society' (p. 3). Indeed, this claim, together with the idea of a leaking 'pool' of talent constitutes the entire underpinning of the proposal made here – that the LERU universities commit to bringing about structural change to increase women's participation, including the earmarking of special funds to support women at critical stages of their careers.

The LERU report, again typically, places much weight in its analysis on forms of bias that are typically 'unconscious' and of inequities typically too small to see, but cumulative in their effects – 'micro-inequities', as Mary Rowe named them (1974). These factors, for which it would be useless to apportion blame, are held to be the major determinants in distorting career outcomes, ultimately to the detriment of both employers and society at large. These factors not only impair judgment of women's true performance, but also have an 'impact on research productivity and are thereby decisive for career prospects' (LERU 2012, 6). It seems to have become important to affirm that these negative outcomes are not the results of any bad intentions, that men and women alike are able to perpetuate them, and thus that the system is in other respects operating properly but requires adjustments of a mechanical more than a political nature if it is to run optimally. Better investment, allowance for periods of reduced productivity, and appropriate incentives will correct the gendered drain of talent.

None of this in any way challenges the norms by which academic activity is conceptualised in market terms; on the contrary, this is a feminism reinvented to match advocacy strategy to the dominant discourses of our time. To assess whether it is likely to be effective is a task beyond the scope of this discussion – certainly it is not at all clear how women in philosophy would benefit if, as I have suggested, success in this area requires a certain distancing from economic goals in favour of laying claim to 'prestige' signifiers. Why invest in women in philosophy if one's goal is to increase a pool of talent with clear socioeconomic objectives? Strategically important though this approach is, what it misses is the need for critique of some aspects of the gendered shape of the neoliberal academy that I have been stressing in the preceding discussion; for instance, how the vocabulary of excellence presumes well-established fields of knowledge into which, at best, women might enter, and to which they might contribute, only as bearers of 'talent' flowing into an existing pool of knowledge.

Contrast the picture drawn by Alison Wylie, a philosopher of science, who argues not simply that we are failing to draw on resources, or that we may be inadvertently overlooking talent – thus not being as 'excellent' as we might otherwise be – but that 'gender inequities can create a cascade of content effects that raise serious questions about the epistemic integrity of a field' (Wylie 2012, 67). Her argument here goes well beyond the idea that we are losing out on some valuable contributors to well-established fields of inquiry to examine precisely the question of how 'epistemic integrity' is constituted. Elaborating the claims of feminist standpoint theory, she argues that disrupting established models of epistemic *credibility* in view of bringing to light their social coordinates is a key stake in achieving a gender equity that itself has epistemic dimensions. The economic factors that establish the language of excellence as the horizon of judgment, are displaced here to make room for demanding critical engagement with the modes of social organisation that provide legitimation to our epistemic practises. These, she argues (2012, 67), must take serious account of both the gendered modes of knowledge transmission (including factors of influence, reputation, resourcing) and production as elements in thinking about how rights of judgment are secured:

> this suggests that the ratification of empirical and theoretical results, as knowledge claims we can trust, must be informed by a systematic assessment of how well the epistemic resources of diverse situated epistemic agents have been incorporated into their adjudication; social-cognitive norms of community practice must bring a critical standpoint perspective to bear on the processes of knowledge production if they are to be epistemically credible.

Where the Repqrt cites an 'unconscious bias' in judging women's performance, for which, as is common in the psychological literature, no further account is given (it seems to be considered sufficient merely to evidence the phenomenon itself), Wylie cites 'testimonial injustice' – linked to the devaluation of women as epistemic agents, capable of giving credible accounts. Here the difference is that Wylie intends to reveal an epistemic issue at the very core of knowledge transmission and reception that reflects how seeing or hearing what one wants to (in 'biased' ways) is secured within relations of power that facilitate the 'ubiquitous partiality of social science' (2012, 55). Her claims run in the opposite direction to the prevailing 'excellence'-based accounts by focusing her critical sights precisely on the problems inherent in the hierarchical ordering of knowledge claims conjoint with the hierarchies of knowers, as these work together to produce profound 'blind spots'. It is less that bias operates on a case-by-case basis than that ruling practices are generally invisible to those who 'operate "centre stage", who benefit from the status quo, and who largely define the agenda of the social sciences' (Wylie 2012, 50).

The two agendas of feminist critique do converge at certain crucial points. Both advocate to: 'create gender excellence in research through building inclusive scholarly communities in which men and women contribute equally at all levels of decision making, policy and defining and carrying out research' (Wylie 2012, 11, citing Schiebinger and Schraudner 2011).

The LERU Report argues that the socioeconomic impacts of failing to factor gender into research implementation disadvantage women, insofar as knowledge of their specific needs is less likely to be met – medicine being the paradigm case. In the context of the Report, however, this is translated as the idea that women bring more perspectives to bear, and its evident implications centre on the paradigm of medial science that functions in a privileged way throughout to bolster the argument that absent women's participation, we may miss something important – women's specific bodily differences no less! Despite all that is valid in this concern, it problematically limits the vistas by which we might take the measure of the epistemic advantages involved in challenging existing practice, these considered less perhaps as indexed to the project of *including* more women, but instead more usefully thought of as *limiting* the hegemony of the masculine.

A 'critical standpoint perspective' precisely does not hold that women need to be included because of the additional perspectives they bring by being women. Such identity-based claims for the value of women's scholarship has indeed led many women to reject an association with feminist perspectives, and with good reason, for the equation of the 'value' of work with originating in and elaborating a particular perspective, as we have seen, makes it particularly vulnerable to denigration within the 'excellence' economy of claims-making – it becomes a 'special interest', and is inflected from the beginning with the disabling connotations of bias. Wylie, however, helps show a different strategy from the one that, by making identity-based claims for including women's perspectives, would risk contributing to the marginalisation of women's work, and relegation to the 'soft' end of the spectrum of knowledge; for she is advocating something more disruptive than 'inclusion of diversity' or an additive model of bringing differently situated perspectives to bear. But she can do so *only* by reopening sociopolitical frameworks for thinking about gender equity as integrally bound up with epistemic values at the level of the *ratification* of credibility, over against the socioeconomic framework appealed to in the LERU Report. The issue Wylie is pressing on in her revision of the key claims of standpoint theory is how a mismatch between experience and theory becomes a provocation to question and how marginalised perspectives thus need to be incorporated into good science, not because they supplement or correct oversights, but because at the level of the ratification of empirical and theoretical results, they establish a practice of transformative criticism.

This practice, I think, directly addresses the problem inherent in global ranking exercises, which I suggested incorporate generous doses of status affirmation concerning the *right to judge* in order to counteract legitimate scepticism about the *capacity to measure* in what is irreducibly a socio-politically constituted field, comprising a wide range of incommensurable needs and differences. On this account, mainstream research tends to reiterate bias when it fails to be questioned by contesting prevailing epistemic hegemony, but this claim runs profoundly against the models of excellence in academic practise, as they are currently being fostered by an irreducibly sociopolitical, pseudo-market rationality. Wylie's account of feminist standpoint theory suggests a model of knowledge acquisition that would seem to require us to encounter and show humility with respect to difference, for epistemic reasons, because it is this that might challenge us to think again. As such, perhaps it promises a very different model of the global university, and the place of philosophy within it, from the one I sketched out above.

# Part II: Markets, Managers and Mandarins

# 4. What's to be Explained? And is it so Bad?

Geoffrey Brennan

## Getting the diagnosis right

The point of departure for the conference 'Markets and the Modern University, from which this chapter arose, is a concern – 'a concern about the way knowledge is being shaped by the commodification of higher education'. And the title of the conference indicates a first-round diagnosis: the intrusion of the 'market' and the re-conceptualisation of knowledge from being a 'public good' to being a 'private good'. The ambition of our collective reflections is to examine all this 'with particular regard for the impact on the social sciences'.

In what follows, I want to address, head on, both this particular concern and the diagnosis of it. To reveal all my cards at the outset, I believe that the concern is ill-specified and that the projected diagnosis is misplaced. There may well be attributes of the modern Australian university that are grounds for concern: I share the view that there are. But in my view, the concern is *not* the 'way knowledge is being shaped' – and not the impact on knowledge in the social sciences more specifically. Frankly, I think that when the concerns are appropriately diagnosed and the source of them properly understood, they may well appear less epistemically and institutionally threatening than the organisers of this conference seem to fear. Moreover, though in some loose way, 'the market' might be implicated in these concerns (when properly specified) I think that the role of markets is considerably exaggerated.

Normally, the 'economics tradition' (which, with appropriate revisionist glosses,[1] I like to think I broadly represent) insists that explanation should begin with a clear specification of the problem to be addressed and then turn to the question of what should be done about it. Economists take diagnosis to be logically prior to prescription. But here, I want to begin with the prescription and then work back to the 'concern'.

## What's the market got to do with it?

So let me begin with the question posed as the title of this section: what's the market got to do with it?

Just to focus for a moment on the Australian university system, it seems to me to be a total mischaracterisation to describe it as an instantiation of a market institution. The number of students in total; the enrolments at different institutions; how many institutions there will be; and to some extent what programs those institutions will offer – all seem to be governed by administrative decisions taken by bureaucrats, reflecting broad political priorities. And what is true of the Australian system is true of every system in the world, with the exception of the US. Even within the US, the role of markets can easily be exaggerated. A large proportion of US students attend State universities, where fees and enrolment numbers and numbers of campuses are determined by State legislatures. And the cost of research activities (apart from the time of academics) is significantly funded from public sources (National Science Foundation and its analogues).[2]

In short, the university system is largely – in many places almost exclusively – publicly run and administered. And most of the changes that seem to motivate this colloquium (or, since I cannot speak for others, that strike me as being proper objects of concern) I see as having originated mainly from government initiatives of one kind or another – not from the operation of markets as such.

---

1   Just how 'revisionist' is a tricky matter. To declare a few aspects: an abandonment of *homo economicus* in several dimensions (in particular the acceptance of a role for moral and related norms and of the desire for social esteem in explaining human behaviour); a recognition of the importance of politics in policy design and execution; a view of democratic political process that is not purely interest-based: to name the most important. But I retain an appropriately qualified commitment to methodological individualism and to agent rationality – features that in my view lie at the Lakatosian core of the 'economic way of thinking'.
2   Moreover, almost no institutions operate by charging a market-clearing price to students. Almost all ration undergraduate places by measured 'ability' to some extent and many of the most prestigious claim to accept students on an income-blind basis (i.e. on perceived ability alone). And almost all graduate students are in receipt of significant subsidies. In important respects therefore, the 'market' in student places is 'self-effacing'.

Let me be clear here. In referring to 'markets', I have in mind an *institutional framework* for coordinating the decisions of relevant players. I am not referring to the basic *economic* realities – the fact that university education and research use up resources, or that those resources have an opportunity cost, or that the time students spend at university is time that could have been spent in other pursuits. Those realities exist whatever the funding details. Of course, these are not the only realities relevant to running a fine university (or a fine university system). And it may be that a view of the university that foregrounds such cost considerations – a view, as we might put it, of the university as a 'site of cost contestation' – serves to occlude those other, no less crucial, realities. This might be, for example, the kind of view that earns economists[3] a description as 'those who lack the imagination to be accountants'!

In a similar spirit, we ought to distinguish carefully between market institutions and what we might loosely term 'market rhetoric'. Although the reference, in the aforementioned conference brief, is to the impact (of such changes) *'on the social sciences'*, it seems relevant to acknowledge the impact *of* the social sciences – and specifically of the role of putatively 'economic ways of thinking' about the university – as a source of many of the changes that most of the commentary here seems to find objectionable.

As I see it (and I concede at once that this may be a highly eccentric view) one of the challenges for economists that arises from the topic of this colloquium is to produce an analysis of the university as an institution that is obedient to the grammatical strictures of rational actor theory, but sensitive to the kinds of considerations that many academics regard as central and that standard economic treatments seem to background (if not overlook entirely). In what follows (and specifically in the [section] addressing the modern Australian university below) I will try to gesture at what might be involved. This is a gesture only: a fuller treatment will have to await a different occasion.

The concession that we economists need to provide a plausible 'economic' account of the institutions of enquiry is not at all to concede that the changes that have occurred in the university system over the last say 30 years and that seem to be the focus of concern here are to be attributed exclusively to the rise of a particular set of ideas – still less that such ideas owe their origin to economics as a discipline. Although I don't concede that claim, I am certainly prepared to entertain it as a *hypothesis*. However, in order to test it out, we need first to get a fix on what the changes to be explained are; and second to

---

3    To the extent that it is a view typical of economists. It shouldn't be, I think, and wouldn't if we were better economists!

speculate a bit more generally about what factors might explain those changes. We will then be in a better position to evaluate the changes – to deplore them, if (but only if) that seems warranted.

# What is to be explained?

I think we should be clear, at the outset, about what we should *not* be trying to explain. If the concern is with the 'shape of knowledge', then the topic is a global one. It cannot plausibly be examined by focusing on the Australian case — since Australia makes up less than two per cent of the world's 'knowledge economy'. In other words, there may be good reasons for querying many of the changes that have occurred in Australian higher education over the last 25 years but a concern based on the effects on 'knowledge' seems megalomaniacal to the point of absurdity; and of course, no less absurd when the focus is limited to the 'impact on the social sciences'.

More generally, we should be wary of extrapolating too quickly from Australian experience to what is going on in the rest of the world. If, as it happens, some of the things that have gone on in Australia are mirrored in other countries then observing which things are common and with which countries offers prospects for explanatory insights. It suggests, in particular, that only if the factors isolated as explanations in the Australian case are replicated in the other countries will that explanation be valid. For example, it seems to me (on the basis of casual observation) that many of the things that have been happening in Australian universities have been mirrored in the UK – where the structure of the university system is very similar to Australia's – but are distinctly less conspicuous in the US. But of course this claim depends on what the 'changes' in question are; and as I say, that just shows why it's important to achieve clarity on that aspect.

So, what are the changes in question?

1.  Increased formality (and associated intrusiveness) in the processes of performance evaluation – most notable in relation to research but also relevant to teaching, graduate supervision and a range of related matters.

2.  A shift in the governance structures within universities away from collective control to more 'managerial' styles.[4] I take it in other words that there has been a significant shift in most institutions away from a 'worker-managed' operation to a more hierarchical form in relation to broad collective decisions

---

4   [Speaking for myself, I now spend much less time in university committees – on professorial or academic boards – than I did 30 years ago (to say nothing of 40) and those committees I do attend are less decision-making than 'information-providing'.]

about the university as a whole. Decisions about research domain and content of courses remain as far as I can tell essentially matters for determination by individual academics. In that respect there has been little change over my career.

3. Greater reliance on 'external' funding for research (mainly through the Australian Research Council (ARC) and the National Health and Medical Research Council (NHMRC), but also on specific government initiatives that lie outside the standard university financing processes).

4. An associated development of interest within universities in 'patentable' research findings'.

5. Larger numbers of non-domestic students.

6. Increased reliance on students as direct sources of revenue (mainly under the HECS scheme in Australia or full fee-paying postgraduate coursework programs).

7. Scale – a significant expansion in the proportion of the age cohort that attends a 'university' and an associated increase in the: number of institutions so designated; and the aggregate cost of the higher education/research system as a proportion of GDP.

8. Increased labour market participation of putatively 'full-time' students (perhaps attributable to the restricted availability and low level of publicly provided student income support).

Not all these changes are independent. As I shall argue later, I think scale has an important influence on many of the other changes. However, I think it is analytically useful to treat the various changes separately – rather than as a bundle.

I have then set myself two general tasks: first, to broaden the standard 'economic' model of institutional performance in a way that enables that model to incorporate at least some of the anxieties aired by many critics of the 'modern university'; secondly, to put this expanded model to work to see how far it can account for at least some of the relevant changes and some of the grounds of critique.

# A modified institutional analysis

## Questions of motivation

It is not a necessary feature of rational actor theory that agents be attributed any specific motivation; but as a matter of fact it is common to ascribe to agents preferences that are predominantly (sometimes exclusively) egoistic in a rather materialistic sense: *homo economicus* (HE) is not so named for nothing! For lots of standard applications, this attribution is probably an acceptable abstraction – but it *is* an abstraction, and becomes seriously strained in lots of non-standard applications. One implication of the HE construction is that institutional analysis focuses on (indeed consists in analysing) the material incentives that that institution invokes. For many purposes that focus is way too narrow: one needs to take account of what Bruno Frey has called 'intrinsic motivation' on the one hand; and the desire for esteem (social approval) on the other.[5]

It is worth noting that the desire to stand high(er) in the opinions of others is itself an essentially egoistic desire: it is MY level of social esteem that 'enters my utility function' – not YOUR level of esteem. In that sense, esteem operates as just another currency of reward (and/or punishment) much like income.

But note that esteem depends on prevailing evaluations – evaluations that track the norms and values that are widely possessed out there in the relevant community. It is true that a person may be driven by esteem considerations to act in accord with values that she herself doesn't hold. But that can't be true for everyone.[6] It probably can't even be true for a majority. That is, the attitudes that observers possess (the attitudes that constitute the esteem or disesteem) reflect the values that the esteem-seeker is induced to track in her behaviour. And those values constitute the norms that govern the activity.

It seems self-evident to me that in virtually all activities, material reward, intrinsic returns and desire for esteem are all in play (though in different proportions in different activities). So, some cricketers may be driven to play the game simply because of the esteem they derive from doing so from people who care about cricket. But most of them presumably enjoy the game themselves, are inclined to play by the rules for the sake of the 'game', and strive to do as well as they can for the sheer internal pleasure of doing so. Certainly, as top cricketers make increasingly large amounts of money (largely from playing 20/20 games in India) purely instrumental considerations play an increasing role in explaining their behaviour – why, for example, they play as much as they do (and, for many, much more often than they would prefer, if it were not for external rewards).

The same could be said for opera singers – indeed, for professional musicians of all kinds – namely, that they derive significant intrinsic reward from the activities they engage in, and considerable public acclaim (specifically in the

---

5   One also needs to keep in mind the manner in which institutional mechanisms of selection operate (Frey 1997).

6   This claim is a bit strong. Under conditions of 'pluralistic ignorance', everyone might believe that others hold value V even when none does: the result can be a kind of 'emperor's-new-clothes' equilibrium. The claim in the text presupposes a certain level of transparency of others' values.

community of opera-lovers whose esteem they especially care about).[7] It would be ludicrous to model their behaviour as if money were all that mattered. Which, of course, is not to say that it doesn't matter at all.

The same is surely true of the 'life of the mind'. Most of us in academic life are driven (*in part*) by the intrinsic satisfaction we derive from the activities that make up that life. We teach our students material we think it will be good for them to know; we make our lectures as interesting and engaging as we can; we do our best to stimulate the imaginations and intellectual curiosity of our students; we write papers because we think (hope) that we have something interesting and/or worthwhile to say to our peers. We have to some extent internalised the norms of our respective disciplines and of the process of enquiry more generally. We admire the really smart and gifted scholars we know. And we struggle to secure their respect. Pathetically perhaps, we even care what our students think of us — and do our best to be conscientious and energetic teachers — in part for that reason! These professional considerations also largely track our interests. Broadly, promotion and better job offers, and conference invitations, and options to give seminars at interesting places, are all connected to our scholarly performance and our reputation as teachers and presenters. We bring to our work the same sorts of motivations that opera singers and cricketers bring to theirs — an understanding of what the activity *is* that we are acculturated into; a love of that activity for its own sake, as well as for the good things it gives us; and a dependence for recognition on our professional peers — not just those in our own departments but across the globe! Or at least, that has been true of most of my colleagues in the various departments, both here and overseas, in which I have worked across my now 45-year career (which I don't regard as over just yet, by the way).

All this seems self-evident to me. But I am lucky to have worked in excellent places with excellent colleagues for most of my life; and I do not regard it as self-evident that all universities (in Australia and elsewhere) are like this — and that not all academics are quite as driven as my immediate peers have been. In short, there is considerable heterogeneity — concerning the weight of motivations of different kinds across different individuals.

In getting a sense of the extent of such differences, it is interesting to reflect on some empirical work that Francis Teal and I did on research output of academic economists in Australia from 1974 to 1983. Over that 10-year period, the top six publishers produced more than 11 per cent of the quality-weighted[8] research

---

7    For an estimate of the size of these non-pecuniary benefits, see Withers (1985).

8    The quality weights are very rough and ready. Another possible metric would be citations rather than publications; but the distribution of citations is even more extravagantly skewed towards those recognised professionally as the 'top scholars'. Citations are a reasonable metric for economics, where journal articles carry almost all the relevant scholarship.

output: the top 15 persons produced a quarter of Australia's research output (Brennan and Teal 1992, 22–30). Out of the roughly 300 names appearing in departmental annual reports over that period, about a half published nothing at all in any given year. (Of those in the sample for the entire 10 years, 14 per cent produced nothing in that entire period.) The bottom half of the distribution produced five per cent of the total (quality-weighted) output. These figures are a reminder that not everything was so very rosy in the 'good old days'! As Teal and I remarked at the time, there are two ways to read this data – one is that there is a huge problem of freeloading at the bottom; the other is that in the research domain at least, one really has to nurture and look after one's stars. Those top 15 academic economists in Australia were punching way above weight!

In short, as one would expect, there is likely to be some heterogeneity of motivation both within and between universities (as in all civil society). But for a significant proportion of the players, non-material motivations (intrinsic and esteem-related) are extremely important. And it seems that these players are far and away the most productive! Equally, the evidence suggests that for many players (more perhaps than one would prefer), non-material motivations play a relatively small role.

## Extending the institutional array

The second feature of rational actor institutional analysis is a tendency to treat the institutional landscape as a kind of choice (or antinomy) between two broad institutional mechanisms: the 'invisible hand' of the market; and the 'iron hand' of government. So, for example, in the more or less standard approach in public economics/public choice, a central normative question is to specify the appropriate domain of government activity. The procedure here is to develop a theory of 'market failure' – based on the properties of goods (non-excludability and collective consumption, in varying degrees and combinations) – and then a general account of 'political failure' (which is essentially good-independent). The standard conclusion is that markets have a comparative advantage in the provision of private goods, while governments have a comparative advantage in the provision of public goods. (Markets may still have an absolute advantage in the latter if the degree of 'market failure' is not too great).

It may be worth noting that the public/private dichotomy in this analysis is driven by the technical properties of the goods in question. Whether university education is a 'private good' or a 'public good' depends on whether the benefits of that higher education accrue mainly to the individual educated or to other parties. One can obtain reasonably ready estimates of the former benefits by examining the future income-earning profiles of university graduates compared with non-university 'equivalents' (as best one can detect them). Such measures do not incorporate the 'consumption benefits' accruing in terms of general intellectual enrichment or better understanding of the social order – and there is little attempt to determine which of these might be associated with 'external' benefits to persons other than the graduate. Nor is there any attempt to assess the consumption benefits associated with access to social activities while on campus with lots of other persons of a similar age and inclination (though I suspect that these latter benefits are an important reason for many to become university students).[9] Of course, different analyses of behaviour (and different attempts at normative evaluation) might variously emphasise the 'private' as against the 'public' aspects of such calculations; but it is doubtful whether any such emphasis amounts to a 'reconceptualisation' in anyone's eyes except perhaps those of government bureaucrats and politicians. These latter are of course important given current institutional arrangements. But I want to suggest that their importance can be overstated. Put another way, I do not think that we in the academy should necessarily take their assessment of their own importance entirely at face value!

Which brings me to the main point of this sub-section, which is to underline the fact that the portfolio of institutional options here is severely limited. What is omitted from the government/market dichotomy is the vast array of what makes up 'civil society' – organisation/institution combinations in which the primary relations are governed neither by market nor political arrangements, but lie somewhere else. For convenience, I have sketched the likely contenders among this 'vast array' in Table 4.1, indicating both the area of activity and the organisational forms associated with it.

**Table 4.1: Institutions and organisations of civil society**

| Activity | Organisation | Institution* |
|---|---|---|
| Religion | Churches | Practices/norms/beliefs |
| Performing arts | Opera companies, theatre companies | Aesthetic rules of fine performance |
| Sports | Various | Rules of the games<br>Conventions that determine best play |
| Language | Analogues of the 'French academy'? | Rules of grammar aesthetics of best usage |
| Law | Courts | 'Rule of recognition'<br>Norms of procedure |
| Enquiry | Academia and research laboratories | *Epistemic and procedural Norms of knowledge/enquiry* |

\* By 'institution' here, I mean something like the rules/norms/conventions that define the activity and that at least putatively govern relations within the organisational forms.

Source: Author's summary.

---

9  Perhaps this judgment relies excessively on introspection. But let me just emphasise that these benefits are, for a utilitarian, no less valid than increases in material benefit.

Now it is not that economists have entirely ignored these activities, or the organisations and institutions that go with them. There are nevertheless only occasional papers that deal with 'the economics of non-market decision-making' (as public choice used to be called – and making a broad ambit claim for things beyond politics). Such analysis has been something of a fringe activity (much like 'rational actor political theory' used to be). The 'economic' element in these cases is constituted by a recognisable application of 'the economic way of thinking' in which rationality; methodological individualism; a concern with relative prices/incentives in explaining changes in behaviour; and an attention to equilibrating forces in social processes, are all characteristic features.

The general reductionist move of treating these institutions as operating either as instances of market relations or political ones (or more typically some combination of the two) is inadequate because it occludes the role of norm-driven behaviour by the participants in the activities in question. The truth is that many 'public goods' of a sort are produced primarily in institutional settings that, though they sit alongside governments and markets and are somewhat involved in both to various extents, are significantly independent of both. This is a point developed at some length (Chapter 5 is devoted to the topic) by Buchanan and Tullock in *The Calculus of Consent,* but sadly the public choice tradition of scholarship since 1962 has not much taken it up.

## The modern Australian university? The issue of scale

To the extent that a significant proportion of academics are driven by norms and subject to institutional constraints that support and mobilise those norms, the university is or can be a largely self-governing institution. One can rely on the intrinsic benefits and esteem-related concerns of academics to motivate them to do what is in their own professional interests. The role of university 'management' on this view is to provide a venue – a venue that might be more or less congenial – for the academics (and their students) to pursue those interests; and otherwise to interfere as little as possible. The idea that the role of university 'leadership' is to 'manage' the activities of the university – say, of the so-called Director of a Research School to 'direct' research activities – is ludicrous.[10] Decisions as to what lines of research to pursue and how best to pursue them can ultimately only be taken by individual academics, influenced as they must inevitably be by their immediate professional colleagues and the

---

10   About as ludicrous as the claim routinely made by successive Treasurers that they are 'managing' the Australian economy!

imagined judgment of those whose opinions they care about. Put another way, the amount of genuine power that university management has over these micro-matters is pretty severely limited.

Or at least, this is true where the norms of academic culture are well-embedded. So, the question of how broadly embedded that culture is becomes an important general question for the operation of the system. And this is where scale enters the picture. Because standard analysis would suggest that the marginal students/academics would be less motivated by intrinsic rewards than the infra-marginal ones. An economist who is drawn by puzzles, strongly motivated by intellectual curiosity, who greatly enjoys the pursuit of learning for its own sake will want to be an academic economist at wages that a more pecuniarily motivated equivalent would scoff at. If the demand for academic economists were to increase, salaries would have to increase in part because the individuals attracted into the sector would tend to be those whose intrinsic motivations are less significant. In other words, other things being equal, individuals self-select into employments according to the level of intrinsic benefits they derive from the activity: those with highest intrinsic returns are the infra-marginal ones. So much is entirely conventional labour market analysis.

The shift from an elite to a mass higher education system has greatly increased the number of students, the number of academics, the number of universities, and the overall cost to government. All of these features are significant. So it should not be surprising if the mix of motivational types on both the teacher and student side of the 'market' should exhibit a shift towards more vocational (and less intellectual curiosity-driven) types.

Nor should it surprise us if the academic culture in many more 'marginal' universities is quite thin. If most of one's colleagues are publishing only occasionally in second-rate journals, then that practice becomes the 'norm' in that department. To earn the esteem of one's colleagues, to the extent that those colleagues esteem publishing at all, one needn't produce very much and what one does produce needn't be especially well-placed. Where the culture is thin, it is not surprising if external modes of evaluation and regulation are put in place.

Nor should it be surprising if, as the scale of operations increases, government increasingly demands that universities justify the size of their operations and the associated costs by reference to criteria that diverge from the academic norms that operate *within* universities. Simply put, the fact that we denizens of the university believe in the life of the mind for its own sake – and to a greater or lesser extent pursue it – is an important fact *for us*. But there is no reason why we should imagine that that set of values will – or ought to – be internalised by the general public or their political representatives. And the fact that the general public (and their political agents) do not internalise our values should not be a source of exasperation to us – or grounds for our modifying the idealisation of the university as a community of dedicated scholars. That idealisation still strikes me as powerfully alive and relevant in many institutions; but it is only to be predicted that it will clash with the attitude to the university held by politicians and senior bureaucrats and the general public.

So I don't think it should surprise us if governments increasingly try to squeeze university budgets, or offload some of the cost of the significant expansion that has occurred onto students, or are increasingly anxious to ensure that scarce public funds are being spent 'responsibly'. Nor should it surprise us if university administrators are responsive to such demands. Doubtless to many within their universities, Vice-Chancellors and their offsiders (considerable and increasing?) will appear to be just agents of governments; and doubtless to governments, those same persons will seem much less responsive than those governments would like. Those in these administrative positions within universities have to walk a tightrope between an external and an internal culture. They have my sympathy.[11]

Still, the clash is not always so clear-cut. At least some of the changes that are occurring and will occur seem to me to be less undermining of academic values than many people seem to make out. Let me mention a couple.

1.  The increased globalisation of the academic labour market has meant that long-standing traditions of uniform salaries across disciplines and across individuals at the professorial level are under increased pressure. This is an example of the increased role of market forces – but Australia has little option here but to respond. Maintaining academic salaries on the basis of averages across the entire system and across individuals within an institution is just a recipe for bleeding from the top. Of course, salary is not critical for many academics; but quality of colleagues is. And over the long haul Australia cannot hope to retain the very best academics without introducing major disparities in academic salaries both between persons and fields. Salary differentiation has already begun in a minor way. Federation Fellowships are one element. Subject loadings are another. But, as in the UK, the system of professorial salary equality will just have to go – unless Australian universities are to commit to a hopeless mediocrity. Of course, Australia has never been much committed to elite activity anywhere except in sports – and the funding of two or three first-class universities across the country faces significant political hurdles. Australia has at best two per cent of the world's English-speaking academics weighted by GDP. If there are 10,000 universities in the world (*Scientometrics* counts 17,000) the top 100 is one per cent of that

---

11  This is, of course, not to deny that some administrators just enjoy bossing other people around and are only too happy to operate in an increasingly managerial university culture.

total. This means that if Australia had one institution in the top 100 it would be doing about twice as well as one could reasonably expect. To have more than that would require either a greater commitment to higher education as a whole or greater concentration of resources across institutions than other countries or both. The truth is that Australia is currently doing remarkably well in the international comparative stakes. But the competition will get predictably fiercer and the need to increase resources and concentrate them more across the best institutions will increase if Australia is to remain in these rankings where it currently lies.

2. Research resources are scarce and there is a major issue of getting resources through to the best researchers – which is going to mean greater differentiation in working conditions across the system (and almost certainly within institutions). The ARC is one mechanism for doing this. No such mechanism is likely to be perfect; but as far as the Research Assessment Exercise (RAE) exercises in Britain are concerned, I have to say that the rankings in the fields I know seem to me to be broadly right. Compared with alternative mechanisms for allocating given research resources, it seems to me that the relation between the academic criteria that emerge from broad consensus within the disciplines and the values of the RAE is pretty close.

In short, the changes in the Australian (and the UK) university system since the late 1980s are in my view largely the result of the shift from an elite to a mass higher education system plus changes like increased globalisation and e-technology that lie entirely outside our control.

Although I am not sure that mass higher education is altogether a good idea, I think that not all the changes that have been associated with that shift are changes for the worse. I think the basic Newman idealisation of the university remains alive and well in many institutions. I certainly do not think of that ideal as 'irretrievably lost'; and it seems to me to reveal a certain lack of imagination to think so. There have been some changes since the 'good old days' of say 1975; but specifically in terms of Newman idealisations, I want to report that the good old days were not all that great.

And even when Deans and Directors and DVCs and Vice-Chancellors seem determined to 'exercise their leadership' via clichés from the latest 'management manuals', most of us can simply lower our heads and get on with our work – engage with questions *we* find interesting; teach what *we* consider important, in a manner that by and large doesn't need to make too many concessions; and simply bluff it out. It may take increasing courage and inflict greater stress to do that than it once did. But it seems to me that there are fewer genuine freeloaders[12] among the academics in universities than there once were; and that we operate in an environment in which it is still possible to captivate students and to do 'good work', and enjoy the esteem of those whose opinions matter to us, and freely bestow that esteem on others who seem to us to merit it. That is largely what has sustained the life of the mind in the past – and living that life has not yet become inaccessible in Australian universities. Saying this is not to deny that a larger proportion of the student body and a larger proportion of academic staff are less engaged by that life than in the past. Moreover, one method of limiting the cost of an expanded system has been to provide more limited time to faculty for activities like research and scholarly reflection. That is a cost associated with the move from an elite towards a mass higher education system. There is, doubtless, much to be said in favour of that move; but it has necessarily imposed some cost on the higher education system. My objective in this chapter has been to lay out the nature of those costs, to emphasise that they are more or less inevitable and to observe that on the whole the system has probably managed them about as well as one might reasonably expect.

---

12   A referee speculates that the number of freeloaders in administrative positions in Australian universities may well have increased. This may well be so, but I am not in a position to judge.

# 5. Higher Education 'Markets' and University Governance

Tony Aspromourgos[1]

It was one theme of my recent critical essay on managerialism in the universities that much loose policy talk about the market and universities has a superficial plausibility only because the conditions required for a genuinely *competitive* market are not explicitly acknowledged (Aspromourgos 2012). It is only some notion of the applicability of the benefits of competition to higher education and university research that can favour a market model for universities. To the extent that standard economic theory justifies 'the market' as a superior way of allocating resources relative to other modes of allocation, it is not the market *as such* that is thereby endorsed; it is the competitive market in particular. Some further implications of this, particularly in relation to the character of university governance, are considered here.

My argument, in part, may be conceived of as complementary to that of Geoffrey Brennan in this volume (chapter 4). His point of departure is that the institutional and policy changes with respect to Australian universities in recent decades have not, in fact, been a move towards greater market organisation of the sector: our position is that, for the educational dimension of universities' activities in particular, a genuinely competitive market is not possible. This is due to two inescapable and unalterable facts about university degree provision: 1) acquiring any particular kind of degree is a one-off act of consumption, per person per lifetime; and 2) it is intrinsic to the situation of a knowledge- or

---

1   The author is indebted to participants in the ASSA 'Markets and the Modern University' Workshop (The Australian National University, May 2013), without thereby implicating them in the final product.

information-intensive consumption item, like a degree, that the consumer lacks substantial knowledge of the product. The latter condition is not an unfortunate contingent circumstance that could be overcome; it is *essential* to the situation.[2]

## Academic markets and competition

Without aspiring here to absolute comprehensiveness in constituting the notion of a competitive market, the conditions notably include: a) multiple agents, or at least multiple potential agents, on both the demand side and the supply side; b) substitutable alternatives to the commodity or commodities being traded in the market under consideration; c) that there be available in common to all potential market participants, a body of information concerning the economically relevant characteristics of the commodities; and d) similarly available common knowledge of the prices at which the various market makers (typically, suppliers) are willing to transact the commodities with known economically relevant characteristics.

In relation to university degree provision, an obstacle to the second condition is the widespread belief (sound or otherwise) that there are no 'competing' alternative employments that are preferable to those requiring a university degree. To overstate the point, 'everyone' wants their children to go to university, if possible. To that extent, the pressure of competition is diminished, from the degree-demand side. In relation to the academic labour market and the second condition, to the extent that suppliers of academic labour are deeply wedded to perceived non-pecuniary benefits of academic life, and therefore discount more remunerative alternatives, competition is enhanced on the supply side of the academic labour market.

But it is the third condition that is particularly violated in the case of the educational dimension of universities' activities, and this is the one that I focused upon in the earlier article. Hence follows from the third condition Adam Smith's (1976 [1776], 77) seminal point, that 'secrets' obstruct the tendency of competition to push market prices toward equality with minimum cost of production (notably, due to a technical innovation known and available to only one producer of a particular commodity). For competition to work its benefits, ideally there should be no economically relevant private information. But in selling degrees, the universities have 'secrets'; that is to say, information about the character of the education and achievements that enable acquisition of their degrees, not available to the consumers.

---

2    To give an intuitive example from another knowledge-intensive consumption domain, when one attends a medical doctor with an ailment, one asks this supplier of medical services, 'what do I need to purchase (or demand)?'

What can result from information asymmetry between potential buyers and potential sellers in a market is explained in a seminal economics article, 'The Market for "Lemons"' (Akerlof 1970). By analogy from the market for used cars (the 'lemons' of the title), it shows how information asymmetry can drive good-quality products (or good used cars) out of the supply side of the market, leaving only bad-quality products (or bad used cars) – in the jargon, 'adverse selection'. This is so even if there is a demand for high-quality product that is feasibly suppliable. The crucial characteristic of the situation – the information asymmetry – is that potential consumers cannot distinguish (ex ante) between good and bad used cars (whereas the potential sellers can). As a result, the potential consumers' offer-prices are so low that potential suppliers of good used cars withdraw from the market.

Along these lines, low-quality university education might well drive out high-quality education, even if there is a demand for high-quality education that could be met. The difference with respect to the used cars parable is that in the case of degree provision, rather than high-quality providers exiting the market, they are induced to transform themselves into low-quality degree providers. This dynamic is reinforced by an information asymmetry at the other end of university education: in relation to potential employees and employers in general, if the latter (ex ante) have difficulty ascertaining the quality of the former, educational credentials can be used by the former as a quality signalling device, increasing the demand for university degrees for an *extrinsic* reason (see three paragraphs above).

With regard to the market for academic labour, the main obstruction in the way of this market producing the desirable outcomes commonly associated with a competitive market is that the supply of recruits to academic life is constrained by its dependence upon a scarce natural human resource: the limited number of highly intelligent human beings suitable to undertake high-quality university research and teaching. This cohort also has potential alternative careers open to it. So, given the pecuniary alternatives available in other careers, one could say that the resource constraint on the supply side of the academic labour market in the long run is the limited number of highly intelligent human beings *who place a sufficiently high value on the non-pecuniary benefits of academic life*, relative to those of other careers.

There has been competition unleashed in at least some segments of the academic labour market by the universities' embrace of a key-performance-indicator (KPI) approach to academic performance and management. But what has this competition achieved? Implementation of research-publications-based KPIs has led to universities' competitive pursuit of some academics – or perhaps, rather, pursuit of some academic CVs – leading to differentiated, supplemented salaries for some, who are regarded as 'star' performers in terms of these KPIs. But this competition does not increase the total quantity of quality research in the world. It simply reallocates academic labour across the global university system (and turns some 'star' researchers into mercenary, academic gypsies). Hence, apart from the reallocation effect, the competition merely delivers economic 'rents' to the academics who are prized by the KPIs – remunerations in excess of those required for their academic labour to be supplied – due to the limited supply of such human talent to academic work. That supply limitation in turn is a result of the natural human resource scarcity, together with the limited number of people of the required intelligence who have also a sufficiently strong preference for the non-pecuniary benefits of academic life. In fact, university managerialism, with its bureaucratisation, and consequent infantilisation, of academic life (in particular, the audit culture), is also diminishing the non-pecuniary benefits of the vocation. This will – sooner or later (there are lags) – reduce the supply of first-rate human beings to the industry.

In fact, in relation to the Australian universities system, in the face of tight revenue constraints that are unlikely to ease, the current world rankings for the top half-dozen of the Australian universities seem only likely to be preserved by shifting those universities further toward a two-class academic model. This would entail a class of relatively well-remunerated 'star' research academics, employed to maintain rankings in relation to the standard research KPIs; and an underclass of low-paid, 'teaching-focused' academics, who will be considerably fixed-term or casual, and who will do what research they can with the residual time available to them. The question, for the viability of this two-class system, is whether – as well as attracting sufficient research stars – a supply of suitable persons to fill the academic-underclass positions will continue to be forthcoming. It *might* be, via what may be called the 'Hollywood' model of labour supply: every year 100 equally beautiful young women go to Hollywood with a view to becoming 'stars'; one or two become stars and the rest become casually-employed bit-players combined with waitressing work or something worse; and so the system is able to continue. The lure of academic stardom might suffice to sustain a two-class university system along similar lines.

The spread of discretionary salary supplementation – selective, and at the discretion of the academic managers – is a consequence of university managerialism, only *partly* due to the associated quasi-competition between universities. It serves also to reinforce managerialism and to reinforce the undermining of collegial governance. There was a time when one could expect or hope that at least senior academic staff, who had no more promotion hurdles ahead of them, would provide forthright and independent counsel in the collective deliberations of faculties, schools, departments and so on. Salary supplementation makes the remuneration of many academics now beholden to the academic managers, and on a regular basis, via annual, biennial or triennial reviews. Under these conditions, to put the point politely, the courage of people's convictions is not always forthcoming.

Of course, salary supplementation is not evenly distributed across disciplines. But for obvious reasons, it tends to be relatively concentrated in those academic areas with the highest revenues per academic; and in an era in which revenue is a pressing concern, these will tend to be the most powerful parts of universities. Hence, the corrupting influence of salary supplementation is relatively concentrated in those parts of the universities that are likely to be most influential in the overall conduct of these institutions. Furthermore, however unevenly distributed salary supplementation is with regard to working academics, it is much more generally distributed among university managers as a whole. This works powerfully to make each layer of the university managerial class beholden to the next level up the hierarchy, further undermining collegial governance.

It was also virtually inevitable that the shift towards managerialism would sooner or later collide with traditional academic tenure. The exercise of unqualified power by the academic manager – unqualified, except by the constraints of external law – is incompatible with such security of tenure of the managed, or at least of the most substantial number of them. Only self-restraint on the part of the managers could stand in the way of that collision. Experience teaches that when human beings are offered power over others, few decline to exercise it. It is true, of course, that, unlike in some other national jurisdictions, academic tenure has no standing in Australian law. But it has always been and remains open to Australian universities' governors to accept a self-denying ordinance of respecting academic tenure as a *convention*, a vital convention, of academic life – and a convention essential to the preservation of academic quality. This is not the place to offer a comprehensive justification for traditional tenure. But one may mention its function in supporting the fearless pursuit of intellectual innovation and, from a more cynical viewpoint, in facilitating academics' appointing other academics more able than themselves. The shift towards top-down governance and line management tends naturally to unbridle power from any self-restraint by way of academic and other conventions and norms – nothing beyond the strict requirements of law.

This is not to say that the previous historical norm in Australian universities, of making continuing academic appointments ('tenure') relatively easy to gain, is desirable. Probably, Australian universities should have been, or should be, moving towards something resembling the US tenure regime. But, to take the example of the 2012–13 termination of a substantial number of continuing academic staff, instigated by University of Sydney management, what has instead happened is a transition from too easy 'tenure' to no tenure at all, for anybody. This is potentially a tectonic shift in the power of the managerial class.

## Research key performance indicators

Some further comments may be added concerning KPIs, with particular reference to research. The recourse to quantity of research publications as an indicator of academic performance obviously militates against quality. Recourse, then, also to journal rankings is supposed to overcome that limitation. The rise of these indicators in research evaluation is an expression of the wider embrace by academic managers of supposedly 'transparent', but therefore also inevitably mechanical, KPIs as governance tools for auditing performance. The motivation and behaviour of universities' senior management in turn have no doubt been governed by various formal and informal KPIs, with global university rankings the biggest and most aggregated KPI of them all — due to prestige rewards to the managers from performance on these 'metrics' and their remuneration being linked to these outcomes. Under these behavioural conditions, the managers' timeframes for 'outcomes', achievements or performance are likely to be just the three, five or 10 years that they intend to occupy their positions, irrespective of the consequences for research, education and the quality of university life beyond those horizons. And in any case, within or beyond these timeframes, damage must be *visible and evident* before blame can be aimed at them or anyone else. As I have argued earlier (Aspromourgos 2012), with respect to education at least, there are substantial reasons why quality decline can be difficult to demonstrate. The issue is always debatable.

But the attempt to incorporate quality into research metrics by way of journal rankings is by no means unproblematic either. Journal rankings appear to be particularly adversely regarded by academics in the social sciences and the humanities — presumably due to the greater scope for subjectivity in these areas — but this is probably an issue upon which sentiment differs across disciplines. In economics, with a relatively monolithic and highly dominant theoretical mainstream compared to the other social sciences, journal rankings are less controversial. But this monolithic mainstream makes the journal-rankings mentality severely prejudicial to survival within the academy of heterodox traditions of theory and policy in economics, and tends also to reinforce conservatism with respect to theoretical innovation. In relation to the question of how much the rise of university managerialism is due to external imposition by government, and how much it is self-inflicted by the universities themselves, it is noteworthy that the Commonwealth Government abandonment of journal rankings in research assessment evidently has not diminished their use by university managers, deans, heads of schools, promotion committees and so on, for judging both academic units and individuals. For a globally peripheral nation like Australia, in the social sciences the conventional journal rankings, being globally oriented, also imply adverse quality judgements with respect to applied and policy-related research on Australia.

When these sorts of research KPIs were first introduced, both in Australia and other countries, they were confronted by the entirely sound charge that there is inevitably an element of arbitrariness in reliance upon such reductionist and mechanical rules for arriving at judgements of quality. Rules do not comprehend exceptions. The KPIs approach was commonly defended against this charge on the basis that it would be used to form judgments about academic *groups* (disciplines, departments, schools and so on), not individuals. And up to a point, that is a reasonable position: in the application of these mechanical rules to comparisons or rankings of groups of individuals, the judgment errors that would occur at the level of individual academics will tend to wash out in the aggregation – the more so, the larger the academic units being appraised.

But in very short time, the journal-rankings KPI, for example, in application to individuals, was happily embraced and internalised by university decision-makers, all the way down the food chain, from vice-chancellors to promotions committees – even, with a perhaps short-sighted opportunism, by large numbers of individual academics (in their promotion and research grant applications). The frailty of journal rankings has been exposed by some serious analysis, but with apparently little effect (Joint Committee on Quantitative Assessment of Research 2008; Frey and Rost 2008; Wall 2009). Recourse to citations – the citation counts of *individuals'* publications, not the citation counts for entire journals – would add robustness to rankings. But even these counts should be handled with caution. What is being cited is by no means necessarily a sound proxy for what is actually being read. Download numbers would provide additional information about what is being at least accessed, and more likely read, and would therefore be a useful addition to the suite of quantitative indicators.

It may be added, with regard to the arts and the humanities in particular, that no cultural dynamism is likely to come from institutions governed by KPIs; cultural innovation will have to come from elsewhere. One is reminded of Robert Crawford's (2013, 30) comment, reflecting on the life and poetry of Les Murray, that, for writers who take employment in it, the contemporary university proves to be 'both patron and padded cell'. Crawford there also quotes Murray's comment, *not* intended as a compliment, that '[a]n academic-led literature is a gentrified suburb'. One may expect the kind of intellectual blandness implied by this comment to be amplified, and across all the arts, humanities and social sciences, in the managerialist university.

# Managerialism and academic ethics

In my earlier article I also argued that the managerialist model – seeking to reduce the conduct of academic life to an exchange process in which rewards and punishments are traded for 'outcomes' at the individual level – is not a substitute for professional ethics and norms of academic collegial life and conduct (Aspromourgos 2012, 48–9). Indeed, the managerialist approach to governance inevitably undermines ethical conduct; it tears away at the civic fabric of collective academic life, eroding the ethical sensibilities of individuals. One may wonder whether, in relation to this, the academic managers have overlooked the fact that the individual-contracting approach may feed back upon, and compromise, the ethical fabric of academic life – as if ethical behaviours could be treated as a given that would be unaffected by the overlay of individualised transacting.

Some might respond that ethical commitments by academic staff are an insufficiently robust basis upon which to ground the conduct of academic life and of universities; the strength of such commitments cannot be relied upon. That of course is true. Other sanctions are also required. But one need not doubt a certain 'frailty' in the conformity of people to ethical principles in order to recognise that the affirmation of ethical codes and embodying them in collegial practices is necessary to the good governance of academic life. Ethical codes are symptomatic, not of naïvety about human beings, but realism. It is the notion that contractual exchange relations could replace ethics in informing conduct in the academy that is naïve.

Some might further respond that if academics, generally, were governed by high ethical standards, then they would not succumb to such temptation to an erosion of civic sensibility. But this is to construe ethics in an overly simple manner. There is reciprocity in ethical behaviour, which is something more than and different from mere self-interested exchange relationships. There is ethical behaviour that is less than unconditional altruism – a realm of ethical life between unconditional selfishness and unconditional altruism. If the leadership of universities makes evident, explicitly or implicitly, that what it really values is performance tables and the KPIs that enter into them – both in research and teaching – then it would be asking a great deal to expect the average academic to accept a more expansive standard of conduct. In the words of an old proverb, a fish rots from the head.

With the embrace of the mores of Management 101 comes also other, perhaps merely irritating but also mildly indecent behaviours, such as the debasement of language that results from the devaluation of superlatives, as each individual academic becomes her or his own marketing consultant. If one had a dollar for every time one is exposed, in the contemporary university, to the terms 'excellent', 'outstanding' and so on (including derivatives), early retirement from all this would be more feasible. Academics are also now commonly being asked to fulfil sets of objectives that are simply impossible. Consequently, in relation to those multiple demands, they must either accept failure or engage in deceit. The latter course might keep them in the game – but at the price of corroding values fundamental to academic life, notably, truth-telling in some sense or other.

## Some concluding thoughts

In the preceding commentary, some adverse consequences of the managerialist model of university governance have been indicated; but this does not address *why* the rise of university managerialism has occurred. This is a more complex issue to resolve than its consequences. It may be suggested that the rise of university managerialism needs to be understood partly in a larger context, as a lagged effect of the conservative shift in social, political and economic culture from the end of the 1970s, initially in Britain and the US. This led to the public sector and public policy being more geared towards the purposes and methods of private enterprise. On another level, but not unconnected, the greater accountability and audit demands placed upon universities can be seen as a lagged consequence of the dramatic enlargement of university enrolments since the 1960s. It could have been expected, sooner or later, that there would be demands to account for the 'return' on the expanding investment in higher education by governments – and by students, as private fees became significant.

At the same time, the shift to mass university education inevitably was going to drive higher education in a more vocationally-oriented direction. This was reinforced as the student population itself became more vocationally oriented, as the era of full employment came to an end in the 1970s. This in turn connects back to the abovementioned conservative cultural shift: the full employment of the postwar quarter-century to the mid-1970s undoubtedly played a substantial part in enabling the social upheavals of the 1960s, to which the conservative political revival from the 1970s was at least partly a response – a response to '1968', to put the point symbolically. In truth, the modern university of recent centuries has not been much at all guided by the notion of 'knowledge for its own sake'. If there is a single principle that captures the spirit of the modern university it is, for good or ill, the Enlightenment notion of knowledge aimed at the material improvement of the human condition – as Francis Bacon (1605 [1951], 41–3) put it, the advancement of learning for 'the relief of man's estate'; or, in the maxim commonly associated with Bacon and his sometime amanuensis Thomas Hobbes, 'knowledge is power'.

The decline in the quality of universities is a global, though perhaps not a universal, phenomenon. In relation to this, what is alarming is not that Australia's best universities – e.g. Queensland or Sydney – might be outside various proposed rankings of the world's 50 or 100 best universities, rankings that are generally derivative from various supposed performance metrics. What is alarming is that they might be *in* those best 50 or 100. Is this as good as can be expected of the best 50 or 100 in the world? To the extent that the quality and the character of Australian universities are being degraded, this does not necessarily entail any *relative* decline in their global standing on conventional measures. This is not offered as a comforting thought.

In these circumstances some solace might be taken from recalling a self-description used in 17th-century England by one group of the pioneers of the Scientific Revolution, calling itself 'the invisible college'. The intent of this metaphor, I think, was to say that the true university or 'college' was not the visible Oxbridge colleges, but rather, the 'college' of those committed to genuine learning (*partly* a subset of the visible university), appealing to a Christian distinction between the visible church and the true, 'invisible church'. Without inviting fatalism, the moral to be drawn from this might be that the corruption of learning is always with us, throughout the ages, the only change over time being the ebb and flow of its tide.

# 6. Transforming the Public University: Market Citizenship and Higher Education Regulatory Projects

Kanishka Jayasuriya

## Introduction

This chapter explores the shifts within mass higher education and its governance over the last three decades. Mass higher education has changed substantially in tandem with the broader changes associated with the social and political compromises over that time. The crisis and transformation of the public university needs to be understood in this context. To this end, this chapter analyses the transformation of the public university as it relates to broader state and governance projects focusing on the crucial shift from the 1980s onwards with the emergence of new notions of market citizenship, bringing with it what has been referred to as 'structured opportunity markets' in higher education. These notions of market citizenship are given shape through an emerging higher education regulatory state, now governed by a range of formal and informal instruments including measures to enhance inclusion and participation within the market. It is these regulatory projects that develop and give legitimacy to the higher education market. Consequently, the development of the regulatory state and market-making has been deeply intertwined. In conclusion, I argue that the 'public' university does not disappear as such, but is reconstituted within these new regulatory arrangements and projects. This argument is illustrated with reference to recent initiatives in the Australian higher education sectors, such as the Bradley Report and the establishment of the Tertiary Education Quality and Standards Agency (TEQSA).

Simon Marginson in his observations on the theme of the workshop that gave rise to this collection suggests – if I read him correctly – that much of the contention on the hollowing out or otherwise of the public university in the Anglo-Saxon world risks going in circles. He proposes that a more productive way would be to explore these debates in the context of higher education changes in East Asia and Russia. In a similar way, Collini (2011) too argues that it is not at all clear that this Anglo-Saxon model of the public research university to which we subscribe – namely, the provision of public benefit, open communication, the nurturing of a scholarly community, the creation of the new knowledge and open public communication – will be adopted by the fast-growing universities of China.

But then, what do we make of the notion of a *public university*? In agreeing with the broad tenor of the critique of the 'historical idea' of the public university, I propose to go beyond some of the sterile debates surrounding the notion of a 'public university'. So how do we define 'public' in the context of the 'public university'? At a minimum, we need to see that the 'public university' is not some 'Weberian' ideal type against which we can benchmark the role of the university. This is clearly evident in the tenor of much of the recent discussion of the public university which, particularly in Australia, Great Britain, and the United States, has been framed in the light of Cardinal Newman's classical ideal of the 'idea of the university'. This much-cited approach to higher education finds expression in the early work of those such as Newman and Humboldt. Newman (1976), for example, argued that the university was central to cultivating the public mind and 'national culture', and training the political elite.

Newman's essay has become a standard reference for those wishing to discuss the nature and purpose of university education. Similarly, Humboldt, writing in the different political economic context of industrial Germany, espoused a notion of the public university that combined industrial and civic elements. These familiar conceptualisations of the university, associated with Newman, Humboldt, and others are products of specific political and economic circumstances. For instance, the case of Humboldt and the consequent German emphasis placed on the state-regulated notion of university and professional autonomy could only be understood in the context of the late industrialisation projects of the Prussian/German state and its promotion of science and technology (Habermas 1987). To the extent that these notions constructed a 'public', it was defined in terms of inculcating 'national culture' and educating a professional and political elite.

It is not possible to read off the 'idea of the university' from its internal history (though this is important). For a more comprehensive picture, we need to see how this sense of the 'public' or the 'publicness' of the university itself has been constituted and shaped by political projects and the broader settlements that underpin them. In other words, politics and contending definitions of the 'public' have always been central to the process of constructing the public university and we need to keep away from reifying an ideal model of the public university that emerged in the 1950s. A good example of this 'ideal type' approach to the public university is found in Collini's much circulated article in the *London Review of Books*. In essence he argues that there has been a major shift from the world of Robbins to the managerial dictates of McKinsey as seen in the recent UK White Paper (Department of Business and Innovation 2011). As such, the principles of the White Paper are only 'the latest instalment in the campaign to replace the assumptions of Robbins's world with those of McKinsey's' (Collini 2011, 14). This is a good point, but Robbins's world was itself a product of a certain kind of social democratic grammar of politics and what this leaves out – in the British context – is precisely the pressures of mass higher education in the 1960s, the role of the polytechnics in this process, and the way these shifts reflect more profound changes in a broader shift from the postwar social democracy, which I refer to below as 'new forms of market citizenship'. In other words, what is missing in this argument is that the state itself has been retooled over the course of the last 30 years in a range of policy areas. The governance of higher education is no exception.

# The changing mission of the public university, state projects, and citizenship

The institutional and ideological context of the public university is constantly being redefined, and to view these changes through the prism of an ideal point of view is to misunderstand the way the notion of the 'public' itself has changed. The broader argument here is that neoliberalism – the project of market reform that has shaped Australian politics and public policy – was not so much a retreat of the state but a restructuring and transformation of the state. The state has remained pivotal to this process of neoliberalisation by creating new forms of market-like disciplines and techniques that were often layered onto other more social-democratic oriented policies and tools. The regulatory state has been the pivotal instrument of this transformation and, in turn, changes in policies, instruments, and tools that govern higher education exemplify a transformation of the state. The higher education regulatory state imposes 'disciplines' through market-like signals, incentives, and accountability benchmarks on institutions designed to increase allocative efficiency and pursue a variety of social objectives. These objectives were often in tension but they were linked together through varied political projects – social-democratic neoliberal or 'allocative efficiency' – of market citizenship. Hence, state restructuring and the diverse forms it has taken is crucial to the understanding of policy changes to higher education including the proposed initiatives introduced by the Abbott government and the Minister for Education, Christopher Pyne (McPhee 2014).

In order to understand the nature of the contemporary transformation of the public university, we need to contrast it with the development the post-Second World War public university and its associated political project of national modernisation. In the postwar period there has been a broad convergence of the institutions and practices of the public research university across the globe. Of course, this is a broad brush statement. The importance of these functions varied across time and place, and was layered on to earlier traditions and institutions. Some of these key functions included national projects of modernisation – the case of the Research Schools at The Australian National University (ANU) in Australia; an emphasis on the importance of the public university as a vehicle of social democratising to promote social mobility; and, a strong research and training mission – particularly evident in the early postwar years in the US public universities – with strong publicly mandated research missions in the basic sciences often linked to, or funded through, the military industrial complex.

In a nutshell, it shaped a notion of publicness which in the case of the Californian Master Plan – driven by its public university system – embodied some of the components of this social citizenship model of the public university. In this context, as Brady and Konczal (2012) note, the Master Plan contained a commitment to educate Californian students with minimal fees and was intended to facilitate the social mobility that was seen as central to the New Deal social settlement that had shaped some of the assumptions about the role of the Californian public university system. This was not simply about the public university but a broader state project of 'citizenship building' (Brady and Konczal 2012; Douglass 2000). The higher education sector in the postwar period emerged out of the domestic politics of broader social settlements that legitimated the idea of higher education as a public good, and the geopolitics of the Cold War which, particularly in the United States, sustained an era of big science.

For this reason, the public university – particularly the notion of the 'public' – needs to be seen in relational terms as it expanded in the postwar period and became the subject of continuing debate and contestation over participation in, and equality of access to, the benefits of higher education. Yet, the point is that various models of the public university not only served to enhance a particular conception of the public good, but also embodied in its institutional practices a nationally framed social citizenship (Robertson 2007).

The question we need to ask is: Why is the public research university seen to be either in crisis or in transformation across the globe? One response to this question is that it is a product of the structural pressures across the advanced industrial states, and includes: (a) a rapid expansion of the university system ('massification'); (b) growing constraints on funding, teaching, and research; and, (c) the growing salience of selection and ranking, especially in research. In turn – and crucially – these pressures on the public universities are themselves located in the 'various crises' of the postwar social settlement across advanced industrial states. In addition, the shift towards a post-industrial service-based economy has transformed the kind of training required for the post-industrial economy. In sum, this move away from the public university as a common source of social citizenship, as Fischman, Igo and Rhoten (2007, 123) astutely argue, is mirrored in a shift in the relative weight of public and private benefit in higher education towards the private benefit. This is a shift which continues to have constrained the impact on what we have called the 'social democratising' effects of the public university. Locating the transformation of higher education in these terms allows us to view the public university – indeed the very term 'public' – in the context of its relationship to broader political projects of citizenship.

From this perspective, the 'public university' and its transformation should be analysed from the viewpoint of the sustainability of state and political projects to transform public universities – as, for example, in the Californian Master Plan – in response to wider social and economic transformations. This resonates with Craig Calhoun's argument (2011, 15) that there is a 'direct connection between the larger societal crises and that in higher education. Universities were central to projects of both the "welfare state" and the developmental state during the decades after World War 11.' During the crisis of the 1970s and 1980s, public universities were the focus for discontent with these programs when they failed to live up to expectations particularly with regard to democratisation, and became the subject of critique from the left and the right (Calhoun 2011, 15). The fate of the Californian Master Plan is a good exemplar of these changes assailed by Ronald Reagan when he was California's Governor, and with the Vietnam War making the university system the site of political struggle between the left and right (Brady and Konczal 2012). It is useful to recall how changes in geopolitical context were central to the emergence and the crisis of the public university and the broader political consensus that sustained the project of the public university in the postwar era.

While the postwar development of the university was dependent on notions of social citizenship, equally pivotal – and this is something that is beyond the scope of this chapter – are the broader geopolitical projects that animated the expansion of the public university system across the world. In the US, the Cold

War geopolitics fed the appetite of 'big science' in major research universities. In fact, the New Deal inspired both the project of democratisation of higher education and the Cold War geopolitical program that spurred the creation of 'big science' research initiatives and formed the cornerstone of the expansion of the public university system in the postwar period. Here, the Californian university system was also at the centre of a key defence-related research enterprise. In Australia, the relationship between 'big science' and 'geopolitics' was never as significant as in the US, but the Colombo Plan (which is now much touted by the Coalition) was a creature of Cold-War politics which sought to encourage members of the Asian elite to inculcate 'Western' values. The broader point is that a trio of forces – (a) the 'massification of the university system; (b) the project of social citizenship, and, (c) the geopolitics of the Cold War that sustained substantive research investment – went hand in hand.

These shifts in higher education played a role – albeit in a different key – in Australia. In her Menzies Oration, Janice Reid (2012) points to how a broad notion of social citizenship was central to the expansion of the postwar university system in Australia. As she points out (Reid 2012, 9), despite their differences, and particularly Whitlam's willingness to use expenditure on universities to promote social equality, both Menzies and Whitlam 'saw universities as central in driving economic advancement and social transformation. Those threads spun out through the generations and though rediscovered and reworked in policy funding reforms every decade or so, can still be traced back to these figures.' Reid's point is well taken but we should not diminish the political distance between Whitlam and Menzies in respect to higher education as it is clear that the Whitlam reforms were designed to promote the social democratisation of higher education, whereas Menzies saw it as an instrument to promote stability and integration among the middle class. Whitlam, of course, made this central to his political project of social democratic modernisation after his victory in 1972. In fact, it is interesting that the changes to the public university have featured prominently in Australian Labor's – each very different – modernising projects from Chifley through Whitlam and Hawke–Keating to the Rudd–Gillard governments. Despite these differences, both Whitlam's and Menzies' approaches to higher education – to use Collini's terminology – were in the world of Robbins located in – albeit different – projects of social citizenship underpinned by the social settlement between capital and labour that marked the postwar period.

Moreover, Reid points out how the peer-driven governance as exemplified by the Universities Commission complemented these notions of social citizenship. As she implies, the bureaucratic governance of the university – which in the postwar period was a lot stronger in Australia than in other English-speaking countries – was often in concert with what Moran (2003) has described as 'club government'. In turn, this 'club government' depended on the use of professional autonomy and the use of 'voice' in shaping the internal governance of the university. Hence the point to be emphasised – and missing in various critiques of contemporary corporate culture of universities – is how these internal processes were connected to wider state projects of higher education.

In several countries, the 'long 1970s' were crucial to the crisis of the various models of the public university. In my view the ongoing crisis and transformation of the public university has to be located in the context of the broader social and economic crisis of the long 1970s. In Australia, the 1970s were crucial to the future evolution of the public university. The Whitlam government abolished fees and sought to increase the capacity of the university system (Marginson 1997c). And in line with Calhoun's thinking, the public university was itself a crucial component of Whitlam's modernising and, we might add, 'nationalising' project. The great irony of the Whitlam reforms is that the model of the public research university that his government consolidated relatively late in Australia was to be so short-lived as the broader ideas and practices of social citizenship and its underlying social democratic grammar of politics came under sustained pressure. These pressures stemmed from both the changing social and economic circumstances with the end of the long postwar economic growth, and the emergence of fiscal crisis of the state (O'Connor 1979). In addition, this was a period of sustained attack on these notions of social citizenship from conservative political movements.

If we adopt this relational framework, we have the advantage of moving away from what is an uncritical analysis of the pre-Dawkins era made by critics, of the recent emphasis on marketisation (Dawkins 1988). This is reflected in the tendency to look somewhat nostalgically at a so-called pre Dawkins golden era. Of course, what this overlooks is the very tumultuous years during the 1970s, which included not just the introduction of free education and expansion of the system, but also the significant university cuts made by the Liberal–National Coalition in the 1970s (Marginson 1997c). It was in this context that John Dawkins introduced his university reforms. The Hawke–Keating reforms and modernisation project sought to achieve democratic objectives within this framework of market reform (Johnson 2000; Jayasuriya 2010a). In this vein, modernisation became a political project that sought to adapt social democracy or its particular Laborist variant to the convulsion of global capitalism that effectively undermined the postwar economic and political regimes and corresponding social foundations (Gamble 2006; Jayasuriya 2006). If we follow this argument, the Dawkins reforms need to be analysed in a broader context of the acceleration of programs of market reform in the economy and in the public sector – neoliberalism if you like – and continuation of the older social democratic objective of expanding mass education.

This social democratic variant of neoliberalism sought to reconcile the 'massification' of the university with the imperatives of market reform. But central to this major project was an attempt to cast the 'public university' within the context of a new notion of market citizenship that sought to meet the dual objectives of expanding 'human capital' and the inclusive participation of citizens in a globally competitive economy. Higher education – as was to be the case with the Rudd–Gillard government – became pivotal to the way in which social democratic parties attempted to embed, and adapt to, the broader processes of neoliberalism or market reform. These changes served to transform the nature and function of the public university.

# Higher education regulatory state and the making of market citizenship

The net impact of these changes – economic reform and the acceleration of university participation – is not so much the hollowing out of the 'public', but rather, the conception of the university framed in terms of market citizenship. In turn, these notions of market citizenship find expression in broader regulatory projects that underpin the reform of the public university. Market citizenship is defined here as promoting the inclusion and participation of citizens within the market economy. As such, market citizenship is not aimed towards redistributing resources but towards enhancing participation within the market. These forms are best described as socialising neoliberal or market reform programs (Jayasuriya 2006; Cerny 2010). Here, the Dawkins reforms were central not just in the modernisation of the university but in the way in which they were seen as constituting an integral part of a notion of a market citizenship. Translating this into the university sector meant that the reforms were designed to enhance individual skills. This process was seen to be essential to participating in the new knowledge economy in a context where innovation was crucial for economic growth. Similarly, there was an emphasis on industry linkages with the university sector. It is important to note that these trends toward market citizenship are part and parcel of what one higher education scholar (Douglass 2009) refers to as 'structured opportunity' markets. According to Douglass (2009, 3), these markets are distinguished by a 'decidedly more differentiated, consumer and market-oriented approach to expanding access and managing enrolment, with various budget and structural limits, and with one goal of supporting greater socioeconomic mobility in society, and economic development'. There are various components of this model: greater global reach of the institutions, more differentiated institutional missions, diversified funding, and providers; and I would add, the growing role of privately managed online education platforms.

A powerful example of this market citizenship was the Higher Education Contribution Scheme (HECS) that sought to reallocate and privatise some of the burden of financing the 'massification' of the university system in order to widen participation. Underlining the notion of market citizenship, the primary rationale for the scheme was not just to shift the burden to private individuals, but to recalibrate the relationship between the private and public contributions. More importantly, the introduction of student fees has provided a powerful regulatory tool to impose market discipline on the university sector. Regulation through fees enables the calibration of both market and social objectives via student contributions. The significance of these policy changes lies not so much on the level of fees but on the way these changes foster a regulatory instrument and form governance arrangements that made market disciplining a central objective of higher education policy. And these market-disciplining forms of governance – via a range of regulatory tools and instruments – have led to a partial reconstituting of the 'public' as consumers of public services.

There has been a differing emphasis by Liberal and Labor on these various components of market citizenship. It is not so much that the world of Robbins had been replaced, as in the UK by McKinsey – to use Collini's evocative phrase – but that the social democratic world in which Robbins operated has now been supplanted by a more neoliberal or market-oriented world where market disciplining through regulation has become much more pivotal, not just in the provision of public utilities or economic governance but also in sectors such as higher education. This has not hollowed out the public university, but has served to underline different notions of 'publicness', particularly with regard to their role in state projects.

Resonating with the earlier Dawkins reforms, there is a social democratic notion of 'market citizenship' that comes to the fore in the Bradley Report commissioned by the Rudd government soon after taking office. The strategic rationale of the Report and the market-citizenship approach is most evident in its approving nod to the OECD statement on higher education. In fact, the OECD has been an important influence in shaping the convergence of higher education policies across both developing and developed countries. The Bradley Report quotes the OECD (2008, 23) to argue that:

> the widespread recognition that tertiary education is a major driver of economic competitiveness in an increasingly knowledge-driven global economy has made high quality tertiary education more important than ever before. The imperative for countries is to raise higher-level employment skills, to sustain a globally competitive research base, and to improve knowledge dissemination to the benefit of society.

But, in addition to this version of the public university as an instrument of human-capital building was the allied notion of inclusion and participation in higher education. Hence one of the key recommendations of the Bradley Report – exemplified by the embedded neoliberal version of market citizenship – was the clarion call for greater participation of disadvantaged groups in the higher education system.

This report (Bradley Report 2008, xiv) went on to argue: 'All institutions in receipt of Commonwealth funds for teaching will be expected to establish initiatives to increase both the enrolment of, and success of, students from disadvantaged backgrounds.' It called for innovative governance projects such as partnership with schools and other educational institutions to enhance participation. More importantly, the report envisaged setting targets for disadvantaged groups, and tying budgetary allocations to such targets in order to enhance their participation within the system (p. xii). At the same time, it advocated a demand-driven financing system (151–74). In all of these proposals, we find that the construction of a regulatory architecture is designed with a view to calibrating the balance between social objectives and market disciplines in order to produce citizens fit for the market.

One of the key means through which these notions of market citizenship were given shape in Australia and the UK was through a broad-ranging regulatory order that enabled both the monitoring of quality and the operation of the demand-led student system. This may be a case of 'Moscow on Molongo' – as described by Corden (2005) – the curious combination of markets and regulation. But Corden's (2005) implication is that somehow regulation is an obstacle to the implementation of market citizenship in higher education. Instead, I would suggest that the two are deeply intertwined. Regulation is the means through which the higher education market is guided to enhance the – often inconsistent – political projects of market citizenship. It is this emerging regulatory governance of higher education that is shaping the internal higher education market and the state.

King (2006), one of the very few writers to conceptualise higher education through a regulatory prism, notes that the close relationship between state and higher education is created by an increasingly rule-governed system of higher education. These rules establish broad directives that regulate the conduct of institutions. Consequently, King argues that it is possible to identify this as a 'higher education regulatory state' (King 2006, 8). The Bradley Report (2008, 97) recommended the creation of the national regulatory system 'on the basis that the regulatory framework for tertiary education is in need of a major overhaul and that the regulation of international education should be considered in a broader context which involves the creation of a national regulatory body'.

The Australian Government has now established the tertiary education regulator – the Tertiary Education Quality and Standards Agency (TEQSA) – that has become the central regulatory agency of higher education. One senior official has described this agency as having more procedural power than any other comparable agency in any high-quality university system (*The Australian*, 6 July 2011). It sets threshold standards for the higher education system and will shape the internal governance of institutions. It is beyond the scope of this chapter to analyse the role of the regulatory state in selecting and sorting research excellence such as the Excellence in Research for Australian (ERA) initiative in Australia, which is a crucial dimension of the emerging higher education regulatory state.

It is important to recognise that the regulatory state works not through direct intervention in higher education institutions – although this is possible – but indirectly through the setting of benchmarks and threshold standards. In this way, regulation is implanted in the heart of institutional structure which in a way mirrors other regulated industries such as finance. In tandem with these changes, universities are now at the crossroads of other overlapping regulatory regimes. For example, they are now key intermediaries in the immigration and visa system, adding a further layer of complexity to regulatory environment in which the modern public university operates. In the UK, an example is the recent experience of a London metropolitan university which lost its capacity to recruit international students after being non-compliant with the regulatory regime of the now defunct UK Border Authority (UKBA). The university has not only become subject to higher education regulatory regimes, but is also the site for a range of complex overlapping regulatory regimes.

Some have sought to describe the modern public university as an institution dominated by a corporate culture, but in my view this description neglects the wider and deeper processes of state transformation which are imprinted on higher education institutions. Hence a better description of these cultural changes is to depict these components of a developing 'regulatory culture' that is deeply entrenched within the university system. A manifestation of this regulatory culture within institutions is the emergence of new regulatory intermediaries, a notion that is used by King (2006) to describe regulatory intermediaries as inhabiting the regulatory space between regulator and regulated key groups which are positioned to play critical intermediary roles. These include the Quality Assurance Agency (QAA), part-time assessors or auditors drawn from the academic community (other '"regulatory intermediaries" for external quality regulation are senior institutional leaders and quality managers in universities and colleges') (King 2006, 11). But these regulatory intermediaries are not merely the external auditors; they are also located within the university itself. The 'audit culture' is part and parcel of the regulatory state that creates and enhances these regulatory actors within the university. The rise of the higher education regulatory state enhances the role and power of these regulatory intermediaries within the university.

For this reason one of the most important implications of this emergent 'regulatory culture' is the increasing marginalisation of 'voice' – peer governance – within the university system. In this regard, TEQSA is as far as you can get from the old peer-driven University Commission, or as Moran (2003) puts it, in a British context 'club governance', towards the more formalised rule-driven system of governance. In turn this regulatory order – and I leave this issue for another day – has considerable impact on professional autonomy and control. Again, the growing regulation of professional activity within the university is complemented by a similar regulation of professions in the areas of law and health. It does suggest that the internal governance of the public university is not due to whims of managerialism, but deeply rooted in the emerging higher education regulatory state.

The thrust of this chapter is to suggest that exclusive focus on the operation markets is to risk losing sight of the rationale and principles around which the regulatory order is being established. Here, it seems to me that the particular social democratic variant of this market citizenship, which can be traced through to both the Dawkins and Bradley reforms, stems from how they sought to incorporate new notions of inclusion within this regulatory order. Yet, such measures eschew the issues of inequality that formed a significant element of the Whitlam project. But my point is this: from the issue of benchmarking participation of disadvantaged students to the differentiated institutional mission statements of institutions, the market-citizenship model of higher education forms part of a larger higher education regulatory project. Regulatory institutions become the mechanisms through which market reform is institutionally embedded, and this includes the kinds of inclusive participation sought by the Bradley Report.

From this regulatory perspective, it is not the market or state that is important, but the way in which the market is constituted through a variety of political and policy instruments. Once established, these new regulatory architectures develop their own institutional and political logic that provides the basis for further reform and experimentation. In this regard, there may well be – regardless of initial intent – a drift towards more intensive forms of market disciplining and expansion, especially so with the election of the Liberal–National Party Coalition government. The Coalition government has already signalled a shift away from inclusive notions of market citizenship towards an understanding of regulation as a project of allocative efficiency to discipline higher education, to build skills and capacities to enable business to operate in a competitive global economy.

An equally important dimension of this regulatory state is the emphasis it places on issues of accountability and legitimacy. Accountability, I would argue, is not simply a technical issue; it is a distinctive political process that helps to give legitimacy to the notion of market citizenship. Audits and quality inspections such as the ERA are the bread and butter of the new higher education regulatory governance. The importance of these 'accountability' measures is emphasised by Adelman (2008, 6) who in relation to the Bologna Process notes that:

> A qualifications framework is a statement of learning outcomes and competencies a student must demonstrate for a degree at a specific level to be awarded. It is not a statement of objectives or goals. It is not a wish list. It is a performance criterion. When an institution of higher education is governed by a qualifications framework, it must 'demonstrate' that its students have 'demonstrated'.

But this is inescapably a political process, and as Harrington and Turem (2006, 201) argue, allows us to see the relationship between accountability discourses and practices – such as, say, a qualifications framework – in the context of its relations and location within the broader patterns of social, political, and legal relations. They also note that framing accountability as a form of political governance has the distinct advantage of identifying and analysing developing forms of accountability and public regulation in terms of 'how it is understood, shaped and ultimately mobilized as a powerful political symbol to legitimate a certain type of regulatory regime' (ibid).

The choice of a particular accountability strategy reflects the strategic preference of key actors in three main ways: first, it rules out alternative ways of conceiving accountability; secondly, it helps to mobilise and favour certain kinds of policy outcomes against other outcomes; finally, it enables the inclusion or marginalisation of private and public actors. This does not preclude the conflict and contestation over the nature of 'accountability', but none of this challenges the parameters of the regulatory order. Here, accountability plays a crucial role in giving expression to the 'public' within this regulatory governance and thereby helps to shape new forms of 'publicness'. I would argue that in the higher education area, these notions of accountability, and the complex regulatory tools of monitoring and enforcement, have helped to promote and expand the notion of market citizenship through imposition of disciplines to benchmark efficiency and social objectives.

Given the recent emphasis on the issues of student mobility, particularly to Asia, we are likely to see an expansion of the higher education regulatory toolbox as a way of enabling Australian universities to compete more vigorously in the knowledge-based geo-economic order. Here, there is a discernible shift from the geopolitics of the Cold War towards a greater emphasis on geo-economic competition in knowledge and innovation. The Asian Century White Paper placed considerable emphasis on enhancing student mobility as a way of building Asia capability. This geo-economic project is echoed in the Coalition's emphasis on a reversed Colombo Plan to send Australian students to Asia in order to build the relevant Asian capabilities which can enable Australian companies to adjust to the new economic order in Asia. Again, this new Colombo Plan will depend on a rather complex series of rules that will feed into a broader accountability architecture.

## Conclusion

The distinctive element of the 'publicness' that underpins market citizenship in higher education is now dissociated from the funding, control, and mission of the public university. Universities are not so much privatised or the 'public' hollowed out, but have increasingly become hybrid institutions consisting of a mixture of public and private funding and control. The 'public' character of the institutions is increasingly secured by notions such as 'public value' benchmarking located within the broader regulatory regimes. This dissociation between the 'public character' of the university and the regulatory regime creates an inbuilt bias towards a continuing shift in favour of increasingly privatised forms of funding. More substantively, it inhibits the collective or common space that is vital for the university to continue as a site of democratic engagement and free inquiry.

To conclude, the thrust of this chapter has been to understand the complex and intertwined links between the transformation of the public university and the rise of new patterns of regulatory governance. I argue that the notion of market citizenship is central to understanding these regulatory projects and how they seek to embed this market process in a particular version of human capital formation and social inclusion. This is, of course, one variant of the regulatory project and, under a Coalition government, we are likely to see some significant changes to the nature and forms of the higher education regulatory order. Whatever the changes, it looks like regulation is here to stay and will increasingly consist of juggling four elements: (a) the massification of higher education, (b) the hard budget constraints, (c) the pursuit of research excellence, and (d) the related importance of the university as a site of geo-economic competition. This will prove to be a difficult quartet to juggle, and one is likely to see a period of constant regulatory change and innovation.

Yet, in all of these changes what seems to be absent is the notion of the university as a site of democratic engagement and contestation in an increasingly globalised world. Rather than going back to various 'ideal types', we need to develop new forms of 'publicness' for the university.

# 7. The State of the Universities

Glenn Withers

## History

Historically the public–private divide matters a lot. Much of the 20th century was devoted to a global battle between public and private ownership philosophies. The difference brought us to the brink of nuclear war.

The so-called end of history said that the democratic liberal market societies were finally ascendant, as evidenced by the fall of the Berlin Wall (Fukuyama 1992). There are all sorts of growing challenges and qualifications to such a generalisation (e.g. Huntington 1996) but, at least in the Anglo-American countries, while political parties do still distinguish themselves a little by greater or lesser dirigisme, a broad convergence to the centre is clear: we are all 'third way' warriors today.

In Australia the public and private spheres are now inextricably mixed. Think of Medibank and private health insurance. Public hospitals and private hospitals. Public policing and prisons and private security, prisons and detention-centre firms. Think of state pensions and privately managed superannuation. Or public and private broadcasters, water companies, railways and electricity generators.

Indeed Australia has a quite distinctive model of the welfare state. It produces an outcome that is one-third public and two-thirds private: an economical welfare state.

Australia actually has one of the lower proportions of public spending and taxation as a share of GDP of the OECD countries (OECD 2014). It is based upon the use of mostly flat-rate, means-tested and targeted social support and it raises the funds for this from a more-progressive-than-most taxation system.

The associated safety net is relatively thorough and state-provided – but with public incentives provided for further private provision in most areas. This is today a quite distinctive 'Australian Way', and it also applies to education.

# Modern Australian tertiary education

In pre-school and child care, there is a blend of public and private ownership and provision plus incentive support from the state for the private provision. Likewise, there are publicly owned and funded government schools and there are private schools with public financial assistance for those choosing the private schools.

In tertiary education too the nation walks on two legs. Universities and technical and further education colleges (TAFEs) are overwhelmingly publicly owned and receive substantial government funding and there is private education and training (PET) which is commercially owned and provided for fees. So we have accepted both public and private components of tertiary education too.

But the university world itself is more nuanced than such broad characterisation would indicate. Thus the Australian university scene does include private universities such as Bond University and the University of Notre Dame, and the Australian Catholic University is established as a company under the Corporations Act. Melbourne University, a public university, established Melbourne University Private, and its Melbourne Business School was established as a separate company from the university. Equally, many universities have private operating entities for foundation programs, executive programs, research commercialisation, consultancy and more, such as Monash College and others.

Many universities also have strategic partnerships with private providers for foundation programs and pathway programs and they contract out an increasing array of functions to private firms ranging from Navitas and Kaplan to UniLodge, for education delivery, accommodation, maintenance, staff and student support, etc.

Most recently, a first for-profit university, Laureate, was accepted in 2011 as a university under the protocols applying prior to the establishment of the Tertiary Education Quality and Standards Agency (TEQSA).

Beyond the individual universities, various universities have over time collectively established private companies for common service provision such as Unimutual, Unisuper, IDP Education, AARNET, Higher Education Services Pty Ltd.

In addition there are many further public and private higher education providers awarding degrees, ranging from Holmesglen TAFE through the Melbourne Institute of Technology to the Moore Theological College and SP Jain School of Global Management.

And there are many public and private research institutes and providers ranging from the Commonwealth Scientific and Industrial Research Organisation (CSIRO) and the Defence Science and Technology Organisation (DSTO) through medical research institutes and 'think tanks' to corporate research entities, including many in 'knowledge parks' associated with universities. Links to universities for all of these are not uncommon.

And what do we make of the fact that public universities receive only 20 per cent of their revenue as direct institutional grants from government (with another 20 per cent being national competitive research grants for academics), while private schools receive 60 per cent of their revenue in direct institutional grants from government (OECD 2013)? Under 'contestability' policies such as in Victoria and Queensland, private tertiary providers receive increasing government support, including participation in vocational education and training (VET) national support programs, access to Australia's fee loan scheme (FEE-HELP) and income support schemes (Austudy and Youth Allowance), as well as access to State and Territory course funding (Noonan 2014).

There is also strong pressure for ongoing change. For example, private providers have sought further access to the Education Investment Fund, Commonwealth Supported Places and more, though sometimes a caution applies that this would be preferred by them without the costly and sometimes poorly administered reporting and accountability burden that can accompany public privilege. Likewise some public VET providers also seek wider access to higher education arrangements ranging from teaching subsidies to university title.

Most recently the Abbott Coalition government proposed in 2014 opening up access to Commonwealth Supported Places for undergraduate degrees to non-university higher education providers, though at a discounted rate to allow for the distinguishing university research function.

In all, any simple distinction between whether Australia should have either public or private as its preferred mode of provision of education is both no longer tenable and is subject to open contestation. We have a quite mixed and fast-changing system in place today in Australia. The distinction between public and private is not nearly as clear as it once might have been.

# Tertiary education reform in Australia

But the changes do not mean that the difference has disappeared entirely, nor that it should disappear.

Indeed it may be argued that a mixed system such as in Australia is a healthy one. Reliance upon either mostly public or mostly private each has its weaknesses as well as strengths.

The Lisbon Council (2008) did indeed say, in one of the rare rankings of higher education systems and one of the few that went beyond heavy reliance upon research metrics as the differentiating factor, that Australia's higher education system was the world's best.[1]

But the Bradley Review of Australian Higher Education (2008) did point out that the achievement reflected in that characterisation could well be unsustainable or compromised. For example, the Review found that Australia was the only country where public funding for higher education as a share of GDP had fallen steadily over much of the late 20th and early 21st centuries, whereas it had increased by over 60 per cent on average for other OECD countries up until the Global Financial Crisis. Australia had attained the highest student-staff ratio in universities for the OECD, yet its higher education students worked in external employment while studying full-time more than most other comparable countries, the flip side of one of the less inclusive income-support systems for students across those countries (Universities Australia 2008a). At the same time, the Australian academic workforce, which had expanded substantially in the 1960s and 1970s, had come to represent the second-oldest workforce in terms of mean age (just behind farmers), which also affects sustainability of tertiary educational provision (Hugo and Morriss 2010).

Also, as the Bradley Review again found, Australia had the highest share of full-fee international students in higher education in the OECD and the share of lower socio-economic status (SES) students in higher education has remained largely static across many years.

For a sustainable future to emerge instead, it was necessary, according to the Bradley Report that the Review's budget recommendations regarding indexation and payment of indirect costs of research grants be implemented in full; that a new tertiary quality assurance framework be implemented efficiently and effectively; that the international education framework be advanced to embrace a 'third wave approach' as recommended in reviews by Baird (2010), Knight (2011) and

---

1   A more recent ranking of systems for the Universitas 21 group of universities has Australia in a more modest eighth place (Universitas 21 2012).

Chaney (International Education Advisory Council 2013); that, again according to the Bradley Report, at least 40 per cent of young adults should hold at least a bachelor's degree by 2020; that at least 20 per cent of students should come from lower SES backgrounds by 2025; and that, according to the Lee Dow Review (2011) student income support needed to be better targeted to support and assist with these equity goals.

In the longer run these ambitions and the need for excellence in standards requires further elaboration in this writer's view. A suitable target would be that higher education funding should move to two per cent of GDP; and that this should be resourced 50:50 public and private.

Cross-country regression analysis for OECD countries relating per-capita income to higher education funding, with appropriate allowance for the direction of causation, as conducted by Universities Australia (2008a), documented the economic benefits of such benchmarks, and the Higher Education Base Funding Review (*Lomax-Smith Report* 2011) also agreed with the general direction of such funding proposals.

## Policy implementation

Reviews are one thing. The implementation of their recommendations is another. It might have been predicted that there would be abolition by a Labor Government of the Coalition's National Governance Protocols and Higher Education Workplace Requirements and the controls they implied over university governance and workforce management, and that there would be the passing of a Student Amenities Bill to help revive campus life under a Labor Government, alhough the latter did take a long time.

But who would have predicted that during a global financial crisis (GFC) there could be a major increase in university funding, both in infrastructure through various fund initiatives such as the Education Investment Fund (EIF), Better Universities Renewal Fund (BURF), Teaching and Learning Capital Fund (TLCF) and through better indexation and enhanced indirect cost support?

Similarly, it would have been brave to predict that, coming out of the Indian student problems experienced in 2009, recommendations to improve the Education Services for Overseas Students (ESOS) Act and make student visa administration better and healthier than before the troubles, would be promptly implemented.

Also coming out of the Bradley Review a new integrated national regulatory framework (under the Tertiary Education Quality and Standards Agency plus an Australian Qualifications Framework Council (AQFC)) might have been seen as the price of increased funding, but less predictable was the acceptance by government that key principles of 'self-accreditation', 'regulatory necessity' and 'proportionality' be embodied in the legislation. Equally, when the resultant regulatory agency showed signs of overreach, government acted quickly to review this (Lee Dow and Braithwaite 2013) and act on the recommendations.

There was also the prompt reform of targeting of student income support that drew heavily on the Lee Dow Review (2011) and the Universities Australia (UA) work in the area. And it was even possible for university representations to turn the Gillard Labor government around on its ministerial titling better to reflect commitment to higher education and to pre-empt planned cuts to the National Health and Medical Research Council (NHMRC) and even recover some of Australian Learning and Teaching Council (ALTC) cuts.

Equally, despite emerging budget deficit issues, the adoption of a demand-driven enrolment funding system for domestic undergraduate places proceeded, permitting university admission of all domestic students meeting their entry standard.

However, despite four years of such change under Labor and indeed in the latter Howard government years too (for example, establishing the Higher Education Endowment Fund), the situation subsequently became uncertain.

There were in the 12 months prior to the 2013 Federal Election proposals by the then Labor government for each of: major delays in allocations from the Education Investment Fund; deferral of scheduled increases in indexation and indirect cost support; imposition of 'efficiency dividends' (i.e. grant reductions) on university funding; conversion of 'start-up' scholarships from grants to loans; elimination of 'up-front' discounts for early payment of official loans; and, continued failure to accept the recommendations of the Bradley and Base Funding Reviews for real per-student funding increases.

Following the election of the Coalition government in September 2013, ideas regarding caps on demand-driven enrolments, abolition of compulsory student services and amenities fee requirements, Australian Research Council grant funding cuts, and controls on types of grants to be funded for research were floated by government representatives, if not acted upon at the time.

By contrast, new provisions for 'Reverse Colombo Plan' studies and improved work-experience visa provisions were also mooted and serious implementation arrangements were pursued as of later 2013. Machinery of government provisions saw VET separated ministerially from higher education and responsibility for research initially left divided and ambiguous, which was not a sign of clarity of vision and purpose in this field.

However, the May 2014 Budget saw the emergence of much more purposive proposals for change. These embraced at least five elements.

The first was expansion. This was to come through increased demand-driven enrolments via extension of eligibility to sub-bachelor degrees.

The second was restructuring. This was to come through reconfiguration of degree subsidy structure and also restructuring of science funding and infrastructure government support.

Third was deregulation. This was to come through removal of caps on tuition fees plus reduced regulatory agency responsibilities, though quotas would be imposed for equity scholarship funding.

Fourth was more competition. This was to come through extension of public subsidy to those enrolled in non-university higher education providers.

Fifth, and finally, there was privatisation. This was to come through reduced public subsidy for undergraduate degrees, new fees for doctoral study, increased student loan costs and lower indexation formulae for future government grants.

These proposed changes were still under consideration in the Commonwealth Parliament as of the time of writing in September 2014.

# The role of universities

From the 1980s through to the early 2000s Australia as a nation went through a transformation under a process of economic reform. It involved acceptance of an 'economic rationalist' view that wider use of liberalisation and privatisation was needed in Australia.

Older reliance upon what Castles (1985) had termed a 'worker welfare state' model, or the 'Australian Settlement' in Kelly's (1992) depiction, was put aside. The outcome has been a major restoration of economic prosperity and resilience compared to most other OECD economies.[2]

---

2   Though various Scandinavian economies have likewise performed well despite their general adherence to a more dirigiste model of policy, and the sustainability of this outcome is at the centre of contemporary economic debate (e.g. Garnaut 2013; Edwards 2014).

However, the momentum of Australian reform is seen as declining from the early 2000s and a phalanx of policy commentators and interest groups have been calling for a resumption of reform. Part of this vision is a view that reform of the non-traded social sectors is at the core of the task that remains. This especially refers to health and education.

As regards tertiary education and especially higher education, one wonders whether the commentators have ever transcended the perceptions that they developed following their own youthful university experience. Certainly, in this writer's view, it is not clear that they talk to their children enough, which may go with a federal politician's role, since they do seem rather unaware of the cumulative extent of reform and change in tertiary education.

For example, even putting aside earlier changes in higher education, the Howard Coalition government's long period of reduced real funding per student and imposition of industrial and governance reform were major vehicles for the transformation of Australian universities, including their growth into larger, more market-based and managerialist organisations that, inter alia, developed whole new areas of remunerative educational practice. The emergence of education exports as Australia's third-largest export after coal and iron, and the top export for Victoria and second for NSW, is only beginning to be more widely understood outside the sector.

During those Howard Coalition government years, the rise of alternative revenue sources saw the government share of university revenue fall from 80 per cent to 40 per cent, delivering the highest share of private revenues for any public university system in the OECD and including the highest share of international revenues in any university system (OECD 2013). Governance and industrial reforms entrenched new managerial power.

The subsequent Labor government reforms from 2007 through 2013 then took the reform process further, altering the foundations for the delivery of remaining public funding and developing a new regulatory rather than self-policing quality-assurance system. But with no increase in real per-student funding and with major new enforceable regulatory requirements imposed, the Coalition imperatives supporting elements of both market and managerial imperatives were arguably reinforced, rather than reversed, under Labor.

Even with the limits to regulatory intervention that the sector managed to have included in its new TEQSA Act (unlike the VET sector) and the successful incorporation of a legislative commitment to academic freedom by way of amendment to the Higher Education Support Act that authorises Commonwealth funding of universities, the balance of reform has been to maintain the market, mandarin and management momentum. It is individual and collegial academic self-determination that has diminished in the process.

Where to next? With some strong advocacy favouring ongoing reform, the pressure for further strengthening of the market and managerial direction is likely to be continued. This prediction has been confirmed fulsomely in the May 2014 Budget proposed by the Abbott Coalition government. Possible developments from this, plus wider developments in higher education, may therefore include: more private universities and other private higher education institutions; the emergence of some public universities that eschew government funded places; more degrees being approved and publicly funded for delivery from non-university providers; more use of blended learning in delivery as accelerated by the attention being paid to the massive open online course (MOOC) phenomenon; more vocational training and education from private providers and within firms, including through ongoing opening of public funds to contestability; more pathways negotiated across the system, including expanded partnerships of universities with private providers for this purpose; more development of new teaching-only university colleges; more inter-disciplinary research to meet growing demand for more holistic views from universities' research; and more acceptance of incentives for impact and engagement by universities with business, government and community.

For universities these trends, if realised, would mean a smaller share of post-secondary education enrolments and more private elements in university operations. They also mean that universities, as other providers, will be under considerable pressure to be even more business-like in their management processes while seeking to maintain a commitment to their core knowledge objectives.

This is likely to take place within a greater engagement with the emerging university and other tertiary education systems of the faster-growing economies, including those in Asia. Two-way student movement may emerge stronger, as may extension into more graduate studies, education partnerships and research collaboration.

## Future response by universities

How should policy and universities respond to these trends and pressures?

First, from the perspective of the tertiary education system as a whole, it is arguable that the major expansion of private provider provision in vocational education and training and in pathway and partnership provision is a potentially healthy one, but subject to careful conditions.

We now have a million-plus students in Australia in each of higher education, TAFE and PET. These are essentially three matched components of our contemporary tertiary education system.

Diversity in forms of provision that helps best meet student choices and needs, and fosters research in all its forms, is to be supported and encouraged. And higher participation rates in tertiary education are beneficial for Australia. Functionalists can take comfort from real rates of return in the 15–20 per cent range, while cost of capital to government is seven per cent or less (Higher Education Base Funding Review 2011).

Tertiary education more than pays its way in terms of employment and earnings benefits – quite apart from wider social and cultural returns that are also or instead a focus for many.

To have one pillar of this system that prioritises flexibility and innovation and responsiveness is arguably a gain. The modern growth of private provision therefore is likely to continue. Large complex public institutions, whether TAFEs or public universities or research agencies, have their limitations as well as their strengths.

For this emergent trend to work best to tap strengths and weaknesses wherever they may lie, one key requirement is an efficient and effective quality-assurance system. This is not yet currently happening and the new national VET regulator especially shows all signs of a bureaucratic, one-size-fits-all, tick–a-box, process-oriented regulatory approach (Withers 2013). TEQSA is still a work in progress but has also given cause for alarm, as Lee Dow and Braithwaite (2013) have convincingly documented. Regulation therefore is ripe for ongoing monitoring, and the pretence that officials can help improve business and education processes rather than maintain threshold output and outcome standards to protect students still needs to be addressed.

Secondly, to determine the appropriate balance in the tertiary education system there does need to be a 'level playing field' for regulation and funding. How a level playing field for such a tertiary environment can be defined is also a work in progress. It should, however, fund providers at cost of public benefit generated, independent of the provider type; that is, follow 'competitive neutrality' principles, including recognition of different cost requirements imposed by government on alternative providers. Present differences between VET and higher education in access to international visa arrangements, in payments for equivalent teaching services via Commonwealth Supported Places, and also actually in provision of research services vis-à-vis non-university research institutes, seem prima facie to violate this principle. Partial reviews of tertiary sector components hide these differences. Comprehensive whole-of-sector examination is called for, despite the federal complications of this, and should proceed under a clear risk assessment framework.

Of course acceptance of public funds may require conduct of activities that are not themselves commercial – for example, specific areas of education and research with small demand but important for the society. Similarly, acceptance of public funds may require adherence to public requirements for transparency and accountability, involving, for example, auditors-general, parliaments, ombudsmen, departmental scrutiny, reporting and contract management. This needs to be understood by those seeking access to university-style funding, just as university representatives need to understand reciprocal obligations such as reinforcement of open-access principles for publicly funded research.

Third, while allowing for competition, some enduring distinctions can remain. These relate essentially to 'truth in advertising'. In this context the term 'university' should remain closely regulated.

This is because a university should be an institution characterised by the pursuit of broadly based higher learning and research for the public benefit (Universities Australia 2008b). The defining characteristics of a university to this end are that it is academically autonomous, and that it operates as follows: it offers rigorous teaching and examination across a substantial range of disciplines and qualification levels (i.e. from diploma to doctorate); it is committed to the systematic development of new knowledge through fundamental and applied research; it undertakes research training at doctoral and postdoctoral level in its areas of research strength; it contributes to public debate and to the advancement of public understanding concerning matters of national and international importance; it engages with its host community to share facilities of community benefit, foster its accessibility to community members and assist in addressing community issues and problems; and it participates in national and international networks to advance knowledge and promote the value contribution of higher education.

The breadth and integration of a university's activities in teaching, research and external engagement in these ways separates a university from other tertiary education providers.

Those providers that wish to develop some or all of these characteristics listed should be able to pursue university status if desired, and this would be welcomed, but only if all the characteristics required are met. To dilute the use of the name would not assist students and other stakeholders in any way.

A university need not be exhaustive in its coverage of all research and teaching undertakings, but it must combine undergraduate and postgraduate teaching and research across a range of disciplines. This principle in no way prevents a university from concentrating on particular areas of teaching and research strength, as many of Australia's universities already do.

It does, however, differentiate a university – so-called – from a more specialised body that should properly be called a college, school or institute. Breadth of coverage also underpins the validity of autonomy and self-accreditation, through the provision of internal checks and balances arising from peer review within a community of scholars, including across disciplines, schools and faculties.

Even great specialised institutions such as the London School of Economics, Caltech or the Massachusetts Institute of Technology do not adopt the title 'university'. This is as it should be, and the emergence of Australia's first specialised university in the form of the Melbourne College of Divinity University is, in this respect, to be regretted. Far preferable would have been the retention of 'School' or 'Institute' for specialised institutions and the simpler adoption of 'university college' title for specialised teaching institutions. The present insistence on such colleges also having research as opposed to scholarship obligations is simple protectionism by existing universities.

Fourth, private universities need not and should not mean for-profit universities. Private universities can be and should be not-for-profit. This is certainly the case already for the vast majority of private universities around the world – and it certainly is the case for those private universities that are consistently at the head of world rankings, such as Harvard, Princeton and Yale.[3]

However, to include the profit motive in the mix is incompatible with the nature of the university – a bridge too far. Such motivation would undermine the public-benefit purpose of the university. This is because commercial provision is inevitably conditioned by the profit motive that drives business at its core and brings its own distinctive but different benefits, but does not and cannot thrive on the production of public goods. Included here is the critical-inquiry function that so characterises all good universities, but doesn't generate much appropriable revenue.

This public-good benefit refers to activities that have wider benefits for society beyond those that can be captured in the excludable and appropriable market contracts necessary for profit-based businesses to operate. It is for this reason that so few for-profit universities have been present in the 1,500 years of university existence – and why related endeavours of contemporary note in Australia, such

---

3   However, private Japanese and Korean universities have achieved less to date, for which a wider historical explanation is needed.

as Central Queensland University business partnership arrangements or even the SEEK corporation's role in IDP Education, seem to have had their distinctive problems in the local environment.

The consequences too of undue reliance on an inadequately regulated commercial imperative are there for all to see in the GFC itself and, in Australian tertiary education to some extent, in the 2009 Indian student crisis. Nevertheless, the latter seems as much or more a government regulatory failure, especially in immigration management, as it was a market problem. Academic self-regulation in universities is an important antidote to over-reliance on both market and mandarin imperatives, providing it is not itself in turn swamped by internal managerialism.

The role of universities therefore in a mixed tertiary system is to work in a complementary way with specialist teaching and specialist research entities, including those that operate through business provisions – for example, within firms and by private providers, through a not-for-profit, comprehensive education and research capacity. The mix can be highly synergistic to the benefit of all sectors in our economy and society in general, but including the field of tertiary education, especially as an area that matters as much for the political, social and cultural dimensions of our national life as its strictly economic aspects (Universities Australia 2008a).

However, for not-for-profit provision itself to work, it must embed substantial autonomy from government too (Aghion et al. 2009). Just as there are consequences from purely commercial motivation in this field, so there are consequences from undue government control, direction and influence. The Australian politicians' ritual denunciation of selected research topics receiving grants would be amusing were it not symbolic of a deeper danger. A pluralist democracy is underpinned by freedom of inquiry.

Creativity in learning and independence in research are key requirements for national progress. There must be systems and culture that ensure substantial professional independence in teaching and research, while still fully complying with all reasonable accountability requirements for the use of public funds and while allowing a reasonable component of private funds to augment this.

Fifth, universities must act responsibly in the use of their autonomy. It is here that managerialism enters the fray again. While defending universities against external control, academic freedom must be respected internally. Institutional autonomy is actually different from academic freedom and the latter is at times also under pressure from within.

Universities are actually managed quite well overall in basic functional areas of administration. A common view to the contrary held by many business managers and politicians is misplaced. Indeed the appearance of twice as many Australian universities in *The Times* top global 500 universities as Australian businesses in the *Fortune* top 500 global businesses, indicates that private business in Australia hardly transcends university practice (Withers 2009). However, there is a great danger that such hierarchical managerialism may be coming increasingly at the expense of freedom of inquiry, as much as by a burden of reporting and administration as from direct intervention in research and teaching, though there are too many instances of the latter too. The modest case study appended below illustrates the unintended effects of managerialism, along with some negative contribution too from mandarins and markets.

Therefore there is still serious scope for better management consistent with the purpose of the university. Above all this involves four components: first, reducing diversion of internal resources to uncreative and unsupportive administration; secondly, better institutionalisation of peer review of academic affairs from practising academics within university decision-making; thirdly, proper respect for staff and student voice in university affairs; and fourthly, improving university integrity codes to ensure conflicts of interest and breaches of research protocols are prevented or dealt with openly and honestly.

# Conclusion

Universities are one of society's most enduring institutions. They have continued to help meet the core human need for the creation and dissemination of knowledge. It is telling that one of the first instincts of the most authoritarian of rulers is to suppress academic freedom.

It is also the case that the ideas and innovations that emanate from universities and the transmission of this learning help underpin economic, social and environmental advancement.

In Australia, traditional university arrangements did seek to provide this under full public funding combined with academic autonomy. However, arguably, this privilege was less respected by its recipients than society might expect for the support provided. To return to old attitudes of entitlement is therefore not what is needed.

New ways under a massified university system do promise more for the citizens who underpin such effort. The capacity to benefit from advanced learning is not restricted to an elite group, but something that can be of wide social gain. But new ways also are full of their own tricks and traps, including the challenges of maintaining academic autonomy and knowledge imperatives while balancing these against the constraints posed by the managers, mandarins and markets.

To meet these challenges requires careful development of the logic and evidence and pursuit of higher values that characterise the university at its best, applied to the problems of the modern university itself too. Hence this collection of essays.

---

### Managers, mandarins and markets: A case study

In August 2012, an Australian Council of Learned Academies (ACOLA) grant of $1.25 million over three years was made for a project to be guided by an Expert Working Group of Fellows of the Learned Academies of Australia. Accommodation for two to three offices to allow conduct of the supporting project research was sought at one of Australia's premier research universities, the home of the Group's Chair.

The outcome was that initial accommodation previously expected from an on-campus Learned Academy did not eventuate as the academy itself was now being required by the university to move to smaller premises if it wished to remain on campus. This was in order to make way for an expanded office of the alumni relations and philanthropy division of the university administration.

A second set of office accommodation promised by the Group Chair's own college was then pursued and then withdrawn when the chancellor and vice-chancellor required the promised space to be instead prioritised for two impact projects related to government linkages and housing administrators for these programs.

A third suite of accommodation then subsequently identified as vacant within another college was removed from consideration when the university central administration required relocation there of the university student equity team instead. A temporary office facility was therefore found in a third college but it too was terminated when it was established that associated rental required of $20,000 annually for offices and IT support could not be paid under the Australian Research Council (ARC) official grant rules behind the ACOLA project's funding.

An off-campus fallback option identified at another learned academy had in the meantime disappeared when that academy found an ongoing commercial market tenancy for rental of its space.

The university concerned had actually been downsizing its staff due to budget issues at this time, making substantial space available in principle but this proved hard to identify as administrators protected space for future possible need rather than immediate use.

Homelessness by Christmas 2013 faced this ACOLA flagship project – the results of which, in addition to associated academic publication, were to be presented at the Prime Minister's Science and Engineering Council to demonstrate academic responsiveness to national needs.

The distortions in delivering on such Learned Academy pursuits in the face of market imperatives, managerial intercessions and mandarins' mandates are evident, even at the cost of work with scholarly imprimatur.

Finally, an academic unit of great distinction and with some independence arising from its standing and external funding and operating via traditional collegial decision-making, provided accommodation for the project after more than a year of searching - a small victory in the end for academic autonomy in a sea of alternative incentives and pressures.

Such is the life in pursuit of veritas in the modern university.

---

# Part III: Education for the 'Real World'

# 8. The Modern University and its Transaction with Students

Nigel Palmer

This chapter is about the marketisation of the modern university and its transaction with students. It identifies opportunities for responding to the challenges associated with marketisation. While appealing to the idea of knowledge for its own sake as a public good is an important part of preserving the idea of a university, more needs to be done if there is to be an adequate response. Responding to the challenges of marketisation requires active and constructive engagement in means as well as ends while resisting their excesses. While the idea of the university is typically constructed as an end worth advocating for, there is growing separation between this and the reality of the contemporary means of engaging with students – in market terms, via the university–student transaction.

## The modern university

The modern university can be characterised as a synthesis of the new and the old, between innovations worth embracing and traditions worth preserving. In essence, universities are as conservative as they are innovative. This is certainly the case with the modern university and, perhaps, it's always been this way. This idea of the new meeting the old can be found in both old and new accounts of the nature of the university (Davis 2013; Marginson and Considine 2000; Newman 1852). This characterisation describes a tension that is in the nature of the university. In the case of the modern university this can be seen between 'the idea of the university' and its brief for innovation. In many respects this tension is constructive. For example, a common point of contestation has been between a comparatively conservative account of the pursuit of knowledge as an end in itself (often citing Newman's *The Idea of a University*) (1852), and the drive for more 'instrumentalist' approaches to supporting vocations and professions, and both pure and applied research (McKernan 2011). Universities are defined through being both innovative and conservative, and continue to evolve both in light of and despite pressures for change, both internal and external.

Universities as communities of scholars provide a vehicle for creativity, innovation and the generation and dissemination of new knowledge. There is also an expectation that as institutions they reflect the kind of ideals we associate with institutions of higher learning. These are the values that often seem to be under threat in the face of continued pressure for change. Areas identified as being at risk and worth defending include academic freedom, equality of educational opportunity and the value and integrity of universities as social institutions. In a broader sense, 'commodification' imperatives have been held to threaten something even more essential to universities: their role as institutions of higher learning. Here, knowledge and commodification are seen as opposed, and 'marketisation' represents the principal threat to the quality and integrity of the academic enterprise.

On many contemporary accounts managerialism, neoliberalism, commodification, and the rise of an 'audit culture' feature among the principal challenges facing the modern university. These are commonly captured under the banner of 'marketisation' and are prevalent to the extent that the modern university now seems to stand opposed to its ideal. While the pressures for marketisation are seen as a function of government policy, these pressures arise as much from within as from without. Conservative imperatives to preserve an idea of the university and to engage in reform for reform's sake are both extremes on a continuum intrinsic to the nature of the institution. Taken to excess, each poses its own threat. There is a substantial literature on the extent to which the pendulum has swung toward the latter, and the threats that marketisation poses to the idea of the university (Apple 2000; Deem and Brehony 2005; Molesworth, Scullion and Nixon 2011; Morley 2003; Shore and Wright 1999; Slaughter and Rhoades 2004; Teixeira and Dill 2011). If this is the case, then where do we look for a viable response to these challenges? Adequately contesting the marketisation of the modern university requires a closer look at higher education 'markets' and the commodification of university degrees.

## Markets

Should universities be engaging with markets differently, or somehow be protected from them? Is it even conceivable for universities to be able to 'resist' the market? It is useful perhaps to make a distinction between the various relations of engagement and exchange that could be conceived of in market terms and the extent to which these might apply (or be avoidable) in the case of universities.

## Ubiquitous markets

There are both 'thin' and 'thick' views of what constitutes a market. At its 'thinnest', a market is simply a way of conceptualising parties interacting for the purpose of exchange. Understood broadly, markets are ubiquitous. A university may be seen to participate in different markets for each of its areas of activity. On this view universities already participate in different markets in different ways, and have been doing so for some time (Jongbloed 2003, 111; Teixeira and Dill 2011, xxi). Institutions have no alternative to participate and, where we adopt a liberal interpretation of what constitutes a market, have been doing so since their inception (Furedi 2011).

The causes of marketisation can be as ubiquitous as the problems they present, as can their agency. Scullion et al. confess that it is possible to hold everybody except the university mascot liable for the marketisation of higher education (Scullion, Molesworth and Nixon 2011, 234). But is this characterisation useful, and does it adequately capture those elements regarded as posing a threat to the integrity of the academy? Describing something as ubiquitous can have the effect of being both fatalistic and useless at the same time. 'Resisting the market' makes no sense where the market has no boundaries, and holding on to the aspiration that you may be able to do so simply reinforces a sense of hopelessness as to its ubiquity. The same holds for other threats to the modern university which might be captured under the banner of 'marketisation', including managerialism, neoliberalism and the rise of an 'audit culture'. Each has been described as 'totalising' in the sense that their influence informs an all-encompassing basis for evaluation. Things only 'make sense' within their prevailing paradigm. Each of these has to varying degrees taken hold in the case of the modern university as a basis for intelligibility, and this makes it very difficult to see where 'resistance' might occur. If we hold that marketisation and its associated phenomena are ubiquitous, then whatever form of 'resistance' we may summon must somehow occur through incremental change from within. If not, then is there still some way that universities can somehow remain 'outside' the market?

## Markets capitalist, free and pure

Deregulated markets by definition entail policies and strategies with the aim of enabling market incentives in areas governments might otherwise seek to influence directly. 'Free' markets sometimes occur in the absence of state intervention, but more often require specific interventions to achieve the desired state of affairs – often through engineering relationships around demand and supply. Jongbloed (2003) identifies eight 'freedoms' as basic conditions for a free market (as outlined in the first column of Table 8.1).

**Table 8.1: Conditions for 'free', 'pure' and capitalist/neoliberal markets**

| Free (Jongbloed 2003) | | Pure (Brown 2011) | Capitalist/neoliberal (Marginson 2012) |
|---|---|---|---|
| Provider | Freedom to specify the product | Legally autonomous institutions | No government interference |
| | Freedom to use available resources | | |
| | Freedom of entry | Minimal regulation of market entry | Markets with free entry |
| | Freedom to determine prices | No regulation on enrolments and fees | Competing institutions/firms financed by shareholder equity, and committed to profit-making and expansion of market share |
| Consumer | Direct and cost-covering prices paid | Full cost recovery for teaching through fees | |
| | | No government-funded tuition subsidy | |
| | Adequate info on prices and quality | Valid and reliable information on programs and providers | Higher education produced as commodities subject to buyer–seller relations |
| | Freedom to choose provider | | |
| | Freedom to choose product | | |

Source: Author's summary.

Jongbloed's conditions could be described as relatively 'thick' in that the conditions for what constitutes a free market are comparatively demanding. Following from these, Brown (2011) developed a comparable set of conditions for what he described as a 'pure' market for higher education (as outlined in the second column of Table 8.1). Brown observed that no developed higher education system has met all of the requisite characteristics for a 'pure' market in higher education, concluding that market theory may have questionable application to higher education (Brown 2011, 12).

Simon Marginson goes further in contending that the marketisation of higher education on the neoliberal model has in fact failed (Marginson 2012). For Marginson the neoliberal market model is only fully realised where the conditions of a 'bona fide' capitalist market are met (2012, 355). These are summarised in the third column of Table 8.1. Some of these conditions are relatively easy to observe – for example where higher education is conceived of as a commodity and subject to the buyer–seller relationship. Others seem more difficult to satisfy, such as an absence of government intervention and shareholder financing (and therefore profit obligations) (Marginson 2012, 355). Marginson points out that despite the rhetoric, it is difficult to identify a single educational system where all of these are in place.

While some of the conditions described above are evident to varying degrees across higher education systems internationally, they are far from universal. While the influence of new public management (and its associated managerialism) has in many respects become ubiquitous, this is not the same thing as saying that neoliberalism has completely taken hold. For Marginson, higher education systems in general fail the test when it comes to satisfying the conditions for capitalist markets on the neoliberal market model. More broadly, it seems difficult to sustain the argument that the provision of higher education would function effectively in a fully deregulated environment. At least some intervention is required for educational systems to function effectively; more is required if governments wish to exercise strategic influence over that system through 'steering from a distance' (Kickert 1995; Marceau 1993; Marginson 1997). This environment has come to be known as the quasi-market model.

## Quasi-markets

The kind of conditions outlined above convey the impression that all markets are potentially imperfect in one way or another. If markets are ubiquitous, so too are the conditions that influence the parameters by which they operate. These include intervention by government, anti-competitive behaviour and even basic social practices. It could be argued that wherever there is negotiated exchange between parties there is price setting – the basic conditions for a very 'thin' view of what constitutes a market. But these would also be accompanied by factors that would render that market imperfect in one way or another. If markets are ubiquitous and perfect markets impossible, then what are we left with? Perhaps all markets are 'quasi' in one way or another – to the extent there seem always to be factors intervening to qualify the market ideal (Akerlof 2003).

Institutional strategies for the modern university are influenced on the one hand by those criteria set by government for regulation and funding purposes, and on the other by market forces. In this sense universities operate in 'quasi-markets'. Quasi-markets have been proposed as a useful means for characterising higher education systems (Bertolin 2011; Le Grand 1991; Lubienski 2009; Niklasson 1996). Here decisions about supply and demand are coordinated by government through 'market-like' mechanisms where market elements may be selectively introduced or withdrawn (Dill 1998; Teixeira et al. 2004). Over the last 20 years there has been an increasingly widespread use of selective regulation of this kind across higher education systems, with market mechanisms increasingly being used to reshape the reality of higher education around the world (Molesworth, Scullion and Nixon 2011, xvi–xvii). Most instances of marketisation in higher education have in fact been sponsored by government intervention rather than inaction. This has been characterised as a transition from state control to state coordination and supervision (Brennan 2010; Clark 1983; Salazar and Leihy 2011).

The incongruity between resisting the market and assuming quasi-market conditions is often reflected in the rhetoric of university leaders. It's not unusual, for example, for university leaders to call for fee deregulation while in the same breath warn of the perilous 'market forces' which loom at the prospect of any decrease in public subsidy. If we permit that universities typically exist in 'quasi-market' conditions, the question when it comes to the idea of the university is not whether markets can be avoided but rather which bits are subject to intervention (and subsidy) by government and which bits are not. Quasi-market government policy entails creating or suppressing (market) incentives (intended and otherwise). In higher education this is typically through selective regulation and performance-related evaluation in support of scale, quality and efficiency. It also supposedly entails strategies to encourage, diversify and inform 'consumer' behaviour.

Jongbloed and Brown point out that a true market for higher education is yet to exist, and as Marginson adds, it is hard to find a single example where higher education is deregulated to the extent that it conforms with the neoliberal market ideal. The pressing issue for higher education is not the debate between advocates for complete market deregulation versus those for protected status, but rather the nature and extent of government regulation in the face of market forces in a quasi-market environment.

## Resisting 'the market'

In summary then, while market forces can in some respects be considered ubiquitous, it seems the more specific forms of market that many might imagine to be in place do not hold. 'Pure' markets in higher education are impossible (Brown 2011, 12), as are truly competitive ones (as noted by Aspromourgos in chapter 5 in this volume), capitalist or neoliberal markets (Marginson 2012, 361) or markets that are truly 'free' (Jongbloed 2003, 134). If we hold that markets are not ubiquitous, then it follows that the path to salvaging those things worth preserving lies in preventing their being subject to market forces, and their evaluation being subject to the market mentality. If they are, then whatever form of 'resistance' we may summon must occur somehow from within. Given the answer lies somewhere between the two – in a quasi-market environment, then prospects for an adequate response lie not in avoiding the market, but in engaging with these things differently, possibly in a more informed way. In this spirit, the following section addresses the marketisation of the idea of the university in practice via the contemporary means of engaging with students – in market terms, via the university–student transaction.

# The university–student transaction

Understood broadly, 'commodification' may be seen to be as ubiquitous as markets: wherever there is a market there is typically a commodity of some kind being exchanged, and thus, the object of exchange becomes 'commodified'. On this somewhat simplistic view one thing stands out: the objects of exchange do not necessarily look the same from the perspective of each of the parties with a stake in the transaction. The dynamics of negotiated exchange in the university–student transaction look different from government, student and institutional perspectives.

Governments now seem to be in the habit of expecting more for less, while institutions seem to be in the business of promising more while offering less. Academics want less 'marketisation' but, given the rise to prominence of the associated idea of 'student as consumer', do students want more or less of all this? Despite all the consumerist rhetoric, many students still subscribe to the traditional ideals of the university – or at least, as they might imagine them. Indeed, these imaginings are a very real part of the university–student transaction, for better or worse. Students are encouraged to embrace the dream (Thornton and Shannon, chapter 10 in this volume). In fact, this makes up a substantial component of what they are getting in their transaction with universities. In this students and universities have differing interests. Universities benefit through promising more and offering less. The idea of the university, ironically features prominently in this.

It's not always clear what is being bought and sold in the university–student transaction. If students are to be considered as consumers of a commodity, then what is it they are being sold? Conceived in market terms, if we were to offer an honest receipt to students accounting for the content of their transaction with their university, what would it look like? Whatever it is, it is no longer principally about the transfer of knowledge. What follows is an account of the engagement between universities and students, in the context of responding to the marketisation of the modern university. In addressing the prospect of marketisation directly, this is described here as the university–student transaction.

## Adequate information on quality

Aspromourgos (chapter 5 in this volume) describes conditions for a *competitive* market. These include multiple agents, the commodities of exchange and a body of information covering the economically relevant characteristics of the commodities (see also Aspromourgos 2012). For Aspromourgos universities have 'secrets' in selling degrees – information about the 'product' not available to prospective students. Higher education has been described as an 'experience good' where quality is revealed on consumption, but about which they have incomplete information at the time of 'purchase'. To be fair to institutions these 'secrets' are often as opaque to them as they are to students. Either way, quality information is asymmetrically distributed between the supplier and the consumer in this transaction, with students participating with 'ex ante' quality uncertainty. Adequate information on quality is commonly identified as a vital ingredient for any market, and on most accounts is a condition for them to function effectively (including those outlined earlier in this chapter). This means more than responding to a liberal ethic for ensuring that students participate as informed consumers (Slater 1997). In the absence of 'quality-revealing' institutions, we end up with the situation described in Akerlof's *Market for Lemons,* where a paucity of information on quality makes it uneconomical to invest in it (Akerlof 1970). Thus, while not only disenfranchising students, inadequate information on the content of the transaction leads to a failure in market mechanisms for quality.

Underlying some market assumptions are that students conduct themselves as rational agents in their transaction with universities and make maximising judgments regarding their destination and type of study. There is an argument that adequate information on quality is redundant in this context, as students often do not make the 'right decision' in market terms – where they fail to make economically maximising decisions. To this extent they fail to conduct themselves as 'rational agents'; therefore providing them with better information on the quality of what they are getting is a waste of time. A more detailed account of student agency and the limitations of its construction as what could be coined *studiosus economicus* would be appropriate for a separate chapter, but in short here are at least two reasons why this does not apply. The first lies in the fact that greater transparency by itself shapes incentives which are independent of consumer agency (Dill and Soo 2004). Thus, adequate information can function as a market mechanism for quality without being contingent on rational consumer agency. Second, students do not 'price' utility in a way that always fits with economic models narrowly defined. That's not a problem with the student, it's a problem with the models – in particular those that provide an impoverished account of value estimation in contexts like this. Students are much more sophisticated in identifying value and in making decisions than is typically captured by narrowly defined economic models.

Evidence on what students do value in decision-making on prospective destinations for study shows that providers are primarily differentiated by cost, course and institutional reputation and selectivity in admissions (Hazelkorn 2011, 3; James, Baldwin and McInnis 1999, ix). Perceived status and market value of the degree and the institution that confers it appear to be consistent factors, though these are often qualified by specific geographic constraints (Baldwin and James 2000; Foskett 2011; Hazelkorn 2007). While the majority of these factors seem relatively stable, students are becoming increasingly sophisticated in their decision-making about prospective destinations for study (Hazelkorn 2011). This increasing sophistication has not always been matched by improvements in the quality of the information available. Institutional rankings have questionable validity as a source of information for prospective students (Dill and Soo 2005; Marope, Wells and Hazelkorn 2013; Stolz, Hendel and Horn 2010). Rather than compare their merits again here, the following addresses what they might reflect if they were to address what students are actually getting in their transaction with universities.

## The content of the university–student transaction

Were we to issue a 'receipt' for what students were really getting in the university-student transaction, it might include content knowledge narrowly conceived. It might include knowledge-and-skills as reflected in the contemporary parlance of learning outcomes. It might include an experiential component through engagement in the kind of activities that universities support that may or may not be directly related to the 'learning outcomes' of the degree. Finally, there might also be some 'client service' aspects to the transaction. These are the sorts of things typically evaluated through surveys of student satisfaction and engagement (Palmer 2011). But a growing component of what students actually get in their transaction with the university is captured by the idea of the university – as communicated in the university brand. Rather than simply being something that attracts the attention of prospective students in recruitment, the university brand is accounting for an increasing proportion of what graduates are walking away with in their transaction with universities on graduation. The following addresses knowledge, the student experience and the university brand and evaluates the extent to which each of these has been 'marketised', and to what extent they constitute the principal components of the transaction between the modern university and students.

## Knowledge

Many authors highlight the student-as-consumer ethos as evidence of the prevailing market rationality associated with neoliberalism and the marketisation of university degrees. Peters, for example, cites Lyotard's reference to the development and exchange of knowledge in accounting for this in transactional economic terms: '[k]nowledge is and will be produced in order to be sold, it is and will be consumed in order to be valorised in a new production: in both cases, the goal is exchange' (Lyotard 1984, 4; Peters 2002, 144). Lyotard's original point was about the depersonalisation and instrumentalisation of knowledge. This may well be the case, but this point is also interpreted as prophesying the commodification of knowledge in a commercial sense – that is, exploited in a market context in exchange for fees. While such interpretations can assist in describing aspects to marketisation, they fail to describe the whole picture when it comes to the marketisation of the modern university, and convey a misleading impression of the nature of the contemporary university–student transaction.

If the university–student transaction simply amounts to the delivery of knowledge in exchange for fees (and possibly also meeting students' 'client service' expectations) then it does indeed sound like the commodification of knowledge and the marketisation of the university degree is complete. But it does not sound like a quality commodity, nor one that would be very highly valued by students. There is more to the university–student transaction than an exchange in regard to the *content* of knowledge – that is, getting factual stuff into students' heads. If we understand universities to be engaged in the commodification of knowledge narrowly understood, then the university that merely conveys knowledge as part of its transaction with students will at best be a budget one at the lower end of the knowledge market.

Consider why Massive Open Online Courses (MOOCs) have so many academics (and commentators) spooked. It's more than just the Baby-Boomers getting freaked out by the technology (Niemelä-Nyrhinen 2007), it's their potential to visibly displace what was once considered unique to the role of a university. You don't need to be a university to run a MOOC – it only helps in terms of branding the product (be it for fee or for free). These courses are 'open' and 'online' in that they enrol students for free via the web, and 'massive' in that enrolments of 30,000 are not unusual (Kolowich 2013) – and it is only early days. At a minimum they invite universities to revisit the content of their prevailing offerings in the university–student transaction, particularly when it comes to the preparation and delivery of structured coursework (Norton 2013). They also signal the potential for the bottom to drop out of any market for university degrees premised solely on the marketisation of knowledge in this way. A recent survey of professors running MOOCs in the United States found that 85 per cent thought courses of this type would have the effect of making traditional degrees less expensive in that market, and half of them thought it would lower their cost significantly (Kolowich 2013). The economics of this will have implications for both demand and supply, with early evidence suggesting that the rise of MOOCs will have the greatest impact on the nature of academic work. They also have implications for how we understand the content of a university degree.

Even at the most basic level the university–student transaction is much more sophisticated than knowledge in exchange for fees. 'Knowledge' no longer realistically captures what universities are really 'selling' to students in the university–student transaction (if it ever did). If there has been commodification via the marketisation of university degrees, it is not simply about the commodification of knowledge. If so, then what are students 'buying', and what are they being 'sold'?

## The student experience

Institutions typically offer what they describe as a 'quality university degree', or even a 'quality student experience'. To say that conceptions of what constitutes 'quality' are central to market dynamics for higher education would be true, but it would be misleading to suggest that the question of what constitutes it and the criteria through which it can be defined, measured and communicated is in any way settled. This is a point of considerable ambiguity that nevertheless remains central to any account of the marketisation of the modern university.

It would be misleading to suggest that either students or universities typically conceive of the exchange of 'content' knowledge as the principal basis for the contemporary university–student transaction. Knowledge does *not* form the basis of the university–student transaction in the same way that students are *not* consumers. As Paul Ramsden put it (2009, 2–3):

> [T]he student experience is created by students in their contact with higher education. They are integral to the formation of the experience. Students are not passive consumers, searching for 'satisfaction'. They are active partners in a relationship … The problem with the consumer model is that it makes the student experience into something that is determined by what the university offers rather by what the student can bring. This is not only out of date: it is both intellectually barren and factually untrue.

There is certainly an experiential component over and above the skills associated with the application and creation of knowledge and a demonstrable increase in the 'knowing of stuff'. The prevailing learning-outcomes approach describes what students know and can do (Kuh 2010). This broadly speaks to 'knowledge' and 'skills', and implicitly captures 'experience' as a third domain in potentially valuable graduate outcomes (Brown 2003, 154; Chalmers 2008, 10). Despite its limitations, the learning-outcomes approach does permit a broader understanding of 'knowledge' in this transaction – something that we can engage with and participate in rather than something that is simply exchanged. Ramsden's dismissal of the student-as-consumer view is in line with accounts of students as co-creators as part of a broader student learning experience. This account is a compelling one, and is one that owes a debt to the more progressive paradigms in learning and teaching (Barr and Tagg 1995; McCulloch 2009).

Survey instruments like the Course Experience Questionnaire (CEQ) are now commonly used to evaluate the extent to which student expectations like this are being met. Scott's 2006 analysis of open-ended responses to the CEQ allowed valuable insight into the salience of aspects of the student experience, either as 'best aspects' or as those in need of improvement. Among the most interesting findings from Scott's analysis was that while personal and intellectual outcomes were ranked among the best aspects, they were outranked by aspects associated with course design, staff availability and assessment when it comes to overall salience and concerns about quality (Scott 2006). While personal, intellectual and 'knowledge' outcomes may indeed be salient for students when things go well, assessment, course design and student support feature prominently among quality concerns, and these combine with the perceived quality and accessibility of university staff as among the most salient aspects of the student experience (Scott 2006). In other words, while students value 'knowledge' outcomes from their degree, there is clearly more to their transaction with the institution for the exchange of knowledge even where conceived of as a broader student learning experience, and this has something to do with the intrinsic value of academic staff and academic work. Despite many inferences to the contrary, these are neither invisible nor merely instrumental to learning outcomes from the perspective of students. These findings suggest that while learning outcomes are valued by students this does not mean that every other aspect of the student experience has only instrumental value to this end. There are other aspects to the experience that are valued by students, and these feature prominently among concerns about what they are actually getting in their transaction with their university.

A quality degree may be one from which students graduate with a sense that they received more than they put in. The 'value add' in this sense is the extent to which students profit from being productively and creatively engaged in their studies. Beyond being 'mostly satisfied' with client-service arrangements that meet or exceed their expectations as consumers, part of this 'value add' is in fact having the opportunity to engage with and benefit from something they did not expect, and something more than they could look up on Wikipedia. This means more than simply offering something over and above that which they could figure out by themselves. It means supporting opportunities for becoming part of an academic and professional community in ways they might not have expected. In a sense, a quality student experience is one where they may confidently expect the unexpected – over and above the delivery of knowledge and meeting their client-service expectations. This is the kind of value that is intrinsic rather than instrumental. The criteria for this are yet to be adequately described, and certainly remain contestable. It certainly has something to do with how we value academic staff, academic work and a collegial environment. These are the sorts of things we would want to find in the idea of the university.

## Reputation and brand

Effectively addressing the problem of information asymmetry in the university–student transaction depends on an important difference between reputation and brand. Reputation is typically informed by the judgment of experts or peers. While not always very empirical, it is nevertheless potentially useful in that it informs judgments about quality in a particular context. Reputation is arguably enhanced through improvements in quality. *Brand* is a construct native to the public relations industry. Branding supports opportunities for enhancing reputation without the need to pay any attention at all to improvements in quality. When it comes to quality it is reasonable to question whether or not a reputation is justified. This is not the case when it comes to the university brand.

A significant part of the university–student transaction includes a premium reflecting the 'brand' or market position of the institution. Here we see a convergence between the marketisation of the university and the *marketing* of the university brand. Those in that profession would of course say that the purpose of marketing the university is to inform prospective students. But communicating the brand is something quite different. As outlined above, most market models are premised on informed consumers making rational choices. The purpose of branding is precisely the opposite: it is to create uninformed consumers making irrational choices (Chomsky 2013, 4). The branding of the modern university is very much an instrument to this end.

Communicating your brand is very definitely not about informing consumers – at least, not in a way that would inform any market mechanisms for quality. 'Quality' (or 'excellence', or 'enterprise') can be made part of a university brand, but this is more about communicating it than actually doing it (Fearn 2010). The terms frequently used in branding the modern university tend to be abstract and semantically vague, to the extent that they might only be imagined, as they are in fact unmeasurable. Replacing demonstrable value with symbolic meaning allows production to be displaced by signification (Sauntson and Morrish 2011, 80–1).

Brand communication is a strategic priority for the modern university. Edward Bernays, widely regarded as the founder of public relations as a discipline, anticipated this as a strategic consideration for the modern university back in 1928. Bernays (1928, 131–2).called it *propaganda*:

> If [the] institution does not produce the mental picture which it should, one of two things may be wrong: Either the media of communication with the public may be wrong or unbalanced; or [the] institution may be at fault. The public is getting an oblique impression of the university, in which case the impression should be modified; or it may be that the public is getting a correct impression, in which case, very possibly, the work of the university itself should be modified. For both possibilities lie within the province of the public relations counsel.

Bernays concluded that the same considerations applied in higher education as also applied (then as now) in politics or in business: 'In the ethical sense, propaganda bears the same relation ... It may be used to overadvertise an institution and to create in the public mind artificial values' (Bernays 1928, 134). In Akerlof's *Market for Lemons* (2003), it is un-economical to invest in quality where there is a paucity of reliable information on it. Following from Bernays, it is clearly more economical to invest in the university brand.

It is ironic then that despite differentiation being among the key economic tenets of effective market competition, universities seem to be in the habit of branding themselves as 'distinctive' in more or less the same way using more or less the same terms (see also Thornton and Shannon, chapter 10 in this volume). This form of identity branding typically fails to capture the imagination of academic staff (Fearn 2010; Sauntson and Morrish 2011, 83). To what extent does it capture the imagination of students? Further to this – how much does this account for what they actually get?

## State and non-state rankings

The influence of university rankings is a notable feature of the current university environment internationally – rankings now have an enormous influence both on the reputation of institutions and the value of the university 'brand'. Rankings have become a 'litmus test' for quality and reputation – to the extent that they have been instrumental in shaping what Hazelkorn (2011, 2) describes as a single global model for a 'world-class university' premised on 'world-class excellence'. In some respects university rankings represent the ultimate commodification of university degrees. It can be argued that rankings work to conceal rather than highlight the 'real' quality of the institution. However, if a significant component of what students are 'buying' in their transaction with universities actually is accounted for in the value of the institutional brand, then it could be said that university rankings are among the most accurate and most honest of metrics.

Rankings perform a dual role when it comes to the university–student transaction. Rankings can convey information on the potential content of a university degree (with varying degrees of validity (Dill and Soo 2005) and often with marginal reference to learning and teaching or the quality of the student experience). They do, however, perform a second function much more reliably. Given that performance in university rankings is having an increasing influence on the strength of the university brand, these rankings can in fact convey a very accurate reflection of a significant component of what students are actually getting.

Rankings provide information on both reputation and brand. Both are potentially useful for students, but only the reputational component is capable of constructively influencing market mechanisms for quality – and only then to the extent that they are able to show demonstrable validity in conveying information about quality. In this sense university rankings (state-sponsored and otherwise) have a role to play in providing adequate information on quality. That is not to say that the current information standards are adequate – far from it. It is simply to say that institutional rankings have a role to play *both* in the marketisation of the modern university as well potentially responding to some of its worst effects.

There are ways in which adequate information on the content of the university–student transaction could support effective market mechanisms for quality, and also offer a response to the some of the problems associated with marketisation. This would require a more sophisticated understanding of the 'quality' being sold to students and communicated in ways that are meaningful. If we unpack the concept of 'quality' from a student perspective we find that the university–student transaction includes more than just the attainment of knowledge. The 'value add' here amounts to more than graduates simply knowing more at the end of a degree than they did at the beginning, and more than simply having their client-service expectations met. It should also mean more than simply graduating with the *idea* of that institution and the brand on the transcript that goes with it. An honest receipt would itemise 'a quality student experience' as accounting for the majority of the content for the university–student transaction. This would entail 'knowledge' variously conceived and capture aspects of their engagement with their institution (and its staff) that were genuinely worthwhile. It would also include a significant premium for the institution's reputation and brand. While branding is becoming increasingly influential, so are the means for evaluating and comparing information on what the institution actually provides – that which justifies its reputation as a quality institution. Here both academics and students have a common interest. If universities are able to simply trade in the brand unchecked then students are short-changed and academics are redundant. Both have an interest in ensuring that a *reputation* for a quality student experience is justified through adequate information on quality.

# Resisting marketisation

In the concluding chapter for *The Marketisation of Higher Education and the Student as Consumer*, Scullion et al. reflect on what can be done in response to the marketisation of higher education. They call for a reimagining of the value of the university, for autonomy and for a critical distance from the concerns of governments and markets. They also call for critical engagement on the part of stakeholders and for greater transparency. They stress that quality must not be jettisoned for extraneous priorities. For Scullion et al., there is no point in improvements in league table performance unless these transparently feed into improvements in teaching and learning practice and scholarly research (Scullion, Molesworth and Nixon 2011, 234–5). Notably, quality, transparency and stakeholder engagement are central to this response. These are not calls to embrace neoliberal managerialism nor are they conservative calls for passive resistance or avoidance. They call for an active, inclusive and transparent (re) engagement in the purposes of the university both in terms of its aims and the means of achieving them.

## Managerialism and quality

Are the growing ranks of academic managers, administrative and policy workers enablers of quality in support of the ideals of the university, or are they simply engaging in their activities for their own sake or for some other purpose? Reflecting on Newman's idea of the university, McKernan (2011, 4) captures this sentiment: 'The problem is that the grey philistines who are "running" our colleges and universities claim, falsely, to be businessmen running enterprises which will bring greater economic growth and riches … They are running universities while having no idea what universities are for.' Are the aims, activities and outcomes supported by the university enhanced *because of* the best efforts of contemporary university management strategies, or *despite* them?

One of the problems in this area is that the means of 'doing business' in a university often come to be taken as ends in themselves. An example can be found in imperatives for measurement for measurement's sake. The use of quantitative indicators can both contribute to and detract from judgments about the things being evaluated, and this is the case with the use of indicators both at the system and institutional level (Chalmers 2008; Palmer 2013). As Linke (1991, 131) put it: 'To the extent that such indicators may influence institutional practice … they will generate a pressure on institutions to direct their performance to the indicators themselves, regardless of what they reflect, rather than to the underlying issues of educational and research excellence, or indeed to any specific institutional goals.' This highlights that in the use of quality indicators there is always the risk of creating perverse incentives. Coupled with a tendency for engaging in measurement for measurement's sake, there is the risk that each new indicator may create more perverse incentives at greater and greater cost without any demonstrable improvement. The point of the exercise is forgotten when the means become ends in themselves.

Tendencies like this have been associated with the rise of what has been described as an 'audit culture' (Morley 2003; Shore and Wright 1999). Aspromourgos (chapter 5 in this volume) holds the audit culture responsible for what he describes as 'the infantilisation of academic life'. Here the interests of the academic and those of the institution appear to be opposed. Students are typically aware of these pressures too, through their engagement with academic and professional university staff. But does this problem extend to measurement itself? The measurement of academic activities and the use of performance indicators have been held to be symptomatic of, and on some views, central to the challenges facing the modern university. Does the path to salvaging those things worth preserving in the academic enterprise lie solely in preventing those things from being measured, or can 'quality' be defined and measured in a way that also aligns with scholarly values?

Ironically, despite the burgeoning enthusiasm for measuring academic activity the nature of the student experience is in some respects becoming more obscure, not less. The content of the university–student transaction is morphing from a quality student experience into an ineffable and indescribable good. This is back-ended by the use of student evaluation surveys and front-ended by branding. Somewhere in between, 'quality' takes place (or not) creating a 'missing middle' in the university–student transaction. If we fail to engage with this 'missing middle', then we are as complicit as anybody in the marketisation of the modern university. To a certain extent the emerging learning and teaching development industry have become apologists for this, where they buy into the discourse of the wonderful, ineffable, indescribable experience of their university without engaging in a defensible account of sound pedagogical practice. The same could be said of quality assurance and evaluation units within universities where they engage in the traffic of measurement for its own sake or simply in support of the university brand. The discourse is inflated at the front end, to be disguised by noise or verified only through the selective reporting of good news at the back end. Here we also see the worst tendencies of quality assurance – where used in support of obfuscation and control as opposed to transparency and continuous improvement. If somewhere in between, students end up being mildly more satisfied than they were the last time this was measured then it's celebrated as a job well done.

The 'audit culture' may only be redeemable where we are able to see that all of the strategies brought to bear in the university environment are instrumental in supporting a defensible idea of the university – both in terms of what it is and what it does, and are not simply engaged in for their own sake or for the sake of extraneous purposes. This may require, as Scullion et al. (2011) suggest, a re-imagining of the idea of the university, how it is valued and how it is enacted in practice.

Is there a way in which the idea of the university may be reconciled with the idea of the 'market'? Perhaps the best way of 'resisting' the market is in fact to participate in a manner informed by the idea of the university. This needs to mean more than simply lobbying government to pick up the tab for any unpriced 'public goods' that could be costed out of the university–student transaction. Perhaps universities as communities should stop thinking that being a university entails avoiding the market (only to be subsumed by it) and actively participate in them *as* universities, openly informed by the idea of the university rather than by misguided conceptions of market-like behaviour.

## Conclusion

The modern university needs to be more realistic and less complacent about how it engages with 'the market'. On the one hand there is a somewhat fatalistic discourse of resistance and avoidance. On the other there exists a discourse around institutional participation in competitive markets through market-like behaviours seemingly for their own sake. While many institutions have become very sophisticated in how they engage in a 'quasi-market' environment, the broader conversation around market participation remains somewhat naïve. To an extent this has remained so for political purposes, as on the one hand, university leaders want more intervention (in the form of tuition subsidy, for example), while at the same time calling for less (in the case of fee deregulation and in regulatory and compliance requirements).

The modern university exists in an era of increasing sophistication. This sophistication extends to engagement with 'the market' and in particular what is described here as the university–student transaction. Reasons not to be complacent include the rise of smaller, niche providers in the higher education marketplace and for different forms of 'delivery' for content-focused knowledge. Each of these signals the demise of the idea of the university as a protected market for privileged knowledge. A flip-side of the evolving consumer culture is that students are becoming much more sophisticated about their purchasing decisions, in how they value and compare things, and why. This will increasingly extend to their decisions regarding prospective destinations for study. Institutions need to be much more sophisticated about how they participate in the 'market' for students – not just for fees, but for students they want to recruit.

Rather than being an undesirable symptom of managerialism, the state and non-state definition and measurement of quality plays an increasingly central role in shaping the dynamics of the markets in which universities participate. Much of the attention to date has been from the perspective of government in the context of regulation and quality assurance. The extent to which adequate information on quality features in the reputational rankings of institutions will also play a determinant role. Here those same drivers for prestige represent both the greatest threat from and the most effective response to the marketisation of the modern university. Rankings and other forms of quality measurement are both part of the problem *and* part of the solution. They are part of the problem where they define an idea of the university that is unrelated to that which gives it value. They are part of the solution where they are reliably able to convey information relevant to what universities actually do. Put simply – rankings need to be more about reputation and less about brand. Most of the time it is hard to distinguish the two, but as the sophistication around rankings and other quality strategies feeding into student choice evolves, relying on brand supported by rhetoric over reputation supported by evidence will become an increasingly risky strategy.

The principal threats to the idea of the university currently lie at the extremes of marketisation. They lie in adopting market-like practices in an unreflective way as much as they do in efforts in the name of 'resistance' that are similarly uninformed. If the pursuit of knowledge for its own sake captures Newman's 'saving grace' for the idea of the university then there's not much of a blessing left. If knowledge for its own sake narrowly conceived really is the principal public good that universities are offering, then MOOCs and Wikipedia seem to signal the demise of this sort of university in a quasi-market environment, as this can be achieved in other ways much more efficiently and affordably. At the other extreme Newman's 'idea' has been also associated with the marketisation of an 'experience' that is wholly intangible. Rather than constitute a response to the challenges associated with marketisation it has been used in support of some of its worst aspects. Somewhere between the two lies an effective response to the challenges associated with marketisation. This requires critical engagement in means as well as ends, and a re-imagining of the value of the idea of the university, and how this might be pursued in practice. Whether this idea be inspired by Newman or Humboldt or Clark Kerr or by the latest thought-bubble of the education minister of the day is contestable. And it ought to remain so.

The *telos* of the university, if there is one, is to be consumed by precisely the sort of angst that is found in the challenge of marketisation. Its demise lies at either extreme: in being so uncritically conservative that it drifts toward irrelevance, or so bent on 'relevance' that it loses sight of the purposes and aims that give it value. If we permit that the modern university is characterised through a dialectic of the old and the new, then we can see that it is in its nature to be under threat. Responding to marketisation is a question of purpose: is it in an ideal of a university that is somehow fixed, or is it in pursuit of market-like behaviours with little or no justification? The answer lies in how we engage these challenges in practice, and that is where we find the nature of the university.

# 9. Markets, Discipline, Students: Governing Student Conduct and Performance in the University

Bruce Lindsay

## Introduction

The university has developed as a substantial and complex regulatory space in contemporary Australian society. Well over one million students are enrolled in the university system, in an environment that has assumed an increasingly commercialised character since the late 1980s. Market principles and norms have become prominent elements of higher education, under the influence of public policy, and hence, as a regulatory phenomenon, the market functions as a juridical and normative order. In this sense, the market is a governmental mechanism, having disciplinary effects.

This chapter takes a socio-legal view of the university system in the contemporary 'market order', and, in consideration of the disciplinary character of the market in relation to its mass student base, particular attention is paid to mechanisms for the regulation of student conduct and performance. Those mechanisms operate through schemes for student discipline and for academic sanction in circumstances of unsatisfactory academic progress. The present analysis considers how those schemes have evolved and adapted to the conditions of market governance in the university sector.

# Market(s), discipline and governance

It is a trite observation that the context in which governance of students now proceeds is heavily influenced, if not dominated, by market principles and models of behaviour. Marginson (1997a) has sought to theorise the rule of market arrangements in the sector, and operation of market mechanisms has coincided with the emergence of corporate ('enterprise') forms of the university as an institution (Marginson and Considine 2000), substantial modifications in expectations, behaviours, norms and legal treatment of students (notably toward experience as 'consumers'), and a treatment of the provision of higher education as an industry and as a major services sector.

The market system in which higher education now operates arguably does so at two levels.

The market in higher education is a market for 'educational services' (Larsen et al. 2002). The transaction at this level is a bargain for admission to the institution, for receipt of instruction, ancillary services and the benefit of collective knowledge and, upon successful exertions and completion (and payment of fees), the entitlement to an academic award (see Deech 2009; *Moran v University College Salford (No 2)* [1994] ELR 187). The substitutable qualities of goods and services in this market (cf. *Competition and Consumer Act 2010* (Cth), s 4E) are met in the competitive demand from students for places in the various institutions ('providers'), which in the language of Hirsch (1976) (and adopted by Marginson 1997; Marginson 2006), entail the 'positional good' of status, especially subsequent status or prestige in labour markets. Substitutable qualities of these markets are also met in the increasingly competitive supply arrangements of institutions, differentiation and contestability for students, especially in the course of accelerating policies of 'deregulation' and trends for public funding to follow student enrolments.

The market, however, not only operates at the level of the market for services; it also operates at the level of the *circulation of capital*. It is this sense of the autonomous circulation of knowledge, capacities, and intellectual practices as forms of *economic and productive power* that is captured in Lyotard's theory of the postmodern condition of knowledge (Lyotard 1984): that knowledge in general and, in respect of education, the figure of skill in particular, has assumed the quality of an independent economic-social force, dissociable from the 'training (*Bildung*) of minds' (Lyotard 1984, 4). Lyotard (1984, 4–5) noted nearly 30 years ago, the purpose of such 'performative' approaches to knowledge is the production and consumption of knowledge for commercial purposes and, in a wider sense, 'optimality' of the performance of social and economic systems (Lyotard 1984, 48). The commercial and performative logic of knowledge is less and less about ideals such as truth, or the 'cultivation' of the person (*Bildung*), or, as was more the Australian approach, the formation of the 'citizen-specialist' (Murray Report 1957, 7–11). Education now concerns knowledge objectified and valorised as an independent productive force; knowledge 'exteriorised with respect to the "knower"' (Lyotard 1984, 4). The student is a principal vehicle in the accumulation and optimisation of that force – and must be managed accordingly.

Lyotard did grasp the tendency of 'knowledge in the form of an informational commodity' to be treated as a marketable and saleable entity or object and for knowledge to be 'mercantilized' (Lyotard 1984, 5). But two further important points need to be considered in the development of the market and the industrial character of higher education. The first of these is that the autonomous economic force of knowledge acquires the *form and character of capital*. This notion that knowledge and competence acquired and reproduced in the higher education system is also to be conceived of as a distinct form of capital has achieved attention in the literature on 'cognitive capitalism' (e.g. Peters and Bulut 2011; Vercellone 2007; Federici and Caffentzis 2007; Boutang 2008). The analogy of 'human *resources*' and the student's accumulation of skills and competences as an 'extractable' base of saleable commodities is a somewhat simplified, but consistent, representation of his/her knowledge base as 'cognitive capital'.

In this respect, the industrialising character of higher education suggests two important spheres of *transaction*. First, the sphere of education and learning itself in which we might contemplate *intellectual/cognitive transactions* in the pedagogical sense: the processes of acquisition, inculcation, practice and reproduction of knowledge. The second sphere of transaction is the operation of the market at the level of the *economic supply chain* of skill, competence, knowledge – embodied in and co-produced with the student – and through which the higher education system supplies graduates onto the market for labour power. In particular, this transaction might be said to amount to the supply of *professionalised* labour power on to the labour market. 'Cognitive capital' is the 'package' or 'base' of certified and accumulated skills and competences embodied in the student (graduate); that is, certified by the university or other 'provider'.

Next, this market for the *supply of cognitive capital*, in which the university plays a central role, is, to borrow from Massimo De Angelis (2005), a dynamic and constitutive process, in which the construction of competence as an independent productive force is intrinsically combined with processes of valorisation and techniques of measure, and with the disciplinary techniques of the market.

As De Angelis (2005, 72) notes: 'The immanent [capitalist] measure of value is constituted by the ongoing working of capitalist disciplinary processes (and therefore value struggles) passing through markets as well as their state implanted simulations.'

De Angelis and Harvey (2009) have considered these constitutive dynamics as applied to higher education in some detail. Higher education is invested with complex and layered forms of quantification and measure (valorisation), which realises and facilitates the 'market order'.

Thus, the market in higher education as a market for 'cognitive capital' involves an integrated circuit of (a) knowledge as an independent productive force (especially as manifest in the quantum of skills of the student/graduate), (b) the valorisation process and techniques of measurement, and (c) disciplinary processes, including processes of governance and regulation of students and institutions.

The market is *disciplinary in its effects*. At the 'macro' level, disciplinary power is exercised and deployed in techniques and norms framing, limiting and directing social relations. For instance, social relations within the university – teacher, student, administrator – are reproduced as economic actors, notably consumers and 'providers' in the supply chain. These tendencies to overarching, market-based normative discipline, especially in processes of 'economisation' (Marginson 1997b), have been considered at length as policy (Marginson 1997a) and juridical phenomena (e.g. Varnham and Kamvounias 2006).

The market also is disciplinary at the micro level – in its 'panopticonic' approach, as Foucault (1979, 195–228) famously described the sphere of disciplinary power. For higher education, the 'market order' operates in and through what De Angelis and Harvey (2009, 17) refer to as the 'fractal-panopticon', or the multiplicity of disciplinary and policing powers. 'Briefly,' they write:

> the market-order as conceptualised by, for example, Friedrich Hayek, has organisational properties similar to that of Jeremy Bentham's 'panopticon'. These essentially disciplinary properties shaping social production are reproduced and extended throughout the social field and the planet. The panopticon of the global market is fractal in that different levels of social aggregation are *self similar* in terms of their disciplinary processes..

So within the framework of the overarching laws and norms of the market, including the singular juridical character of the student as consumer or as 'hybrid' institutional actor (cf. Rochford 1998), there exist within the university what Foucault (1979, 222) termed 'all those systems of micro-power that are essentially non-egalitarian and asymmetrical that we call the disciplines.' Foucault was looking to the real bases of control and ordering and 'panopticism constituted the technique, universally widespread, of coercion' (Foucault 1979, 222). Disciplinary techniques at this level constitute the basic sub-stratum of forces, mechanisms and arrangements for order. It is in this context that the question of the conduct and performance of students, and the regulatory mechanisms for their governance, should be situated. Zwagerman (2008), for example, has analysed university schemes for student discipline in terms of 'panopticism' in some detail. At the level of juridical character, it has been held that the formal legality of a student contract with the university may import the real complex of rules, regulations, policies and architecture of institutional order (*Clark v University of Lincolnshire and Humberside* (2000) 1 WLR 1988; *Bayley-Jones v University of Newcastle* (1990) 22 NSWLR 424).

The growth and intensification of market principles, rules and norms within higher education is also accompanied by expansion of formal rules and the juridical character of practices, dealings and relationships (Rochford 1998; Witteloostuijnand and de Jong 2007). This juridification of university life follows historic trends within other social and economic sectors, such as labour relations and social welfare. In higher education, the processes of juridification accord with the 'expansion and differentiation of law' into new spheres (Blichner and Molander 2008) and an incremental colonisation (cf. Wade 1969). Arguably, the process has accelerated in the recent decades of market reform. The growth of formal and semi-formal (e.g. administrative or 'soft law' (see Creyke 2010) regulatory systems governing higher education, as well as deployed by the university, is a key part of the disciplinary architecture of the 'enterprise university' (Marginson and Considine 2000) and its underpinning economic model.

## The student

The student is a central subject of governance in the university. At the empirical level, the student–university relationship has been characterised by certain defining trends. These include:

- eclipse of the student experience as a distinctive (pre-work) experience in the lifecycle and the integration of student experience with the labour force and family responsibilities (e.g. Devlin et al. 2008);
- fragmented and diverse student base, including substantial cohorts of older ('mature-aged'), off-campus students, students from lower socio-economic status backgrounds, and overseas students, especially from non-English speaking countries;
- the so-called disengagement of student from the institution (McInnis 2001), including decline of the campus as a site of activity;

- long-term radical changes in pedagogical experience, including the revolution in online and technological mediation and sources of information and the construction of mass higher education on high volume programs, such as the rise in student-staff ratios (e.g. *Bradley Report* 2008, 72) and the casualisation of staff;

- the hegemony of economic models, commodity forms and consumer norms and expectations.

Governance of student subjects confronts the problem of a rapidly expanding, diversifying, anonymous, and technologically-mediated student base, operating in a radically new informational and intellectual landscape. These trends imply a managerial or technocratic 'student problem', of which issues of student conduct and performance – such as is the form of academic misconduct or unsatisfactory academic progress and attrition – form just one, albeit significant, dimension.

The process and discourse of governance is extensively influenced by administration. As Readings (1996, 152) argued, administration is now hegemonic and this includes the construction of the student as an administrative subject:

> The administration of knowledge is, of course, the only point at which anything like a question of content enters: the question of what knowledge is to be managed by teachers and administered to students ... Teaching administers students. It accredits students as administrators, and it trains them in the handling of information. It probably does all these things rather successfully.

Administration is deeply insinuated into the logic and practice of academic life. Even if we limit observation to decisions that contain some element of academic judgment, administrative functions and procedures are prolific. Review of results, special consideration, complaint-handling, enrolments, reviews of higher degree by research students, extensions, course development and review, grading, peer-review decisions, disciplinary decisions and unsatisfactory progress, the awarding of degrees: all of these actions are administrative in character. They do not account for the mass of decisions made about fees, contracts, building works, finance, marketing, human resources, and so on.

Following Readings and Foucault, Alicia Evans (2011) has considered the effects of the pervasive qualities of administration on the Australian university, posing the student *qua* 'performer' within the administrative machinery, as against the student as an educational subject. The 'performative' character of the student, however, only partly grasps the changed subjective, disciplinary and governmental/administrative situation of the student in the 'market order'.

As Foucault (1979, 135–69) theorised, disciplinary techniques and powers, the apparatuses of administration and governance, are played out, unfold, and/or are applied to 'bodies', with the object of producing and reproducing 'docile bodies'. The purpose of governance or management is not simply repression. It is to render the 'body' useful and to achieve some form of optimality as well as utility. 'A body is docile that may be subjected, used, transformed and improved' (Foucault 1979, 136). For Foucault (1979, 165, 178–81, 186–87), the relevant 'docile body' representative of the educational sphere was that of the 'pupil'. That is arguably also the ideal student subject of the university system prior to the period of market and industrial transformation. The model of the pupil, subject to the mastery and authority of the tenured academician – the professorial ideal – was the guiding institutional relation in which disciplinary mechanisms operated. It is a discursive model that continued to relatively recent times:

> The context of educational societies involves a special factor which is not present in other contexts, namely the relation of tutor and pupil; that is to say the society is charged with the upbringing and supervision of the pupil under tuition, be the society a university or college, or a school (*Glynn v Keele University* (1971) 1 WLR 487, 494).

The 'body' to which the contemporary disciplinary forces of the market order apply is no longer the 'pupil', or youth in training to the academician. The fragmentation, diversity and complexity of the student base are evidence of a breakdown of that hegemonic, corporeal person.

Rather, the 'docile body' to which the university's governmental systems and controls now apply is a new type of person, perhaps best and most commonly expressed in the term 'learner' (see, for example,Candy et al. 1994), which is the student integrated directly into (at least in the virtual sense of functioning and acting within a broad simulation of) the workplace and labour market. Discourses of skill, employability, graduate attributes and academic performance are all integral to the 'body' of the student *qua* 'learner'. This new educational 'body' on which markets, institutions and regulatory machinery of higher education work is less the young person 'in formation', or the 'citizen-specialist' in training, than the burgeoning *homo economicus*. The model of the student is as an instrumental subject, acquisitive, a site of accumulation of professional skills and qualities. The person of the student becomes equated with a form of 'micro-firm', an 'enterprise of oneself' (Marginson 1997b, 123), or 'basin of immaterial labour' (Lazzarato 1996, 136) within the cycle of professional work. Yet, given the increasing complexity and diversity of the student population, the 'body' of the student – that is, of the 'learner' – is to be measured, characterised and disciplined according to models and standards of conduct and performance. Foucault (1979, 181–83) notes that the disciplinary system is corrective and normalises (including for the pupil) a duality of sanction/punishment and privilege. This is productive of docility and utility. For the contemporary student, the ubiquitous 'learner', the system of reward and punishment and its disciplinary effects apply more to the 'cognitive body' than the physical body of the student (see, for example, Boni and Walker 2013). The governance of the 'cognitive body' of intellectual capacities and behaviours is, in this sense, parallel to Nikolas Rose's reading of the regulation of self and subjectivity as 'governing the soul' (Rose 1990). That is, the rationality of academic systems, now pervasively inculcated and moulded to administrative systems (Readings 1996; Evans 2011), is the science and practice of governing the higher cognitive powers of the individual.

## The regulatory system for student discipline and academic exclusion

Universities have regulatory powers for the governance of student conduct ('student discipline') and academic performance ('unsatisfactory progress'). These are formalised, quasi-judicial procedures that can provide the basis for termination of a student's status as such and even, collaterally, their right to be in the country, given visa conditions requiring enrolment and satisfactory academic progress. Other than voluntary withdrawal or graduation, these are the sole means of severing a student's status and relationship with the university. The consequences of adverse decisions can be grave, although there are many levels of intervention and/or sanction in this sphere short of exclusion from the institution.

For the sake of context, it is useful to distinguish these quasi-judicial mechanisms of university governance and regulation from the wider academic-administrative terrain of 'everyday' governance of students. Within the university, the masses of decisions and institutional actions that are disciplinary *in the discursive sense* are those such as decisions of routine academic judgment, assessment, grading and allocation of students thereby to an intellectual hierarchy. This is a process of ordering and classifying cognitive powers and abilities, according to the frameworks of academic programs, 'learning outcomes', assessment procedures, systems and codes of knowledge. This is not to suggest an absence of countervailing norms, practices and communities in the wide sphere of academic discretion (including matters of assessment, pedagogy and administration) (see, for example, Harvey 2004; Lambert et al. 2007). But these latter forces, while potentially turbulent, innovative or resistant, remain presently confined and marked by overarching disciplinary frameworks.

Powers of student discipline and sanction for sustained poor academic performance might be said to be *secondary regulatory powers*, which is to say action available subsequent to decisions such as those of 'pure' academic judgment. Other than for actions in response to 'non-academic' misconduct, these secondary powers are typically dependent on primary academic decision-making. Primary powers are those exercised either to establish the programs, standards and decision-making frameworks of the academy (e.g. courses, rules, pedagogical techniques, intellectual norms), or those, as noted above, deployed to assess and evaluate the performance of students and their exercise of intellectual/cognitive abilities (e.g. academic judgment, grading, certification).

Schemes for student discipline and unsatisfactory progress have long been held to be subject to judicial supervision (*University of Ceylon v Fernando* (1960) 1 All ER 631; *R v Aston University Senate; ex parte Roffey* (1969) 2 WLR 1418; *Glynn v Keele University* (1971) 1 WLR 487) and, whether operating on the basis of a student contract or the university's administrative-legal authority over its 'members' (including students), institutional conduct under such schema is subject to the ordinary legal norms of fairness, rationality and lawfulness (see also *Simjanoski v La Trobe University* [2004] VSC 180; *Bray v University of Melbourne* [2001] VSC 391; *X v University of Western Sydney (No. 3)* [2013] NSWSC 1329; *Bell v Victoria University of Wellington* [2010] NZHC 2200).

Both student disciplinary schemes and academic progress schemes, therefore, adhere to certain basic procedural requirements of fairness and impartial decision-making. There will be a form of 'tribunal' – usually in the form of committee or panel – charged with conducting a hearing, before which the student may make submissions and call evidence (see generally Lindsay 2008b). Disciplinary scheme are ordinarily accompanied by an express disciplinary code. Academic progress rules will turn on certain rules or thresholds of 'satisfactory' progress. Further points on each body of rules are noted below.

Prior to the period of 'mass' higher education, the smaller, elite enclaves of universities in Australia (as in, for instance, the UK) tended to combine general, informal supervision and management of students, under customary academic codes and norms, with occasional, formalised disciplinary or exclusionary arrangements. From the 1960s, there were pressures to adopt reasonably formal, quasi-judicial procedure (see, for example, Forbes 1970–71). These levels of formality were perhaps also a residue of the magisterial authority held by vice-chancellors in the ancient English universities (see, for example, Cripps-Day 1894). This stark dichotomy between general informality and occasional formal procedure was perhaps also consistent with the circumstances of the universities as small 'educational societies', or voluntary institutions analogous to self-governing 'social clubs' (see *R v Aston University Senate; ex parte Roffey* (1969) 2 WLR 1418).

Contemporary regulation of student conduct and performance represents a break with older, more paternalistic models of the university and past concerns in relation to student supervision (see Lindsay 2008a). Contemporary approaches are reflective of the industrial character of the institution, as discussed above, and the reproduction of market discipline and regulatory measures applying to the 'cognitive body' of the student.

## Student discipline and misconduct

Contemporary concerns with misconduct have generally focused on academic misconduct, such as plagiarism or collusion or exam cheating. There is a growing number of studies investigating motivations and behaviours relating to misconduct, which suggest high rates of transgressive behaviour or at least, arguably, a high level of non-conformity with academic norms (e.g. Franklyn-Stokes and Newstead 1995; De Lambert et al. 2006; Marsden et al. 2005; Norton et al. 2001).

In a study of seven Australian universities, it was found, on average, around one per cent of enrolled students in the sample were subject to some kind of disciplinary action for misconduct (Lindsay 2010). The overwhelming majority of cases involved allegations and/or findings of academic misconduct, such as plagiarism or exam cheating. Recent media reports suggest that cases of formal misconduct in Western Australian universities are in the hundreds, if not thousands, and largely concern forms of academic misconduct (Hiatt 2013).

In relation to student misconduct, there has been an historic shift by institutions in the manner of engagement with students over issues such as plagiarism, collusion and use or misuse of the information technologies. This shift has been variously panoptoconic (Zwagerman 2008) and militant (Zobel and Hamilton 2002; Briggs 2003). Three main techniques are evident. First, there has been widespread use and adoption of so-called plagiarism detection software such as Turnitin. Use of these technologies may be a precursor to marking of papers, or available where any suspicion arises as to 'originality' of work. Notwithstanding problems that may arise with concepts of 'originality' in students' work (Richardson 2002; Chandrasoma 2004), these technologies are now key means of surveillance over students' intellectual output (Zwagerman 2008). They may also now be used as means of student self-policing and surveillance, whether as a basis of fear or threat to students or to be used directly by them to verify and analysis the 'originality' of their own work.

Secondly, alongside 'back end' technologies of surveillance and the prospects of punitive action, universities have undertaken concerted 'educative' campaigns, aimed at circumventing academic-disciplinary problems. These range from provision of notices prior to submission of student work or prior to exams, online warnings, dedicated 'practical skill' training sessions in academic norms and conventions, and development of 'academic skills' programs and staff, especially (but not exclusively) for international students.

Thirdly, as in common with regulatory approaches to the policing of norms, universities apply graduated and proportionate responses to transgressions. This may have informally applied previously but no doubt the present scale of academic-disciplinary issues has led to more formalised guidance and rules. Graduated action ranges from clearly punitive responses to cases of intentional and/or calculated misconduct (e.g. exclusion) to educative or pastoral approaches at the marginal end of the spectrum where, for example, poor writing or expression skills may be at issue (e.g. warnings, resubmission of work) (see, for example, Deakin University *Student Academic Misconduct Procedure*, Schedule A).

## Academic progress

Rates of exclusion or other remedial action by institutions for poor student performance appear not to be commonly reported or available (Department of Education, Employment and Workplace Relations 2011; Wimhurst et al. 2006, 133–34). However, student attrition and progress rates are known. 'Attrition' and 'progress' indicators combine various factors, including failure, withdrawal, and course transfers, hence are only a very rough guide to exclusion for poor performance. Over the 2001–09 period, student progress rates for all undergraduate students have remained stable and attrition rates (student non-return to study) have fallen. Student progress rates were around 85 per cent in 2009 (i.e. around 15 per cent of students failed or withdrew) (Department of Education, Employment and Workplace Relations 2011).

There are grounds to argue that actions for poor academic performance are more prolific than for student discipline. Part of the reason for the occurrence of academic exclusion is that it is a routine extension of the academic process and typically triggered by numerical thresholds: for example, when a student fails (receives a grade of less than 50 per cent) in a fixed number of subjects, a process for review and decision-making on the basis of academic performance is triggered. Also, disciplinary processes are accusatorial and arguably attract a greater level of opprobrium.

Institutional responses to rates of exclusion for poor academic performance now include pre-emptive and graduated strategies (e.g. University of Melbourne *Academic Performance Policy*, cl 2). Pre-emptive strategies include early identification of students considered to be 'at risk' of later exclusion for poor performance; for example, where a student fails a substantial number of subjects in a particular semester, especially early-year students (University of Melbourne *Academic Progress Review Procedure*, cl 7). Adoption of the language of risk implies, in this instance, a problem applicable both to the individual student, manifest for example in external issues impacting on performance as well as intellectual shortcomings, and applicable to the institution insofar as accumulations of failing grades reflect on the reputation of the university in the market.

As with disciplinary practices, graduated responses to poor student performance typically span exclusion from the university, re-enrolment conditional on meeting prescribed performance targets, and re-enrolment accompanied by provision of pastoral or academic assistance or advice.

Overseas student regulation now influences institutional approaches to academic performance, requiring systematic approaches to early intervention and hence ongoing monitoring or performance (*National Code of Practice for Registration Authorities and Providers of Education and Training to Overseas Students 2007* (Cth), Standard 10). Institutions enrolling overseas students have express surveillance obligations, given further effect by their function in migration regulation, such as in requirements to certify that student visa holders have achieved satisfactory academic performance (or not, as the case may be) (*Education Services for Overseas Student Act 2000* (Cth), ss 19(2); *Migration Regulations 1994* (Cth), Schedule 8, Condition 8202(3)).

Regulatory influences on misconduct and progress procedures have increased over the past decade. This includes direct influence, such as for 'at risk' intervention strategies and codification of appeals and review, as well as the indirect influence of pervasive and far-reaching regulation of the sector generally, especially 'consumer protection'-type regulation (e.g. *Education Services for Overseas Students Act 2000* (Cth); *Baird Report* 2010, 5) and institutionalisation of an academic 'quality assurance' regime. Further, methods of academic policing of students have become far more systematic and explicit, especially in the use of technological surveillance, early-intervention procedures and the rhetoric of risk (e.g. *Tertiary Education Quality and Standards Agency Act 2011* (Cth), s 15), transgression, and anxiety (Zwagerman 2008, 683–86). Finally, universities have developed a range of 'soft' techniques aimed at ordering, organising and influencing conduct and performance (see, for example, McInnis 2003). These are more akin to 'welfare' measures and include, for instance, substantial counselling, welfare and academic 'advisory' staff.

# The evolution of purposes for regulatory controls over student conduct and performance

The market-disciplinary character of university surveillance of, and powers over, student conduct and performance reflects the now dominant industrial-economic project of higher education. The policing mode of these powers is a strategic response to these conditions and the multifaceted 'student problem'.

## Confidence in the supply chain of cognitive capital

First and foremost, this 'problem' is the student as bearer of 'cognitive capital', as the 'cognitive subject', and consequently the problem of supply of cognitive capital onto the labour market. Student discipline and academic progress, in their contemporary focus on academic 'integrity', 'standards' and performance, contribute significantly to the discourse and practice of institutional 'quality' and cultures of audit and surveillance entailed in these agenda. These are approaches now incorporated into statutory form (see, for example, TEQSA *Higher Education Standards Framework (Threshold Standards) 2011* (Cth), ss 4, 6), although reflective of the extensive machinery of 'quality assurance' now well-established in the higher education sector (e.g. Harman 1994; Vidovich 2002; Shah et al. 2011). The actuarial discourse of 'assurance' and 'risk' was emphasised in the Bradley Review for instance (*Bradley Review*, [4.1]). As noted above, it underpins the approach of the sectoral regulator (*Tertiary Education Quality and Standards Agency Act 2011* (Cth), s 15; TEQSA *Regulatory Risk Framework*). 'Risk' reveals the sentiment that in the student – at least in their objectified behaviours and intellectual practices – there is the spectre of threat. It is a multifold threat: of transgression, incapacity (incompetence) and/or reputational damage. The threat may be manifest in immediate modes of crisis, such as in reputational damage of the institutional 'product' in the market (see, for example, Victorian Ombudsman 2010; Victorian Ombudsman 2011; Independent Commission Against Corruption 2005), or longer-term senses of secular crisis (Senate Education, Employment and Workplace Relations Committee 2001, Chapter 5). Regulation and policing of conduct and performance is one important dimension of dealing with the question of market and state confidence (see, for example, *Bradley Review*, [4.1]).

## Response to motivational crisis

The second basis for emergence of the policing mode on the part of higher education institutions relates to the subjective crisis of the student. While there have always been rates of student misconduct and non-performance, the present context is heavily influenced by the disjuncture between instrumental goals attached to knowledge, performance and learning (e.g. grades, qualifications) and intellectual norms (e.g. academic ethics).

In part, this phenomenon might represent a rupture in older organising principles in the university, such as relatively stable intellectual communities, campus experience and the professional acculturation process of university life. Student 'disengagement' or 'negotiated engagement' (McInnis 2001) is a complementary symptom of the wider subjective reorganisation.

Clearly, there is engagement by students in higher education. It is really the nature of that engagement and the values, expectations, discourse and norms underpinning it that is at issue. The question is the extent to which higher education is primarily, or even substantially, a self-determining intellectual exercise (as the *Bildung* or 'citizen-specialist' models presupposed), or rather the postmodern experience in which the student, reduced to being the manager of their accumulated skills, competence and motivations within a highly transactional (provider–consumer) relationship, is a sort of highly competent and strategic game-player. Arguably, the horizon of the student is deeply pragmatic and may be subject to substantial external forces and pressures (e.g. Victorian Ombudsman 2011, [234]).

Students are not amoral. Rather, there are contradictory and complex rationalities and pressures at issue, including acquisition and adherence to norms, uncertainty or instability in those norms, high-stakes outcomes, and complex practical realities and opportunities (see, for example, Sattler et al. 2013; Maher et al. 2009). Additionally, the university as the source and mediator of intellectual knowledge – including the authority as to technique (e.g. 'critical and independent thought' (*Higher Education Standards Framework (Threshold Standards) 2011* (Cth), s 4.1) and norms of its acquisition (e.g. academic conventions) – are under challenge from the saturation of knowledge in electronic sources and possibly from the trend of some institutions to mass, relatively indiscriminate delivery (e.g. MOOCs).

If the motivating force of students' relationship with the university (and its governing intellectual project) is under challenge, external discipline and policing modes, as distinct from internalised self-discipline, arguably step into the breach – to the extent they provide alternative motivating forces. These may be negative, such as in terms of fear of exclusion or disciplinary action.

Or they may be positive, in the ranks of advisers, counsellors, facilitators, 'early intervention' programs and other 'support services' – all deployed to guide students and optimise performance and results.

## Managing permanent crisis and selective austerity

Finally, policing approaches serve as a response to long-term ('secular') dynamics of institutional crisis, especially evident in austerity and applied to teaching and learning (the pedagogical space). Informal policing of standards was, from a practical point of view, a viable strategy in smaller, close-knit, sometime paternalistic institutions. The erosion of such conditions is indicated in, for instance, the comparison of staff to student ratios over a 60-year period. University statistics in the 1950s showed ratios between 1:3 and 1:12 (*Murray Report* 1957, 39–40). Vice-chancellors at the time apparently complained that Australia was not comparable with the UK, where ratios were around 1:7. By the 2000s, those ratios were approximately 1:20 and have steadily risen since the late 1980s (Universities Australia 2006). Concurrently, there have been long-term constraints on funding to resources such as libraries and long-term shifts in the academic workforce toward casualisation and increased work intensity. The constraints on teaching and learning noted by the Senate Employment, Workplace Relations and Education Committee (2000, [5.55]–[5.68]) more than a decade ago are unlikely to have improved fundamentally in the meantime.

The policing function is a response to austerity at two levels. It displaces the proportionately declining institutional space of teaching with technological, regulatory and/or therapeutic ('student support') machinery. It also is practically and logically consistent with the shift toward administration.

# Conclusions

The administrative and regulatory technologies of the university are also technologies of the market. Quasi-judicial mechanisms applying to student discipline and academic progress are particular models of academic administration crafted in the shadow of law and with procedures mimicking or adapted from legal models. They are now applied and adapted to an institutional, cultural and epistemological terrain profoundly changed over the course of several decades. This chapter has argued that these mechanisms need to be viewed in the context of the industrial and economic revolution in which the central productive force of the university – knowledge manifest in the cognitive and intellectual powers of the student – assumes a strategic role in capital accumulation. It is well to argue, from the perspective of law, that regulatory mechanisms for the governance of student conduct and performance should be applied fairly and with real adherence to principles of formal justice (e.g. Lindsay 2012a; 2012b). If we take a deeper view, from the perspective of social and cultural theory and radical political economy, juridical concepts of justice are only part of the equation. Governance, administration and law in the university need to (re) consider and engage critically with the models and forms of education and knowledge – that is, function beyond (and against) the models and conditions of capital. If that is to be achieved, universities will also need to think beyond functions and techniques of academic policing (see, for example, Chandrasoma 2004) and in resistance to the market.

# 10. 'Selling the dream': Law School Branding and the Illusion of Choice

Margaret Thornton and Lucinda Shannon

## Introduction

In a little over 20 years, the number of law schools in Australia has tripled – from 12 to 36. The catalyst for this revolutionary change occurred in 1988 when by a stroke of the pen the then Minister for Employment, Education and Training, John Dawkins, declared all Colleges of Advanced Education (CAEs) to be part of a new unified national system of higher education with the option of becoming universities (Dawkins 1988). The intention was to increase school retention rates and enhance the calibre of the Australian workforce so that Australia might be more competitive on the world stage. Despite the transformation of the tertiary sector, which resulted in 16 new universities in four years, government funding was not proportionately increased (Marginson and Considine 2000, 28–9).

Indeed, such phenomenal growth could not be sustained from the public purse. To generate additional revenue, the Dawkins reforms heralded a shift away from free higher education to a user-pays regime in which students themselves assumed partial responsibility for the cost of their education (Marginson and Considine 2000, 56–7). While initially resisted, the new regime was quickly normalised. Public acceptance was ensured by, firstly, eschewing the language of fees and referring to the charge euphemistically as a 'contribution' (the Higher Education Contribution Scheme or HECS); secondly, setting the initial cost for domestic undergraduate students at a modest A$1,800 per annum across the board; and, thirdly, making HECS repayable only when a graduate reached a certain income threshold. Of course, once a fee regime is put in place, it is inevitable that fees will be ratcheted up, and disciplinary differences soon emerged, with law being charged at the top rate. The shift from an élite to a mass system, supported by a user-pays philosophy, dramatically changed the character of legal education (Thornton 2012).

CAEs were formerly teaching-only institutions which generally did not include professional programs, but once they had become universities they were anxious to legitimise their new-found status by offering professional degrees. As universities had already been partly deregulated,[1] they were free to choose what courses they wished to offer – with the exception of medicine. To boost the knowledge economy, it was hoped they would offer courses with clear career paths. Law was a popular choice. In addition to attracting well-credentialed students, university administrators believed that a law degree required few resources. Indeed, it was a longstanding myth that law could be taught 'under a gum tree' (Martin Report 1964, II, 57). The persistence of this myth ignored the notable pedagogical shift that had occurred in legal education away from the large-lecture model of course delivery (the 'sage on the stage') to an active learning model of small-group discussion, critique and interrogation of legal knowledge – a superior pedagogical model, but one requiring substantially more resources.

Many new law schools were established in the early to mid-1990s, not only in the new universities (for example, Southern Cross, Western Sydney and Victoria) but also in the 'third generation' universities established in the 1960s (for example, Flinders, Griffith, and La Trobe). The parlous financial situation in which all the law schools soon found themselves compelled them to take in more and more students to meet budgetary shortfalls. This set in train an endless spiral and caused them to espouse once again the outdated but cheaper pedagogies that had so recently been cast aside. Income generation and cost cutting became the primary concern of law deans everywhere.

In a volatile climate beset with risk, a law school, particularly a new school, could not passively wait for students to apply for admission. Through a range of marketing tools and the creation of a distinctive 'brand', law schools set out to woo students/customers and persuade them to choose *their* institution over others. This chapter examines the ways in which Australian law schools present themselves to the world as attractive and desirable in a competitive market. The first port of call for prospective customers is likely to be the law school website, on which we propose to focus.

---

1   The Commonwealth Tertiary Education Commission was abolished in 1987 and its functions transferred to the Department of Education, Employment and Training (Marginson and Considine 2000, 31).

While purporting to present themselves as distinctive, law schools tend to emphasise similar things in their advertising. Attractiveness and desirability are construed in terms of consumerism, with advertising often redolent of a tourist brochure. The student who undertakes a law degree is promised employability, prestige and wealth; he or she is also assured of a glamorous and fun-filled career. As a result, the serious and difficult aspects associated with the study of law are sloughed off, as well as the centrality of justice and critique. But first a word about competition policy in legitimating the pre-eminent role of the market in reshaping the legal academy.

## Competition policy

In accordance with the values of social liberalism, the prevailing political philosophy extols the role of the market, rather than the state, as the arbiter of the good. Freedom for the individual within the market is the fundamental social good, according to neoliberal guru Friedrich Hayek (1960, 92–3), as it fosters competition. The philosophy of Hayek, which was applied to universities by his colleague Milton Friedman, assisted by Rose Friedman (1962; 1980), underpins the commodification of higher education in Australia and is particularly relevant to legal education. Friedman was of the view that students who enrolled in professional courses should not be the recipients of public funding because it was assumed they would subsequently earn high incomes. The loan system that Friedman advocated, which would be repayable throughout the taxation system (Friedman 1962, 105), was precisely the one that was implemented in Australia.

Competition, however, is by no means peculiar to higher education, for it is an inescapable dimension of the 'market metanarrative' (Roberts 1998), which permeates every aspect of contemporary society. Competition became an official plank of Australian government policy with the *Hilmer Report* (1993), the main recommendations of which were incorporated into the *Competition Policy Reform Act 1995* (Cth). In accordance with the philosophy of Hayek and Friedman, competition policy endorses the view that the operation of the vectors of supply and demand within a free market is the best way for society to generate greater efficiencies in production as well as a superior outcome for consumers. In other words, the effect of the marketising reforms required universities to reposition themselves as the 'simulacra of business' (Sauntson and Morrish 2011, 73).

Prior to the Dawkins reforms, Australian law schools had been largely immune from competition. For decades there was only one law school in each state, but the landscape was to change irrevocably. The proliferation of law schools has inevitably meant increased competition for 'market share', particularly for top-performing students. Competition also means that some schools will succeed while others will founder. To date, however, no Australian law school has been compelled to close. This is because the most vulnerable – the regional universities – are generally located in marginal electorates. It is nevertheless within a competitive social-Darwinist environment that law schools operate, perpetually haunted by the possibility of third-ratedness and non-success. As the now classic work of Ulrich Beck (1992, 19) has established, risk is the inescapable corollary of entrepreneurialism and the production of wealth.

The ideological underpinnings of the transformed environment have been secured by the emergence of a new marketised language in which it is accepted that students are 'consumers' or 'customers' in a 'higher education market' and universities are 'higher education providers' delivering a 'product'. Like consumers generally, the consumers of higher education are expected to exercise choice as to which law school 'product' would best equip them with the means of realising their dreams. To the student/customer/consumer, legal education is the 'bridge to [the] displaced meanings' of an idealised future career (McCracken 1988, 110). That is, legal education is understood as the pursuit of knowledge not for its own sake as articulated by John Henry Newman (1966), one of the most famous theorists of the *idea* of the university, but because of what it promises. But how are students to know which law school to choose?

## The standardising imperative

While there is a modicum of diversity in Australian law schools (Johnstone and Vigaendra 2003, 56), there is simultaneously a propulsion towards homogeneity which constitutes a particular marketing challenge, as sameness is anathema to the ideology of choice. The imperatives in favour of sameness are not mere abstract exhortations but prescripts emanating from the profession and the state, underpinned by the rhetoric of competition at the international level.

First, as a professional discipline, law is subject to the requirements of the admitting authorities. Acceptance of the 'Priestley Eleven', the 11 compulsory areas of knowledge necessary for the accreditation of a law degree, is regarded as non-negotiable by all Australian law schools – a factor that straightaway ensures a significant degree of sameness in the curriculum. Secondly, the state itself is playing an increasingly interventionist role in ensuring the curricular and pedagogical standardisation of higher education through auditing and accountability mechanisms.[2] The most notable recent instance is the Australian Qualifications Framework (AQF), which is designed to ensure consistency in the provision of all tertiary and vocational qualifications. For law schools to be compliant, the AQF (2013) requires distinct learning outcomes for the LLB,

---

2  In response to the Bradley Review into higher education (Bradley et al. 2008), the Tertiary Education Quality and Standards Agency (TEQSA) was set up in 2011 and is charged with ensuring compliance with the Higher Education Standards Framework.

LLB Honours, LLM (coursework) and JD programs. Thirdly, the contemporary trend in favour of the international ranking of universities further encourages sameness and entrenches stratification.[3] League tables assume that universities, like football teams, all compete on a level playing field regardless of differences in aims, age, resources and student catchments. Hence, if a wealthy private American Ivy League university is No 1, the aim is to emulate its characteristics in the hope of elevating one's own institution in the global rankings, whether that is appropriate for a public university in Australia or not. League tables, with their obsessive focus on rankings, also reinforce the tendency to see higher education as 'a product to be consumed rather than an opportunity to be experienced' (Brown 2011, 16).

Competition policy and the market embrace both emphasise the division between older and newer law schools. While the former have substantial positional goods emanating from their age, wealth and status, often as the sole provider of legal education in a State for as long as a century, the latter, with none of these benefits, are struggling. However, such differences are discounted on a supposedly level playing field. The move to standardise, referred to as *isomorphism* by Marginson and Considine (2000, 176) and, perhaps more evocatively, as *McDonaldisation* by Ritzer (2000, 2010) is a way of describing how the creation of an identical product is required with only a frisson of difference, a surface variation, to set it apart for the purposes of marketing (Thornton 2012, 43). As students are not 'reliable long-term clients' but 'fickle customers who may be difficult to attract and retain' (Ritzer 2002, 20), law schools must purport to offer something special. While sameness is accepted as a tacit criterion, it is difference that is marketed (Ariens 2003, 349).

## Marketing and the illusion of choice

At its simplest, marketing is 'the provision of information to help people make decisions' (Lowrie and Hemsley-Brown 2011, 1,081). Possessing the means to access information to inform their choices, individuals supposedly become autonomous rational actors in accordance with the prevailing ethos of neoliberalism. But this faith in the idealised freely choosing consumer to which the dominant market paradigm subscribes is questionable. Bauman (2005, 58) contends that choice is the 'meta-value' of a consumer society and that it enables the evaluation and ranking of all other values. He suggests that the

---

3    Some of the better-known global league tables are: the Academic Ranking of World Universities, retrieved 28 September 2014, from www.shanghairanking.com/index.html; QS World University Rankings, retrieved 28 September 2014, from www.topuniversities.com/university-rankings/world-university-rankings; Times Higher Education World University Rankings, retrieved 28 September 2014, from www.timeshighereducation.co.uk/world-university-rankings/.

conjunction of the discriminating consumer and the market as the purveyor of free choice are essentially myths that nourish each other. Marketing does not simply disseminate information; it actively works to 'create' the appearance of difference and to encourage favourable associations with a product. Vast resources are mobilised by big business in the construction of a product's uniqueness through advertising and branding (Smart 2007, 172). Despite the asymmetry between business and individual consumers, the presence of 'different' products transforms choice into what Holt (2002, 79) terms an act of 'personal sovereignty'. The products being chosen then become authentic resources in the establishment of the consumer's identity (Holt 2002, 83). Nevertheless, the promotion of the 'cult of *difference* and choice' effectively obscures the marked similarity between goods and services (Bauman 2005, 59). Thus, while commonplace products such as washing powders all perform basically the same function, each manufacturer aims to persuade consumers that their product possesses some unique quality. This paradox of sameness and difference is similarly exemplified in the marketing of legal education.

## Branding and the aesthetic of work

Law schools may claim to be 'excellent', 'the best' or 'world class' but such claims alone are unlikely to entice well-qualified applicants (Ariens 2003, 337). In any case, Readings (1996, 21) effectively demolishes the concept of excellence as the 'watchword' of the contemporary university. While no one can be against excellence, no one really knows what it is, because it not only lacks a fixed standard of judgment (Readings 1996, 24), it lacks cultural content altogether (p. 38). Excellence, then, is a pre-given in the marketing of legal education, but there needs to be some additional feature that is distinctive, or an element of 'niche marketing' to create a unique identity or 'brand'. The need or desire for branding has emerged as a result of increased competition in conjunction with consumer choice.

At its simplest, a brand is a name, mark or symbol which denotes a particular seller's product or service (Doyle 2001, 166). A successful brand will involve a product with a recognisable identity and represent a particular set of values that is important to the consumer. Even if the claims made are spurious, as has long been the case with myriad prophylactic products, consumer perception is the key to a successful brand. Hence, as Temple (2011) argues, branding as a route to success is an illusion. Law schools must therefore work hard to associate their product with the idealised futures imagined by prospective customers. Branding is not merely about uncovering the 'essence' of an institution; it is also about creating certain associations with the brand in accordance with the dominant ideology of the consumer culture (Holt 2002, 80).

Professional credentialing is an ever-present consideration in law school marketing (Ariens 2003, 329). Even if students elect not to practise law, the majority like to qualify for admission 'just in case'. But advertising a law degree requires much more than the promise of credentialism. It also requires access to professional labour markets — but not any job. Zygmunt Bauman (2005, 34) argues that the consumer society has radically altered the perception of work, which has shifted from production to consumption. Rather than providing security and a stable identity of the kind associated with modernity, work is now expected to produce an aesthetic of pleasure through excitement, adventure or happiness. The line separating work and life is thereby corroded.

This aesthetic of pleasure, which is a mark of the contemporary culture of 'youthism' (Thornton and Luker 2010, 165), can be discerned as a leitmotif in law school advertising, where law schools increasingly represent themselves as the gateway to a satisfying and fun-filled career. No consumer exercising free choice would choose a boring job 'devoid of aesthetic value', as Bauman (2005, 34) points out. Needless to say, repetitive and routine work, which may characterise a great deal of the work undertaken by junior associates in large law firms,[4] is accorded short shrift in advertising material. Potential students must be tempted and tantalised by the idea that a law school can make their dreams come true (Haywood et al. 2011, 184). Branding, therefore, is less about the consumption of a product than about 'the social relations, experiences and lifestyles such consumption entails' (Aronczyk and Powers 2010, 7).

The time spent at law school studying law is frequently glossed over in advertising, being represented merely as a means to an end — a mere blip between the reality of the present, the receipt of a testamur and the realisation of the dream. It is the campus culture rather than the content that receives attention in marketing because it comports with the prevailing aesthetic of pleasure. Inger Askehave (2007, 739) likens the rhetoric of advertising in the student prospectus to that of the tourism industry. An example from Southern Cross Law School illustrates the point: 'Embrace the sun, sand and surf. Study law this summer at Byron Bay or the Gold Coast.'[5] Indeed, the 'vibrant campus culture' was what appealed most of all to two University of Western Australia alumni, according to the Law School website.[6] There is no advertence to the fact that intellectual engagement with new ideas requires effort and commitment, or that law students will have to spend hours reading (cf. Broadbent and Sellman 2013, 62). Neoliberal rhetoric in conjunction with a consumerist mentality has

---

4    The Chief Justice of NSW, Bathurst CJ, was compelled to resile from a controversial reference to new recruits in corporate law firms as 'mindless drones', which he subsequently replaced with 'mechanical drones' (Merritt 2012, 33).

5    Retrieved 12 September 2012, from www.scu.edu.au/schools/law/.

6    Iona Quahe: retrieved 11 September 2013, from www.studyat.uwa.edu.au/courses/business-law; Cameron Barnes: retrieved 11 September 2013, from www.studyat.uwa.edu.au/courses/law-and-society.

contributed to an 'intellectual shift from engagement to passivity' in higher education generally (Williams 2011, 172). Student/consumers expect their 'service providers' to ensure that they pass the course with minimum effort. The point was made by numerous academics interviewed in both Australia and the UK for *Privatising the Public University* (Thornton 2012).

## Websites

In the marketing of legal education, promotion of the idealised work/lifestyle mix is found in most contemporary media (Symes 1996, 137). Universities produce a range of physical materials in the form of glossy brochures highlighting attractive features of the campus or student life. Professional and academic staff, students and alumni engage in various forms of direct marketing through events such as open days, information nights and university fairs at home and abroad.

However, as the impact of the Internet is deep and far-reaching, it requires special consideration. The nub of Marshall McLuhan's famous aphorism 'the medium is the message' is that the use of any communications medium has an influence far greater than its content (Levinson 1999, 35). One aspect of the Internet's potency is derived from the fact that it is made up of 'all or at least most media that have come before it, with writing ubiquitous in the driver's seat' (Levinson 1999, 38). The webpage holds great potential because the message can be conveyed in a range of formats in the one place. For many students, a visit to the homepage of a university or faculty will be the first campus 'visit' (Opoku et al. 2006, 32), and the global reach of the Internet may be especially useful in attracting full fee-paying international students. Prospective students can view video clips of student testimonials, take a virtual tour of the campus and the law school, find out about the course and career options, and read online brochures together with the profiles of lecturers and successful graduates. Websites allow users to navigate this content in a way that is relevant and interactive (Simmons 2008, 551; Song and Zinkhan 2008, 99) which enhances an individual's 'relationship' to the brand in question (Simmons 2008, 553).

It takes significant resources to produce a high-quality website which incorporates a range of media and creates a unified and compelling statement, but not all websites are created equal. For instance, some law school websites contain only written text, with a few pictures and the university crest. The information contained on these websites relates mainly to course content and structure rather than an attempt to lure students with powerful imagery and the promise of opportunities. The 'success' of online branding depends on a cluster of rational and emotional values that enable the consumer to recognise the 'promise experience' (Chapleo et al. 2011, 30).

Websites may be the 'virtual face' (Meyer 2008) of an institution but the divergence in quality has implications for a law school's ability to harness effectively the language and imagery of the aesthetic of work. Hence, a lack of resources may limit a school's ability to sell itself as a pathway to a bright future. However, there is no necessary correlation between the amount expended on marketing and students' choice of university. An investigation by the *Times Higher Education* of universities in the United Kingdom found that despite the significant increase in expenditure by nearly a quarter, they suffered a 7.4 per cent fall in applications the following year. It is notable that the new universities (post-1992) were among the biggest spenders on advertising, while those belonging to the Russell Group, the most prestigious, were the lowest (Matthews 2013). As might be expected, Oxbridge attracts students regardless of marketing expenditure, while large sums spent by the new universities will not necessarily prove to be a wise investment. While the international marketing of Australian undergraduate law degrees has been limited because of the largely municipal nature of the law degree, the globalisation of legal markets is inducing a change. The full fee income received from international students is the main reason they are being targeted, despite the curricular and pedagogical challenges posed by diverse student cohorts (cf. Lo 2012).

## Legal education and the 'golden ticket' to employment

Perhaps unsurprisingly, law school marketing is strongly correlated with the vocational aspects of legal education. Vocationalism is described by James (2004, 44) as 'the set of statements about legal education produced by law schools and by legal scholars which emphasise the importance of the teaching of legal skills and prioritise employability as an objective of legal education'. The development of commercially focused law programs, the emphasis on applied skills for the 'real world' and the marketing of law schools as a branch of the legal profession are salient features of law school websites as schools strive to build a brand that can tap in to the consciousness of prospective students lured by élite careers. The emergence of the global law firm as a key stakeholder in the educational enterprise and the demands of the global new knowledge economy more generally have become key selling points for law schools. Although precise data are not available, a 2010 survey by Graduate Careers Australia revealed that only 43.7 per cent of law graduates started work in law firms (Berkovic 2011).

While some law school websites advert to a wide range of possible careers,[7] the overwhelming focus is directed towards conventional private legal practice, which is similar in the UK (Broadbent and Sellman 2013, 60).

## The commercial focus

A symbiotic relationship between law and business is not new but it has been accentuated with the neoliberal embrace in which the market has become the measure of all things. Understanding the marketability of the commercially oriented law school requires an interrogation of the drivers of law school behaviour, including the pressures that students and the legal services market place on law schools. This encourages law schools to stress their strengths in commercial, corporate and taxation law.[8] The commercial orientation, as well as providing a pathway to legal practice, demonstrates to the corporate legal labour market the 'marketability' of a law school's graduates.

The élite corporate firms, including the emergent global conglomerates that evince a particular interest in Asia,[9] represent the most desirable destinations for law graduates and there is an attempt to shape the curriculum accordingly. Sydney Law School, for example, offers specialised postgraduate courses in areas such as Law and Investment in Asia or US International Taxation.[10] Other law schools are careful to show that commercial specialisation is one of several core areas on offer.[11] Alumni profiles often showcase individuals who have risen in the ranks of top-tier law firms or have pursued high-flying international corporate careers as a means of emphasising the accessibility of such careers to the graduates of a particular law school.

Employment with an élite law firm is prized by students, both for its high earning potential and the glamorous and youthful lifestyles held out in the firm's own marketing materials (cf. Collier 2005, 61–4). As a result, student/consumers may place pressure on law schools for more commercial options, to the detriment of critical or social justice approaches (Thornton 2012, 71). Nevertheless, as a concession to the sense of altruism that many students

---

7   E.g. UNSW Law: retrieved 11 September 2013, from www.law.unsw.edu.au/current-students/careers; UTAS: retrieved 11 September 2013, from www.utas.edu.au/law/about-the-faculty-of-law.

8   E.g. Deakin Law School: *Welcome from the Dean and Head of School, Professor Mirko Bagaric*. Retrieved 11 September 2013, from www.deakin.edu.au/buslaw/law/about/.

9   A flurry of amalgamations occurred between super-élite London-based and Australian firms in 2012. They include Allens Linklaters, Ashurst, Norton Rose, Clifford Chance, DLA Piper and King & Wood Mallesons (e.g. Spence 2012, 39).

10   Sydney Law School: retrieved 11 September 2013, from sydney.edu.au/law/fstudent/coursework/buslaw.shtml.

11   *School of Law Mission Statement*, University of Canberra: retrieved 30 September 2014, from www.canberra.edu.au/faculties/busgovlaw/school-of-law/school-of-law-mission-statement; Victoria University: *Bachelor of Law, Course Objectives*. Retrieved 30 September, from www.vu.edu.au/courses/bachelor-of-laws-blaw.

retain, law school websites may link social justice initiatives with the pro bono programs of commercial firms.[12] Students, conscious of their HECS (now FEE-HELP) debt and wooed by the luxurious offices and prestige of the super-élite global firms, are inclined towards those law schools which position themselves as conveyor belts to these and other large firms. Invariably, these law schools are likely to be the oldest and most prestigious in a state.

## Skills, experiential learning and the 'real' world

> One of our aims has always been to have graduates known for what we call 'real-world readiness'.[13]

In the new knowledge economy, it is 'know-how' rather than 'know-what' that is valued (OECD 1996). This shift in favour of applied knowledge is clearly discernible in the law curriculum as law schools include more practical skills in the curriculum. In the United States, the global financial crisis has induced a scathing attack on law schools for favouring esoteric scholarship over the training of 'practice ready' graduates (Segal 2011; Illinois State Bar Association 2013; cf. ALRC 2000, 36–9). The view is that the American law degree, the JD, not only takes too long, it is too expensive and contains insufficient 'useful knowledge'. As the Australian LLB/JD is a prerequisite for admission to practice and does not entail a separate Bar exam, there is a greater consciousness of the needs of the profession, but the neoliberal turn has accentuated the desirability of practical skills over theoretical and critical knowledge (Thornton 2012, esp. 59–84).

Accordingly, a salient theme in law school marketing is the provision of skills through experiential learning and contact with the 'real' world. Sally Kift (1997, 58) argues that in developing skills for practice, 'experiential learning is the best (and possibly the only effective) way to prepare students'. Experiential learning is also often understood as the centrepiece of progressive education as it engenders an active rather than a passive approach to learning (Rankin 2012, 22–3). However, law schools market experiential learning not so much because it will result in better lawyers but because it accords with the market's demand for graduates with 'job-ready' skills – that is, the neoliberal imperative which

---

12    E.g. Sydney Law School's social justice page for undergraduate students outlines a range of initiatives that students can take part in, many of which are accomplished through partnerships with large law firms: *Sydney Law School Social Justice Program*. Retrieved 30 September 2014, from sydney.edu.au/law/fstudent/undergrad/social_justice_program.shtml.
13    University of Wollongong: *Where a UOW Law Degree Can Take You …* Retrieved 11 September 2013, from www.uow.edu.au/law/uowllb/index.html.

favours 'know-how' over 'know-what': 'Experiential learning is a high priority for UniSA Law. We aim to develop not only students' knowledge in Law, but also their practical skills so that they are job-ready when they graduate'.[14]

External placements and clinical legal education are the main ways in which experiential learning is undertaken. Clinical legal education is usually accomplished through either a partnership with a local legal centre or, in cases where the law school is perhaps better resourced, through a legal centre run by the law school itself. While law schools attempt to show these clinical experiences as an aspect of their 'unique' brand of legal education,[15] experiential and skills-based learning is widespread and its validity is rationalised using a common theme of access to the 'real':

> Working on real cases with real clients you will be under the expert supervision of our legal practitioners at one of Monash Law School's two community legal centres.[16]

> ... a unique opportunity for law students to apply their studies to actual legal practice with real clients.[17]

The relationship between the 'real world', practical legal skills and law school 'uniqueness' is best encapsulated in the QUT online advertisement entitled *Real Graduates*.[18] This consists of testimonials from three graduates employed by large corporate law firms. Each testimonial begins with the graduates smiling reassuringly into the camera and holding up a sign that reads 'REAL'. Each graduate goes on to detail their story and extol the virtues of QUT's unique practical, skills-based focus, which prepared them for the workforce and made them attractive to employers. This is part of QUT's broader branding strategy, which positions the institution as 'a university for the real world' in accordance with its slogan. While QUT is exceptional in its articulation of such a clear message, appeals to the 'real' are widespread. Implicit in these appeals is the notion that theoretical and critical knowledge is arcane and irrelevant; it is not real.

---

14   University of South Australia School of Law: *Experiential Learning*. Retrieved 30 September 2014, from www.unisa.edu.au/Business/Law/About-us/Experiential-learning/.

15   E.g. in 2013, Newcastle Law School provides its students with a legal clinic called 'Law On the Beach' which consists of free legal advice for the public provided by students under the supervision of a lawyer. The unique setting, with its appeal of sun and sand, is intended to appeal to young people who may be otherwise denied access to legal advice. Retrieved 11 September 2013, from www.newcastle.edu.au/school/law/unlc/law-on-the-beach.html.

16   Monash Law School: '*Real* cases with *real* clients'. Retrieved 11 September 2013, from www.law.monash.edu/future-students/undergraduate/course-guide/law-undergrad-courseguide-2013.pdf.

17   Newcastle Law School. Retrieved 11 September 2013, from www.newcastle.edu.au/school/law/unlc/law-on-the-beach.html.

18   QUT Law: *Courses and Study – Work Placement and Projects – Real World Placement Program*. Retrieved 30 September 2014, from www.qut.edu.au/law/courses-and-study.

Bond University's video advertisement for its accelerated law program contains images of well-dressed, capable, go-getting young people winning trophies, finishing their degrees in record time and connecting one-on-one with knowledgeable and charismatic teachers, all performed to a rocking upbeat soundtrack.[19] At the point of 'World-Class Facilities', the video shows law students mooting in a state-of-the-art moot courtroom, complete with its own Leo McKern doppelganger on the bench.[20] The idea that this university is geared towards preparing students to get out there into the 'real world' is the key message.

The language of the 'real world' or situated learning is also known as problem solving or problem-based learning in the legal education literature, for it seeks to create an educational context reflective of the complexity of actual practice (Rankin 2012, 24). As with colloquial speech, the phrase is used glibly on websites reinforcing the idea that the time spent at university is a break from normal life and the process of studying for a degree is less important than the outcome (Williams 2011, 175). The discourse of the 'real world' instantiates the stereotype of the university campus as an ivory tower cut off from ordinary life; its primary use value in the market being the award of a testamur.

## Links with the profession and beyond

At a time when law schools were anxious to secure their acceptance as legitimate constituents of the academy, they sometimes regarded close relations with the profession with suspicion, but this has now crystallised into an essential selling point. While the legal profession generally does not play other than a minimal role in the design and delivery of legal education, except for specifying the criteria for admission, intimate relations may now be emphasised by a law school anxious to assure prospective students of its legitimacy as a 'real' legal educator, and links between the two are made clear in the law school's promotional texts.[21] For instance, the 'well designed curriculum' means one that is 'developed in consultation with the legal profession and other key stakeholders'.[22] Further, the professional credentials of law school staff are seen as vital:

> The strongest [aspect of Sydney law school] is the links it has to the current legal community outside of uni. So you go into a lecture and you're tutored by

---

19   Bond University: *Ten reasons why Bond Law* (video clip). Retrieved 30 September 2014, from www.bond.edu.au/faculties-colleges/faculty-of-law/about-the-faculty/why-bond-law/index.htm.

20   In their study of UK law school websites, Broadbent and Sellman (2013, 61–2) note the disproportionate prevalence of images of mooting, although the limited visible potential of law is acknowledged.

21   RMIT, for example, emphasises 'work integrated learning'. See, RMIT Graduate School of Business and Law, *Be the leader you want to be*. Retrieved 11 September 2013, from www.rmit.edu.au/bus/schools&groups.

22   UTS, Law: *Information for Future Law Students*. Retrieved 11 September 2013, from www.law.uts.edu.au/students/future/index.html.

barristers, you're tutored by practising judges, you're tutored by practising advocates. And having that link to the legal community is really useful because they draw upon their own experience ... they give you that realism.[23]

I've gone to seminars here, you know, with professionals from all around Queensland, and I sit down at a table and there's one of my lecturers ... Just the other day my supervisor had said, 'Go and call this barrister, he's the best in Commercial Law,' and I looked at the name and I thought, 'Hang on, I know him,' and I Google him and he's a QUT lecturer ...[24]

While academics may be 'experts' in regard to a substantive field of knowledge, it is more appealing if they practise law, as it is assumed that they will then be able to transmit the values and knowledge needed for students to move seamlessly into the élite, high-paying careers in the global economy which they desire. Members of the practising profession are characterised as the definitive legal 'knowers' and the closer the law school is able to position itself to the kernel of practical legal knowledge, the more persuasive its claims to expertise appear. That a school's graduates are 'highly prized by the legal profession'[25] is a feature that demonstrates the value of the degree. Such statements reveal the endurance of the profession's 'magnetic pull' over legal education (Sugarman 1986, 27). Like the commercial focus and the emphasis on 'real world' skills, links to practising lawyers are believed to be highly marketable. These links effectively vouch for the fact that a law school's educational product is a bridge to the coveted and prestigious careers to which prospective students aspire.

## Internationalising the curriculum, internationalising the appeal

Spurred on by the internationalisation of law and legal markets together with the attendant demands of employers, the impetus to internationalise legal education is 'gathering momentum' (Coper 2012, 4; cf. Lo 2012). Internationalisation entails a range of approaches from augmenting the curriculum to increasing the numbers of international enrolments (Coper 2012, 4). While an increase in enrolment of fee-paying international students is one of the aims of marketing, it does not in itself necessarily internationalise Australian legal education (Lo 2012). As early as 2004 the International Legal Services Advisory Council (ILSAC) drafted a report that called for a greater focus on and coordination of

---

23 Sydney Law School: The Sydney LLB - Combined Law — Jared Ellsmore (video clip), Retrieved 30 September 2014, from www.youtube.com/watch?v=VmlyEnheAGc&list=UUKXY_RwWHOpg2vo3lOldTDw&index=5&feature=plcp.

24 QUT Law: *Courses and Study, Real Graduates,* Natalie Taylor (video clip). Retrieved 11 September 2013, from www.qut.edu.au/law/courses-and-study.

25 James Cook University School of Law: *The law program.* Retrieved 30 September 2014, from www.jcu.edu.au/law/JCUDEV_002404.html.

internationalisation efforts in Australian law schools in order that graduates and institutions could be competitive on the global stage. In 2012, a thoroughgoing report was commissioned by the Australian Office for Learning and Teaching, which was strongly of the view that the law degree should be internationalised, although it did not prescribe how this might be done. A number of law schools have already embarked on curriculum redesign projects that encourage international perspectives. The University of New South Wales Law School, for example, has redesigned its entire curriculum to reflect the global imperative:

> This is one of the strongest characteristics of the new curriculum that it's going to reflect the new international dimensions that anybody who studies law or who works in law in the future has to be familiar with. So we will have a new compulsory course on global perspectives in law and we will be introducing and expanding more and more international opportunities for our students to go and study law overseas ...[26]

While websites stress the academic value of the global content of the law curriculum, this pales in comparison with the allure of international postings: 'It's not just a university, it's a global community. You'll join a network of Bond graduates now working in Dubai, Kuala Lumpur, London, New York, Paris, Shanghai, Singapore, Toronto ... the sky is the limit.'[27] Many law schools offer educational exchanges with overseas universities (Johnstone and Vigaendra 2003), and placements and internships with organisations overseas also come across as a means of linking the law degree with excitement and adventure, both personal and professional.

The appeal of overseas travel and the prestige of élite international careers underpin the marketing of international placements and educational exchanges by presenting them as pleasurable activities facilitated by the law school. Exchange programs with overseas universities are a response to the idea that students will be required to connect with 'trans-national' legal knowledge (Chesterman 2009, 881–82). Such programs are sometimes rationalised by drawing on discourses of personal development. To use the words of Sydney University on its 'The Sydney LLB Advantage' webpage, an exchange not only internationalises the degree but also 'challenges [students] academically; facilitates the development of new skills; and enhances their personal growth and self-confidence.'[28] Beyond such statements, the accent is on exchanges as an

---

26   UNSW Law: David Dixon, Dean, *Studying Law at UNSW – Part 1* (10 May 2012) (YouTube). Retrieved 30 September 2014, from www.youtube.com/watch?v=dG9NzN2Milk.

27   Bond Law School. Retrieved 11 September 2013, from bond.edu.au/faculties/law/about-the-faculty/index.htm.

28   Sydney Law School: *The Sydney LLB – Study Abroad and Exchange*. Retrieved 30 September 2014, from http://sydney.edu.au/law/fstudent/undergrad/exchange.shtml.

'exciting' opportunity to incorporate overseas travel into the degree,[29] and the testimonials of students stress the opportunities for fun, adventure and new experiences:

> All in all, it was a magical experience, and an unforgettable summer. More than rules and regulations, tagliatelle and one-euro pastries, what has stayed with me since Tuscany is how diverse the study of law can be, and what incredible places a law degree can take me.[30]

> [Studying in Japan] was a lot of fun. I think a whole different experience, a whole eye opening experience … being able to explore a country … you don't really get to see until you've been there and experience it for yourself.[31]

International internships and placements often take place in the context of human rights or international governance organisations, such as the Khmer Rouge trials[32] or defending the rights of prisoners on death row.[33] Furthermore, the notion of 'where a law degree can take you' is articulated powerfully in the choice of law alumni profiles that law schools share on their websites and online promotional material. While the alumni profiles of judges, barristers and corporate lawyers are to be expected, strong contingents of alumni profiles are also made over to those operating at the highest levels of international law and governance. The profiles of graduates working for the UN or for international courts are held out as proof of a direct causal relationship between having attended a particular law school and the attainment of a career in international justice:

> Terry said he chose to study law at UQ because of its reputation, and since completing his degree he hasn't looked back: 'University was great. It was hard work but I wouldn't be where I am today without UQ', says Terry. 'More specifically, I wouldn't be here [at the United Nations] without the guidance and knowledge I received from the staff at the TC Beirne School of Law.'[34]

These international careers accentuate employment as a portal to 'enriching' experiences that involve travel and adventure:

---

29    E.g, Monash University Law School: *Undergraduate Course Guide, Law International Programs*, 8. Retrieved 30 September 2014, from www.law.monash.edu.au/future-students/undergraduate/course-guide/law-undergrad-courseguide-2013.pdf.

30    UNSW Law: *UNSW Law Undergraduate Guide 2013*, Katrina Geddes, 5th Year Commerce/Law student (online brochure) 31. Retrieved 21 March 2013, from www.law.unsw.edu.au/future-students/undergraduate/why-study-law.

31    Sydney Law School: *The Sydney LLB – Combined Law, The Sydney Law Advantage*, Rebecca Tan (video clip). Retrieved 30 September 2014, from http://sydney.edu.au/law/fstudent/undergrad/advantage.shtml.

32    Melbourne Law School, *JD, Experience* (video clip). Retrieved 11 September 2013, from www.law.unimelb.edu.au/jd/experience.

33    Sydney Law School: *Alumni and Friends, Naomi Hart*. Retrieved 30 September 2014, from http://sydney.edu.au/law/alumni/profiles/hart.shtml.

34    T C Beirne School of Law, UQ: *What Students Say, Terry Slight*. Retrieved 21 March 2013, from www.law.uq.edu.au/what-students-say.

I am an associate legal officer in the Rwandan Criminal Tribunal's Chambers … but having the opportunity to learn first-hand and in detail about the Rwandan genocide is extremely enriching. The opportunity also to work at an international level and in such an amazing country as Tanzania is an obvious highlight in my career path.[35]

During university I worked in the international office of a global firm and also undertook an internship at the United Nations in New York … I am currently based in Paris, but my clients and colleagues are in The Hague, London and the Middle East.[36]

Such texts evoke images of globetrotting careers pursued for pleasure and are often accompanied by a photo of the smiling graduate at his or her workplace. In this way, alumni profiles visually and textually embody ideal careers in a way that plays into the desires of students for pleasurable post-law school employment. There is no acknowledgement that these roles, particularly those involving the examination or prosecution of human rights abuses, are premised on the suffering of the world's most vulnerable people. In order to set up these idealised visions of future employment, the routine and disturbing aspects of international opportunities and perspectives are excised. To be desirable to consumers of legal education, the international career appears as a glittering prize that is attainable by any graduate of *that* law school and it is one that is devoid of the mundane, the distasteful or the difficult.

## Critique

As James (2004, 377) has illustrated, there is little consistency in the meaning of 'critique' in legal education discourse generally. It is frequently confused with unwarranted criticism, and the favouring of a positivist and doctrinal approach to legal education and adjudication has coincided with 'know how' and the favouring of applied knowledge currently in vogue. A passive pedagogy encouraged by the lecture method also discourages interrogation and critique. It encourages students to search for 'right answers' rather than accept the law as a canvas comprising many shades of grey which demand interrogation (Thornton 2012, 85).

James (2004, 377) claims that terms such as 'critical thinking', 'critical reasoning', 'critical evaluation', 'critical perspectives' and 'criticism', while having potentially different meanings, are often employed in Australian legal

---

35   UNSW Law: *Graduate Profile, Miriam Mafessanti* (online brochure). Retrieved 10 September 2012, from www.law.unsw.edu.au/student/miriamn-mafessanti.
36   UNSW Law, *Law Undergraduate Guide 2013, Philippa Webb* (online brochure). Retrieved 21 March 2013, from www.law.unsw.edu.au/future-students/undergraduate/why-study-law.

education discourse interchangeably and refer to an understanding of 'critique' as criteria-based judgment. The ambit of the concept shifts depending on the broader ideological framework in which it is deployed. In the promotional monologue of legal education a particular vision of 'critique' as a practical skill has emerged. The texts of websites equate critical thinking with the 'skills for life'[37] and 'the skills employers really look for in a graduate'.[38] Where critical thinking is not clearly marked as a skill, it is paired with practical skills in order to have value:

> [the law] program is distinctive in that it blends critical thinking and enquiry with the development of sound legal practice skills.[39]

> Our unique approach to legal education will provide you with a critical and questioning attitude, broad perspectives and the skills and knowledge required for whatever career you may choose.[40]

This casting of critique in the service of employability is a central feature of what James (2004, 385) refers to as the 'vocational critique' in which critique becomes merely the ability to 'supplant sloppy or distorted thinking with thinking based on reliable procedures of inquiry'. But absent from this technical understanding of the definition of critical thinking is any assessment of the broader theories of knowledge that go to the heart of the discipline to consider how law might contribute to the creation of a more just society for all. The idea that critique involves the application of a wider lens that can encompass a socio-political interrogation of law or an understanding of theoretical knowledge receives short shrift when employability is deemed to have far greater use value in the market. Despite the responsiveness of law to the politics of the day, the law school has been tardy about incorporating significant curricular change. Indeed, the core curriculum has evinced little change over a century.

The social liberalism of the Whitlam era succeeded in bringing about a degree of modernisation to the curriculum, but the inclusion of critical perspectives on law occupied a prominent place for only a brief moment before there was a resiling induced by the neoliberal turn (Thornton 2001). Student demand, in conjunction with consumerism, has played a key role in the retreat from the critical and the recasting of law as a purely vocational skill. Within the current marketised environment, as we have suggested, corporate subjects, taught from a largely functional perspective, are regarded as vastly more desirable as

---

37   James Cook University School of Law, *The aim of the school*. Retrieved 21 March 2013, from www.jcu. edu.au/law/JCUDEV_002404.html.

38   Macquarie University Law School: *Future students*. Retrieved 21 March 2013, from www.law.mq.edu.au/future_students/.

39   Southern Cross School of Law and Justice: *The School*. Retrieved 11 September 2013, from www.scu.edu. au/law-justice/index.php/4.

40   University of Wollongong Faculty of Law: Professor Warwick Gullett, Dean, *Where a UOW Law Degree can take you*. Retrieved 11 September 2013, from www.uow.edu.au/law/uowllb/index.html.

they are deemed to have greater relevance to students' imagined careers than critical perspectives or subjects focusing on critique. As shown by this study of websites, the tendency of law school branding is to slough off critique with its suggestion of abrasive and ponderous scholarship that is unlikely to help realise the dream of a fun-filled career.

Most significantly, critique is a destabilising concept (Robins and Webster 1998, 128). Feminist, racial, queer and critical legal studies provide frameworks that shine a bright light on the socio-political undersides of identity and power. When deployed in the study of law, critique unmasks the myth of legal objectivity and demands that attention be paid not just to the impact of administrative and judicial decision-making at home but also to the imperialistic designs of multinational corporations elsewhere. This now includes global law firms pursuing the interests of powerful clients with mining and resource interests all over the world, without regard as to whether they are in Mongolia, South Africa or the Middle East. The version of critique contained in the marketing materials of websites constricts its political reach by focusing on the aesthetic of pleasure.

## Conclusion

Freedom of choice is regarded as an unmitigated good within a liberal democratic society. The concept has been effectively deployed by neoliberalism and its market embrace so that consumer choice, by metathesis, is accepted as an unproblematic good. The result of virtually unlimited choice is that it blunts the critical capacity of students and induces a conservatism among them (Nixon et al. 2011). This is because choice favours the easy, pleasant and attractive path rather than one that is complex, challenging and reflexive (Broadbent and Sellman 2013, 59). Indeed, critique is not a word that features in the marketing repertoire because it induces 'the sort of dissonance and angst that good marketing works hard to eliminate' (Nixon et al. 2011).

The essays in Molesworth, Scullin and Nixon's collection (2011) show compellingly how a consumerist culture is eroding the civic role of higher education generally in the UK in favour of hedonism. Building on *Privatising the Public University* (Thornton 2012), and examining Australian law school marketing on websites, this chapter has suggested that the shift has also been marked in law. Rather than aiming to produce critical thinkers who can contribute constructively to public debate on the pressing issues of our time, law school marketing encourages consumerism as the ultimate telos of the good life.

Academics have undoubtedly been complicit in the sea change that has occurred in the legal academy as a result of widespread acceptance of the market metanarrative (Roberts 1998). Academics, no less than student/customers, are neoliberal subjects shaped by the relentless demands of the market. Not only are they (we) enmeshed in the prevailing consumer culture with all its fictions, but their (our) attention has been effectively deflected by institutional demands to teach ever larger and more diverse cohorts of students while being ever more productive in terms of research 'outputs'. Cutting corners in teaching by adopting an uncritical, minimalist approach is therefore functional for academics as well as for students.

The market, the branding of law schools and the seductive illusion of choice have effectively combined to consign the scholarly pedagogical project of the legal academy to the margins. As Askehave (2007, 725) puts it, we no longer '*teach* courses to *students*' but we '*sell* courses to our *clients*'. Of course, there are legal academics who are committed to including critical thinking in their teaching and imbuing their students with a sense of the possibilities of realising a more just and responsible society through law. However, the task of committed academics has become progressively harder as good intentions are frustrated by the fantasy world of marketing.

We have sought to draw attention to just how pervasive this fantasy world of law school marketing has become and how difficult it is to resist as marketing has become a key rationality of the corporatised university. Despite the pressures confronting law schools in a competitive environment, however, we should not abandon hope. Critical engagement – involving academics, students and the wider community – is the only way to challenge the new orthodoxy. A mere nanosecond ago, neonate law students wanted to change the world but many have been captivated by the ubiquitous message that consumerism epitomises the good life. There is no point in rueing the passing of free higher education in the belief that its reinstatement might resolve the market malaise, for those days have gone for good. Nevertheless, there are always spaces in the legal academy in which to animate the spirit of justice that many students still secretly long for in contrast to the vacuous dreams spun for them by university marketing departments. We need to pay heed to those spaces.

# Part IV: Conditions of Knowledge Production

# 11. Disciplining Academic Women: Gender Restructuring and the Labour of Research in Entrepreneurial Universities

Jill Blackmore

This chapter examines the 'gendered nature of the social organisation of research and scientific knowledge production' and in particular the gendered nature of the corporatisation of higher education (Knorr-Cetina 1999, 9). It argues that the conditions of labour of the entrepreneurial university and underlying market-oriented instrumentalism has changed the nature of the relationship of higher education with the public, with the individual student and the academic, in ways that are gendered. 'Markets do not make social distinctions disappear, they regulate interaction between institutions e.g. families and education, and "instrumentalist" status distinctions, bending pre-existing cultural value to capitalist purposes' (Fraser and Honneth 1998, 58). The dominant neoliberal policy 'doxa', with its economistic view of higher education in relation to the knowledge economy, is an ideology which shapes a range of constantly changing discursive and material practices (Epstein et al. 2008). This is 'not so much a "new" form of liberal government, but rather a hybrid or intensified form of it' that works through and on subjectivities that are racialised, gendered, classed and sexualised (Bansel et al. 2008, 673).

Neoliberal reforms have produced new forms of governmentality premised upon comparison. Within the social field of higher education, the rules of the game have changed over the past two decades (Naidoo 2004). Internally, elite universities seek to maintain their comparative advantage relative to newer universities in the Australian market as external pressures intensify. These pressures include the entrance of new players (Singapore, China, Indonesia) and increased competitiveness of established players (USA, UK, Germany) in the international education market. All strive for 'world excellence' status. The sector has also had difficulty maintaining its boundaries as market principles have penetrated into the structures, processes and language of higher education (Lingard and Rawolle 2011), with the blurring of boundaries between higher education and other fields (politics, journalism, publication, business) as well as the pressure to gain new sources of funding that provide more immediate economic benefits (Bourdieu 1990, 1988, 1986). The doxa of higher education as a public good has been unsettled as universities are no longer the only source or producers of knowledge legitimating what counts as valued knowledge (Marginson 2011).

Within global higher education markets, research remains critical to the distinctiveness of both the field and the status of an individual university and its positioning relative to the state and other educational providers. Bourdieu (1986) refers to the research activities of academics as scientific (research) capital that includes symbolic capital in terms of esteem, international networks and material capital or findings. What gets researched, how it is researched and how that research is valued, the symbolic capital, is also indicative of gendered power/knowledge relations within the gender regime of the academy and gender order of the wider society (Connell 2006). The following analysis draws from a three-year Australian Research Council (ARC) project on *Leadership in the Entrepreneurial University: Diversity and Disengagement*. The study involves intensive case study research through interview, documentary and policy analysis in three universities – a Group of Eight (Go8), a university of technology and a regional university – to identify differences between how institutional cultures, scale and disciplinary scope impact on who gets to lead and the nature of that leadership. It follows 15 years on from an Australian Research Council (ARC) study investigating educational restructuring in universities, schools and TAFE in post-Dawkins Australia in the mid-1990s. The chapter's title appeals to Foucault's notion of the dispersed disciplinary power relayed through discourse and power/knowledge relations. Policy texts and institutional practices have discursive and material effects in terms of how they discipline the humanities and social sciences more harshly as well as in the production of particular academic subjectivities (Bansel et al. 2008, Clegg 2008).

This chapter argues that we are experiencing a second phase of higher education restructuring that is also reconfiguring the social relations of gender within the field (Brooks and Mackinnon 2000, Currie et al. 2000, Deem 2003). The first phase of restructuring that unified, marketised and managerialised higher education systems (Blackmore and Sachs 2007) in Australia and the UK was nation-centric. The second phase emerges from the context in which academic capitalism has gone truly global, fuelled by new technologies and increasingly mobile students, academics and content (Slaughter and Leslie 1997). Higher education research is now closely tied to the national economy through priority setting by government research funders — the ARC and the National Health Medical Research Council (NHMRC). Quality, now *the* measure of distinction in education markets, is signified in research through research assessment (e.g. Excellence in Research for Australia (ERA); and the Research Excellence Framework (REF) in the UK) (Besley 2010). Quality in teaching and learning is being driven through a standards-based agenda of the newly established Tertiary Education Quality and Standards Agency (TEQSA). Market distinctiveness is also produced through individual university compacts leading to greater institutional differentiation. This globalised phase of restructuring is characterised by the intensification of the processes of corporatisation (managerialism, marketisation and privatisation) that were emergent during the 1990s (Brooks and Mackinnon 2000; Blackmore and Sachs 2007; Marginson and Considine 2000). This resulted in a blurring of public/private provision, a renewed focus on branding and ranking, moves towards institutional restructuring to encourage interdisciplinarity, demand-driven online curriculum, industry partnerships and the intensification of academic work (Shapper and Mayson 2005; Epstein et al. 2008; Menzies and Newson 2008).

Serial restructuring and rebranding over two decades have had gendered effects because of the assumptions underpinning the processes, structures and practices work within the frame of gendered organisations. Universities are characterised in particular by a unique historical allocation of values associated with knowledge legitimation, production and dissemination that are reconfigured over time. Gender is evident in how research is understood and enacted in the:

- policy discourses and images of research that equate science and technology with innovation as the driver of economic growth to the neglect of the social and cultural;

- policies premised upon a normative science that fails to recognise the nature of quality research in different disciplinary fields where women are concentrated (Gillies 2008);

- redistribution of time and space in terms of how and where academics work, leading to work/life conflict more than balance and the impact on those with caring responsibilities (Pillay et al. 2013);

- individuals' capacity for mobility is becoming increasingly important in academic careers with women more bound to place (Menzies and Newson 2008; Jons 2011);

- gender division of labour in research management and practice with regard to who does what and who gets recognised in terms of esteem and leadership (Bell 2009; Coates et al. 2009);

- institutional cultural ethos and heightened expectations about research;

- competing policy discourses about teams and collaboration and competitive individualism of 'star' systems (Blackmore 2009a); and

- reward systems where potential beats substantive record in promotions (Chesterman et al. 2003; Dever et al. 2008).

Markets also are socially constituted, despite the discourse of rational choice theories, produced through policy and often without any pre-existing demand. Markets allocate value and distribute resources and rewards. In particular, markets produce 'social settings that foster specific types of personal development and penalise others' (Bakker 1994, 4). In the case of the performative university, they encourage self-interest and self-promotion, being seen to be performing, thus producing an entrepreneurial intellectual habitus and managerial leadership habitus (Metcalfe and Slaughter 2008; Blackmore and Sachs 2007). Markets produce and exploit emotions of anxiety and desire. On the one hand, there is anxiety arising from the volatility of higher education markets of students, academics and providers. On the other, there is the passion of academics as researchers to achieve, to make a difference and to contribute, as many academics are ethically disposed to 'do good' (Macfarlane 2011). Markets are also gendered. Bakker (1994, 3) sees 'markets as institutions imbued with structural power relations and those have an asymmetrical gender dimension to them'. Gender is central to how the 'managed education market' works differently in terms of what is valued, images of academic or entrepreneurial leadership, the division of labour, and who has the opportunity to become the internationally mobile strategic academic.

# Research, quality and the global market

Australian universities during the 20th century were nation-building enterprises with a strong public commitment, funded largely by government, a reactively autonomous social field in which research was considered to be part of everyday academic practice. Jane Kelsey (1995, 58) saw universities in the 1990s as primary sites of critique of the ideologies of neoliberal market theory, and therefore they were an 'obvious target for radical market oriented restructuring'. Post-1989, the Dawkins reforms set in train the processes of corporatisation of the academy – managerialisation, marketisation and privatisation – that restructured the higher education sector nationally. Universities are now transnational corporations with global reach and they are again being restructured within increasingly diverse and complex global higher education markets. The context is of heightened competition from older Anglo competitors and recent Asian players. Higher education markets also arise due to the lack of government funds and are thus increasingly driven by external demands of industry, government, NGOs and students. This means fewer research-driven agendas internal to the disciplines. External and internal education markets increasingly determine the value of knowledge, create reputations, distribute rewards, promote images of success, and form more entrepreneurial academic identities (Clegg 2008).

Bourdieuan scholars now argue that decisions about the field of higher education are being made by those outside of the field more than those inside due to the globalisation of higher education policy, research, increased cross-national institutional arrangements, and international labour markets of students and academics (e.g. Naidoo 2004; Lingard and Rawolle 2011). This is evident with reduced numbers of academic and student and increased numbers of business representatives on university councils (Rowlands 2013). Internally, the field is increasingly porous not only due to greater seamlessness between the sectors of TAFE, universities and schools but also a blurring between public and private providers with the trend to privatisation (Marginson 2011). Other policy trends and institutional responses are emerging that impact on the social organisation of research and the positioning of women as academics and as future leaders in research, such as:

- shifting from quantity and capacity building to 'quality' and 'excellence' as defined by proxy citation indicators (ERA);
- shifting from merit and pure research to applied research with measurable use-value (industry partnerships);
- focusing on research concentrations, institutional environment and capacity building (ERA and ARC);
- encouraging differentiation between universities (global ranking and compacts); and
- producing the intensification (scope, scale and depth), diversification of academic labour (research only/teaching and research/teaching only), and the blurring between academic/professional roles.

## Gendering academic labour

The internal higher education labour market comprises a well-defined historical gendered (and in many instances racialised) horizontal division of labour in which women academics are concentrated in more junior and casual or contract positions (Coates et al. 2010; Junor 2004; ABS 2012), undertaking more teaching than their male counterparts (Bell and Bentley 2005). Bell (2010, 48) reports that 'significant international studies are providing evidence of persistent patterns of horizontal segregation (by discipline) and vertical segregation (by level of seniority and measures of esteem) of women in higher education'.[1]

---

1    In Australia, in the period 2003–11 women have increased from 19.1 to 27.3 per cent representation in above senior lecturer levels, from 33.7 to 42.2 per cent senior lecturer, 46.4 to 51.5 per cent lecturer and 53.2 to 54.9 per cent below lecturer full-time or fractional full-time positions, not including casual staff. Women increased from 62.2 per cent to 65.6 per cent full-time and part-time non-academic staff; an increase from 52.2 to 55.9 per cent of all staff (ABS 2012).

Women's numerical increase obfuscates the changing nature of the research enterprise (Chesterman 2008). Pipeline theory assumes that a critical mass of women, particularly with the feminisation of the academy, will be promoted into managerial and research leadership. Yet many women do not progress past senior lecturer, or associate professor or head of school (Bell 2010). Even when women achieved numerical parity in the Australian Research Council grants in 2013, they were not usually principal investigator and they peaked in ARC successes a decade later than men, at 65–70 years (ARC 2012). The Federation of Australian Scientific and Technological Societies concluded that gender segregation contributes to the attrition of women from the scientific professions (Bell 2009), as in the UK (Guderley 2013), particularly since women are paid on average less than men internationally (ranging from 75 per cent to 90 per cent) (Welch 2012). Even highly successful female research leaders continue to feel excluded from the networks that build research capacity. An MIT study of women in science and engineering concluded that marginalisation increases as they progress, because they endure 'differences in salary, space, awards, resources, and response to outside offers … despite professional accomplishments equal to those of their male colleagues' (cited by Bell 2009, 442).

Importantly, this horizontal and vertical gendered division of labour repeats itself inter-generationally. Any increase in Australian women's participation has been in traditional subjects, with three per cent increases in science, engineering and technology from a low base. Yet female participation in the professional fields generally has increased over 11 per cent (Bell 2009):

> As is the case across most of the developed world, women have long held top spot in the 'typically female' professions of education and health (where women are three out of four Australian students and a quarter of professors), food and hospitality, the arts and humanities, and creative arts (where two thirds are female) (University World News 2009).

The UNESCO Digest (2009) found that men outnumber women 'in engineering, manufacturing and construction in all countries for which data were available', with the opposite proving true 'for the cohort of graduates in education, humanities and arts, social sciences, business and law, and health and welfare, where, in almost nine out of ten countries women outnumber men'. Even then, a concentration of women does not necessarily translate into research leadership. Collins et al. (2011) found multiple factors explained the difference to female academics' advancement as leaders in New Zealand universities: university environment; invisible rules; work relationships; proactivity; and personal circumstances. To this I would add increased institutional differentiation and the changing nature and intensification of academic labour.

# Institutional differentiation and branding

Heightened global competition in higher education has changed the rules of the game, making research *the* indicator of quality in university rankings (Marginson 2010). National research discourses focus on quality (world excellence) and innovation (applied research and entrepreneurialism) on the one hand and efficiency and alignment with national priorities on the other. Both governments and funders demand more immediate returns for investment. The 1990s emphasis on research capacity building and quantity saw an increase in female participation as students and academics. But research assessment (ERA), with its focus on quality, institutional differentiation and research performance, together with compacts, has encouraged university executives to specialise and strategically position each university in niche markets. The argument in the Australian context is that universities can no longer afford to offer everything to everyone, thus putting the notion of a liberal comprehensive university under threat. Re-branding and the identification of strategic research foci produces more differentiated systems of education, such as in the US and Canada, between research-intensive, comprehensive teaching and research and undergraduate or teaching institutions. In terms of equity, these usually produce gender-gap salary differentials, with women in the majority in the colleges, non-research, more generalist or third-stream institutions (Gordon and Whitchurch 2010). Already the ERA repositions smaller and newer universities without strong research environments as struggling to survive (e.g. the amalgamation between the regional University of Ballarat and the Gippsland campus of Monash in 2013). Greater differentiation within the system will impact on the quality of teaching when dissociated from a research base and creates an underclass of students, largely in regional and newer universities, which recruit most of the students from lower socio-economic and more educationally diverse backgrounds.

# Leading research: Normative science and the unbundling of academic labour

Policy creates markets, and allocates values as well as resources. Policy is symbolic of what counts, discursively conflating science and technology with innovation in public discourses. The 'quality' and efficiency government agendas have also led to reductionist measures based on metrics in research assessment (Besley 2010). ERA is just one driver that enhances the advantage of those in the male-dominated material or 'hard' sciences relative to the social sciences. Particular forms of 'scientific capital' (Bourdieu 1988) are valued more. These agendas have changed the disciplinary practices of research in the social sciences and humanities, with large concentrations of female scholars and students where quality and esteem factors, the game changers in the field, are often individually-written books and even edited collections, not journal articles.

Institutional policies also skew towards the hard sciences as more 'productive' while contributing lack of student demand to the downsizing of the humanities and social sciences (e.g. Latrobe University, University of Melbourne). In anticipation of some form of research assessment since 2003, universities foregrounded research in strategic plans; created distinctiveness through research centres and built capacity; reconfigured disciplines to create research concentrations; formed collaborative research networks; intensified and sped up research training; recruited star graduate students and researchers; and heightened competition for research funds (Blackmore 2009b). 'Big science' is where women are not research leaders (e.g. Collaborative Research Centres). Cross-institutional and international collaborations rely on big money through industry networks and academic mobility, which women tend not to have to the same degree (Jons 2011; Metcalfe and Slaughter 2008).

Research assessment has had flow-on effects. First, the audit culture means universities now require individual academics to align their research with faculty, university and national priorities through performance appraisal. In practice, performance management becomes a form of internal and internalising control of academics by managers in the production of the high-performing (and conforming) academic (Bansel and Davies 2010). Implicitly, the threat in enterprise bargaining is that research and teaching positions can be made 'redundant' to university priorities. Managers now scrutinise those organisational units defined by ERA as 'low-quality', even though they do not coincide with fields of research (FoR) codes. Often poor performance of a FoR was more a consequence of misjudged institutional tactics and poorly constituted fields of research categories than poor quality research. The audit culture also means that academics need to be managed better through centralised strategic plans so they do not research 'whatever they want'. The well-managed researcher now strategises in performance plans what research they do, who they do it with, how they do it, where they publish it, and ostensibly whether it aligns with institutional and national goals. Much of this performative work requires some fabrication to achieve the necessary alignment (Ball 2000; Blackmore and Sachs 2007).

Secondly, all universities are emulating the research-intensive universities, resulting in an increased diversification and unbundling of academic labour. Because ERA 'counts' the 'output' of all research active academic staff within a field of research named by the university, universities are increasingly differentiating between academics based on level of research 'activity' and use-value (active researcher/teacher). An academic's notional core work of teaching, research and service has been unbundled into research-only, teaching and research, and teaching-only positions (Macfarlane 2011). This trend favours research-intensive universities with well-established science and technology concentrations and industry, government and philanthropic partnerships (Metcalfe and Slaughter 2008).

Thirdly, research assessment has paradoxically reinvigorated disciplinarity through abstract fields of research codes at a time when knowledge economy discourses and university restructuring focus on interdisciplinarity, applied research partnerships and collaboration in large teams. At the same time, institutional restructuring has led the social sciences, humanities and arts to be amalgamated into larger faculties redesigned into new 'disciplinary formations' (e.g. creative industries) while seeking efficiency. Individual sociologists, historians and anthropologists are increasingly embedded within interdisciplinary centres, focusing on applied problems with social, medical, material sciences and technology. One consequence is that disciplinary training in the numerically feminised fields of social sciences and humanities is increasingly reliant on elite institutions. Another is that the social sciences and humanities as heterogeneous disciplines are assumed to have one voice among multiple voices of the material, biological and cognitive sciences at the executive table. The shrinking of the fields of social science and humanities, as languages previously, not only skews university priorities and profiles towards the 'hard' sciences but endangers long-term sustainability in terms of building disciplinarity capacity in what have traditionally been feminised fields. At the same time, ERA highlights ambiguity in the notion of what constitutes a discipline or field of study and the contradictory policies around interdisciplinarity. For example, education characterised as a field of research never 'scores' well in research assessments internationally or in Australia (Furlong and Lawn 2011). Education is characterised by its multidisciplinarity, its inclusion of scholarship on teaching practice, its professional orientation and its high level of feminisation (Seddon 2013). Women's studies, highly interdisciplinary, are under threat. Torr (2006, 60) argues that in the UK:

> full-time positions in women's studies departments are limited and subject areas outside of women's studies are still largely organized along traditional disciplinary lines ... the setting of stricter guidelines for postgraduate training at a national level ... limits the extent to which graduate level programmes can be interdisciplinary in nature.

# Implications for women as research leaders

Research assessment in Australia as elsewhere has led to a focus on research leadership and recruitment, quality and excellence. Workloads are increasingly based on incremental point systems that require sustained if not escalating performance in terms not only of publication and grant churn but also leadership and service. Universities have ratcheted up expectations of all academics to publish in particular journals and to measure their achievements by citations while also informing policy and practice. Promotion committees utilise measurable indicators (ranking of journals, student evaluations, citations) as proxies for quality. A new academic habitus is being produced as academics internalise these expectations and processes of assessment (Bansel et al. 2008). This ratcheting up of expectations of 'quality' research *and* teaching *and* service has led to academic overload with a number of gendered effects. While both men and women enter postdoctoral research-only appointments, the early trend suggests that teaching-only appointments will become the default positions for tenured early-career women academics, impacting significantly on their academic status and career prospects as traditional teaching and research appointments decline (quoted in Lane 2012). International studies indicate that women are exiting the sciences as a consequence of these rising expectations and conditions (Bell 2009; Guderley 2013).

Furthermore, the increased scope, scale and depth of what constitutes research leadership means track record 'relative to opportunity' that recognises women's broken career trajectories is often ignored in committees where sustained track record dominates. Having children is not the norm. Yet:

> life choices (to delay entering the academy, to undertake periods of part-time or casual work, to commence a career as a research assistant, to have children, to care for aging parents) do not alter one's capacity to produce high quality research outcomes, nor indeed to produce 'breakthrough research', but they may impact on the quantum of research productivity, the strength of research networks and mentors, professional mobility and therefore profile (Bell and Bentley 2005, 1).

A sustained research record is not only unsustainable for most, but also limits how we understand excellence and quality. 'Although research is only one strand of academic work (in tandem with teaching and community service) research has, in the modern university, been accorded higher status as the defining feature of the academic enterprise' (Bell and Bentley 2005, 358). Furthermore, research policies are premised upon a normative model of big science – large teams, scaled-up projects, industry partnerships, individual and institutional collaboration and research concentrations. Yet reward systems are premised upon academic hierarchies with a few individual winners.

The logic of sustained research record encourages the unbundling of research from teaching and is most evident in the research-intensive universities where women in research are in decline.

## % academics who are women (excl. casuals)

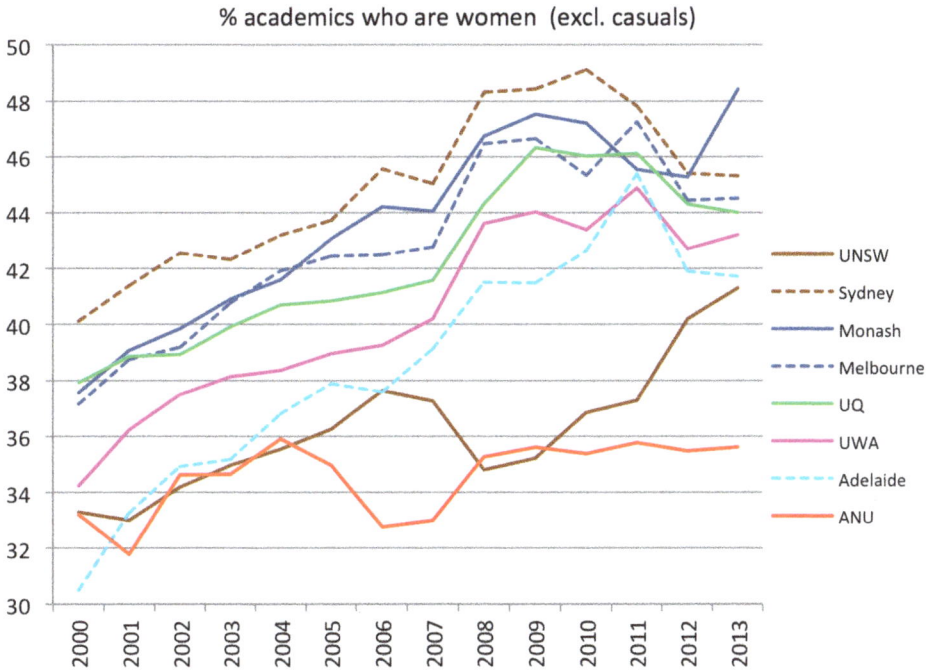

**Figure 11.1: Gender bender: Women in academic decline**

Source: Susan Feteris, with permission. Retrieved 17 February 2014, with data from http://education. gov.au/staff-data.

Feteris (2013, also cited in Lane 2012) argues that the decade of expansion of funding and capacity post-2000 saw female academic numbers in the Go8 universities increase to 50 per cent, followed by a post-ERA decline in research-only roles and an increase of women in teaching-only roles of 10 per cent. 'Many Go8 staff who took voluntary departure or forced redundancy packages were women' (Feteris cited in Lane 2012). Women lose out as they tend to do more teaching and pastoral care and thus are readily made redundant. Students also lose out as key researchers focus on research-only and not research and teaching, as opposed to the US where star professors are also expected to teach (as evident in MOOCs).

Finally, research leadership is contingent on mobility, flexibility, industry and government connections to source funding. Metcalfe and Slaughter (2008) argue that private funds tend to be in the areas of technology, and material and biological sciences, while women tend to be concentrated in the health sciences, law, social sciences, arts and humanities – fields more reliant on community, government and social philanthropy. As higher education becomes more globalised, mobility is necessary to attend conferences, teach and develop research collaborations: 'Higher education is increasingly a globalised occupation in which workers are expected to participate in global activities and to have skills, expertise and attributes that are of world standing' to gain promotion to the professoriate (Boden and Epstein 2006, 252; Boltanski and Chiapello 2005). While internationalisation and cross-national research collaborations offer new possibilities, this is often at a financial and personal cost to academics, particularly early-career academics with young families as they tend not to have discretionary research funds to draw upon. At the same time, university employers push in enterprise bargaining for flexibility by extending the hours that academic (and professional staff) work with online technologies, allowing teaching to occur any place any time. Technologies are a two-edged sword: facilitating working from home and therefore more family-friendly, but also invading private time and space. Again, research indicates that women tend to do more domestic work when working at home than male academics due to the lack of change in the domestic gender division of labour: the workplace is respite (Coates et al. 2010).

## Managing research and the gender division of labour

The focus on research has produced a proliferation of managers of research (academic and non-academic) as it now requires 'managed alignment' of the individual to the collective research enterprise, institutional plans and specialisms, and national priorities stated in university compacts. The intensified focus on managing research has produced a proliferation of pro vice-chancellors (PVCs) and deputy vice-chancellors (DVCs). While there is recognition that research managers at DVC and PVC level need to have credibility in terms of a research profile, that credibility is associated with science. Scott et al. (2011) in a large-scale study found that of the 21 who identified as being in PVC and DVC positions, 19 were male with disciplinary backgrounds in the Natural and Physical Sciences (13/31) followed by Society and Culture (6/31), Education (4/31) and Health (4/31). Most DVCs of Research have backgrounds in the material and biological sciences and most are male. This reproduces the gender division of labour between Humanities and Social Sciences (HASS) and Science, Technology, Engineering and Maths within research management and hegemonic mindsets that impacts on the rules of the research game institutionally in terms of the distribution of funds (e.g. scholarships, post-doctoral fellows, grants and awards). It confirms the invisible micro-politics of gender that associates particular forms of knowledge, authority and leadership within the academy (Morley 2013a).

# Reconfiguration of the academic workforce: Diversification, de-professionalisation and casualisation

The focus on research is occurring at the same time that academic work is being reconfigured, marked by its casualisation and feminisation (ABS 2012). Teaching is being unbundled into instructional design, tutoring, assessment and technical support, all undertaken by 'experts' with blended learning (multimodal online/ face-to-face) (McWilliam and Taylor 1998). While this provides scope for the professionalisation of administrative work (itself feminised) and the emergent field of e-learning and ICT (Gordon and Whitchurch 2010), arguably it signals a de-professionalisation of academic work (Shapper and Mayson 2008). Research is also being unbundled due to the blurring/merging of academic and administrative roles. Women with doctorates are moving into research administration rather than staying as academics, as it is understood to be a more 'controllable' environment (Whitchurch 2013). Meanwhile, academics have become amateur managers of research supported by an ever-expanding cadre of specialist full-time research management professionals (Whitchurch 2013). 'Contradictory tensions surrounding the historical and cultural meaning of female identity and female work are played out' (Dillabough and Acker 2005, 129) as new fields of feminised administrative work in research are developing at the same time that teaching is being feminised and de-professionalised and research is re-masculinised.

Overall, the conditions of academic work are radically altering with the rise of contractualism. Institutional flexibility is reliant on the casualisation and intensification of academic labour (Reay 2000).[2] The rapid increase of research-only contract positions is reliant on soft money, encouraging grant churn to attract funds to maintain their employment. Contracts are also being proposed for the professoriate as they are increasingly incorporated into line management in performance appraisal and pseudo-employment relationships. Researchers now recruit, manage and undertake performance reviews of staff as management/ administration has been dispersed down. New learning and management technologies and the accumulation of big data for digital archives are upscaling the management work of research. This intensification drains academic time and energy, produces anxiety, and diverts and detracts from research. Bexley et al. (2011) found that two-thirds of Australian academics in their sample feel the job is now overwhelming.

---

2   In Australia, the staff:student ratio has trebled since 1996, a trend exacerbated with the caps removed from enrolments, with casual staff accounting for more than half of staff increases while continuing staff decreased from 63.6 per cent to 59.3 per cent (Junor 2004; Coates et al. 2010).

# The next generation?

Academic life is marked by ambivalence, contradiction and paradox (Hearn 2000; Blackmore and Sachs 2007). The self-managing academic both opposes and accommodates the corporatisation of their everyday practice as they struggle between the dulling effects of compliance regimes and their desire to excel, being both competitive and collegial (Bansel and Davies 2010). At the same time, they are sidelined as decision-makers, experts and creative agents within their own institutions (Boden and Epstein 2006). Due to the normative pressures of science, particular fields of research are becoming redefined, offloaded or more difficult to do, in terms of who does research with whom and what research gets done.

This has implications for the future generation of researchers. First, in terms of the pipeline from graduate into the academy. While there are significantly higher numbers of women in undergraduate programs, this decreases in areas of science, technology and engineering as they progress to postgraduate. From 2002–10 a higher proportion of Australian graduate students are in information technology (29 per cent), agriculture, environment and related studies (28 per cent) and management and commerce (25 per cent), with the greatest expansion in engineering compared to smaller expansion in health and education and a small reduction in social science and larger fall in management (ABS 2012). Thus research resources and university infrastructure have moved significantly towards the 'hard sciences' and technology, where there are fewer women.

Secondly, the image of the star female academic moving up to become a professor by building a sustained research record is becoming more distant for many young women (Diezmann and Grieshaber 2009). A Berkeley study of one thousand graduate students (Mason 2008) demonstrated a significant gender gap of 10 per cent between male students who saw an academic career, and female students who saw choices between having children and being a research professor, of more likely moving to follow a partner and being less able to maintain sustained research, and therefore more likely to be in teaching. Furthermore, female graduates are much more likely than their male counterparts to complete their PhD as a solo project and less likely to be part of a research group and to pursue their PhD for intrinsic motivations such as intellectual and academic development, personal satisfaction, or interest rather than career (Dever et al. 2008). Being involved in a research group for four years develops the collaborative and networking skills most likely to impact on future employment opportunities and career paths (Dever et al. 2008, 1). Among graduate students, a higher proportion of women were in insecure and part-time jobs, with the gender difference most pronounced in research-intensive universities and for those with children. Fewer females were in supervisory or managerial positions and 90 per cent of male graduates and 69 per cent of females with children were working full-time (Dever et al. 2008). Bexley et al. (2011) found that most early-career researchers, while committed to their discipline, to research, and to teaching, have long-term plans of exiting the sector or moving overseas due to levels of stress, lack of tenure and work overload.

## Conclusion

The above trends have implications for both gender equity and universities. Universities are less family friendly for everyone, but more so for women. Current workloads and expectations exacerbate existing incompatibilities between work and life (Pillay et al. 2013). The skewing of Australian universities towards the sciences and technology also means there is a shrinking pool of available courses and supervisors to build research capacity in HASS and limits the ways in which HASS provides different ways of understanding the world. Equally, Scheibinger and Schraudner (2011) argue that science, medicine and engineering cannot claim excellence without greater involvement of women researchers.

But this is about more than increasing the percentage of women into science and technology or leadership. It is about the nature and role of the 21st-century university and the challenge to notions of the liberal comprehensive university. As MacIntrye (2010, 36) argues, the Bradley Review mentions briefly the importance of universities 'as a cornerstone of our legal, social, economic and cultural institutions' then fails to elaborate on what that means. Policies around the knowledge economy refer to responsiveness, relevance, rankings, international best practice and instant, obvious and measurable use-value but not the public good. Macintyre (2010) argues that the distinctiveness of the university in a democratic society is that it encourages independent critical thinking and is not totally framed by advanced capitalism. This distinctiveness requires both academic freedom and critical inquiry – both central to innovation – and a degree of institutional autonomy (Blackmore 2003; Marginson and Considine 2000). Macfarlane (2010) argues for the need to revive the notion of intellectual leadership within the academy, to reassert the role of the academic to be a critic and advocate. Academic leadership informs critical professional practice, critiques policy, and provides an intellectual forum that widens the notion of public interest and public good. Neoliberal policy reduces universities to the production of instrumental knowledge premised upon economic values that ignores the social and political role of universities, renders them as just another transnational corporation out to make a profit. Marginson (2011, 411) comments: 'If the work of higher education institutions is defined simply as the aggregation of private interests, this evaporates the rationale for higher education institutions as distinctive social foundations with multiple public and private roles. The private benefits could be produced elsewhere.'

Martha Nussbaum (2010) argues that the focus on profit offers an impoverished view of education and of what constitutes powerful research, which can produce a good society for everyone. Ackers (2000, 2) identifies a 'tie between gender and an organisation's most fundamental values and practices ... that contributes to such problems as inefficient decisions, unclear expectations and excessive controls'. The deep instrumentalism and functionality of neoliberal policies lacks any understanding of collegiality, collaboration and the premises of academic professionalism based on mutuality and trust or how diverse ontologies, epistemologies and politics are more likely to lead to greater 'productivity', and are more conducive to research and a better society. Ohrn et al. (2009, 4) reflect in the European context on the contradictions within contemporary gender relations in academia that 'on the one hand traditional masculinities are losing ground as growing numbers of women position themselves in research, and on the other hand ... pressures from a performative culture strengthen structures working to the disadvantage of women and other groups not traditionally in power'.

# 12. Functional Dystopia: Diversity, Contestability and New Media in the Academy

Jenny Corbett, Andrew MacIntyre and Inger Mewburn

## Introduction

Many scholars in the Social Sciences today are concerned that growing pressures for applied or policy-relevant research, and the importance placed on external research funding, are having systemically negative influences upon academic life. Academics generally are expressing concern that reduced public funding, more reliance on student fees as the mainstay of revenue and a rise in 'managerialism' in response to closer regulatory scrutiny, divert universities from their core business and traditional values. Our view is more positive. We make three arguments to this effect. First, we believe implicit comparisons with a notional happier past are themselves problematic. Secondly, the multiplicity of funding sources now underwriting academic research has created greater contestability in the market for ideas – something we believe is strongly positive. Thirdly, while there are certainly unwelcome constraints on researchers at the margins of casual employment (a growing portion of the academic population), we do not see increasing marketisation and the rise of new technology as necessarily oppressive – indeed, they can generate new modes of academic practice. In this chapter, we offer a preliminary sketch of our main contentions, rather than a detailed elaboration and defence.

In the first section of the chapter, we address the myth of a golden age of university independence. To many it feels as if along with changed, and generally tighter, funding, has come a greater demand for accountability and scrutiny plus an uncomfortable exposure to competitive market pressures even though the social value of education means that it cannot be judged solely by economic criteria. But the evidence of history and international comparison tells a different story. The balance between external intervention and academic independence changes over time and place. If the immediate post-Second World War period was one of relatively relaxed oversight of universities, accompanied by a belief in the role of governments to provide public goods and rebuild cultural and social capital in the Anglo-Saxon world, that was specific to a time and place in history. It was not a norm and it is no longer the basis for realistic policy. Nostalgia for a particular historical moment can create myopia and confused thinking.

In the next section we weigh the disadvantages of less certainty of funding against the advantage of independence from a single source of support. Over the last two decades we have certainly witnessed a changing balance in sources of funding, with increasing importance of student fees and the associated pressure for responsiveness to student preferences. Alongside this has been a surge in regulatory controls on government research funding schemes together with the growing importance of contract and consultancy funding for research. Combined, factors of this sort generated sharp concerns within the academic community ranging from perceived rampant managerialism and excessive commercialisation, to degradation of scholarly independence (Ginsberg 2011; Hil 2012; Nussbaum 2010; Thornton 2008, 2009). As we will discuss, while funding changes have certainly brought challenges, such arguments understate the fact that reduced reliance on a single source of funding can bring advantages of increased contestability and independence.

In the final section, we note the exciting opportunities brought by new technology. Coupled with the changes in funding sources and accountabilities is the growth of new technology and digital media, particularly social media and content-management systems that enable educational materials – once the closeted preserve of the individual professor who hiked across campus with their slide carousel – to be released, open and free of charge on the internet via large, corporate providers such as EdX and Coursera. This trend, which Weller (2011) calls a turn to the 'pedagogy of abundance', signals a world where, as he points out, talent is no longer scarce or hard to locate, content has been translated from the slide deck to intangible (and infinitely transportable) 'bits', available on demand 24 hours a day to a global audience.

In conclusion, we do not entirely disagree with the many who have pointed out the damage – even violence – these technological and workplace changes have done to traditional notions of academic identity and freedom – but we take a tempered view and hope to move the debate beyond this stage. Clegg (2008) outlines a range of responses to what she calls (after Barnett 2003) 'pernicious ideologies' of the contemporary university, including quality and audit controls, the 'seemingly malign influence of managerialist practices', consumerism and undermining of autonomy and respect for academics and their work. There is a large and growing body of literature that identifies (and bemoans) the 'casualisation' of the academic workforce. Kimber (2003) claims that structural changes in Australia have brought into being a two-tiered system with a 'tenured core and a tenuous periphery' and the end of clear career paths for academics. This literature has had little, if any, tangible effect on changing the workplace practices it criticises. It is clear that new lines of critique need to be developed, ones that acknowledge growth, increasing complexity and change as ever present and inevitable within our universities, and recognise the new possibilities they raise.

Well-reasoned, elegantly-argued critiques, as valid as we think they are, have not been accepted by politicians and the public. In part, it must be acknowledged, this is a product of the chronic obstacles to university leaders speaking with a strong and unified voice. More broadly, too often academics come across in the media as seeking to preserve entitlements in an era when others are having to go without job certainty or the ability to pursue the work they really want to do. Why should academics and universities be treated differently? This is a hard argument to counter and one that has not been well served by much of the analysis to emerge from universities themselves. We do not answer those questions here but we do bring an understanding of the role of the new in the contemporary university to bear on these old problems.

## The myth of the golden age

In their entertaining history of The Australian National University (ANU), Foster and Varghese (2009) paint a picture of the Honourable John Dedman laying the foundation stone of University House on the 24 October 1949. The then Vice-Chancellor of ANU, Sir Douglas Berry Copland, sitting in the audience, listened to a speech that would have warmed the heart of any contemporary vice-chancellor. The university, opined Dedman, should continue to operate without the messy intrusion of party politics. Free to pursue knowledge for the highest purpose, said the minister, ANU should have no strings attached to its income, other than in the broadest terms. Vice-Chancellor Copland leaned over, so the story goes, to congratulate Dedman's boss, Prime Minister Ben Chifley, on this fine speech from his minister. We can only imagine Copland's chagrin when Chifley treated him to a dose of cold, hard political reality.

Yes, it was a great speech, Chifley agreed, but the trouble with Minister Dedman was 'he really believes it' (Foster and Varghese 2009, 114).

The little vignette is telling: from almost the first moment the national university was tangled up in politics – as are all Australian universities and most others around the world. This is also a reminder that some of the discussion about what is wrong with universities today may be guilty of nostalgia for a mythical golden age of the university, when individual scholars engaged in uninterrupted creative thought on deep questions of their own devising, free of external oversight. Furthermore, the backward-looking argument that we should return to a time that was more conducive to academic life is unlikely to be helpful in considering whether we now have the right policy settings to get us where we need to be. Contemporary universities' tasks are complex, with objectives ranging from technical and vocational training to solving the moral and practical challenges of our age by brave, iconoclastic thinking, sometimes within the same institution. Inevitably, this means that in defining 'what universities are for', measuring their performance and designing their governance, regulation cannot be easy. Any pursuit of single, standardised models by either academics or government will be quite problematic.

Marginson and Considine (2000) outline new trends in governance structures which include the rise of executive power and corresponding decline of 'disciplinary' (academic) power to set priorities and direction for academic work. However, the problem of the modern 'multiversity', as Collini (2012) dubs it, has old roots – there never was a golden age when universities were pure seats of higher learning unfettered by the demands of practical masters, whether church or state. Governments have, for centuries now, pulled the university's strings all around the world. The desire by the paymasters to exert 'remote control' over what academics do and how they do it is nothing new. In his book, *Academic Charisma and the Origins of the Research University*, Clark (2006) discusses the German system of the late Enlightenment, from which we draw many of our academic traditions, including the PhD. Clark cites the work of Johann Justi from the 1760s, whom he calls the 'Adam Smith of Prussian "police science"' (what today might be called political science). Justi noticed that the academics of his time tended to ignore financial rewards and he stressed the need for academics to have the freedom to pursue their work in the way they saw fit – *so long as these aligned with the needs of the state*. Justi foreshadowed the role of higher education auditing agencies, such as the Tertiary Education Quality and Standards Agency (TEQSA). As Clark (2006, 12) puts it, Justi argued that:

> The state must set up inspectors for wares, as well as a system of seals or labels to indicate ranges of excellence in products. When the state notices that some products, including academic ones, are inferior, then prizes and payments ought to be instituted to encourage invention.

In a move that echoes contemporary public servants carrying out government objectives from within an education department, Justi argued that, if needs be, external experts should be brought in to enforce these standards, since 'for money one can attain anything' (2006, 12). The practice of oversight on academic work pre-dates even the beginnings of the 'police state' in northern Europe. Clark outlines the processes behind 'visitations' of the clergy to the proto-university cathedral schools in the 13th and 14th centuries. The visitation practice involved senior bishops and officials travelling around the countryside inspecting the conduct of teachers and monks and looking for 'improvement' since their last visit. Interestingly, there is evidence that these early academics resisted such audit-like practices. Clark claims that the visitations to Franciscan foundations in 1232 and 1239 'appeared so inquisitorial that the poor friars took the visitors for spies and hated them' (2006, 341).

Clearly, we cannot plausibly hark back to a golden age when the state, or the church, provided unlimited funding and left us alone to pursue whatever 'pure' research we wanted and when students studied whatever we told them to. Life was never thus. And we also cannot champion such a system and, having been left alone to develop new lines of enquiry and fields of research and make remarkable discoveries, then be appalled by the fact that the users of research increasingly want to engage with the production of research both inside and outside universities.

Within universities too, simplistic thinking about 'value-free', 'pure' research is surely a thing of the past. The self-aware researcher recognises that there is, and should be, a constant struggle about how much our inherited norms enter all academic work. At what point does the mainstream way of thinking become an impediment to originality and what is the fate of the iconoclast who challenges too soon? There is no right answer about who should choose the questions for research or how they should be researched. A subject is not made irrelevant or illegitimate for academic study because a policymaker (or the Queen) poses the question. The danger is when the pursuit of apparently 'irrelevant questions' (i.e. not immediately of practical relevance) is blocked. But in fact current critics overstate this danger: present policy settings in Australia, particularly those concerned with ERA research assessment and impact, for the most part do almost the opposite. They do not reward media professors and impact does not, in any of the variants, mean being on TV responding to the issues of the moment with no underlying research evidence. The new regulatory, management and governance regimes are not killing the culture of academia – but they are certainly changing it; for the worse in some respects and for some individuals, but also for the better. Most of us would agree that regulatory change that reduces male and white privilege is a positive step, as are checks to ensure minimal teaching standards and the transparent storage of scientific data to facilitate experimental replicability.

This historical perspective is important in considering the cocktail of pressures facing Australian and other higher education sectors: tight public funding, increased regulation, greater competition for students, faculty and professional staff, together with major technological change. As Sharrock (2012, 324) points out, institutional leaders 'must handle a Rubik's cube of Rubik's cubes', where growth in the size and complexity of institutional management has resulted in 'elaborate systems' which are required to manage (and report on) the activities of the contemporary university. As Sharrock puts it (2012, 323), universities face the 'eternal strategic dilemma of infinite mission and finite means' without the 'avuncular mix of funded growth, low competitive pressure and loose performance expectations, which characterised the 1970s'.

Our quick tour of the history of universities shows that while these are not new pressures, it is now more clearly understood by academics and private citizens (who are increasingly consumers of higher education) that the multiplicity of functions of universities leads to a variety of outcomes that represent both private and public benefits. The public benefit, while hard to define in developed countries (easier to demonstrate in developing ones where the impact on growth is clear), is not completely dismissed in principle even by the most ardent managerialist free-marketeer, though its scale is contested. It underpins the case for some element of public funding for at least part of the higher education sector. The private benefit to individual recipients of university education (in terms of generally higher salaries for graduates than non-graduates) is similarly not disputed but its value, too, is much debated, leading to dispute about how much the user should pay. The very complexity of the university as a contemporary institution adds to the difficulty of knowing whether universities are 'doing their job' and who should pay.

## Funding and freedom

If ongoing change in the university sector is a constant, one of the most widely discussed dimensions of recent change is the funding of universities. As former Stanford University President Gerhard Casper (2010, 1) has put it, 'these are the best of times and worst of times for universities'. These are the best of times as, almost everywhere, the dominant discourse is of the centrality of universities in a globalised knowledge economy. And these are also the worst of times especially for public universities, 'because as governments face extraordinary budget shortfalls due to their spendthrift ways and the sharp economic recession, they do not generally assign higher education and research funding the priority that their emphasis on innovation would suggest. They do not put their money where their mouth is.'

The recent circumstances sharpen the old question of the value of the university, which matters because it affects societies' views of who should pay for universities. The economic view that beneficiaries should pay is 'incentive compatible' and therefore efficient. This means that those who benefit have an incentive to pay for the service and, if the provider fails to deliver, to cut their support or vote with their feet. That is why the argument has become influential in global policy circles. The logic is correct but there is a big risk that the public benefit of universities is undervalued, with the result that too little overall investment is made, since private beneficiaries will not pay for the public externalities. This is one, but not the only, fear of those who decry the move to 'co-payment' by students (the other being fairness and impact on poorer students). Another concern about heavy reliance on student fee income is that the academic purpose will be distorted (deflected) towards the demands of 'customers' who, in the extreme view, do not really know what is important and valuable in the enterprise in which they are engaged.

At the same time the opposite fear, that publicly-funded universities will be interfered with and misdirected towards activities determined by the paymasters (governments – and ultimately tax payers), is often voiced by the same critics. By implication, there is some other world in which universities are funded by benefactors who require no accountability and who express no views about what universities should do. As Capano (2011) shows, across a range of different models of university governance, the one constant is a continually changing balance between government or market control and the 'independence' of the university. Yet the plethora of models still produces quality outcomes assessed against objectives of increasing access (student numbers), original research, technical advances and economic benefits. No single governance or funding model, it seems, outperforms all others. While there are some global common trends, there is no convergence. This does not imply that governance and funding models are irrelevant but that we need to look elsewhere to understand what makes great universities and what kind of interference inhibits them.

In Australia, we are currently seeing the generalised phenomenon of funding pressure played out starkly. Indeed, if anything, Australia has been out of step with other wealthy countries in that government funding for universities in general, and research in particular, has actually increased in recent years (Commonwealth of Australia 2011, 17–8). We are now moving painfully into the very much tighter budgetary circumstances of many other countries. No less contentious than the issue of the quantum of government funding is the profile or character of funding. A recent Group of Eight discussion paper (2013, 4) sets the matter out clearly:

> … many universities are operating in a funding environment that requires them to become more responsive to the immediate needs of business or society, a situation exacerbated by the growing cost of research and the increased reluctance of all funding bodies to pay the full costs of the research they commission. In seeking financial support from a broader range of sources, universities are coming under pressure to produce short-term practical outcomes, to commercialise, and to chase funding, no matter what the implications of winning it …

Taken to its extreme, this approach could prevent universities from making their really significant, fundamental contributions to economic, social and cultural development or environmental sustainability; and could ultimately lead to more fragile and less resilient societies.

We agree with this assessment. However, we also believe that the current situation is not as bad as often depicted and need not necessarily be taken to anything like its possible extreme. There can be little doubt that, other things being equal, the greater a university's dependence on short-term funding, the less the scope for the type of research that requires sustained independent scholarly inquiry. This is a particular challenge in the physical and natural sciences, given the typically high infrastructure costs and multi-investigator projects, but is nonetheless a challenge too for the social sciences.

Certainly we must ask to what extent the expanding phenomenon of contract grants and consultancy work is compromising the character and independence of scholarly research. While it is true that some entities commissioning research seek to define very tightly the subject of research work, its outcomes and even ownership, this is not a universal phenomenon. Indeed, our personal experience and wider anecdotal evidence suggests a growing awareness on the part of research-funders of the changing dynamics and challenges of the contemporary university environment.

For instance, there appears to be widespread recognition among government agencies that the era of education and/or science and technology ministries adequately funding the full range of research needs is long past. Specialised agencies right across the public spectrum are increasingly reaching out to universities and investing in multi-year agreements in order to stimulate research. We have experienced this with agencies ranging from social security to finance, from environment to defence, from international development assistance to taxation. In our experience, the primary motivation of the funding agency is very often to sponsor new and creative thinking. It is precisely the independent and uncontrolled nature of academic thinking they are seeking to fund; they have highly educated staff of their own (not infrequently with doctorates), but these staff think and work within the tightly specified incentive structures and hierarchies of officialdom.

Furthermore, prospective funding agencies are drawn not just to the reality of independent analysis, but also to the perception and prestige of independent analysis, for the powerful legitimating benefits this can bring to their intramural policy battles within the government sector as well as their efforts to lead public thinking on particular issues. So strong is the interest of government agencies across the spectrum that not only are they increasingly prepared to invest substantial sums from their own operating budgets, but they are writing funding agreements specifically delegating very high levels of research independence to the scholars involved: for example, only designating a minor portion of the budget for research on topics requested by the funder – with the rest explicitly at the discretion of the researchers. Speaking again from our direct experiences and those reported by colleagues in other universities, somewhat surprisingly, investments in research from the business sector seem to come with, if anything, fewer – rather than more – strings attached. In part this is likely to be a function of stricter reporting and accountability requirements on the use of public money and the greater freedom that businesses have to decide on the use of their own money. But we have also experienced remarkably enlightened thinking among corporate decision-makers about the importance of independent and long-range scholarly research capabilities and a preparedness to mobilise funds in support of it.

The advent of new technology raises the intriguing question of whether we could think more broadly about what constitutes a funding base. Could we use the internet as an additional strategy to widen funding for academia and academics, and loosen the grip of funders with other agendas? The experiment in research crowdsourcing by Deakin University is an interesting development. Here researchers make a pitch directly to the public to fund research for its intrinsic worth. Some might see this kind of private money from citizens as more 'pure' than the national priorities of the government or donations from large private companies.

As this chapter was being written, Deakin University researchers were trialling the use of Pozible.com, a crowd-funding site, to generate seed funding for short research projects. The 'kick backs' to the crowd-funders are transparent on the site. Along with a 'pitch' explaining the value of the research was a clear outline of what you could expect for a $2, $30 and $50 donation. The project, led by Professor Deborah Verhoven with a multi-disciplinary team, concentrated on enhancing the researchers' social media strategies, thus building an 'audience' for their research both with social media. Of the seven projects which pitched through Pozible.com, six reached their funding targets.[1]

However exciting the Pozible work done by Deakin is, for now, the most desirable position for a university is to have a large portion of its resource base being made up of reliable longer-term funding. This underpins its ability to recruit and retain the most sought-after scholars and house them within a critical mass of intellectually diverse colleagues who can sustain long-term data-gathering, debate and theoretical inquiry. But given that such funding is becoming scarcer in relative terms, universities and individual academics are seeking alternative forms of funding in an effort to improve their ability to pursue institutional and individual academic objectives.

We certainly do not mean to suggest that there is a readily accessible and abundant supply of 'academic-friendly' research funding waiting to be harvested. Nor are we under any illusion that a substantial (if unspecified) portion of contract-type research funding does not come with very significant controls. And, above all, we are acutely mindful of the heightened challenge presented by contract-type funding to the prestige of universities if individual academics leave themselves open to the perception and reality of material conflicts of interest by failing systematically and proactively to publicise their sources of funding. But these considerations notwithstanding, we do maintain that this new funding frontier is much less bleak than often portrayed and, moreover, is one that, as both individual scholars and university officers, we approach with a good deal of optimism.

Finally, we also contend that there is something inherently healthy – in terms of academic vitality – to greater diversity of funding sources and greater contestability of these sources. Put differently, while a core of predictable longer-term funding is a necessary ingredient for universities, we do not believe the quality and independence of research is maximised by that funding all coming from a single Ministry of Education-type source. The examples of leading North American public and private universities are one illustration of this. What matters is that there needs to be reasonable predictability about resource flows over the medium to long term, and a multiplicity of contestable funding sources is probably a preferable option. It is the task of university leaders to navigate these waters and assist individual academics – whether privileged with a tenured appointment or not – in seeking the resources they need to pursue their research ambitions.

---

1    Deakin University. Retrieved 17 December 2013, from http://t.co/8dTkcLslfq.

# Marketisation and technology

No investigation of change in Higher Education would be complete without an examination of new technologies, which open up unexpected opportunities for innovation. Of particular interest is the group of interactive technologies collectively called Web 2.0. These include social media and cloud-based technologies, which together bring the means of production of academic 'stuff' back into the hands of the academic who no longer needs access to large enterprise systems to do authoring and distribution of content. Free online tools enable academics to craft teaching material, generate research data, and share knowledge and expertise on cloud-based, open-sourced software platforms.

With this kind of control over the means of production – and access to the public as direct sponsors of research – academics truly can become 'technopreneurs': making, sharing, remixing and even selling their academic expertise in a worldwide market. For example, the academic who makes a blog and builds an audience may leverage this social media reach by selling books, downloadable resources or their services, as speakers and teachers.

Building academic peer networks also becomes easier in this online environment. The conference circuit used to be the primary vehicle for academics to meet and build relationships outside their institutions; social media sites like Twitter enable peers with mutual interests to meet and build relationships without the cost of an airfare. These peer networks echo existing academic cultures in that they tend to be reciprocal and rely on a common understanding of an academic 'gift economy' (Mewburn and Thomson, 2013). This is most visible on platforms like Twitter where information 'bundles' are offered and taken up on an ad hoc basis and, over time, operate to build networks of trust online (often dominated by a number of opinion leaders). The kind of literacies required for casual academics to take advantage of these new spaces of opportunity are different from those which were required prior to the turn of the century, when many tenured academics entered the academy.

The 'publish or perish' mantra is increasingly being replaced with the imperative to 'be visible or vanish' (thanks to Dr John Lamp for this phrase). However, there may not yet be general recognition within the academic community of this imperative.

What way forward for the individual – and the academy – in such a world? In *Gutenberg to Zuckerberg*, John Naughton points out that we are bad at predicting the disruptive impact of technology. Although bibles were the first things cranked out on Gutenberg's new printing press, the Catholic Church ended up the loser in that particular industrial revolution. Naughton argues that, especially when it comes to technology, we can over-emphasise some changes and entirely miss others.

We are just entering the age of a 'post scarcity' academic economy, characterised by what Weller (2011) deems a 'pedagogy of abundance'. Massive open online courses (MOOCS), which make it possible to access educational material and techniques from premier institutions without paying, challenge the very business model of the university itself. Another challenge is presented in the form of 'micro-credentialism' such as Mozilla's open badges project. Open badges are essentially bits of code that can be issued by anyone (individuals or institutions) to individuals as recognition for participation in learning activities and the attainment and demonstration of skills. Given that there is plenty of teaching and learning material online available for free (including, but in no way limited to, MOOCs), open badges are a way to create a legible learner identity without a singular institution to do the credentialing work.

To see the marketisation of the academy as something to be resisted risks wiping out these new spaces of innovation, which are breeding forms of academia that may help the academy survive the coming abundance crisis. There is obvious potential for conflict between our scarcity model and the abundance of online spaces. Micro-credentialing such as open badges, which turn anyone into an education provider, holds the potential to seriously disrupt our current business model. As the technology commentator and blogger Clay Shirky points out, Napster didn't kill the old music industry — it was the idea of Napster (that you can get just one track, whenever you want, online), that contributed to the collapse of an entire industry. It wasn't the technology, Shirky (2012 blog) is at pains to point out, that is the real issue here — it is the failure of imagination of those within the industries being threatened by new technology. The music industry:

> ... just couldn't imagine — and I mean this in the most ordinarily descriptive way possible — could not imagine that the old way of doing things might fail. Yet things did fail, in large part because, after Napster, the industry's insistence that digital distribution be as expensive and inconvenient as a trip to the record store suddenly struck millions of people as a completely terrible idea.

Journalists are dealing with the disruptive effects of an abundance economy in the form of 'new media' — academics are just late to the digital party. One thing we can learn from the industries that have gone before us is that those who do not embrace change may die.

# Conclusions

What does the debunking of the myth of the golden age, when academia basked in unlimited funding with no strings attached (or at least an avuncular laxity in paying the bills), and a harder look at the pros and cons of diversified funding and the 'marketisation' of the university, tell us about the sense of crisis and frustration that so many academics claim to feel? Principally it suggests that universities and the subjects they research and teach constantly change. There are no 'right' structures to decide what are appropriate subjects for academic study and inclusion in university syllabi. Questions about the value of any particular discipline to the modern university or to society at large (such as the recent attacks on the Humanities and the value of pure and applied Social Science research) come and go and are not closely connected to funding or governance structures. They occur in both publicly- and privately-funded systems and require thoughtful and constant explication and rebuttal. Academic inquiry inevitably leads to questioning the questions, so that new fields of study emerge and their emergence is testimony to the health of the institutions. Designing management and governance structures which allow that to happen is critical to both the wealth-creation and intellectual functions of universities. As in any other field of regulation, regulators will always be one step behind the innovators. Social science, as researched today, was not conceived in the mediaeval university yet it owes its origins to the then core disciplines of moral philosophy, mathematics and the study of the natural world (see, for example, de Ridder-Symoens 2003). Is it useful? That depends on what we think we need to know now. Its full value will probably not be known until the next set of questions emerges and new fields evolve.

If our current solutions to these issues are 'managerialist' and narrow-minded (as some believe), they are already under challenge from new technologies. These put tools in the hands of newer entrants to the academy with power that is not yet fully clear and is certainly underestimated or feared by many entrenched incumbents. Contestability of ideas and challenge to the traditional guardians of university practice may appear to usher in dystopia but in our view this is necessary, desirable and unavoidable.

Another lesson to take to heart is that the gap between academics with little experience of administrative and policy responsibilities, and those in 'middle management' or in leadership positions, is potentially dangerous. 'Middle managers' are stuck deep in what Donald Schon would call, 'the swamp of practice' where decision-making is not clear-cut or easy to perform. Geoff Sharrock (2012) has identified four distinct domains that characterise this swamp and to which managers must attend:

- programs: the diverse array of academic projects in student learning, research and third-stream activities that academic enterprises exist to pursue;
- people: the various professional groups who play direct or indirect roles in supporting and delivering academic programs and related functions of the enterprise;
- systems: the authority structures, technologies, policies and procedures that enable people to manage their programs and support functions effectively such as enrolling students, timetabling classes, paying staff, providing research facilities, and planning workloads and budgets; and
- strategy: plans to develop and maintain the capabilities needed to sustain the entire enterprise and its programs, people and systems.

These different domains are full of competing demands and argumentative voices. It is extremely difficult terrain to negotiate and there is precious little in the way of training (it's no surprise that the best book we have found on the topic is called *Herding Cats* (Garrett and Davies 2010). In our collective experience, academics who have not experienced middle management of some sort can have a limited understanding of what it takes to hold the university together. This is part of what leads to nostalgia for the golden age and produces the accusation that 'the administration' is full of pedants determined to burden overworked academics with administrivia (and here we single out Richard Hil's book, *Whackademia* (2012), for special mention). It contributes to an unhealthy polarisation of the academic workforce. The responsibility for opening the debate and bringing the passion for the core values of universities into the discussion about how to pay the bills should be shared by all of us.

# Part V: Telling It How It Is

# 13. A Design for Learning? A Case Study of the Hidden Costs of Curriculum and Organisational Change

Diane Kirkby and Kerreen Reiger

Like the sector itself, the study of higher education has expanded exponentially in recent decades. There are now many scholarly accounts of the impact of neoliberal and post-neoliberal policies on teaching and learning practices in universities internationally, and of the managerialist forms of governance accompanying them (e.g. Blackmore and Candiko 2012; Lorenz 2012; Blackmore et al. 2010; Olssen and Peters 2005; Slaughter and Rhoades 2004; Marginson and Considine 2000). There has, however, been relatively little theoretical and empirical work which builds on critical scholarship in comparable fields and, other than identifiably feminist scholars (e.g. Thornton 2011; Blackmore 2005; Evans 2004; Kenway et al. 1994/2006), few bring a consistent gender lens to analysis of the impact of neoliberal managerialism on universities. Analysis of workplaces in non-academic organisations, such as hospitals and other organisations, shows how complex patterns (of gender and cultural diversity, as well as of class) shape identities and interactions at the local levels of social practice and policy implementation (e.g. Connell et al. 2009; Halford and Leonard 2001). Management scholars in particular have demonstrated that building social trust and relationships is central to institutional success, including in higher education (Vidovich and Currie 2010; Tierney 2008; Gilson 2003). As hegemonic forms of masculinity in the public world have meant that women traditionally carried much of this 'hidden work' in organisations (Reiger 1993; Pringle 1998), it is, we contend, essential to study how implementation of neoliberal change initiatives impacts on the social relations and trust processes operating in specific institutional settings.

Accordingly, in the first section of this chapter, we establish an interdisciplinary framework for understanding the relevance of trust and relational networking for productive academic workplaces, and then, in the second part, use it to assess the impact of recent organisational change in one university workplace. We argue that not only are traditional forms of collegiality in universities now threatened, but that recent managerialist reforms risk damaging the taken-for-granted relational work which makes them 'successful, productive enterprises', even as understood within an economic paradigm – those making optimal use of the skills of a diverse and equitable workforce to provide effective services to their 'customers'. So-called reform of 'knowledge work' that is driven 'top-down' by managers with little appreciation of complex, and gendered, organisational dynamics, we conclude, poses a risk to the very creativity and critical thinking still acknowledged as being central to a university's purpose (e.g. Universities Australia 2012). It actually *undermines* proclaimed university objectives such as those articulated in La Trobe University's 2012 'Future Ready' Strategy – 'the advancement of knowledge for the public good'; giving students an 'identifiably modern, globally relevant education' allowing them 'to be successful and to make the world a better place'; and offering staff the capacity for 'risk-taking, creativity and innovation in teaching and research' (La Trobe University (LTU) 2012).

## Universities under fire

Accounts of contemporary universities point to the transformative political, economic and technological forces driving the international 'reform' assault on institutions of higher education – commonly seen by critics as the 'neoliberalist marketisation' of higher education. While not all agree with commentators still nostalgic for a past in which 'older white men' largely ran universities, or in which students' academic pursuits were accompanied by political and cultural endeavours (e.g. Hil 2012), there is considerable consensus on the largely negative impact of politically motivated demands for increased 'production' and improved educational 'performance'. Despite differences of emphasis, the extensive international higher education literature is largely pessimistic, frustrated and often very angry about these developments (Lorenz 2012; Marginson 2012; Wildavski et al. 2011; Zipin 2010; Wildavski and Slee 2010; Davies 2005; Kenway et al. 1994/2006; Readings 1996). Irish academic John Harpur, for example, has argued that we are now seeing an insistence on 'changing both the cultural and organisational ontologies of universities'. In what he terms this 'new alchemy' (Harpur 2010, 21), a narrative is being constructed and disseminated about universities as 'knowledge management' companies: 'economic return, entrepreneurship and innovation, knowledge delivery and scholarship are braided together' in a 'happy-ever-after' account of the future, one which he acknowledges has a 'powerful pull on the human imagination'. As Western policymakers grapple with the shifts in global power, higher education is coming to be seen as too important to be left to academics. Instead, 'belief in *brainpower* ... is [seen as] the last natural resource that the west has at its disposal' (2010, 13). Others are concerned about the resulting commercialisation of scientific research, especially of biotechnologies, and the liberalisation of commercial access to university research findings (Mowery and Sampat 2005).

Increased managerial control over academic labour is reported to be producing loss of professional autonomy and deteriorating working conditions for Australian as for British academics (Fredman and Doughney 2012; Blackmore et al. 2010; Anderson 2006; Evans 2004; Davies 2005). The result appears to be a culture of increasing acquiescence to intensified management demands, of diminished trust and widespread demoralisation and bullying (Zipin 2010; Vidovich and Slee 2009; Zabrodska 2011). Most worryingly, although the problems resulting from twenty-five years of efforts to transform or 'reform' higher education are now well documented, they remain completely sidelined or ignored at the policy level (e.g. Universities Australia 2012; Bradley et al. 2008). Few decision-makers are paying any attention to scholars' concerns, and, importantly, the general community has not been engaged in meaningful debate about the purpose and value of higher education. This shortcoming was brought home forcefully in the La Trobe experience of organisational 'reform' undertaken in 2012.

## Making invisible work count: Trust, emotional labour, and leadership

Questions of institutional trust have been major focus of debate in organisational studies for some years (Kramer and Tyler 1996), especially 'the many ways in which individuals, organizations, and societies benefit from high levels of trust – and pay a steep price for its absence' (Kramer and Pittinsky 2012, Intro.). Gilson (2003), for example, analyses health care institutions as comprising 'a complex web of relationships' in which trust plays a central role at many levels (Gilson 2003, 1,463), and Tierney (2006, 2008) has examined the varying systems of trust shaping US universities. He concludes that 'a culture where trust is embedded in the organization's fabric is likely to be better prepared for dealing with the myriad problems that exist on the horizon than those institutions that reach for bureaucratic and hierarchical solutions' (Tierney 2008, 40). This is especially the case for highly trained, specialised workers such as the research scientists studied by Sitkin and Stickel (1996), who found managers imposing a 'total quality management regime' had no grasp of the *nature* of their work. In line with organisational studies which show that distrust and even revenge not only undermine morale but sabotage reform, it is precisely the destruction of trust and mutuality in social relationships that is central to critiques of the managerialist transformation of educational institutions (Vidovich and Currie 2010; Avis 2003).

It is trust and the emotional dimensions of academic work cultures, however, which are reportedly suffering: as Bronwyn Davies (2005, 7) puts it 'neoliberalese' has 'inserted itself into the hearts and minds of academics'. She and others have noted with alarm the deteriorating collegiality and increase in incivility and outright bullying amongst academic colleagues (Anderson 2006). Building on the insights of international critics of neoliberal pressures on universities, Lew Zipin (2010) offers a troubling and deeply troubled account of the emotional fate of those within the universities in our present 'post/late modern' *dark times*. Keeping people in line in accord with an increasingly punitive audit culture requires an increasing array of managers to oversee compliance and indeed to break the resistance to managerial directives of those accustomed to traditional professional autonomy. He argues that this results in 'undercurrents of pedagogically violent intent' and the danger of increased bureaucratic demands producing less flexibility and innovative thinking (Zipin 2010, 156–7; see also Reiger, Schofield and Peters 2015).

Discussion of academic leadership has also therefore taken on new significance with regard to managing the changes in contemporary universities (Morley 2012; Scott 2008). What is the effect on the academic workplace when the style of leadership that wins followers through moral authority and influence is replaced by imposing compliance through managerialist positional authority? A corollary to that question concerns the qualities of those rising to positions of leadership in the new corporate university - or as Morley puts it, 'who self-identifies and is identified to existing power elites as having leadership legitimacy?' (Morley 2013b, 118). Like others in management studies (e.g. Kotter 2002; Stacey 2010; Stacey and Griffin 2005; Scott 2008, 11) places particular emphasis on relational capabilities in leaders: the 'emotional and cognitive capacity to figure out when to draw upon specific competencies, and the capacity to learn from experience', arguing that 'those institutions that manage the growing change pressures best' ensure they develop and support effective leaders. The role of leadership is particularly pertinent when it comes to the question of how to attain gender equity and diversity. As US social scientist Phillipa Strum (1989, 221) has succinctly summarised it: 'Equality is not a natural phenomenon: it comes into existence only when a leader is present to guide society toward it. Yet reports suggest that an aggressive, punitive even 'muscular' style of leadership is being fostered in 'post-late' times universities, one widely discussed in the literature on new public management and on the 'masculinisation' of managerial cultures (Hearn and Parkin 2001; Wacjman 1999).

Somewhat ironically in view of the attempt to make the public sector emulate the corporate world, there seems to be little engagement with alternative perspectives on leadership advanced by advocates of 'bottom-up' consultation and effective change management, including those who are recognised and respected in the private sector (e.g. Hoffer Gittell 2009; Kotter and Cohen 2002). In research on high-performing companies like some hospitals or aviation exemplars such as South West Airlines (Bamber et al. 2009), key factors in success include: improving coordination across parts of the organisation, seeking solutions from frontline workers; treating people with respect and emphasising courtesy both towards clients/customers and employees. Several corporate change-management frameworks stress the importance of organisational cultures and 'sense-making' (Weick 1995) and of skilled, facilitative leadership and engaging employees' *emotions* (Kotter and Cohen 2002). In their varying ways, they call attention to the centrality of mutual trust and respect, of understanding complex work cultures and of effective leadership of change (Kramer and Pittinsky 2012). Importantly, they offer a markedly different way forward from the management model currently dominating universities. Indeed, they are being employed in higher education in some cases (Tierney 2006; Blackmore and Candiko 2012). As Tsui (2012) reports concerning a major reshaping of curriculum at the University of Hong Kong, the process was not just 'top-down' but widely debated and contested. Eventually, agreement was reached on the flexible curriculum and student-centred approaches needed to prepare students for contemporary challenges as citizens. Even an OECD report on higher education (HE) noted that 'The experience of countries participating in the review suggests that mechanisms of regular and institutionalised consultation – which are inherent to consensual policymaking – contribute to the development of trust among parties' (2008, 317). What happens, however, when an institution lacks the required leadership and effective process?

A range of feminist accounts has demonstrated that more than what Connell (2006) terms a 'categorical' approach to gender – one based merely on women and men as numerical categories – is required to make sense of how *institutions* operate. Forms of knowledge and practice in higher education, as in society in general, reflect deeply held assumptions about what Butler (1993) terms 'doing gender', that is as a social practice performed in personal and public life. Power relations that privilege masculinity continue to shape patterns of social inclusion/exclusion, in close and fluid intersections with inequalities and identities associated with class, 'race'/ethnicity, sexualities and dis/abilities. From the extensive scholarship on gendered workplaces and social relationships produced in recent decades (e.g. Acker 1990, 2012; Adkins 1995; Halford and Leonard 2001; Wajcman 1999), we have ample evidence of the complexity of the gendered social relations of paid workplaces as well as of households. The importance of women's invisible labour has been widely documented, including emotional labour undertaken by those in service sector roles, such as flight attendants, along with the challenges women face in seeking equity in paid jobs and to avoid being squashed by the 'work/care' collision (Pocock 2003) presented by family demands. In terms of universities, Morley (2013b) describes the patterns whereby women's *presence* in universities has risen, both as academics and students, and explores why they nonetheless continue to be under-represented in university leadership positions. Similarly, Ross-Smith et al. (2005) report interviews with senior women in academia, as well as in business, which point to the challenges for women of being in 'not doable jobs'.

Evans goes further than the 'depressing tables of how many women are vice-chancellors' to consider the politics of gendered *knowledge*. She argues that even the ideal student of the corporate university is an 'essentially female subject', one who conforms nicely to requirements of the audit culture (2004, 89); that deeply gendered forms of knowledge remain embedded in the academy; and most significant of all, that a mere pretence of institutional gender neutrality is internalised by many women as well as men (2004, 97). She insists (2004, 102) that gendered power and difference still matter, not in essentialist ways but that the real prejudices and disadvantages faced by women remain both structural and symbolic:

> [S]tructural in the sense that women are included in a debased, but more demanding, form of academic life without any of the traditional support systems of men; symbolic in that the apparent erosion of gender difference disallows the investigation of that difference and the radical discussion ... which might result.

Evans' warning resonates with several concerns of other feminist scholars.

Many have pointed to the lack of social recognition accorded in paid workplaces, as in the home, to the relational and emotional labour commonly undertaken by women, whether as wives, secretaries or service sector workers (e.g. Adkins 1995; Pringle 1998). Several years ago Marilyn Waring's influential *Counting for Nothing* established the argument that the entire system of modern economics, systematised in the international accounting system, ignored questions of real human and environmental value: the dominant economic system, she argued, made no sense (Waring 1988). Similarly, feminist economist Nancy Folbre (2001), has argued powerfully that mainstream economics lacks any appreciation of the complex ways in which Adam Smith's 'invisible hand of the market' can only operate because it is underpinned by the 'invisible heart' of unrecognised and unvalued care labour. Though sometimes lacking this critical structural lens, attention to informal, interactional dynamics has increased in workplace studies, including research into the personal and financial costs of bullying and vindictive behaviours (Pearson and Porath 2005). Both the critical literature on the politically and economically driven transformation of contemporary universities, and other accounts of effective change management, point to the significance of social relationships in the academic workplace, and hence the need for detailed exploration of local organisational cultures and practices. It is no longer adequate, if it ever was, to conceptualise 'neoliberal reform' only as a linear, rational and managerially driven process. Each higher education institution is responding in distinct ways to the changes being imposed across the sector. As we will now argue, the La Trobe experience demonstrates how messy and complex the outcomes can be.

## The La Trobe University Faculty of Humanities and Social Sciences (FHUSS) Organisational Implementation Strategy (OCIS)

There is not space here to provide a full account of the context and detail of the restructuring processes associated with the 2011–12 implementation of the FHUSS OCIS. In view of our stress on context, leadership and complexity of processes and outcomes, some background to our investigation of its impact on staff is necessary. Drawing students from the northern, less privileged, ethnically diverse areas of Melbourne and, in recent years, from rural campuses in Victoria's north, La Trobe has been proud of its long tradition of commitment to social equity and community engagement: for example, as the first local university to enrol applicants without Year 12 accreditation, notably women – a legacy still emphasised by La Trobe vice-chancellors. As some of our LTU colleagues have commented in recent years, La Trobe came late to the audit culture and 'new times' in HE. Protected through the 1990s–early 2000s, but also made vulnerable by a traditional collegial regime and senior leadership turnover, more than one wave of voluntary redundancies (in 2002 and 2006) was undertaken. Although these were difficult, they were not overly traumatic for most Humanities and Social Sciences staff, with several taking early retirement. In another faculty, however, the impact was severe, especially for critical feminist scholarship (Thornton 2006). The academic community was soon confronted by even sterner warnings about the radical changes needed in curriculum, finance and structures. As one academic commented (Interview, November 2012):

> La Trobe's problem is that from about 2006 to now they've tried to do a technological revolution – all the IT systems, a major overhaul of all the management systems, and they've tried to introduce more recently, a teaching and learning revolution. It was like a parody of Trotsky's permanent revolutions, [but] the only one occurring was inside the university! And, can I say it, all the fuck-ups in the world occurred because you can't do it.

The implementation of an across university 'Design for Learning' (DfL) initiative sought to streamline curriculum within degrees and, most importantly, to implement new forms of accountability directed at 'measurable outcomes'. Many committed teachers were supportive of such 'quality improvement' initiatives and devoted a great deal of (often unpaid) time to their implementation, while others resisted, resenting the imposition on their professional autonomy. Reorganisation of teaching was needed and subsequent new appointments, especially those designed for 'generational renewal' offered new opportunities. However, with new senior managers, and a new faculty management team in 2010, different systems and orientation produced tighter managerial authority and a decline in collegiality such as input into regular faculty and school board meetings.

By 2011, escalating concerns about the faculty's financial situation were further triggered by an apparent decline in enrolments and the impending government-driven open market in higher education. An external consultant undertook a 'review' of the faculty in mid-2011, producing reports which were widely regarded as seriously lacking in understanding of the disciplines in the faculty or the relationship between them, weak or no evidence for claims made, hence lack of transparency and bias and overall intensely negative tone. As submissions to the faculty concerning the Irvine Review made clear, destruction of trust was already under way. The subsequent organisational change process was being discussed in meetings called in early 2012 but was then fully presented as OCIS in June 2012, bringing to the fore simmering tensions and serious concerns about the processes involved and lack of understanding of the impact of planned changes. This OCIS stage 1 was then followed in September by OCIS 2, which followed industrial disputation and resort to Fair Work Australia. OCIS 2 introduced a new level of confusion and struggle by nominating, seemingly quite arbitrarily, the desired staffing profiles for each teaching (i.e. disciplinary) program and a designated process for 'matching' academic and some administrative staff to positions, and hence matching the required redundancies in 'affected' areas.

As external commentators Bode and Dale (2012) have provided a valuable detailed critique of OCIS in its broader context, one which resonated with the LTU staff who read it and accords with our reading of the documentary evidence, we will use and extend its analysis it here. They deconstruct the slides of meaning in the OCIS texts through which university structures are reinterpreted through 'a narrative of separation, internal division and unification', so that 'the university' becomes senior management and it is left unstated just what the disciplines and programs are if not part of 'the university'. Where 'the faculty' fits is subject to a further slide insofar as it becomes largely responsible for its own fate in inadequately supporting 'the university' financially. Bode and Dale note that in seeking to answer what the university 'is', the OCIS positions the faculty both as actor and its management as victim of circumstances, yet the authors of the document are not named and the passive voice camouflages any possibility of responsibility. In terms of curriculum planning, similarly, Bode and Dale astutely note ambivalence about disciplines and the separation of academic staff from planning of teaching and learning, and from the entity called 'the faculty'. Most ironically in view of the external pressures, they also point to the seemingly 'baffling lack of interest in − or at least, of detailed attention to − the nature of "the market"': students too are outside the 'university' as consumers, whose shifty allegiances occasion considerable anxiety, but little, it seems, effective research and analysis (Bode and Dale 2012).

# Exploring the impact of the OCIS

Our analysis here is based on qualitative evidence from approximately 50 teaching, research and administrative staff in the Faculty of Humanities and Social Science (HuSS). In late 2012, we sent an email message around the faculty inviting people who wished to speak with either or both of us to get in touch and assured complete confidentiality. Some interviews and discussions were undertaken by Kerreen Reiger in the role of 'insider-outsider' critical friend for use as material for a planned publication on innovation in universities (Reiger, Schofield and Peters 2014, in press). Diane Kirkby's involvement was in accord with the EO Committee (for Equality Diversity and Wellbeing)'s terms of reference, viz: 'to ensure staff and students work in an environment free from harassment and discrimination' and 'to monitor and report ... on the implementation of the university's Equal Opportunity for Women in the Workplace (EOWW) Strategic Plan'. Motivation for the investigation was informed by discussions over working conditions which had been taking place in an informal women's network since it first began meeting in 2010 amid growing concerns over the direction of the faculty, managing the work-family balance and of the handling of some specific instances of sexual harassment and assault. The OCIS process raised serious concerns among this group, especially when specific areas like Gender Sexuality and Diversity Studies and Art History were targeted for cuts, despite being financially successful and having a rising level of enrolments. The implications for women staff and for the possibilities of maintaining and growing feminist theory and knowledge (Morley 2013b) were too stark to be ignored.

In informal and semi-structured conversations, some recorded, and email exchanges with staff across the faculty, together or singly, we consulted with a range of our colleagues, first always gaining their permission, which was often enthusiastically given, to listen to 'their story'. Those who came forward were staff on both regional and metropolitan campuses, those formally deemed 'affected' by staff cuts and also 'unaffected' staff, women and men, research-only and teaching staff, those who took voluntary redundancies, those whose redundancy was involuntary, those who were matched to remaining positions, senior and junior staff, program coordinators, postgraduate students, and senior managers. In corridor chats as well as through participant observation in meetings at varying levels but especially through the data through which we were privileged to gain personal accounts, we found a depth of grief and depression among the staff that is consistent with what Zipin (2010) has described as the *dark* side of managerialism: a consequence of managerial efforts to break academic power and spirit. Although we sought to ensure that a range of views was represented, no one came forward to offer any real defence of the OCIS or of current governance of either the Faculty or the University. In the following discussion we focus on three issues, the overtly gendered implications, criticism of poor processes and (masculinist) leadership, and the resulting emotional damage and impact on work cultures and social relationships, some of which fell most heavily on women, including administrative staff.

## Identifying gender dynamics at work

The OCIS experience revealed the difficulty of rendering gender dynamics visible as a social process which clearly involves more than simply the relative positions of women and men. It brought home the shortcomings of an EOWW policy that has no allowance for the complexity of gender dynamics interwoven in institutional decision-making or the social and especially trust relationships central to workplace and disciplinary cultures. Nevertheless, there are times when relative numbers of women to men are important. In relation to the consideration of redundancies and the process by which those decisions would be made, requests by staff for information on the processes to be followed did not indicate any awareness of ensuring effective gender equity. This was partly a shortcoming of an EOWW policy which is based on numerical representations of women vis-à-vis men as the measurement of institutional success. When the redundancies (voluntary and involuntary) were announced, the numbers of men to women were equal but this statistical equality was not consistent with the proportion of male to female staff in the faculty, where women outnumber men. It did not allow for variations across disciplinary, geographic or age areas. While it is not clear if a disproportionate percentage of women or men were among the 'affected' staff, it seems more men were retained in key curriculum areas identified for future development, more women were retained on regional campuses where the future is still uncertain, more men were among the younger and more women among the junior levels. Although the term 'relative to opportunity' was included as a relevant criterion, there was no evidence of design or forethought concerning how the numbers were achieved and can be maintained, nor of attention being paid to future mentoring/leadership needs.

Not surprisingly, responses to the OCIS reflected common gendered life patterns and expectations. Both men and women volunteered to take voluntary redundancy, but some women chose to do so because of the increasing difficulties of maintaining their family responsibilities within a perceptibly (and rapidly accelerating) deterioration of a 'family-friendly' workplace. In interviews and informal conversations men tended to emphasise the financial incentives that were offered to go, while many women stressed their responsibilities towards family, colleagues and students. Women spoke of 'a culture of expectation making it very difficult', the 'lack of flexibility' and no options for making it easier to maintain a level of productivity and of their anticipation that in the reduced faculty staffing, increased teaching workloads would accelerate a decline of conditions. Some women found the balancing act now 'just too hard'. Others reported discouragement and disincentives being placed in their path, and sometimes overt discrimination by senior men, as causes in their decision-making; that maternity leave had been treated as 'complicating' their careers, and a barrier to their promotion, a reason not to apply for external grant funding. Of the men who went voluntarily, some apparently did so out of a willingness to retire or a preference to take a risk on starting a new career or relocate to another institution rather than stay in what they described as a poorly-managed workplace where disillusionment prevails and the future looks bleak. Some women saved their jobs by indicating their willingness to job-share with their colleagues. One program saved jobs by three women negotiating collaboratively to take a significantly reduced fraction of employment. However, other women who indicated their willingness to go part-time were instead offered involuntary redundancy, raising the prospect they had made themselves vulnerable. Some observed that senior women had been treated very badly within the changing culture, thus proscribing their own aspirations or modifying their behaviour. They were given the impression that seniority was no guarantee of respectful treatment for women and no protection from losing their jobs.

Although the final cuts were in the end a little different, the curriculum areas first announced to be excised by the OCIS had all or largely female staff, and were areas where diversity was most concentrated. Of particular concern was how OCIS devalued gender-and-diversity research and teaching in the curriculum at the expense of areas employing men (e.g. sports journalism). As a successful area, one of importance to a university priding itself on its diversity and radical identity to attract students, one might assume that the Gender, Sexuality and Diversity Studies (GSDS) program would be promoted as a key interdisciplinary area vital to contemporary global challenges. Not so. While the coordinator of

GSDS was eventually saved after a major community surge of support, it was at great cost to its coordinator and to the then truncated program. Assurances that 'People who were regarded as having strategic value to the future of the University were not accepted' for redundancies, did not apply to a staff member teaching a core subject in GSDS, and an active researcher in the field of sexual and family violence. Thus the gendered assessment of 'what counts' shaped the processes in complex ways, and to other aspects of such dynamics we now turn.

## Processes and leadership issues

As recounted to us, many responses to the OCIS were overwhelmingly critical, and surprisingly united in expressing anger at the ineptitude, confusion and frustration that the process entailed. Recurrent themes in interviews included the absence of respect for and trust of staff, of meaningful rather than 'techno'-communication, and the damaging impact of the negative tone in which much information was conveyed and meetings conducted, as well as the silence with which staff communications were greeted. One commented that emails were often sent from faculty management after 5pm, often on Fridays, as though this 'was an intended plan to give them important information when people were not together' to discuss and respond. Accordingly, there was a significant decline in essential institutional trust: '[T]here was more fight in people early on, but we later lost the fight, as though it was strategically engineered information leading to people becoming demoralised, so eventually we did not really know if the financial crisis was real or manufactured' (interview, November 2012).

There was criticism of the management's over-reliance on outside experts and legal advisers, an approach which also appeared to be a defensive strategy showing lack of respect for, and ignoring the experience, expertise, knowledge and goodwill existing within the faculty. It set up, or perhaps was instigated by, increased distance that was maintained throughout the process between academic and many administrative staff and management. Other forms of division intensified. In view of the loose networked character of universities (Bento 2013; Blackmore and Candiko 2012), change processes do not work in rational, linear and predictable ways. In this case, internal conflicts between previously harmonious disciplinary groups such as Sociology and Anthropology, and between rural and city colleagues were fostered, damaging collegiality although the projected curriculum developments, notably redevelopment of the BA, actually required enhanced collaboration across fields. Moreover, for those on the ground, said one program convenor, 'there was no thought about how we might have to manage it, and it was like a war zone'. Another recounted 'waking up at night and worrying about Bendigo [campus]', saying that the ways the 'indicative structures' were imposed was 'just appalling'.

Concerns about lack of effective senior leadership and lack of accountability at that level were pervasive: 'there was no one player and no overall vision', as one academic said. There was a widespread sense of confusion as 'to who was ultimately responsible' especially as the VC was new to the job; so 'any resistance from below was floating up and going into space' and people felt that those 'up the "top"' could do anything they wanted', said another informant. These concerns were exacerbated by the gendered dynamics involved in the changes to the culture and to the power structure within the faculty which went hand-in-hand with the perception of a 'highly personalised process — that people were going not because of their record but because of who was in their corner'. Although women outnumber men in the faculty, there has been a loss of women from faculty management positions (Head and Deputy Heads of School, Associate Deans, Deputy Dean) and their replacement by men, which has led to a concentration of men in positions of authority and power, and a loss of leadership opportunities for women. Another program convenor said that respect was missing, especially for women, and that the faculty leadership seemed to have 'a fiefdom here'.

Those promoted seemed to be 'yes-men or -women', according to several of those interviewed, people who would 'not rock the boat', said some administrative staff. Furthermore, 'the university did not seem to have a diversity principle', unlike many private-sector boards. Instead, there was 'a certain element of a boys' club, both at faculty and university level … in effect all like-minded people', which can be useful, but 'in terms of effectiveness is not so … it leads to "uncritical support"'. Greater diversity, both ethnic and gender is needed. It seemed that leadership has become more hierarchical, 'running it like the Army' rather than expecting responsible school and program-level colleagues to participate effectively in decision-making. The example of a senior assertive woman being marginalised and pushed out left a lesson for others; as one said, 'I therefore won't be as loud politically, as a senior female can't operate like that in this environment. I'll have to exercise judgment on when to be assertive.' Another said there are 'double messages when reporting sex harassment and bullying. "Yes we care", and "don't make trouble for the organisation"'. Women staff thus expressed feelings of unease at the apparent empowerment of masculinity they have observed in the corridors and meeting rooms. They face the troubling issue of whether there is a role for senior women in the new managerial university: 'There used to be transparency in getting into managerial structures of the Faculty. That is no longer the case.' Staff, especially women, who asked hard questions such as wanting detailed financial evidence, were characterised as difficult personalities resistant to change, rather than as trusted employees exercising their critical expertise in the faculty's interest.

## Grief, loss and suppression of dissent

In light of debate about the declining capacity for opposition to managerialist imperatives (Lorenz 2012; Davies 2005), the experience of La Trobe HuSS staff suggests this occurred through complex and, as Zipin (2010) suggests, emotionally troubling processes. A series of losses were mentioned often – a fostering of ill-feeling, undermining of collegiality, loss of their capacity to recruit and work effectively with postgraduates, loss of valuable staff, and the loss of the reputation of HuSS Faculty seen to be important in the community, and in future competition for research grants and staff recruitment. Staff complained that the management saw academic staff as 'problems' and treated them accordingly. They asked why it was done this way. They were not alone. One reported being told by a consultant brought in to offer advice to those considering or taking redundancies, that he had never seen anything like the OCIS process in many years working in the field: he described his work for organisations as usually 'like using a clean scalpel to assist healing, but this was like it was being done with a rusty bread knife'. Many staff said they felt they had not been heard, and no one knew if anyone even read the many submissions they spent nights and weekends preparing. As no effective collegial support had been provided to them during the OCIS, in spite of 'counselling' opportunities for those directly affected, they welcomed the opportunity to speak to us and were grateful that we were listening.

Their stories revealed the devastating impact of the OCIS implementation on the morale and productivity of staff and postgraduate students, with undergraduates demonstrating, even violently. All reported experiencing unusual levels of stress and anxiety, with attendant physical symptoms of insomnia, disruption to their normal routines and personal relationships, and reduced professional performance. Some individuals sought medical treatment, or reported self-medicating with alcohol. One, who rarely drank alcohol, reported astonishment that the bottle of whisky was suddenly gone after a week rather than a year, and feeling so stressed that family suffered, as well as teaching. Some feared their recovery would be very slow. Reflecting this sense of trauma, many staff who survived the redundancies are now speaking of feeling 'survivor guilt', and are pessimistic about the faculty's and the university's future. Not only academic staff felt the burden. We have been told that many faculty administrative staff, most but not all of whom are women, feel depressed and demoralised in the current regime, even months after the OCIS restructuring. They expressed concerns about the lack of transparency in appointment processes in the restructure yet, although they have been told 'it is not personal' and they are 'entitled to ask for information', that is contradicted because when someone queries processes, such as in a public forum, 'they are jumped on as being disloyal'. Genuine questioning of decision-making processes and effective recording of meetings for transparency and good governance is no longer seen as legitimate. As one colleague noted in an email follow-up to an interview, 'concern to maintain positional power' at senior levels meant:

> that the people who do the work and have the knowledge and experience to come up with innovative solutions are disempowered and then blamed for the problems – e.g. out-of-date curriculum. There was enormous frustration that the innovative and critical strengths of people in the Faculty were not able to contribute to solving the problems.

The shift from flatter governance structures to top-down and positional power was both completely demoralising and counterproductive in the face of the very real external pressures on the university.

The emotional responses that our interviews disclosed could be (and were anticipated by management to be) expressions of opposition to change, a failure of staff to recognise the writing on the wall. By contrast, we argue it was a failure of senior and faculty management to understand the substantive issues and provide the necessary detailed evidence, not to mention coherent vision, to underpin change. Most importantly, as a subsequent external consultancy report articulated (KPMG 2013) effective leadership and change management were seriously inadequate. What staff at La Trobe resisted was not change per se, or even downsizing, which had happened before, but they sought supported opportunities for curriculum innovation and respectful collaboration that could underpin future viability. In spite of recognition of the external pressures on the university, the need for radical upheaval was experienced as arbitrary. Importantly, and especially galling for academics, it was not grounded in actual *evidence* of the productivity, potential and financial viability of particular units and programs. There was also little recognition of the distress, even devastation, caused by loss of a valued institutional culture, workplace environment and social relationships, all of which are built up in time and in 'place'.

The La Trobe FHuSS experience bears many of the hallmarks explored in studies of the restructuring of corporate workplaces (Kotter and Cohen 2002; McCabe 2007) but many are particular to the de-professionalisation of educational work (Fitzgerald 2009). In the case of LTU's OCIS, however, they were made much worse by bewildering contradictions within management's demands; inconsistent, ambiguous and shifting exercises of power; the differential and sometimes contradictory work experiences of both administrative and academic staff. Power and control infuse the strategies, innovations and technologies that managers employ, and these operate in both intended and unintended ways, but their overall impact can be to 'impoverish working life'. Many leaders of the corporate workplace, as McCabe (2007, 221) claims, 'lack the imagination, courage and empathy for others' needed to optimise the creativity and ingenuity of the workforce. As an astute interviewee observed in November 2012: 'Our faculty was the scapegoat, the guinea pigs for the experiment. Such waves of change are not going to stop and I think unless we can work out ways to survive, "brand ourselves" as they like to say, they'll keep coming back.'

Some staff reported trying to find ways to forge new working relationships with their colleagues, united in having shared a difficult, highly stressful experience. They point to the staff and La Trobe's highly diverse student body as the best hope for the future: 'There are a lot of talented people here which is the only reason this faculty still has credibility.' Others by contrast point to increased individual self-interest, keeping doors closed and still feeling vulnerable, even many months after the major impact of OCIS had passed. As one administrative staff member remarked recently, 'there is no trust left'.

## Conclusions

The analysis we have offered in this chapter exposes the centrality of good leadership, trust in governance and high staff morale to an effective change process, one that is capable of sustaining a productive learning and research environment. Drivers of the OCIS process at La Trobe showed insufficient knowledge of organisational processes, of how the daily work of learning and teaching was achieved, or a grasp of the social relations that allowed the local workplace to function productively. The organisational restructure and associated curriculum and staffing changes did not prioritise staff knowledge or wellbeing, nor recognise the close correlation between those factors and success in moving people forward. Staff complained that the administration and management of the university saw academic staff as problems and accordingly treated them with distrust, rather than examining issues of competence of leadership and management practices at other levels of the faculty. Clearly too much change was attempted at once and several staff said that linking organisational restructuring to curriculum redesign was a major mistake. It became clear that the OCIS process undermined the good social relationships and productive work culture that had been a hallmark of the faculty and underpinned its reputation for scholarship. The experience of La Trobe HuSS staff suggests that the outcome of poorly managed change can be a high cost to the institution: fostering of ill-feeling and resentment, the loss of capacity to recruit and retain postgraduates, the loss of respect by valuable staff and care for the reputation of the university in the community, which can impact on future competition for research grants and staff recruitment. The fear of extinction remains strong among humanities and social science staff who survived the 2012 cuts at La Trobe. The recovery process can be painfully slow and impede further initiatives.

How to provide a new form of networked institution to allow the critical capacities of Humanities and Social Science scholars to flourish in new ways in a changing context is, to use complexity theory's premises, an 'emergent' possibility. The role of renewed disciplines and inter/trans-disciplinary fields, such as studies of peace/conflict, social and environmental sustainability, and gender and sexuality offer promising opportunities. These cannot be realised, however, if only narrow economic criteria and limited ideas of 'quality' dominate change efforts in higher education, and knowledge based on local institutional experience is demeaned. Notwithstanding the damning nature of critiques of neoliberalist assaults on the academy as 'killing thinking', to use Mary Evans' evocative and pessimistic term (2004), we need to seek out glimmers of contradiction and thus any grounds on which to base not merely resistance, but an alternative vision. In view of the major challenges of the 21st century, the essential starting points of reform need to be, first, genuine commitment to the social as well as economic value of education, and, second, recognition of the importance to institutional success of fostering social trust, equitable relationships and effective leadership in university workplaces.

# 14. 'Smoking Guns': Reflections on Truth and Politics in the University

Judith Bessant

## Introduction

This chapter offers an insight into the contemporary management practices and neoliberal culture found in many of our universities, and it raises questions about academic authority and how it secures its legitimacy by way of a participant's case study or auto-ethnographic account. I tell how after making complaints about the style of management of the primary protagonist I was 'sacked' by the university, which misused the redundancy provisions of the enterprise bargaining agreement (EBA). After nearly four years the matter ended up in the Federal Court which in May 2013 saw Justice Gray issue a damning judgment, order my immediate reinstatement and fine the university.

This story centres on an extreme case. Yet like most stories about modern organisations it cannot be explained just by framing events in terms of neoliberalism and managerialism. It is also a story about conflict between the authoritarian character of contemporary university versions of managerialism and an academic ethos of positive freedom and public scholarship grounded in the idea that academics have a right, even an obligation, to engage in debate, and to seek to hold people, including their managers, accountable to certain ethical and rational criteria. It is also a story about dissent and conflict as it highlights opposing concepts of authority regarding ideas about education and academic practice. It is about rival claims to legitimacy grounded in contesting intellectual and ethical traditions.

As never before, universities have become sites of contest about who gets to say what they are for and who gets to establish the standards by which they are evaluated.

# Background

In the late 1980s as a young academic, I was keen to have a future in what I saw as a prestigious and honourable profession – the academy. With a crisp new PhD in hand, and a couple of infants in tow, I got my first academic job. Starry-eyed and with great expectations, I looked forward to working in an environment that valued good teaching, that engaged in intellectually rigorous research, and that promoted well-informed debate. Later I would call this the idea of the 'university as public conscience' and the practices that make possible 'public scholarship' (Mitchell 2008). I was also committed to the value of being able to speak out as an exercise in positive freedom. I assumed I could and would relate to colleagues and students in a straightforward way, including those in positions of authority over me. As I learnt some time later, courtesy of Foucault, the Greek word for this, speaking truth to power, is *parrhesia*, described as establishing an ethical contract with others in a hierarchy of power: the speaker tells the truth without concealing anything while the 'figure in authority' listens to any critical truth without punishing the speaker (Tamboukou 2012, 849–65).

How far I had travelled and how much had changed since those early career days in the late 1980s is highlighted when I fast-forward to 16 May 2013. After four hellish years at Royal Melbourne Institute of Technology University, I was in the Federal Court of Australia on a wet and wintry day in Melbourne to hear Justice Peter Gray hand down his judgment in *NTEU & Bessant v RMIT* (*NTEU*).[1] Seated in the tastefully modern Federal Court, on my left were my National Tertiary Education Union (NTEU) colleagues who stood beside me through it all, among them NTEU's Senior Industrial Officer, Linda Gale, who remained a strong and stable figure throughout what turned out to be a four-year calamity. To my right and behind me were my family and dear friends. Our talented barrister, Joel Fetter, stood at the bar table alongside our on-the-ball solicitor, Elizabeth McGrath, and opposite the university legal team. Representatives from the university were sitting further down the pews.

We all stood as the Clerk of Court banged his gavel to announce the entrance of Justice Gray. It was a big day for us all. Appointed to the Federal Court in May 1984, it was Justice Gray's last day before retiring. I was there to hear his judgment on a trial which ran from October 2012 to February 2013, which followed many days in Fair Work Australia.

---

1  *National Tertiary Education Union and Bessant v Royal Melbourne Institute of Technology* [2013] FCA 451. Retrieved 8 September 2014, from www.judgments.fedcourt.gov.au/judgments/Judgments/fca/single/2013/2013fca0451. In what follows I draw on the judgment of Gray J, official transcripts of that case (Transcript), documents tendered in evidence during the trial and other records of events and correspondence obtained through FOI, Rights of Entry and discovery.

Justice Gray began reading his judgment, beginning with his conclusion and orders. He found the university took unlawful adverse action against me when they terminated my employment in April 2012 because I exercised my workplace rights. Specifically I made complaints about the behaviour of my immediate supervisor (NTEU [139], [140], [141], [145]). Justice Gray's judgment was that the university breached s340(1)(a)(ii) of the *Fair Work Act 2009* (Cth). In addition he found that the university contravened s50 of the *Fair Work Act 2009* by failing to comply with the RMIT Academic and Professional Staff Union Collective Agreement when at the time certain managers knew my 'position was likely to have an uncertain future', they failed to offer the option of voluntary redeployment. A substantial fine was imposed for each of the proven offences. Justice Gray also ordered my immediate reinstatement, specifying that I be treated 'as if I had been employed continuously by the respondent from 20 April 2012 up to and including the date of [her] reinstatement' (NTEU [147]). Copies of the 64-page judgment were handed to relevant parties, the judge stood, bowed and left the courtroom. RMIT University had three weeks to appeal his decision, but there was no appeal.

## Events leading to the judgment

As I remarked earlier, implicit in my identity as a young academic in the late 1980s was the idea of the university as a space of public scholarship where the distinction between managers and academic work was improbable. By 2012, after an extended period of being treated poorly and finally losing my job because I complained about my manager, it became apparent that a sharp distinction between managers and academics had evolved.[2] Over those decades academics had been stripped of the intellectual authority they once seemed to enjoy. In part, this story highlights how in many instances managers rather than academics now make judgments about academic practices and speak on behalf of the university.

One significant feature of this case is that we cannot presume that our public universities are necessarily managed by officials with a strong regard for the rule of law, or for truth safeguarded in an ethos of open, intellectually and ethically rigorous deliberation. On the issue of whether we have seen a decline in deliberative decision-making forums that are inclusive of academics, I suggest that such a decline is evident. This is reflected, among many other things, in changes such as the new laws and practices pertaining to the membership of university governance bodies. I refer, for example, to Victoria's *Education Legislation Amendment (Governance) Act* 2012 that removed requirements for

---

2   Most, but not all, of what I detail below came out in the court proceedings.

elected academic and student representation on university councils, and the 2012 *University of Tasmania Act* that similarly reduced academic and student representation and changed the composition of the university council. These developments point to a steady push towards reduced shared governance, and towards reduced deliberative practice that is inclusive of key stakeholders and those with a direct interest in decisions made. Whether we have seen university officials become less constrained by the rule of law is far more difficult to determine. All I can say is that in this instance it was demonstrated in a court of law that the fact we have laws prohibiting certain kinds of conduct did not constrain decision-makers from acting in unlawful ways.

Whether we describe it as the 'enterprise university', a 'neoliberal ethos', 'managerialism', or 'New Public Management', what is also clear is that some management-cum-governance problems now affect the integrity of academic teaching and research in a number of our universities. This is *not* to overlook managers who are committed to the idea of a university in which academic authority and legitimacy are taken seriously. I have direct experience of many good university managers who remain effective guardians of the integrity of 'their' institution but, in the context of the modern university, they are a minority.

As Arendt (1967) argued, it is by telling stories that we can grasp the truth of events and thereby disclose practices which enlarge freedom. Here I tell a story of how I found myself that day in the Federal Court of Australia, and do so mindful of the fact that this approach enables some understandings and insights formed after the event.

The trial vindicated my conviction born from harsh experience, that certain normal and useful provisions for redundancy established in Australian industrial law were misused. The court found that arguments by university representatives about 'a business case' were spurious. As Justice Gray noted in his judgment:

> As I have already found, Professor Gardner was well aware that Professor Hayward wished to have Professor Bessant dismissed from her employment for reasons that were entirely unconnected with the financial difficulties … The personal nature of the conflict between Professor Hayward and Professor Bessant, which included the complaints Professor Bessant had made about Professor Hayward, was well-known to Professor Gardner … In such circumstances, on receiving Professor Hayward's memorandum of 2 March 2011 (which was clearly directed to securing the ultimate removal of Professor Bessant) and his memorandum of 28 June 2011 (which sought her approval of the removal of Professor Bessant), it might have been expected that Professor Gardner would take steps to ensure that the 'business case' that was being made was not designed to conceal an ulterior motive on the part of Professor Hayward. Professor Gardner did no such thing (*NTEU* [120]).

As I show in this chapter, the redundancy provisions were used to punish and silence me.

I begin with a brief outline of Justice Gray's judgment.

## The judgment

Justice Gray found that redundancy provisions were misused to terminate my employment because I exercised my workplace rights and because I formalised complaints against Professor Hayward when he was my supervisor. Professor Hayward was also found to have displayed animosity toward me soon after his appointment to the university in 2009 and, as mentioned, the Vice-Chancellor (VC) was aware of that:

> There is no doubt that Professor Gardner was well aware that Professor Hayward harboured animosity towards Professor Bessant. Professor Hayward's memorandum dated 18 March 2010 ... made Professor Gardner well aware that Professor Hayward was keen to have Professor Bessant removed from the School. Although she regarded it as inappropriate that she should be called upon to deal with an issue of the kind raised by the memorandum, Professor Gardner did not say that she put it out of her mind when she came to make her subsequent decisions. Nor did she have any discussion with Professor Hayward about the inappropriateness of his approach. She spoke only to Professor Fudge, to tell him that she did not want to see a memorandum like that of 18 March 2010 on her desk again. (*NTEU* [101])

In short, Justice Gray found that the story advanced by the university for terminating my employment, namely that there was a financial crisis and no work for me, was inauthentic. Evidence was given how Professor Hayward, without notice aggregated my salary (which for budget purposes was originally allocated on a 50 per cent basis to two discrete work units) into a single discipline area. This meant my 'remuneration was allocated entirely to the budget' of one small program area. The immediate effect of this action was to exacerbate the budgetary stress in that unit. That was then used to support the 'business case' for my dismissal (*NTEU* [34], [112]).

Additionally, Justice Gray found there were no contemporaneous criteria or reasons developed or used to identify my position as redundant – as required by law:

> One of the most disturbing aspects of this case is the absence of any contemporaneous account of the reasons of Professor Gardner for deciding that Professor Bessant should be made redundant (*NTEU* [110])

Justice Gray continued:

> Anyone with a background in the discipline of industrial relations, which Professor Gardner had would understand the importance of recording decisions for dismissal. No such reasons were recorded. (*NTEU* [110]).

Moreover, criteria that were finally developed were drafted *ex post facto*, after I had been targeted and after it was pointed out to the university in Fair Work Australia that criteria did not exist (*NTEU* [72], [82], [116]). Justice Gray observed that had those *after-the-fact* criteria been applied impartially it was highly likely my position would have been secure:

> The criteria presented to Deputy President Hamilton (Fairwork Australia) with the letter dated 23 September 2011 appear to have been created by somebody to answer the obvious criticism that there had been no criteria applied in the choice of the position of Professor Bessant as the one to be made redundant. If there had been criteria of the kind specified in September 2011, there is every reason to suppose that Professor Bessant would have fared well if judged honestly by reference to them (*NTEU* [115]).

The judgment pointed to substantial evidence of adverse action. Without notice, my title and work-plan were changed to restrict my work (*NTEU* [49], [39]). I was stood down as Discipline Leader by the Dean via email without any notice or consultation. This occurred immediately after I made a complaint about him. As a result of the Dean's action, I blacked out, fell and suffered a physical injury (*NTEU* [43]). Soon after, a formal notification of an Industrial Dispute was lodged. That dispute related to Professor Hayward's treatment of me and an 'Issues Resolution Committee' was established to resolve the dispute. That Committee found in my favour. As a result a formal 'Settlement and Release Agreement' was signed by all parties, including the university which, amongst other things, agreed that I undertake a period of three years' research work. However *on the same day* (29 April 2011) that the *Settlement and Release Agreement* was signed, redundancy papers were prepared which abrogated that Agreement (*NTEU* [61], [81]).

In addition the conventions of due process were ignored. A second internal university review mechanism, a Redundancy Review Committee (RRC), also found that the university had acted unfairly and that rules of natural justice had not been applied (*NTEU* [80], [121]). The VC overrode those findings. Justice Gray found that:

> ... she [Professor Gardiner] did not undertake anything like the examination of the documents which she said she undertook following the receipt of the Redundancy Review Committee's report. In justification of her failure to investigate whether Professor Hayward was hiding his true motives behind the 'business case', Professor Gardner gave evidence that she was concerned only

with the question whether the financial case stood up in its own terms. In other words, on her own evidence, Professor Gardner was not concerned with the possibility that Professor Hayward was using the financial case as a pretext to seek the dismissal of Professor Bessant for reasons of his own. Professor Gardner's approach was not that of the impartial decision-maker (*NTEU* [120]).

Justice Gray's decision finds that 'Professor Gardner's reluctance to delegate anyone else to consider the report of the Redundancy Review Committee (RRC) is also significant' (*NTEU* [121]).

> Her evidence is that she was surprised by the findings of the committee. This was the first occasion on which a Redundancy Review Committee had made findings critical of one of Professor Gardner's decisions in relation to the redundancy of an employee. Despite the finding of the Redundancy Review Committee that the process in relation to Professor Bessant had been unfair, Professor Gardner did not see any need to have the process conducted again. Although she spent some time in Indonesia following her receipt of the report, she did not consider delegating the decision to anybody else. There is no doubt that she could have done so. Clause 3.14 of the Enterprise Agreement defines 'Vice-Chancellor' to mean the Vice-Chancellor of RMIT or her or his nominee. Her evidence indicates that Professor Gardner did not wish the ultimate decision on Professor Bessant's case to fall into the hands of anybody else (NTEU [121]).

He continued that the VC's own actions in responding to the RRC's findings suggested that:

> Professor Gardner was committed to making Professor Bessant redundant. She was attempting to put out of her way the issues raised by the Redundancy Review Committee, without having to consider their substance, because a proper process might have resulted in a different decision (*NTEU* [123]).

> Professor Gardner's approach to the processes involved in making Professor Bessant redundant suggests that she was setting out to achieve a pre-determined result and would not allow herself to be diverted by anything that might prevent that result from being achieved (*NTEU* [124]).

Justice Gray found that 'Professor Gardner was well aware that Professor Hayward wished to have Professor Bessant dismissed from her employment for reasons that were entirely unconnected with the financial difficulties' (NTEU [120]). 'The personal nature of the conflict … which included the complaints Professor Bessant had made about Professor Hayward, was well known to Professor Gardner at least from her receipt of Professor Hayward's memorandum of 18 March 2010' (NTEU [120]; see also NTEU [101]).

In what follows I describe some of the events and processes which lie behind this case.

# Ticking all the boxes (2004–2009)

In mid-2004, I was recruited to RMIT University as Professor in Youth Studies and Sociology. I was appointed to two discrete discipline areas: Youth Work and Social Science, with half my salary coming from the Youth Work budget and the other half from the Social Science budget. My brief as Discipline Leader in Youth Work was to concentrate on renewing and consolidating that area, after which I would move to another discipline in the School. I note that while renewing the program was a priority in the first four years of my employment at RMIT, most of my academic work was outside the Youth Work area.

From mid-2004 I continued being an active researcher. In that time, I was Chief Investigator on three large ARC grants, published five books, authored dozens of book chapters and many articles in refereed academic journals. I was formally identified as one of the top researchers within a very large school. I also carried a full teaching load, I taught into 'common courses' across the School and into Youth Work. I was also a successful manager. For some of that time I was the School Research Director. From 2004 until 2009 I chaired the university-wide committee that oversaw the examination and classification process of all research degrees within the university. From mid-2004 until 2009 I was also an active member of the university research committee and a member of Academic Board. For all that time I also served on the School Research Committee (and for some years I also chaired that committee). I was on the School Learning and Teaching Committee and on the School Executive. I renewed the Youth Work undergraduate program, developed new courses and developed a new postgraduate degree. I was also the Discipline Leader for Youth Work. In addition I was active in 'community outreach' work that included developing a new sociology curriculum for the State Education Department for years 11 and 12, had been on Board of Management Committees and an adviser to NGOs and government agencies, etc. I was ticking all the boxes and took my responsibilities seriously.

My work effort, capacity or accomplishments were never an issue. It was recorded as a 'fact' that I had 'an impressive curriculum vitae as an academic', that I had 'experience as a scholar across a wide range of disciplines in the social sciences', that my 'list of publications indicates that [she] is a scholar of high standing' (*NTEU* 33). University managers in the witness box concurred. As Justice Gray observed of Professor Hayward's evidence:

> Notwithstanding that he [Professor Hayward] described Professor Bessant as 'a very good researcher', as 'scholarly and of international standing' and as 'an impressive teacher', Professor Hayward recommended against relocation [to another area in the School] (*NTEU* [46]).

Between 2004 and August 2009 senior staff in the School and in the university had been committed to developing the youth work area. Among other things, it was evident in management decisions in 2008 to appoint new senior staff and to develop a postgraduate degree in 2009 designed to bring in revenue to sustain the area. By mid-2009, my task in building and consolidating the area was near complete. I had just finished developing and guiding a new postgraduate program through the maze of university vetting processes and committees and obtained final approval. Marketing the new program had begun with an overwhelmingly positive response from prospective students. I was looking towards bedding that new Master's program down before exiting youth work and focusing more of my work in other areas in the school.

In August 2009 all that changed when David Hayward was appointed as Dean of the School.

## Bad times begin …

In August 2009 the new Dean and I had several meetings. In those early meetings he displayed what became a persistent pattern of behaviour. This including making innuendoes referring to what he described as 'historic events'. Unbeknown to me at the time, those 'historic events' referred to my whistleblowing some 20 years earlier. Over the following months, and indeed years, I asked Professor Hayward for details. He refused, but continued with allusions to 'those events'.

Some time later I discovered, after reading internal university memos,[3] the 'historic events' referred to a darker story relating to my early history at RMIT-PIT[4] in the early 1990s. They referred to reports I made about certain disturbing disclosures made to me by young people who sought my help. Those young people reported inappropriate sexual conduct towards themselves, and towards others, by a then senior university staff member and another person working in child protection. I reported the matter to RMIT university senior management and later to the Human Rights and Equal Opportunity Commission (HREOC). This whistleblowing was being ominously alluded to by Professor Hayward 20 years later and was cited by him in his (18 March 2010) memo to the VC as one of the reasons why my dismissal was a good option.

---

3   Hayward 18 March 2010, 3. See also, for example, memo (HR, RMIT, 14 October 2010).
4   Phillip Institute of Technology (PIT) amalgamated with RMIT.

The substance of those disclosures was later confirmed by a number of internal and external inquiries.[5] At the time, however, there was no public acknowledgement of any wrongdoing or unlawful conduct relating to the person in question. Instead the individual was quietly 'moved on'. I was disappointed by the response although, as responses to revelations about equivalent abuse in other organisations came out over the years, I soon realised that the practice of saying nothing and quietly moving people on was the norm.

What I did not fully appreciate at the time was that the failure to make public what had happened would have significant implications for me later down the track. Twenty years later the matter reared its ugly head. Unbeknown to me it became a topic of conversation and indeed a rationale used to terminate my employment. This, I discovered very late in the piece, is what the Dean was referring to in his innuendos about historic issues.[6]

Very soon after the Dean's arrival at RMIT he sent me an email advising that he had cancelled the new postgraduate program. This was done without consultation or prior notice. He chose to communicate that information to me by email even though my office was adjacent to his. (I note that I just spent the two previous years developing the new program. David Hayward's decision came just months after the program had received final university endorsement and after we had embarked on a marketing program).

Following that communiqué came a quick succession of similar surprises. In November 2009 the Dean informed me he had organised an external review of the undergraduate Youth Work program that would begin immediately, before Christmas 2009. Again this was done without any notice or consultation. I politely expressed surprise that neither my colleagues nor I were consulted about the fact a review of a program (that had only recently undergone a curriculum renewal) was to take place, that we hadn't been consulted about the terms of reference, timelines, or who was best placed to carry out the review. I also expressed disappointment we had not been afforded the opportunity to review the program ourselves as a first step. I pointed to the errors in the documentation the Dean had prepared for the external review, and described how some of his commentary in the document was likely to be offensive to the staff named.

Within a week or so the Dean changed his mind, agreeing that staff could undertake an internal review. He said the program area was in deficit and that savings needed to be made. While not disputing his claim, I pointed to the

---

5 E.g. by university inquiries (one led by Faye Marles) and by a State Government inquiry involving the former Minister for Youth Affairs, Vin Heffernan, that led to a Review of Youth Work education in Victoria in 1995.

6 See, for example, David Hayward to VC, Margaret Gardiner, 18 March 2010.

other program areas in the school that were in deficit and asked why they were receiving different treatment. I also referred him to the university's earlier plans to invest in the youth work area, suggesting it would make good sense to reap the returns on that investment already made in its development by proceeding with the postgraduate program that would generate income. Finally, I proposed that after we completed the review I move out of youth work into another area in the school, as was the original plan, and that this would help ameliorate 'the fiscal problem' he identified.

These unexpected decisions and the various chopping and changing that took place within a relatively short timeframe affected staff, and some became ill. The Dean interpreted this as an industrial strategy and resistance to his authority and to his plans. I point out on many occasions that no-one was resisting change, nor was I organising a 'political campaign' as he insinuated. I set about finding savings. I note that at the time the Dean was restructuring the entire school and that 'my group' was the only academic unit not included in the new administrative restructure.

In late 2009 all this took a toll on my health; I became unwell and took leave for one week. I recovered and returned, ready for work. Nonetheless I was instructed by the Dean not to return until I had provided a 'certificate of fitness to work', which I experienced as another form of harassment. I saw his 'instruction' as differential treatment, noticing that other staff in the school (some of whom had been seriously ill) had returned to work and not been required to produce a fitness-to-work certificate. I read the university guidelines on 'fitness for duty' and sought union advice. My circumstances did not fit those described in the guidelines, and the NTEU advised me the doctor's medical certificate confirmed my capacity to work and that no further proof was required. I communicated that information to the Dean.

At this time I submitted incident reports to RMIT Human Resources and sought advice from the university Ombuds. My concerns related to the Dean's erratic behaviour (e.g. taking me off the school executive then, soon after, reinstating me), his ongoing innuendo and references to what he described as 'historic issues', the constantly shifting goalposts, unreasonable timelines, intimidation, failure to consult, stigmatisation and a dictatorial management style. In late 2009 and early 2010 four academic staff in 'my' program area and I complained to the occupational health and safety officer.

In December 2009 just prior to taking Christmas leave, I met with the Dean in the hope that a frank conversation might assist and I tabled an informal complaint to him directly. In that meeting I explained to him why his decision to exclude some staff from a school 'academic restructure' that included everyone was problematic and how it made those people feel stigmatised. I asked for a decision to be made over the summer break about location of those staff into the new academic structure and said I would like to be included in that decision. He gave an undertaking that would happen before my return to work in early February 2010.

Also in that meeting, I repeated my request for information about his continuing references to still unspecified 'historic issues', raising the idea of natural justice, and saying I would like the opportunity to respond to what was said. He refused to provide any detail. I explained how I experienced his practice of repeatedly removing me from the school executive and then immediately reinstating me as erratic and disturbing. Finally I asked whether he thought it was possible for us to work in ways that avoided the grief of the last few months. At the end of the meeting he thanked me for not formalising a complaint.

Over the Christmas break I worked to make immediate budget savings. On returning to the university I met the Dean and detailed an initial savings plan that I had developed with colleagues. In response, and much to my surprise, he didn't want to talk about the savings. Instead he retrieved a telephone bill from a red folder on his desk and read out that I had spent $40 on my work phone downloading documents over the Christmas break. This, he said, demonstrated I was not serious about making savings. I considered his response bizarre, and was disappointed given the work I had done over the summer holidays to achieve the agreed-on financial goal.[7] In that meeting I also drew attention to the fact that staff in 'my' area remained outside the new organisational restructure while all their colleagues were well and truly integrated into the new arrangements. I reminded him of the undertaking he had given in our last meeting that they would be included. I explained that those staff were complaining to me, as their immediate supervisor, about what they experienced as exclusionary treatment.

The situation did not improve. The innuendo and references to 'historic issues' and 'things people were saying' continued.

On 18 February, several youth work staff and I met the school health and safety officer to make a complaint and seek advice. Soon after, on 22 February 2010, I had my annual work-plan meeting with the Dean. As was standard practice, I provided a written plan and we discussed my role as Discipline Leader. There was detailed discussion about how that role would evolve and the kind of support I might need. We spoke of the savings already made and I provided a written summary of the savings. I explained my plans to meet with the school finance officer to establish how more savings could be made.

---

7   Despite that discouraging response, I remained committed to making the savings, and made appointments with the relevant finance officers to seek their assistance.

In a bid to resolve outstanding matters, I also met with RMIT HR staff on 26 February 2010. In attendance were two HR staff, the occupational health and safety (OHS) officer and a union official. I remained cautiously optimistic, thinking that with a little good will we could navigate what had become a difficult situation. I was assured by HR staff that the meeting was confidential until they themselves had time to get advice and until I had time to consider their advice and the options available. Unfortunately, however, that evening the OHS officer sent out a group email and copied in the Dean. In that email she revealed to him that a meeting took place that day between myself and HR and revealed the content of that meeting.

Two working days later, on 2 March 2010, just as the semester's teaching was about to begin and without any prior notice or consultation, I received an email from the Dean that he was standing me down as Discipline Leader. Given the way the decision was made and communicated, and despite the fact that my role as Discipline Leader was discussed at a work-plan meeting just one week earlier and nothing had been said of any changes to my role, I was literally shocked. On reading the email I stood up and collapsed, hitting my face on the chair as I fell. I sustained facial injuries and knocked out one of my front teeth. On medical advice I took two weeks' leave, had dental treatment and was advised by my doctor to avoid the Dean.

While on leave I submitted an OHS incident report to RMIT HR, notifying them of the email and my injury. I received no reply. Over the following weeks and months I attempted to contact RMIT HR more than two dozen times by email and phone seeking their assistance in my return to work. My primary concern was that the Dean's action made it unclear what my work-plan was. I was no longer Discipline Leader, and while I was on two weeks' leave recovering from the injury, my teaching was assigned to others.

When I returned to work, the Dean asked me for another 'fitness to return to work certificate'. I reminded him of our last conversation about that matter and that a doctor's certificate verified my capacity to work.

## The Hayward memorandum 18 March 2010

Little did I know at the time, however, that plans had already been hatched by my Dean and communicated to the VC which argued for the termination of my employment.[8] As Justice Gray observed:

---

8  Memo from Professor David Hayward to Professor Margaret Gardner, cc Professor Colin Fudge, 18 March 2010.

> The contravening reasons for Professor Bessant's dismissal were kept secret. Even in Court, they were not addressed by Professor Gardner, and others who could have shed light on them were not called to give evidence (*NTEU* [141]).

Justice Gray described this as an 'options paper' (Transcript 14 February 2013, 589). I would call it a chilling example of what, unknowingly, I was facing.

On 18 March 2010, and 16 days after standing me down from the Discipline Leader role, the Dean wrote to the VC. He advised her that my position was 'no longer tenable for a mixture of inter-personal, organisational and financial reasons' (Memo from Professor Hayward to Professor Gardiner, 18 March 2010, *NTEU* [45]). That sentence alone gives the lie to the official story that my redundancy was motivated purely by financial reasons. In justifying his conclusion the Dean cited what he saw as my political orientation: 'It was clear to me that a core part of the problem was Professor Bessant. In the continuum of leadership styles in universities, Professor Bessant sits at the left and is strongly anti-managerialist' (Memo from Professor Hayward to Professor Gardiner 18 March 2010, *NTEU* [45]).

It was an email that signalled his approach to dealing with lawful complaints I had made about his treatment of me after his appointment in August 2009. In that memo Professor Hayward unaccountably failed to inform the VC that I had made complaints against him. Instead he claimed that I was a troublemaker referring to the whistleblowing action I took 20 years earlier. Professor Hayward also unaccountably failed to inform the VC about the content of those complaints regarding patterns of inappropriate sexual conduct towards young people (mentioned above).

This memo from Professor Hayward foreshadowed the storm to come. At that time and for the next few years I had no inkling that correspondence or similar papers existed and thus had no opportunity to correct the record or to prepare myself for what was to come. That document and others like it were obtained later through a Right of Entry inspection by the NTEU and 'discovery' processes relating to the court case. Those documents, which were either misleading, overly selective and/or factually incorrect, worked to prejudice the VC and others who knew of their content. Documentation like that also gave the lie to the official university line that my position was terminated for purely financial reasons.

In respect to this and another similar early document, Professor Hayward stated under oath that he had not considered the option of terminating my employment until mid-to-late 2011. Justice Gray did not, however:

> accept that a document of this size and detail would have been prepared just in case Professor Hayward ever wished to use it, which was his explanation for it.

In my view, it demonstrated Professor Hayward's desire to see Professor Bessant dismissed from RMIT, a desire he harboured at least as early as March 2010 ... and that he sought to implement (*NTEU* [53]).

And later Justice Gray reiterated the point that contrary to arguments about finances, from day one plans were afoot to have my employment terminated: 'Well, I can read it, Professor [Hayward]. It's very clear. The position is untenable because she won't do what you want' (Transcript, 14 February 2013, 600).

In his questioning of the VC, Justice Gray also put to her:

So you've got Professor Hayward who has been gunning for Professor Bessant for some time. He has finally got himself a business case that you accept. He has got himself a targeted redundancy that you accept. It's all a bit iffy (Transcript, 14 February 2013, 670).

## Seeking assistance from the VC and WorkSafe

In mid-April 2010 and not knowing about the Hayward memo, I met the VC (at my request) to seek her assistance. I described to her the recent events, their impact on me and requested that I be moved away from Professor Hayward to another part of the university. This I argued would also help address the financial problem facing the youth work area. In that meeting, the VC made no mention of the fact she had just received 'advice' from the Dean proposing the termination of my employment. At the end of that meeting she said she would discuss the matter with Professor Colin Fudge, the Pro Vice-Chancellor in charge of my College. Thereafter I attempted to seek assistance from Professor Fudge: however, on most occasions when I did so he was overseas and unavailable.

After months of trying to contact HR and receiving no response, I contacted Worksafe. I wanted advice, given that the university's Human Resources had failed to respond to any of my requests for help in returning to work. They had also not responded to any of the incident reports I submitted. I had also asked HR how I might respond to the issues about the Dean that I raised with them in early 2010. As a courtesy I notified HR and RMIT senior management that I was meeting with Worksafe and explained why.

Worksafe advised me that 'poor management' *per se* was not unlawful and that, given I had received no response from HR about my complaint, the best way to proceed was to submit a bullying complaint. I was advised that because the university had statutory obligations to react to such complaints, such action would force the university to respond. I took that advice and on 17 June 2010, I submitted a bullying complaint to the university.

## Secret surveillance and smoking guns

As with many cases like this, there are always larger back stories than the more narrowly construed issue of adverse action might suggest. It is clear from the evidence presented in court that from at least March 2010 the Dean was committed to terminating my employment, which he achieved in April 2012. It was a commitment that also saw him organise covert electronic surveillance of me in a bid, to use his own words, to find a 'smoking gun' that would further his case against me.[9]

When the Dean stood me down as Discipline Leader in early March 2010 it was just days into a new semester. Apart from my own health issues, other colleagues also become ill (Transcript, 31 October 2012, 317; 1 November 2012, 414–7; 2 November 2012, 516, 524–5, 554–5).[10] The Dean was also informed that his actions were breaching the Occupational Health and Safety Act (Transcript, 2 November 2012).[11] The Dean seems to have interpreted their sick leave as an industrial strategy, one which I was orchestrating using my 'charismatic' power. The suggestion was offensive and indicative of a failure to appreciate the impact of the Dean's behaviour on the health of staff. For the record, I had neither the power nor the interest in trying to influence staff to take leave, nor were the staff in question the sort of people who would allow themselves to be so manipulated.

The poor timing of the decision about my removal as Discipline Leader and staff illness caused by 'environmental risk factors in the workplace' resulted in major disruptions to students and classes in the initial weeks of the semester (Worksafe, 4 March 2011). Some students inquired about causes of those disruptions and voiced their objections. Those 'upheavals' also attracted media attention. Over the following months some students began taking various actions that included establishing websites.

---

9   The smoking gun' reference comes from an internal email from Professor Hayward in which he wrote: 'here is the report. Is it the smoking gun we need?' The Dean has sought assistance from IT staff to surveil my emails. I understand he was looking for evidence of misconduct that might provide the basis for disciplinary action (email from Hayward to PN cc GB, JF, 6 September 2010). Unfortunately for him there was no evidence because I had committed no offence.

10   Other staff had submitted 'Incident Reports' to HR about the Dean's actions. On this matter Justice Gray said: 'it seems odd that HR go into a spin when there are a lot of incident reports coming in, because a lot of incident reports might just indicate that something is really, really wrong' (Transcript, 14 February 2013, 586).

11   See also findings from Worksafe inspector: 'I have formed the reasonable belief that there are work environment risk factors in your workplace, such as poor management actions and a poor consultation process in relation to the restructure of the area you work within, and your removal from the Discipline Leader position' (L Dekic, Worksafe Report, 4 March 2011).

Without my knowledge, certain 'informational cascades' about the responses were gathering momentum. Unbeknown to me at the time, the Dean organised electronic surveillance of me. As I discovered later the Dean believed I was conspiring with students to carry out a political campaign directed at him and the university.[12] To be clear, I had little knowledge of the student responses at that time and was certainly not involved in them.

By late 2010, relations between the Dean and students had become so difficult that he applied for an intervention order against one student. The student reciprocated with an application for a Personal Safety Order against the Dean.[13]

In late September 2010 an internal RMIT document came into my possession that shocked me deeply. It was an RMIT report instigated because it was 'suspected' I might have encouraged students to complain and that I might have 'disclosed documents' in ways that 'breached policy'.[14] The surveillance was to undertaken in an attempt to discover evidence to support this claim and provide the basis for initiating disciplinary action against me.

In spite of the fact there was no evidence for these claims, the report wildly speculated that I 'could have' used my work credit card to pay for the establishment of a student website and that I 'could have' used my RMIT-funded mobile phone to upload documents on to a student website (Bristow to Harwood memo, 6 September 2010). No evidence was found because those things did not happen. The allegations were untrue, offensive and defamatory. Nonetheless, some people wanted to believe them. Having said all that, I add that I believe students have a right to make complaints and to protest about matters of direct interest to them.

I recall thinking at the time how this charge against me seemed so large and fanciful that those who heard about it would say 'he couldn't have made that up, it must be true'. The timing and cascade effect of the story provided opportunities and time to adorn the story, to create a damaging representation in the minds of those privy to the whispers and secrets. Concealment of the charge meant I had no opportunity to respond. At the time I was reading Cass Sunstein's *Infotopia* (2006) which helped me understand a little better what was going on, particularly Sunstein's account of 'informational cocoons' and how they enable damaging stories to flourish because they are not challenged. Sunstein notes such practices are especially virulent in workplaces characterised

---

12   E.g. email from Noonan to Hayward, Bristow, and Fergusson, 7 September 2010, Youthworks investigation v1.0.doc. See also Bristow to Bramwell, 2 April 2012, subject PC.4.12 Privacy complaint.
13   This intervention order came on the cusp of similar action by another RMIT Head of School (*Sydney Morning Herald*, 14 April 2011).
14   Memo to B Harwood from G Bristow (Manager, IT Security), 'Investigation into Youthwork.biz email and website', 6 September 2010.

by silos inhabited by like-minded people who mostly talk and listen to each other and who self-censor in ways that inhibit their capacity to ask questions and consider things clearly.

I was also reading the story by the academic, Owen Lattimore (2004, 8), who was persecuted in the USA in the 1950s by McCarthy for his alleged Communist tendencies. His account of being lied about and how it destroyed his career resonated with what I was experiencing:

> A big lie of this kind would not stand just by itself ... Clearly I had to face the danger of supplementary lies, perhaps it would go as far as perjured evidence, I would have to face that possibility. I had yet to learn that McCarthy is a master ... of the little ball-bearing lie that rolls around and around and helps the wheels of the lie machine to turn over.

Similarly Ellen Schrecker's book *No Ivory Tower: McCarthyism and the Universities* seemed to have a few lessons for Australian higher education (Schrecker 1986).

Scandalised on learning what had happened, and with my faith that rationality would prevail still intact but somewhat tattered, I wrote to the VC expressing concern and informing her that what was claimed was untrue and damaging to me. I asked her to take action to stop the spread of those stories.

## Notice of dispute: Issues Resolution Committee and the agreement

In August 2010, the NTEU sent the Dean a formal notice of dispute about his action in standing me down as Discipline Leader. Some eight months later, in March 2011, an Issues Resolution Committee was established in accordance with the EBA to resolve the dispute. It consisted of one staff representative and one NTEU representative and was chaired by a Pro Vice- Chancellor.

On 30 March 2011, I provided evidence to the Issues Resolution Committee about the erratic management style I had been subjected to, how I was stood down, and spoke of the impact this had on me. On hearing the evidence, from me and Professor Hayward, members of the IRC, through the Chair, moved to resolve the issue in dispute and to mitigate the damage. The Chair (Pro Vice-Chancellor Kirk) formalised an agreement that I be located in a research position for three years, that research seed funding be made available and that my dental bills be paid for by the university. All parties agreed and a formal written agreement was signed.

During that process there was no indication that my redundancy was planned, although the NTEU and I raised the question of redundancy in the IRC proceedings. The reply we were given by Professor Hayward was that 'no-one in the university was immune from redundancies … not even the Vice-Chancellor or the Dean were immune'. The idea that a VC or Dean of a School could be made redundant in a university seemed so preposterous to me that I took that statement as an assurance that 'a three-year research' position meant what the words said. If I had formed the view that it was Professor Hayward's intention to terminate my employment, I would obviously not have agreed to sign the dispute settlement. On 29 April 2011, all parties signed the formal 'Settlement and Release of Agreement'.

I thought things were finally resolved and that I could go back to work. I took four weeks' annual leave. Unbeknown to me, *on the very same day* that the Agreement was signed, documentation was signed off that resulted in the termination of my employment.

About this, Justice Gray said:

> It does seem odd to the outsider that one minute there's a job for you, it's a research job … and the next minute, you are being made redundant …. It looks odd to me (Transcript, 14 February 2013, 645) … It seems so utterly irrational to me that one arm of the university enters into an agreement with a professor, in a particular situation, and within a very short time, another arm of the university does away with it altogether. It doesn't add up to me … Don't you have to say you have a bit of a problem here with redundancy coming hard on the heels of this agreement? (Transcript 14 February 2013, 649).

He continued: 'the thing that to me makes this case so exceptional is that so recently before the redundancy, there was an agreement on behalf of the university and you can't run away from it' (Transcript 14 February 2013, 654).

Listening to this discussion in the courtroom, I couldn't help but think of Alan Ryan's (2012, 329) account of Hobbes' condemnation of intentional breaches of such a formal agreement. It was like a message from the dead:

> Hobbes thought that injustice was literally illogical … to say, 'I promise that I will do such and such, but have no intention of doing so', comes very close to saying , 'I shall and I shall not do it' … saying 'I promise' while having no intention to do so, is not self-contradictory but wicked. The contradiction between what I say and what I know I shall do is, as with lying, the essence of deceit, not a defective logic.

## More secret business: Changing my title, restricting my work and salary relocation

It was around this time that I noticed three developments had taken place without my knowledge. First, on 13 May 2011 I noticed my official title on the university webpage had mysteriously changed. My title, Professor of Youth Studies and Sociology, had been changed to 'Professor of Youth Work'. I sought to have the title corrected. After much ado, I received a memo (21 June 2011) explaining that it was decided the correction could not be made 'on advice from Human Resources'.

Secondly, I noticed my salary had been reallocated entirely to the Youth Work budget. Since my appointment in 2004, it had been divided 50:50 between Youth Work and Social Science. Again I was not informed or consulted about this change. This move was significant because locating 100 per cent of my salary into the small Youth Work area had the effect of both inflating the budget deficit of that area and lowering the student:staff ratio. Thirdly, in July 2011, I was notified that my work was restricted exclusively to Youth Work (Correspondence from Marcia Gough, Executive Director HR, 21 July 2011).

These three developments pointed to differential treatment. Restricting me to Youth Work only worked to deny me opportunities for redeployment within the school, something afforded to *all* other staff in Social Sciences. Staff in the Social Science discipline had been formally advised by the Dean that they would not be made redundant, but any staff surplus to requirement could be relocated to other areas in the school.[15]

I replied, providing Ms Gough (Director of HR) with an account of my work activities since my appointment at RMIT, noting the multidisciplinary nature of my work and pointing out that it was mostly outside the area of youth work. I referred to my position description and the fact I had a dual appointment in Youth Studies *and* Social Science. I pointed to my work-plan which detailed many cross-disciplinary projects. I also drew her attention to the university's declared commitment to the principle of academic freedom which supported an academic's right to inquire into, write and speak freely without being treated adversely.

On 25 August 2011, the NTEU notified the Dean of a formal dispute over the change to my title.

---

15    In a PowerPoint presentation to staff, the Dean estimated there would be five Social Science redeployments (Hayward, Powerpoint, 21 August 2012, 2). While my own position was being made redundant because there was said to be no work, staff in the Social Science program were told they could pick up what had been my work, to quote Professor Hayward: '[the] Balance of staff would join staff in Youth Work to form new unit' (Hayward, 21 August 2012, 4).

After many trips to Fair Work Australia (FWA) my title was corrected. Nothing more was said about prohibiting me from working beyond the confines of Youth Work.

A myriad of similar incidents took place along the way, including threats that I would not be paid when I was on sick leave, all of which give a flavour of the treatment I was receiving.

## Employment terminated: July 2011–April 2012

With the April 2011 'Settlement and Release Agreement' in place, I took four weeks' leave. On the day of my return to work on 18 July 2012, I opened my email to find a message from the Dean notifying me that my employment was to be terminated.

The NTEU lodged notice of another dispute on 8 August 2011. That was followed by many more trips to FWA and many conciliation meetings, all to no avail. In FWA, a number of academic vacancies that existed in the school and university that I could have filled were identified but rejected by Professor Hayward in his capacity as the university representative.

I wrote to the VC on 25 October 2011 requesting another meeting to discuss the situation. She declined. On 28 October 2013, I received a couriered letter from RMIT terminating my employment on grounds of redundancy.

## Redundancy Review Committee (November 2011)

In mid-November 2011, I applied for a review of the redundancy decision. A Redundancy Review Committee (RRC) was formed comprising three members, all professors.[16] The review began in late 2011 and finished in February 2012. It was long and gruelling and extended by a suspense-ridden summer interval.

On 3 February 2013, the RRC issued a report on its findings. Like the 'findings' from the first internal Issues Resolution Committee, the RRC also found in my favour, stating that: 'The decision to terminate Professor Bessant's employment was not fair' and members gave their reasons. They also found that 'the rules of natural justice have not been applied ... in making the decision to terminate Professor Bessant's employment'.

Those findings were forwarded to the VC on 16 February 2012. She replied by asking me to make a submission to 'rectify the deficiencies in the process'. I responded (22 February 2012) expressing concern about her assumption she

---

16   One was a university nominee, another an NTEU nominee, and a chair appointed by the VC.

could rectify *ex post facto* what were substantive flaws in the process. I pointed to the fact that the investigative committee mandated by the university's own enterprise agreement, the RRC, confirmed the process was problematic. I reminded her of the history of animus between the Dean and myself and the history of adverse treatment. I also pointed to flaws in the 'budgetary analysis'.

I reminded her also that in April 2011 the university had entered into a formal agreement resulting from the Issues Resolution Committee which provided an assurance of work for at least three years (Settlement and Release Agreement of 29 April 2011), and pointed out how on the same day that document was signed the university initiated formal redundancy procedures targeting my position. I described that action as a breach of faith, and vindictive on the part of the Dean. Finally, I said that the university had failed to meet the simple test of fairness and transparency required by its own policy, the EBA and the law. None of this had a salutary effect.

The VC replied, informing me that she had overturned the Redundancy Review Committee's decision, and that my employment would be terminated on 20 April 2012. On this, Justice Gray found that she 'did not undertake anything like the examination of the RRC'S documents' (NTEU [120]):

> Despite the finding of the Redundancy Review Committee that the process in relation to Professor Bessant had been unfair, Professor Gardner did not see any need to have the process conducted again … following her receipt of the report, she did not consider delegating the decision to anybody else. There is no doubt that she could have done so … Her evidence indicates that Professor Gardner did not wish the ultimate decision on Professor Bessant's case to fall into the hands of anybody else (*NTEU* [121]).

> Professor Gardner's approach to the issues raised by the report of the Redundancy Review Committee was to reject its findings. Both her evidence and her letter of 8 November 2011 … made clear her determination that there should be no criteria for the selection of the appropriate person or persons to be made redundant. She rejected unequivocally the proposition that the reality of Professor Bessant's position, following the Settlement and Release Agreement of 29 April 2011, should have been taken into account. Professor Gardner made it clear that she did not like the terms of that agreement (*NTEU* [122]).

> Professor Gardner's letter to Professor Bessant of 16 February 2012 … is also revealing … She was attempting to put out of her way the issues raised by the Redundancy Review Committee, without having to consider their substance, because a proper process might have resulted in a different decision (*NTEU* [123]).

After considerable effort to reach a resolution, on 4 September 2012, Commissioner Ryan of Fair Work Australia (FWA) issued a Certificate under the *Fair Work Act 2009* certifying that he was satisfied that all reasonable attempts to resolve the dispute had been unsuccessful. We proceeded to court.

On 18 September 2012, the NTEU and I lodged an application to the Federal Court of Australia through our barrister, Joel Fetter. The matter was listed for 15 October 2012. We sought an injunction with the idea of securing my employment until the matter could be heard. However, the presiding judge, Justice Gray had other ideas. He dismissed the application for an injunction and much to everyone's surprise announced the matter would be heard immediately. Lawyers on all sides were stunned and appeared a little panic-stricken as they faced the prospect of preparing for a large and complex trial within a very short timeframe.

Justice Gray announced the matter would proceed on the following day (16 October 2012). My legal representative explained to him that I could not attend because I had major surgery scheduled that day. In response, Justice Gray scheduled the trial to proceed in late October 2012. We all left the courtroom a little shell-shocked.

I walked from the Federal Court opposite the Flagstaff Gardens to the hospital in Carlton for my pre-operative consultation with the surgeon. This came hot on the tail of a visit to my GP days earlier. I had been feeling poorly for some time. To cut a long story short, a very large tumour was discovered and I was listed for urgent surgery. I had been feeling unwell for many months, something the doctors put down to a psychological response to workplace stress, for which I was prescribed medication and sent off for counselling.

When I visited the surgeon that afternoon in October 2012, he informed me that the MRI results indicated the possibility of cancer. The next day, a four-and-a-half-kilo tumour was removed. As is standard practice, a frozen section was taken and sent to pathology. I was in hospital for five days. A few days after being discharged, the surgeon called me with the pathology results, reporting that I had cancer and that he would refer me to an oncologist in six weeks.

On 22 October there was a directions hearing at the Federal Court but I was too unwell to attend.

# The trial begins

It was two days later – 25 October 2012. With a 'knock, knock' of the gavel, everyone stood as Justice Gray strode to the bench, head down, with his robes billowing behind. It was announced, 'the Federal Court of Australia is now is session'. The day began and I was in the witness box. In acknowledgment of my medical condition and discomfort, I was given the opportunity for rest breaks. Over the next couple of days, I was subject to examination and cross-examination.

Six weeks after surgery I visited the surgeon who confirmed the cancer diagnosis. He said I would require treatment for the rest of my life and that he had scheduled an appointment for me to see the oncologist the next day.

The following day, I visited the oncologist who looked at me, checked my records, and contradicted the surgeon, saying that I did not have cancer; the tumour was benign and had been successfully removed, and I was now discharged. What happened after that is another story, and I am pleased to say it was the oncologist and not the surgeon whose diagnosis was right. Somehow a mistake had been made. It was the first of two big wins.

Back to the court case: there was a long adjournment over Christmas. We were directed to attempt mediation over that period, but it was an exercise in futility as the university's lawyers denied there was a case to answer.

On 13 February 2013, I found myself back in the Federal Court overlooking the beautiful Flagstaff Gardens on a hot summer's day. We sat waiting for the judge. Evidence was given by NTEU officers who had supported me over the years, Wayne Cupido and Linda Gale. The Dean gave evidence for just under three days. After the Christmas adjournment the Dean re-entered the witness box for his third and final day. The VC and an HR member of staff who oversaw the redeployment process also gave evidence.

# In lieu of a conclusion

The fact that two internal university review-resolution panels found there were serious problems with what had happened did not help the university's case. Their respective findings and recommendations had been disregarded. Justice Gray's incredulity at the way the formal Agreement was effectively annulled on the same day that it was signed off and the VC had overlooked the findings of reviews, stands out in my memory of this case.

Whether we call it the enterprise university, neoliberalism, 'New Public Management', or corporate re-engineering, a deeply corrosive influence is eating into the ethos of our universities (Sennett 1998). Propelled by the rhetoric about 'efficient business' practices, we see can see how excessive rule-bound hierarchical organisations antithetical to a sustainable academic community can have deleterious consequences (Balfour and Grubbs 2000, 570–84).

While 'efficiency' was always on the tip of the tongue of certain university managers, the entire episode was an enormous exercise in very costly inefficiency. The direct financial impost of the legal case itself in lawyers' bills and with the fines handed down, as well as the costs of associated activities such as staff being sent repeatedly to Fair Work Australia, the expensive internal administrative processes and so forth, to say nothing of lost productivity, cost the university, or the Australian taxpayer, a tremendous amount of money. In fact the evidence revealed how easily a university could use a masquerade of financial exigency, manufactured by management choices about how to move costs and revenue streams around within a budget, to disguise an attack on an individual employee. RMIT got caught out, but is far from being the only university, or the only employer for that matter, to dress up as redundancy the targeting of an individual employee. As Justice Gray noted:

> There was no display of contrition on the part of RMIT, particularly from Professor Gardner. She maintained to the very end of her evidence that the decision to make Professor Bessant redundant was fully justified. She made no concessions as to any impropriety. (*NTEU* [143]).

> The need for specific deterrence is quite high. Unless the effect of a penalty is felt, RMIT might again succumb to the temptation to make use of its redundancy processes to rid itself of an employee when it desires to do so for reasons that would be prohibited by the Fair Work Act. There is also a need for general deterrence (*NTEU* [144]).

According to Tamboukou (2012), this development has been aided and abetted by the failure on the part of too many academics to respond when universities are entering 'dark times'. As she notes (p. 865), when 'academics withdraw from practices of acting and speaking together' about the political, we fail in 'our task as teachers to inspire our students in the pursuit of freedom'. This absence of positive freedom, she argues, is a political failure.

My own experience points to much self-silencing. Once it became known I was under attack from my manager and as it became clear what norms mattered under the new regime people simply complied and silenced themselves. Competing views, disagreement or critique were described as 'political' and unwelcome. As Sunstein observes, a belief that one's reputation will suffer, that 'we' will be punished or not rewarded for speaking, is what engenders self-silencing (2006, 202–3).

Among the instances of the new norm-setting practice, I refer to one directive to staff from the Dean that he communicated very soon after his appointment. It was a directive instructing senior staff 'not [to] send or participate in group emails of this type from now onward' (Hayward to various staff, 29 October 2009). My understanding was that such 'group emails' were deemed to be political. It did elicit a critical response from one senior member of staff that same day: 'Dear David, I disagree entirely. I maintain that I have every right to talk to my fellow discipline leaders; that email is often the only way, and that my staff have the right to know what I am saying/doing.'

That lone dissenting response sank without trace.

I conclude this chapter by briefly addressing three questions: why did this situation ever happen? what lessons are there? and why did I seek reinstatement and not a financial settlement? My explanation for the ordeal points to a mixture of reasons. It is a story of what happens when a manager deeply committed to an autocratic style of management meets someone with a different worldview. First, what happened can be understood in part in terms of organisational politics, some of which can be explained by referring to new public management or a neoliberal mindset.

As Nussbaum (2013, 164–5) observed, understanding some prominent human tendencies to engage in deliberately cruel and bad behaviour towards others requires thinking about political emotions such as anxious competitiveness and pride, and cultures that shape and sustain those tendencies. This is not to be explained simply by reference to thoughtlessness, neglect, or even fear-tinged suspicion; it also involves 'some active desire to denigrate or humiliate'. This tendency she argues is central to in-group discrimination. Even when we manage to develop capacities for genuine concern, 'insecurities make us prone' to 'the subordination of others as people learn to split the world into favoured and stigmatised groups'.

Ultimately, I understand that what happened is illustrative of what happens when practical wisdom and good judgment are absent. By practical wisdom, I refer to the practice of listening to good counsel (and the capacity to determine who can offer it). I refer to the capacity to judge what is the right, what is a good thing, and the ability to judge what is false and malicious from what is true and decent. The lack of this capacity on the part of some key managers and the tendency to act 'as if' everything is functioning well, to my mind helps explain why this unfortunate series of events took place. Stanley Cohen (2001, 64) offers some insight into this in his account of certain kinds of social relations. Writing about environments in which control by the more powerful is exercised by manipulating loyalty through fear and collusive forms of denial which works to encourage mistreatment, he describes how at 'a subterranean level everyone knows what is happening, but the surface is a permanent "as if" discourse'. The social group is drawn together in a web of denial which frees members from the inconvenient truth or 'troubling recognition' of wrongdoing while the more powerful get to 'shrug off the responsibility' for the harmful effects of their action, thereby ensuring legitimacy for further wrongdoing.

Secondly, with regard to the lessons learned from this experience, I note that since the judgment many people have offered advice on how to avoid a repeat of this scenario. The biggest lesson for employers is simple: employers and managers need to ensure that the lawful processes put in place for redundancy are not abused.

Thirdly, I chose reinstatement rather than taking the money – up to $1,994,284 – because I did not believe managers ought to be able to use taxpayers' money to buy themselves what they want. And, while a judgment vindicating me plus a lot of money may have assuaged my hurt, returning to that same workplace and being present within that university was an important public statement and a reminder of what happened. It was my own way of reclaiming the university back – at least symbolically. My work does matter to me, which is not to suggest that I have no life beyond my work, but that researching, writing and teaching are critical to who I am.

In conclusion, the final lesson relates to institutions and organisations committed to the idea and practice of securing justice – in my case it was a good judicial system and the NTEU. Specifically, my experience points to the value of a good union, to the way they are integral to our democratic culture and importantly to the value of individuals in them who know exactly *why* they do *what* they do.

# Part VI: University Futures?

# 15. Seeking the Necessary 'Resources of Hope' in the Neoliberal University

Jane Kenway, Rebecca Boden and Johannah Fahey

If academics cannot defend the university as a democratic public sphere, then who will? (Henry Giroux 2011)

If you do not resist the apparently inevitable, you will never know how inevitable the inevitable was. (Terry Eagleton 2011)

## Beyond dirges of despair: A biographical introduction

At the 2008 American Association for Geography conference in Boston, Jane and Rebecca gave papers at a symposium on global knowledge nodes and networks in higher education and research. Later, at dinner, they discussed the emergence, normalisation and changing inflections of the neoliberal university over the last two or three decades in Australia and the UK. Rebecca explained that writing about contemporary universities had a profound emotional impact on her and others she knew because it meant that they exposed themselves critically to the causes of personal discontent and distress. She proposed a multinational research project designed to explore systematically the affective aspects of neoliberal reforms in universities. Jane and Rebecca agreed they were tired of the constant descent into critique that characterises much progressive analysis of the contemporary university. They felt then, and even more in 2014, that even as such analyses and critiques multiply, and as their depth and sophistication increases, the situation just gets worse. There is no dialogue between such critiques and the universities, policies and practices that are the subject of them.

They pondered why, given the widespread problems of morale in our universities, academics remain in workplaces that often feel personally injurious and where teaching and research are increasingly colonised by simple-minded managerialist agendas and ruthless financial policies. Rebecca thought we might be a little like the victims of domestic violence who hope, often against hope, that things might get better: we remain, in part, because we often love aspects of our work and because some of us still hold onto the increasingly frayed fantasy of 'the ideal university' and the social good to which it might contribute.

It was not lost on us that we pondered these issues while enjoying conference leave overseas and that, as established professors, we have less reason to be miserable than academic colleagues on casual or short term contracts — 'academia's indentured servants' (Kendzior 2013), whose numbers are swelling in step with their unpaid workloads. In a National Tertiary Education Union (NTEU) report to an Australian public parliamentary hearing on insecure employment, Grahame McCulloch (2013) observes: 'On conservative estimates, of the 200,000 employees of public universities, around 68,000 have continuing employment, around 45,000 are on fixed term contracts, and roughly 86,000 are "regular casuals". Around half of undergraduate teaching is undertaken by casuals.'

He calls such casualisation 'the dirty little secret' of university expansion. But we should not engage in misery competitions and perhaps secure, senior academics have different reasons to be miserable. Later-career academics have witnessed the type of university we value in freefall and have experienced the bitter pain of this (see, for instance, Kenway 2011). For many, the university has not only been our life's work, but also the vehicle through which we have sought to contribute to the betterment of the human condition in socially and environmentally just ways. We share a mounting concern that many academics seem so weighed down by mind-numbing performative and compliance pressures and the constantly changing demands for 'change', all under the imperative of urgency, that many of us are losing a sense of agency.

Jane and Rebecca pondered Raymond Williams' (1989, 118) incisive claim that 'to be truly radical is to make hope possible rather than despair convincing' and feared that our constant critiques had helped make 'despair convincing' and, thus depressed and debilitated, we were barely capable of meeting Williams' demand to make 'hope possible'. We agreed on the need for a project that critically, imaginatively, positively and optimistically might help to provide 'resources of hope', to use another powerful Williams (1989) phrase.

We thought that the conference we were attending provided 'resources of hope'. It seemed relatively free of neoliberal nonsense and included inspiring people and presentations that provided fresh resources for thought, teaching and activism.

For example, Catherine Gibson and the late Julie Graham, collectively known as Gibson-Graham, talked about post-capitalist politics (2006). David Harvey, with a group of the early radical geographers, compared the conditions of possibility that they experienced as junior scholars with those of current graduate students and early-career academics. Harvey's *A Brief History of Neoliberalism* (2005) and *Spaces of Hope* (2000) were on display. And Noam Chomsky, arguably one of the most important social critics of our time, spoke to a packed auditorium and received a standing ovation.

We talked of building a project called 'Spaces of Hope in the Neoliberal University', where we would scamper around, full of youthful excitement again, working out what constitutes a space of hope, identifying and documenting those that exist and asking how more might more be created. As the evening wore on, and the wine depleted, our thinking was that, despite our customary gloom, it would be possible to identify particular research centres, research fields or sub-fields, teaching programs, conferences, even universities, that have either managed to maintain critical/creative/thought-full research and teaching agendas and that have managed to elude audit logics (or that have used them in clever insubordinate or mischievous ways). We also imagined that it might be possible to find small spaces within the academy where, despite the overall oppressive conditions, academics still manage to find various orders of 'old-fashioned' satisfaction, even pleasure, in their working worlds. And, most of all, we wanted to identify spaces of resistance to neoliberal agendas – spaces where academics have stood together against the powers and ideologies in the university sector and policy circles with positive outcomes. Our ultimate aim was to contribute to a new economy of hope, where these precious resources and their strategic utilisation combine so as to achieve a multiplier effect, spreading hope back through the university sector globally.

It is a fact of academic life that such exciting conference ruminations often evaporate once back in the boiler rooms of the neoliberal university. But, this conversation has stayed with us, and each has pursued these issues with others, including Johannah. We turn to these shortly when we begin to identify some 'resources of hope', but first a few harsh words about the neoliberal university, hope and hopelessness.

# The cold embrace of the neoliberal university

It is worthwhile reminding ourselves of the brutal reality of neoliberalism, if only to recall that there are alternatives. Neoliberalism is a form of political economy that validates and valorises the so-called free market as the primary mechanism for all human exchange and interaction. Market exchange thus becomes:

> an ethic in itself, capable of acting as a guide to all human action, and substituting for all previously held ethical beliefs, it emphasizes the significance of contractual relations in the marketplace. It holds that the social good will be maximized by maximizing the reach and frequency of market transactions, and it seeks to bring all human action into the domain of the market (Harvey 2005, 3).

If the free market is the warp and the weft of our life, then social institutions and organisations must also play their part. Thus, the neoliberal university is marketised, privatised, commercialised, franchised corporatised, managerialised, vocationalised, technologised, surveilled and securitised, and increasingly individualised, infantilised and casualised. It is anti union (both staff and student), free speech and activism (Epstein et al. 2007). While the fine detail of these practices varies between universities, countries, faculties and disciplines, to a significant extent they have become almost ubiquitous. All aspects of institutional life are 'badged' or 'branded' in their terms: teaching and research, governance, institutional ethics, academic freedom, academic and student work and identities, even social inclusion, and much more. As Collini (2012) documents so well, few traces remain of Newman's 'idea of a university', even with its associated problems. But notions of public good – where universities are resources that cannot be charged for, where use cannot be restricted and does not diminish their value (and indeed, enhances society) – are anathema to the neoliberal, free-market economy.

The guiding ideologies of the neoliberal university, including its epistemological hegemony, have become so normalised that many can't think beyond them. That the neoliberal project in universities continues unabated despite the global financial crisis bears testament to the normalisation of this ideology. As scholars, we have startlingly little to offer to replace that which has been so resoundingly found wanting. Rather, the austerity engendered by the crisis has been embraced by universities, which are now intent on downsizing 'unprofitable' disciplines or fields, shedding tenured staff and casualising an even larger percentage of the academic labour force.

Those fields and disciplines most dissonant with the neoliberal project have suffered the most – for instance, the humanities and social sciences, where a degree is less able to be converted into the personal quality of 'employability' in the commercial economy (Boden and Nedeva 2010). In the UK, the withdrawal of virtually all state funding for undergraduate provision means that students have to pay around £9,000 a year in fees, plus living expenses, out of money usually borrowed from the state and to be repaid from subsequent earnings. The clear disciplinary focus being encouraged (but not necessarily being achieved) is that the 'wrong' choice might result in lower earnings and 30 years of debt. Because teaching earns the dollar that pays for research in such areas, a decline in student numbers leads inexorably to a decline in staffing and other research resources. Problematically, these are the very intellectual areas where, most often, critical agendas find a space and which help give voice to subaltern knowledges and people; fields from which 'dangerous knowledges' can emanate.

Giroux (2008, 1) advises that '[n]eoliberalism is not just a system of economic power relations but also a political project of governing and persuasion intent on producing new forms of subjectivity and particular modes of conduct'. As Jane, Johannah and others argue in 'Haunting the Knowledge Economy' (Kenwayet al. 2006), the 'subjectivity and particular modes of conduct' it seeks to produce in universities is that of the 'techno-preneur'. Specifically, the primary and interrelated research imperatives of the globalising neoliberal university are a techno-scientific orientation to knowledge, an emphasis on 'knowledge networks' for the explicit purpose of 'knowledge transfer', and the commercialisation and commodification of knowledge. The ideal researchers implied (but probably never realised) are the techno-scientist, the instrumental and strategic knowledge networker transferring applicable knowledge to 'end users' and the knowledge entrepreneur, skilled at branding and making profit from knowledge.

Harvey (2008, 3) observes that neoliberalism involves:

> a shift away from the historic ideal of government as responsible to the people (in this case, for educating a national populace), towards a model in which *the people owe it to the nation* as well as to their own well-being to strive by any means necessary to educate themselves within a ruthlessly competitive struggle for which government provides the settings and the benchmarks of success [our italics].

This resonates within universities. Techno-preneurial academics' deepest loyalties are to 'their' university and they are expected to be ruthlessly competitive in advancing its, usually defensive, often absurd and sometimes paranoid agendas within the homogenised policies and benchmarks of nation-states and supra-national agencies such as the OECD. As we have argued (Kenway et al. 2006; Boden and Epstein 2006), the present conditions of knowledge production, with their reductionist notions of the knowledge economy and national innovation, have contributed to a crisis not only of the research but also of the moral imagination.

The stronghold of power and privilege that exists at the top of universities exemplifies this problem of the moral imagination and of the structural factors that allow the managerial classes to extract personal rent from 'their' organisations. A list of vice-chancellors' salaries was published in *The Australian* (6 June 2012): those with annual salaries over a million dollars were the VCs from Macquarie ($1,185,000), Monash ($1,105,000) and the University of Western Australia (UWA) ($1,005,000). And as Paul Frijters from *Core Economics* (15 May 2013) explains, in addition there are various bonuses and perquisites such as chauffeur-driven cars and business-class travel. The situation is similar in the UK, where governance issues allow vice-chancellors to enjoy significant personal financial benefits – even in 'underperforming' universities (Boden et al. 2012). In 2012–13 (the academic year when full tuition fees were introduced), the leaders of the 27 Russell Group universities – which regard themselves as the élite – enjoyed an average 8.1 per cent pay increase, bringing their average remuneration packages to £318,500 (Grove 2013). While direct comparisons are hard to make, this story of the pecuniary greed of many senior university managers is replicated in many other countries. The justification is clear: the neoliberal university has clear rationales and performance targets and these individuals are successful within those. In a free market (and, certainly in the UK, emphasis is placed on market factors when justifying these salaries), those who are organisationally entrepreneurial, which means doing as bidden, are rewarded handsomely.

In her Open Letter to the Vice-Chancellor of Sydney University, Raewyn Connell says:

> It's not encouraging to see university managers across the country increasingly resembling the executives of big corporations – in pay and conditions, in language, in techniques of running an organization, and in hard-handed approaches to the workforce. Corporate managers are an increasingly powerful, rich and selfish group in Australian society. The more that university managers integrate with them, the bigger the gulf that will open with the staff of the universities (Connell 2013).[1]

And as Libby Page (2014) points out in *The Guardian*, anger is mounting in the UK against VCs' salary hikes at the very moment when they are cutting universities to the bone.

---

1   The university management's response to Connell can be found at http://images.smh.com.au/file/2013/03/26/4142308/Open%2520Response.pdf?rand=1364286577433.

# Hope and 'structures of feeling'[2] in the hope-less university

The concept of hope gained enormous popular currency during Barack Obama's rousing first presidential campaign and through his book *The Audacity of Hope* (2006). But, as Chomsky predicted in his Boston address in 2008, it was ultimately devoid of political content. In contrast, we offer a sociological, cultural and political reading of hope, drawing on the work of Ghassan Hage, Harvey and Giroux, which casts hope as that which provides an alternative to the hegemonic present.

Hage (2003) argues that societies distribute hope and that the type of 'affective attachment' produced by particular societies is closely linked to their 'capacity to distribute hope':

> The caring society is essentially an embracing society that generates hope among its citizens and induces them to care for it. The defensive society, such as the one we have in Australia today as a consequence of neoliberal ideologies, suffers from a scarcity of hope and creates citizens who see threats everywhere. It generates worrying citizens and paranoid nationalism (2003, 3).

Commenting on Gramsci's use of the aphorism 'pessimism of the intellect, optimism of the will' Harvey (2000, 17) asserts:

> we are not in prison cells. Why, then, might we willingly choose a metaphor drawn from incarceration as a guiding light for our own thinking … Do we not also owe it to him, out of respect for the kind of fortitude and political passion he exhibited, to transform that phrase in such a way as to seek an optimism of the intellect that, properly coupled with an optimism of the will, might produce a better future? … and if I parallel Raymond Williams's title *Resources of Hope* with the title *Spaces of Hope*, then it is because I believe that in this moment in our history we have something of great import to accomplish in exercising an optimism of the intellect in order to open up ways of thinking that have for too long remained foreclosed.

For Giroux (2012, 38), as for Harvey, hope is potentially 'a subversive force'. He talks of 'educated hope' which is:

> more than a politics, it is also a pedagogical and performative practice that provides the foundation for enabling human beings to learn about their potential as moral and civic agents. Hope is the outcome of those educational practices and struggles that tap into memory and lived experiences while at the same time linking individual responsibility with a progressive sense of social change. As a form of utopian longing, educated hope opens up horizons of comparison

---

2   This concept is from Raymond Williams (1977, Chapter 3).

by evoking not just different histories but different futures. Educated hope is a subversive force when it pluralizes politics by opening up a space for dissent, making authority accountable, and becoming an activating presence in promoting social transformation.

We see the neoliberal university as, in many ways, a paranoid, defensive institution that has lost 'the capacity to distribute hope' to many of its staff and students. In so doing, it may have fatally undermined our capacity to contribute to the redistribution of hope more broadly – to fulfil the broader social function of the university. It does not seem to care about staff opinions and values and certainly shows us little respect. The neoliberal university fosters both the techno-preneur, who knows the rules of the game and plays ruthlessly to win and also harbours academics who don't necessarily like the rules of the game but are compliant politically, fulfilling the fantasies of the 'science of compliance' (Creed 2013). Audacity is in short supply, but cynicism, fear and even hostility and despair are not.

Our view is that some academics feel a sense of shame about their quiet compliance, particularly those who have seniority and relative security, those who have more room to manoeuvre and who have an implicit responsibility to be altruistically active to try to protect some of the values of the university as a 'democratic public sphere' in which:

> critique, dialogue, critical theory and informed judgement constituted a pedagogical necessity through which the institution could develop a public awareness of itself and empower administrators, researchers, teachers, and students to act in socially responsible ways that made such an awareness to those both inside and outside the institution meaningful (Giroux 2012, 113).

True, many on the Left in academe have written critical pieces about the fates and futures of the university; pieces that speak about 'the ruins', 'the end of', 'the future of', 'the purposes of', 'repositioning', 'beyond' and so forth. But too few accept the responsibility that Giroux speaks of to develop a wider public awareness. Maybe they are just too tired or too alienated, or both.

Academic staff do not necessarily have confidence in or trust those further up the management chain, those who are separated by their well-remunerated privilege and who are nonetheless busily engaged in merciless practices of 'cutting' and 'tightening'. Such negative affectivity is exacerbated by the ever-increasing, time-consuming, mind-numbing, energy- and morale-sapping audit demands of the job. The cold embrace of the neoliberal university has smothering effects. As a friend said recently 'I feel I can't breathe'.

All of this points to the importance of recognising that universities have become highly emotional spaces. They are greedy and needy, as Susan Franzway (2001) makes clear, but also they can be toxic, and such toxicity is often contagious, not just among staff but also graduate students. Speaking of the situation for anthropology PhD students in the USA, Sarah Kendzior (2013) says:

> Graduate students live in constant fear. Some of this fear is justified, like the fear of not finding a job. But the fear of unemployment leads to a host of other fears, and you end up with a climate of conformity, timidity, and sycophantic emulation. Intellectual inquiry is suppressed as 'unmarketable', interdisciplinary research is marked as disloyal, public engagement is decried as 'unserious', and critical views are written anonymously lest a search committee find them. I saw the best minds of my generation destroyed by the Academic Jobs Wiki. The cult mentality of academia not only curtails intellectual freedom, but hurts graduate students in a personal way. They internalize systemic failure as individual failure, in part because they have sacrificed their own beliefs and ideas to placate market values.

Our views about the structure of feeling in contemporary universities have been reached not through the sort of systematic research that Rebecca originally proposed, but through observations and conversations in many different university circumstances over many years, complemented by Zipin's (2010) powerful chapter on the 'ethico-emotive ground tone' of the contemporary university. It is instructive to put our views alongside those expressed in the powerful, poignant open letters written by Sydney University staff to senior management explaining why they supported the NTEU's enterprise bargaining campaign and industrial action and about their hopes for the future of the university.[3] In telling the university of her intention to strike and to resign, Sue Woolf (2013) of the Department of English, in which she taught Creative Writing, wrote:

> I looked up from my research and teaching, and realized that the educational institution I'd joined so joyfully had become a severely hierarchical corporation that I hadn't a hope of approaching in a democratic way. The style of management of our university – management defined, it seems to me, solely as the managing of systems, structures, finances and building, never people – has robbed the colleagues I've been proud to be amongst, colleagues chosen for their brilliant scholarship and eagerness to share it, of any hope of democratic governance, even of the courage to speak out. I mourn almost as in a romantic dream the old days when our then Head of School asked us creators of literature – I work closely with a major poet and a celebrated screenwriter – what was required in our Creative Writing unit – which is why, I believe, we flourished, for as in all units, the people who know what's most needed surely are the people who've been employed for knowing. That seems a truism too obvious to be contestable.

---

3   More such letters can be retrieved from http://www.nteu.org.au/sydney/article/Open-Letters-14308.

Now, in this corporation, what we teach and the way in which we are to research and teach seems imposed on us, and continually under surveillance, as if we're infants and don't know what we're doing. For a terrible contagion has gripped all levels of management, where management seems considered only efficient if it's remote, suspicious and authoritarian.

Other letters speak of love of the job, the institution and of enabling learning. Raewyn Connell draws these themes together in her lecture *Love, Fear and Learning in the Market University* (2013).

In the UK, academics are less willing to speak loudly. But research has shown that academic staff in UK universities are unhappy in their jobs, have little perceived control over their environment and feel very stressed (Edwards et al. 2009). Likewise, the University and College Union (UCU), the academics' trade union, found similar issues in 2012.[4] But there is a relative public silence from individual academics – and perhaps the muffling of their voices aids the sense of stress and toxicity.

Hage (2003) points out that, along with 'the end of society' associated with the neoliberal project, has come the end of the notion that any social collective might distribute hope. Commenting on Bourdieu, Hage (p. 18) maintains that:

> what characterised neo-liberal economic policy in his eyes was not that it was shaped by a society marred by inequality, but that the very idea of society, of commitment to some form of distribution of hope, was disappearing ... the greatest casualty, and the one that has most bearing on the quality of our lives, is neither the decline of sovereignty nor of identity as such, but the decline of society.

We argue that the neoliberalisation of universities and the attendant onslaught on academic autonomy, freedoms and imagination have destroyed the society of the academy. The techno-preneur is the ideal neoliberal subject, trained and honed to the task. Nose to the grindstone, s/he is the antithesis of the academic flâneur, purposively wandering the streets of the academy to explore, imagine and hope.

## Resources of hope

We feel obliged, at this point, to disembark from the descent to critique and to take our own advice to be hope-full. But hopefulness requires resources with which to think, imagine and act. We therefore offer some possible, but very real, 'resources of hope'.

---

4   See www.ucu.org.uk/index.cfm?articleid=6344, retrieved 28 September 2014.

## Spaces of hope

Documenting and suggesting alternative types of organisations and practices that speak to different and preferable ethics, and making them visible, is a well-established activity amongst progressives and radicals. This is one direction in which Rebecca has taken her work. She works at the University of Roehampton, which she feels is becoming a space of hope as the result of the determined efforts of a senior management team dedicated to fostering a collegial university and an ethic of social justice and responsibility. She has been locating and documenting the practices of other universities around the world that she describes as 'alternatives to current reforms'. In a field report on Mondragón University, an integral part of the massive Mondragón Co-operative Corporation in Spain, she and her colleagues say (Greenwood et al. 2011, 41):

> Gibson–Graham (2006) argue cogently for such a postcapitalist future (as they name it). They do not deny the need for capital, or business activities, but posit a different sort of capitalism – new ways of combining money and people to produce the tangible and intangible goods that society needs. They also advocate exploring current practices to find spaces of hope for reordering the world, and breaking the hegemonic paradigm of private market supremacy. Although the Mondragón co-operatives are avowedly capitalist, they have combined capital and work in quite a different way to the current neoliberal trend and have worked consistently for sixty years to generate a solidary economic and social order.

Mondragón University is a self-managed organisation, where elaborate governance structures allow its owner academics, staff and administrators to participate effectively in decision-making. The university sees itself in the service of the local community – which itself is largely organised on a cooperative basis.

Some spaces of hope might also be aspirational. For example, Rebecca's paper *Trust Universities? Governance for Post-Capitalist Futures* (Boden et al. 2012), proposes the creation of 'trust universities' as non-revocable trusts under which the beneficial use of university assets would only be allowed to students and staff on condition they pursued socially, culturally and economically useful goals, explicitly negotiated with surrounding society.

## Intergenerational hope

'The draining of many bright young people into purely market-oriented activities' is something that concerns Connell. She sees this as fuelled partly by their 'difficulty in seeing worthwhile careers following on from the research higher degree' and by the 'squeeze on public sector funding generally and on higher education specifically'. All of this, she argues (2008, 70–2), is having a deleterious effect on the production of 'future generations of intellectual workers'; those with 'the skills, the interest and the institutional capacity' to undertake the sorts of socially engaged work that she herself undertakes.

Like Connell, Jane and Johannah have addressed the manner in which the research imagination is being stifled and how to construct a 'defiant global research imagination'. In the opening chapter to *Globalising the Research Imagination* (2008), they explain the ways in which the research imagination is being globalised from 'on high' and ask what possibilities exist for defiant research theories, practices and identities, how such alternatives might be conceptualised in the globalising circumstances of current universities and what this might mean for the next generation of researchers.

In so doing, they offer some pedagogical principles designed to help doctoral supervisors/advisers support students in developing a defiant global research imagination. These principles include seeking and provoking 'uncomfortable thought', examining 'unexamined habits of looking', trying 'to see from elsewhere' and 'striving for complexity'. These ideas are drawn from Greek-French thinker Cornelius Castoriadis, a philosopher, economist, social critic and psychoanalyst. In translating his ideas about the imagination, Jane and Johannah develop an argument for a research imagination that is rich with critical, creative and ethical, individual and collective possibilities and responsibilities. They contend that such an imagination should seek to unsettle the global hegemonic research imagination associated with neoliberalism.

Rebecca, as part of a team of like-minded scholars, has recently received substantial funding (€4.3 million) to do precisely what Jane and Johannah discussed in terms of the next generation of researchers. Rebecca is part of a team of researchers from six universities representing five European countries that won funding for an EU Marie Curie *Initial Training Network* program called UNIKE (*Universities in the Knowledge Economy*), which addresses the changing roles and scope of universities in emerging global knowledge economies and regions. The team will train a networked group of critical researchers, consisting of 12 doctoral and three postdoctoral positions. Although the proposal was cloaked in a knowledge economy discourse, the project will concentrate on the identification and canvassing of new alternatives, to be carried forward by the early career researchers. One of the doctoral students works on alternative forms of university ownership, finance and organisation – specifically cooperatives. One of the postdocs is exploring new landscapes in publishing and knowledge dissemination, and another is looking at academic entrepreneurialism, civil society and democracy. Overall, the objective is to produce new and imaginative thinking that proposes how universities might be reconstituted away from the neoliberal model.

## Figures of hope

Social activists often share stories of other like-minded activists in different times and places to both pay tribute and to provide inspirational resources for present times. The neoliberal university needs such figures of hope. They might be characterised, using Harvey (2000, 234), as the 'insurgent architect' who has certain emotions and desires, including hope, 'all of which play out through social activities and actions' and who is 'endowed with certain powers and skills that can be used to [offer alternatives and] change the world'.

> The architect can (indeed must) desire, think and dream of difference. And in addition to the speculative imagination which he or she necessarily deploys, she or he has available some special resources for critique, resources from which to generate alternative visions as to what might be possible (Harvey 2000, 238).

Jane and Johannah are currently writing a book, *Moving Ideas and Mobile Intellectuals*, where they invoke the figure of the insurgent intellectual, drawing on the ideas of some of the feminists involved in the study,[5] who seek to create spaces of hope in their universities, in classrooms and in thought. Here are some 'tasters', in their own words, of their practical theories that arise, in part, from their own mobility and the hope-full lessons it has taught them.

Meaghan Morris, now living in Australia, was Head of Cultural Studies at a Hong Kong university when interviewed. She explains the frame of mind that informed her work there, including developing new cultural studies courses, in her keynote address for *Moving Ideas and Research Policies: Australian intellectuals in the Global Context* (2008), the conference arising from the ARC project:

> At this point of uncertainty in advance of any reform, we have two ways to go. One is the way of cynicism: we can go through the motions, adding new tasks to the 'compliance' pile of chores while changing nothing fundamental to the work we do as teachers. The other, more adventurous, way is that of creativity: taking these tasks as an opportunity to further what my colleagues call 'a project of hope', we can use them to realize dreams and goals of our own.

With her colleagues, Morris has avoided the politics of pessimism and nostalgia and sought to identify the possibilities for progressive educational practice in the nooks and crannies of neoliberal higher education reform in Hong Kong. This is seen as a move from 'cultural critique to critical pragmatics' (Hui Po-keung 2006) in which the insights of cultural studies are put to work politically (see further, Chan and Hui 2007).

---

5   This arises from the ARC project, 'Moving Ideas: Mobile Policies, Researchers and Connections in the Social Sciences and Humanities ⊠ Australia in the global context, 2006–2010'.

As an example of a travel story in which 'floating notions' provide 'creative occasions' for her, Morris talks about 'difference', which she points out is a 'new humanities keyword that often signifies 'the West' in Asia' (2008), hence it is a story 'of difference about difference' (2008). *Traces* is a 'multilingual journal of cultural theory and translation', published in Chinese, English, Japanese and Korean editions, that was founded by Naoki Sakai and of which Morris was the senior editor for five years. Each issue appears in all four languages and the journal as a whole is collectively edited by scholars, who work in these and other languages. *Traces* is distinctive as there is no 'base' language of enquiry — every issue is multilingual in composition from the very beginning. *Traces* therefore takes today's management talk of process metaphors of circulation and flow seriously, in the sense that the approach is seriously creative. The journal is representative of a hope-full 'experiment in a collaborative mode beyond the simple version of "travelling theory" understood as thought originating in the Euro-American academy and then circulating elsewhere' (Morris 2008). And, it points to work practices that are very different from those valorised by the neoliberal university.

Sneja Gunew, now working in Canada, grew up in Australia from the age of four. Although all of her schooling was in Australia, she still felt like a migrant on the margins. This led to her idea of 'stammering pedagogy' – using a major language in a revolutionary minor mode, following Deleuze's minoritarian status within majority. She said to us, 'I have always been very aware of habitual ways of thinking which can be very paralysing without you realising it. You can fall into certain habits of thought, certain assumptions, and I invariably try to test this constantly (as much as one can)' (2008). Gunew's teaching and research have always challenged the heartlands of the dominant.

Stammering pedagogy is:

> an attempt to suggest a model for teaching that does not claim to have absolute answers, indeed, is sceptical of the discourse of answers, the position of 'those who know'. Such a pedagogy is attuned to the ghostly dimension of other meanings in any pursuit of a definitive meaning (2004, 132).

To Gunew this approach to teaching:

> is a matter not only of constantly crossing borders but of drawing attention to their presence – the ways in which their barbed-wire fences, their cells of solitary confinement, suddenly appear in the heart of the homeland, the metropolitan centre (2003, 53).

> It is tuned in to the stammering, the dislocations which seethe beneath the surfaces, whether these be of globalization or nationalisms. Within this framework, and

when used strategically and critically, those multi-multiculturalisms help to sustain such a stammering pedagogy, allowing it to disrupt the gathering menace, once again, of monolithic models of knowledge (2004, 132).

In Gunew's research work in Australia, she sought to reveal 'the foreign within Australian culture itself' (2003: 44) by rereading canonical Australian literature (a particular manifestation of the dominant culture) from an outsider position constructed in non-Anglo-Celtic Australian writings (Gunew 1994). She set up the first courses in non-Anglo-Celtic Australian writing and orature, immigrant histories, library collections and bibliographies and also framed the first (multi) cultural arts policies (Gunew and Rizvi 1994). In her teaching in Canada, she seeks 'to find ways of expressing the alertness to differences' (2004, 125). For her, the 'stammer' is a pedagogical model she uses in her classroom where she seeks to make her North American students aware of the 'foreignness' of another culture while at the same time 'destabilizes their own cultural assumptions and certainties in producing meaning' (2004, 126). This intervention challenges hegemonic practices of thought.

Rosi Braidotti, now working in the Netherlands, came to Australia aged 15 and her experiences of migration contributed to her idea of 'nomadic consciousness', most recently elaborated in *Nomadic Theory: The Portable Rosi Braidotti* (2011):

> It is an ethics based on the necessity of meeting the challenges of the contemporary transformations with creativity and courage ... *The challenge is how to put the 'active' back into activism*. In so far as this position entails accountability for one's historical situation, it expresses not only a sense of social responsibility but also an affect. Hannah Arendt used to call it: love for the world (Braidotti 2005, 178 [our italics]).

Throughout her work, Braidotti insists on the importance of deploying philosophical debates in the interests of making practical social and political contributions, stressing what she calls 'positive ethics'. In terms of feminist thought, Braidotti recognises that feminism has opted for an 'optimism of the will' whereby 'feminist intellectual and political energies are converging on the ethical project of contributing to the construction of social horizons of hope' (2005, 178).

The Gender Studies Network that she set up in Italy in 1988 and which she ran until 2005 is part of this social horizon of hope. Today it has 130 universities in 27 countries and it is still the largest gathering of gender studies/feminist networks in Europe, and perhaps the world. By including Korea, China and South Africa it contributes to a particular construction of the European space. Braidotti says, 'our role is to keep it open, keep it tolerant, to keep the exchange of ideas in a non-commercial way, free universal education. If we can't stop the commercialisation of universities then at least we can try and contain it'.

For these three insurgent intellectuals optimism of the will, intellect and spirit with regard to teaching and research involves such things as refiguring difficulties as opportunities, constantly challenging 'monolithic models of knowledge' and generating theoretical innovations that reach towards alternative practices.

## Hope-full student activism

University staff have some reasons to be optimistic when students conduct highly visible, energetic and clever campaigns. In 2013 alone, around the world but especially in various parts of South America, many campaigns have opposed the neoliberal agenda in universities. Specific issues have included fee hikes, the privatisation of student loans and services, the closure of student unions, the debt burden, the poor pay and conditions of university academic and non-academic staff, the diminution of the university curriculum particularly in the humanities and social sciences, VCs' excessive salaries, and university repression of student dissent (including the use of heavy-handed management, and security guards and police on campus). In the UK in 2013, there were student actions at the universities of Birmingham, Sussex, Edinburgh, Sheffield, Exeter, London and Warwick and a mass rally was held in London in late 2013 opposing 'cops on campus' (Grove 2013).

One such protest, and the path it took, points to some of the very real concerns of students about curriculum diminution and the discursive and punitive strategies of university management. The students' protests at La Trobe University in Australia in 2012 were against proposed budget cuts in the Humanities and Social Sciences (HUSS) Faculty and against the proposed loss of up to 45 staff; a sorry story documented poignantly in this collection by Kirkby and Reiger, whose 'affective attachment' has been sorely tested. Art history, gender, sexuality and diversity studies, Indonesian, linguistics, and religion and spirituality were all to be axed (*The Age*, 20 June 2012). These fields potentially contribute to what Giroux (2012) calls the 'formative cultures necessary to a vital democracy'.

The students of the 'Stop the HUSS Cuts Collective' demands included that 'The VC, other members of University Council and senior management take cuts to their pay; the money saved to be spent on retaining staff and subjects in the HUSS Faculty' (@ndy, *Slackbastard*, 22 August 2012). According to *The Australian*'s list of salaries for 2012, the previous La Trobe VC's annual salary was $705,000. It is likely his successor, Professor John Dewar, receives similar remuneration. During a noisy, but non-violent, student action in a university foyer, when accidentally coming across the students, Dewar studiously avoided any contact with them. According to Kirsten Veness (2012) of ABC News, he later said he supported students' right to protest as 'it adds colour and movement to life on campus'. However, the university insisted that 'protests must be officially approved' and that the university could suspend or expel students for protesting on campus without permission until after Open Day (Lee 2012). This indicated that the VC's predilections were more for beige and stasis than 'colour and movement'. And his later remarks on *The Conversation* (Dewar 2012) confirmed his keenness to take the active out of activism.

After intense lobbying from staff and students, the senior executive made some concessions on Indonesian, gender studies, linguistics and art history (Trounson 2012), but still punished student protesters on charges that were eventually dismissed. More recently, the VC still wants to restructure and cut jobs to 'make the university modern and agile to meet the needs of the community and industry' and to allow it to adapt to the changing tertiary environment (ABC News, 21 October 2013). Giroux (2012, 123) notes that universities once 'provided a space for the nurturing of democratic ideals and offered a shelter for radical intellectuals and mode of critique that vigorously defended higher education's public role and the formative culture and modes of literacy that were that were essential to its survival and promise'.

Student anger at what is happening to universities is on the rise and is exhibited on the streets sometimes in quite playful ways, such as the Victorian College of the Arts students, who, drawing on *Les Miserables*, waved the red flag in a 2013 protest and offered a stirring rendition of 'Hear the People Sing'.

Image 15.1: Hear the students sing, 14 May 2013

Source: Adam Howard, Colby College, Waterville, Maine, USA.

Close by was a provocative art installation by Van Rudd.

**Image 15.2: Student cuts, 14 May 2013**

Source: Artwork by visual artist and activist, Van Thanh Rudd. Courtesy of Adam Howard, Colby College, Waterville, Maine, USA.

One of the least remarked upon features of these 2013 rallies is that they attracted such comparatively good numbers despite the many factors militating against student activism (Pitman 2014). These factors include the fact that in Australia the nature of student guilds/unions has altered so significantly since the Liberal government introduced voluntary student unionism in 2005. Since then, most student unions have been subject to the same neoliberal pressures as universities; their 'hosts' now largely govern them and many have tailored their practices and philosophies accordingly. This has made it much harder for more progressive and radical students to gain a foothold and for them to organise on campus. Interestingly, due to student resistance, Western Australia did not follow down the same path. As a consequence, students still effectively control and have access to serious resources. A 700-strong on-campus crowd during these rallies was made possible at Curtin University because of this but also because a socialist and highly activist ticket won the student elections.

Hage (2003, 30) says: 'The caring society is essentially an embracing society that generates hope among its citizens and induces them to care for it.' It is clear that student campaigners have actively embraced such a notion. And, as these and many other campaign examples indicate, student activism is a resource for hope for the academy as a whole and for academics. But this begs the question of how often university staff consider this and work with student activists.

## Hope as collective action and civic courage

Recent activities at Sydney University speak to the benefits of collective action as a resource for hope. In the recent enterprise bargaining round, the VC (on an annual salary of $905,000 in 2012) and his senior management team proposed an enterprise agreement that ruthlessly attacked the staff's working lives and conditions and also sought to cripple the NTEU (Connor 2013) The measures and their likely effects are revealed starkly in staff members' public letters to management. On the same day as the national student strikes against the cuts noted earlier, Sydney University staff also went on a 24-hour strike. Altogether, in 2013 there were seven staff strikes and there was an important overlap between the students and the staff. Bronwyn Winter, in her open letter, points out that 'many students have expressed their strong support for me and my colleagues' and that 'a number have also been attending pickets'. Such 'coalition building' is one of the many techniques currently being deployed in the revitalisation of the union movement worldwide as it faces the changes wrought by neoliberal globalisation (Burgmann 2009).

But spaces for hope are not always pretty, as the 'cops off campus' campaign with regard to the University of London demonstrates (Grove 2013). But the example that shocked the world was in the USA in 2011 when University of California, Davis student protesters were pepper-sprayed. The images of a security officer, wearing riot gear, spraying pepper directly in the faces of a line of protesters who were seated on the ground, went viral. Gabbat (2013) reports that '[t]he university had paid out $1m to settle a lawsuit filed by demonstrators who were pepper-sprayed during the protest. The sum represented $30,000 per demonstrator and an additional $250,000 in legal fees.' If nothing else, what a waste of money in times of austerity.

A shocking feature of the actions at Sydney University was the use of police and security guards. They roughly evicted activist students from lecture theatres during 'lecture bashes' and were very heavy handed in their response to students and staff on the picket lines. Students developed a petition that was sent to the VC demanding that he not use the police on campus.[6] They outlined the physical assaults students experienced and the dangerousness of the police tactics: 'One student had his leg broken and is currently awaiting surgery. Other students and staff seem to have cracked ribs and one has a broken nose. Several students and staff members were trampled. Many others were shoved, grabbed, bruised or struck.'

---

6   www.change.org/en-AU/petitions/to-the-vice-chancellor-of-the-university-of-sydney-refuse-to-allow-cops-on-campus. Retrieved 11 February 2014.

*My Wonderful Day* (Raue 2013) is a student's account of his own experiences of police brutality on 14 May 2013. He tells of being choked: 'I was frightened for my life. The grip around my neck never wavered, and I feared that I would pass out or even die, unnoticed …' He says he 'can't stop crying and shaking' and points out that his subsequent distress was made worse by those who blamed him for being there in the first place.

This, and other examples around the globe, led us to the view that the use of police and heavy-handed security staff is an underacknowledged feature of the corporate university. As Fitzclarence (2012–13) points out, modes of policing dissent are becoming increasingly militaristic around the world. The fact that people are still prepared to put their bodies courageously on the line under such circumstances is certainly a resource of hope.

Clearly, collective action as a resource for hope requires courage and pride. About her decision to strike at Sydney University, Nour Dados, a Senior Research Associate on a short-term contract, said this:

> It is no easy decision for staff to commit to fourty(sic)-eight hour strike action. That decision is all the more difficult for those of us who cannot be sure that we will have work next semester, or next year. Yet it is a decision that I am proud to make. I know that those of us who will be on the picket lines on Tuesday and Wednesday are not fighting only for our own work rights today. We are honouring the struggle of those who were here before us, and creating pathways for those who will come after us.[7]

The pride people take in hopeful activism and civic courage extends beyond the self and the more restricted matter of working conditions. Dados is concerned about 'those who will come after us' and this sentiment was echoed in a YouTube video in 2013 called *A Message from Staff at the University of Sydney*,[8] where staff and students point to the implications for others (teachers and social workers, thinkers and inventors, for example) now and in the future, of the attacks on their working conditions. As this suggests, our teaching and research often involves those whose work has the potential to challenge the misdistribution of hope in a society marred by inequality.

In October 2013, university staff at Sydney University finally reached an acceptable enterprise agreement with management after what was nearly a year-long campaign,[9] one that was creative, not just defensive, in the techniques deployed. One of the oft-remarked-upon side-effects of this campaign has been the sense of university community it helped to build. This bridged many of the

---

7    www.nteu.org.au/sydney/blog/University-of-Sydney-39/tag/open%20letters. Retrieved 11 February 2014.
8    www.youtube.com/watch?v=oP5CR_B4MhE, 12 May 2013. Retrieved 11 February 2014.
9    www.nteu.org.au/sydney/bargaining. Retrieved 19 November 2013.

so-called silos that university life often erects between faculties, administrative and academic staff, casual and tenured, senior and junior staff as well as between staff and students. As Hage (2003, 15) says:

> If hope is the way we construct a meaningful and dignified social life. If hope is the way we construct a meaningful future for ourselves … such futures are only possible within society, because society is the distributor of social opportunities for self-realisation. We can call this hope societal hope.

## Hoping with others

These resources speak to the importance of academics developing extended connections and communities as resources for hope. Of course, this involves all manner of organisations challenging the widespread political inertia brought about by so many years of neoliberalism, mobilising staff and students alike. Rebecca and her colleagues (Boden et al. 2012) argue that an effect of neoliberalisation has been to negate the social relations of universities with surrounding society, instead turning them into a set of customer–contractor deals. Meaningful and hope-full relationships with the societies in which universities are situated need to be rebuilt. After all, as Connell (2008) observes, university academics:

> have a speaking position that allows you to … do hopefully more progressive things than simply reproduce that privilege. To use that privilege to advance consciousness and social justice in other spheres such as school education, gender politics. But it's an inherently contradictory position, and I feel emotionally in solidarity with movements that are contesting the whole system of global privilege that produces that intelligentsia. I'm now old enough and ugly enough to live with contradiction.

As she also says (2013), neoliberalism in education 'has its own contradictions and weaknesses; educators face the task of making these clear, and putting together new agendas for just and inclusive education, and pro-education, rather than pro-profit, coalitions'.

Giroux argues that the reduction of universities to contracted providers in a knowledge economy should provide special impetus to academics to be in the vanguard of hope, forging coalitions to build better alternatives – we have everything to fight for. For Giroux, the crisis in universities is part of the crisis in democracy.

There are so many alliances that we can forge by working in an engaged way with others, outside the university. We applaud the European continental notion of the public intellectual, speaking, writing and acting outside of the constraints imposed by neoliberal pseudo-scientific methodologies and performance criteria that demand and delimit modes of publication.

## Images of hope

In 1974 the young French tightrope walker Phillippe Petit, with no safety net or harness, walked, and sometimes even danced, for an hour along a wire suspended between New York's Twin Towers. Despite the subsequent destruction of the buildings, Petit's glorious and audacious act cannot be erased and remains in the public imagination as a hopeful and courageous, but, of course, precarious, moment. But further, the documentary *Man on Wire* (2008) highlights the bureaucratic resistance Petit experienced and his and his team's ultimate manner of getting around it, which was, in the end, not to ask for permission and to evade security.

Some, of pessimistic inclination, might think that in neoliberal times hopeful optimism is outright foolish. But as the man on the wire indicates, apparently foolish acts can be beautiful, sublime and inspirational. They speak to what unifies hope 'optimism, fear, desire, wishing, wanting, dreaming, waiting and confidence'. These 'express in one way or another modes in which human beings relate to their future' (Hage 2003, 10).

Such symbolism might be seen as a resource of hope, reminding us that the seemingly impossible is possible, and of the importance of optimism of the will, intellect and spirit. The towers were signifiers of Western global capitalism. Their collapse now signifies the beginnings of current forms of paranoid nationalism in many nation-states. Certainly creating and sustaining spaces of hope in the neoliberal university is akin to tightrope-walking in the space between the twin towers of institutional and individual neoliberal sensibilities.

# Concluding thoughts ...

In our view, 'hope' in the neoliberal university will not be redistributed from above – positive change will not come from that direction. Hope requires identifications and imaginations that take us well beyond the techno-preneurial subjectivities so favoured and the acts of compliance that we have come to practise so reluctantly but nonetheless so expertly. It involves using our own ideas and developing alternative mechanisms for the distribution of hope; it involves becoming insurgent and defiant and a changed 'structures of feeling'. We leave the last words to Giroux (2012, 38–9):

> The goal of educated hope is not to liberate the individual from the social – a central tenet of neoliberalism – but to take seriously the notion that the individual can only be liberated through the social. Educated hope as a subversive, defiant practice should provide a link, however transient, provisional, and contextual, between vision and critique on the one hand, and engagement and transformation on the other. That is, for hope to be consequential it has to be grounded in a project that has some hold on the present. Hope becomes meaningful to the degree that it identifies agencies and processes, offers alternatives to an age of profound pessimism, reclaims an ethic of compassion and justice, and struggles for those institutions in which equality, freedom, and justice flourish.

# Bibliography

@ndy, Slackbastard, 22 August 2012. Retrieved 11 February 2014, from http://slackbastard.anarchobase.com/?p=32138.

ABC News, 'Union warns against La Trobe Uni job cuts', 21 October 2013. Retrieved 15 December 2013, from http://www.abc.net.au/news/2013-10-21/union-warns-against-la-trobe-uni-job-cuts/5034680.

Academic Ranking of World Universities. Retrieved 28 September 2014, from http://www.shanghairanking.com/index.html.

Acker, Joan, 'Gendered Organizations and Intersectionality: Problems and Possibilities' (2012) 31(3) *Equality, Diversity and Inclusion: An International Journal* 214–24.

—— 'Inequality Regimes: Gender, Class and Race in Organizations' (2006) 20(4) *Gender and Society* 441–64.

—— 'Hierarchies, Jobs, Bodies: A Theory of Gendered Organizations' (1990) 4(2) *Gender and Society* 139–58.

Ackers, Louise, *Participation of Women Researchers in the TMR Marie Curie Fellowships*, 2000. Retrieved 23 April 2013, from ftp://ftp.cordis.europa.eu/pub/improving/docs/women_final_rpt_3march2000.pdf.

Adelman, Clifford, *Learning Accountability from Bologna: A Higher Education Policy Primer Issues Brief*, Washington Institute for Higher Education Policy, Washington, 2008.

Adkins, Lisa, *Gendered Work: Sexuality, Family and the Labour Market*, Open University Press, Buckingham, 1995.

Aghion, Philipe, Mathias Dewatripont, Caroline M Hoxby, Andreus Mas Colell and Andre Sapir, 'The Governance and Performance of Research Universities: Evidence for Europe and the United States', Working Paper, National Bureau of Economic Research, Cambridge, Massachusetts, 2009.

Aitkin, Don, 'Research Policy in Australia 1989–1999: A Retrospective' (2000) 8(2) *Research Evaluation* 151–4.

Akerlof, George A, *Writing the 'The Market for "Lemons"': A Personal Interpretive Essay,* 2003. Retrieved 16 April 2014, from www.nobelprize.org/nobel_prizes/economic-sciences/laureates/2001/akerlof-article.html.

—— 'The Market for "Lemons": Quality Uncertainty and the Market Mechanism' (1970) 84 *Quarterly Journal of Economics* 488–500.

ALRC (Australian Law Reform Commission), Managing Justice: A Review of the Federal Civil Justice System, Report No. 89, Australian Law Reform Commission, Sydney, 2000. Retrieved from www.alrc.gov.au/sites/default/files/pdfs/publications/ALRC89.pdf.

Altbach, Philip, 'The Dilemmas of Ranking' (2006) 42 *International Higher Education* 2–3.

Anderson, Gina, 'Carving Out Time and Space in the Managerial University' (2006) 19(5) *Journal of Organizational Change Management* 578–92.

Anderson, Ryan, 'Savage Minds Interview: Sarah Kendzior' 2013. Retrieved 13 May 2013, from http://backupminds.wordpress.com/2013/05/12/savage-minds-interview-sarah-/#more-404.

Anonymous, 'Technology Transfer Centre to Aid Industry', *The Australian Higher Education Supplement*, 24 April 1985.

—— 'Industry and University to Meet', *The Australian Higher Education Supplement*, 5 September 1984.

—— 'A Parting Shot at "Mediocre" Universities', *The Australian Higher Education Supplement*, 1 August 1984.

—— 'Overseas Job Models Praised', *The Australian Higher Education Supplement*, 6 July 1983.

—— 'Competing for Student Advantage', *The Australian Higher Education Supplement*, 27 January 1982.

—— 'A Bigger Bang out of Every Buck', *The Australian Higher Education Supplement*, 25 June 1980(a).

—— 'Problems of Campus Promotion', *The Australian Higher Education Supplement*, 16 April 1980(b).

ANU Research Office, *Intellectual Property*, The Australian National University, Canberra. Retrieved 22 April 2013, from www.anu.edu.au/commercialisation/intellectual-property.php.

Apple, Michael W, 'Between Neoliberalism and Neoconservatism: Education and Conservatism in a Global Context' in Nicholas Burbules and Carlos Alberto Torres (eds), *Globalization and Education: Critical Perspectives*, Routledge, New York, 2000, 57–77.

Arendt, Hannah, 'Truth and Politics', *The New Yorker*, New York, 25 February 1967.

Ariens, Michael, 'Law School Branding and the Future of Legal Education' (2003) 34 *St Mary's Law Journal* 301–61.

Aronczyk, Melissa and Devon Powers, '"New Branded World" Redux' in Melissa Aronczyk and Devon Powers (eds), *Blowing up the Brand: Critical Perspectives on Promotional Culture*, Peter Lang, New York, 2010, 1–26.

Ash, Mitchell G and Alfons Sollner, *Forced Migration and Scientific Change: Emigre German-Speaking Scientists and Scholars After 1933*, Cambridge University Press, Cambridge, 1996.

Ashby, Eric, *Challenge to Education*, Angus & Robertson, Sydney, 1946.

Askehave, Inger, 'The Marketization of Higher Education Genres: The International Student Prospectus as a Case in Point' (2007) 9 *Discourse Studies* 723–42.

Aspromourgos, Tony, 'The Managerialist University: An Economic Interpretation' (2012) 54(2) *Australian Universities Review* 44–9.

Australian Bureau of Statistics (ABS), *Australian Yearbook 2012*, Commonwealth Government, Canberra.

Australian Government, Department of Education, *Higher Education Provider Guidelines*, 26 November 2013. Retrieved 14 April 2014, from https://education.gov.au/higher-education-provider-guidelines.

—— Senate Education, Employment and Workplace Relations Committee, *Universities in Crisis*, Canberra, 2001.

—— *Study Assist*. Retrieved 14 April 2014, from http://studyassist.gov.au/sites/StudyAssist/.

Australian Qualifications Framework, Australian Qualifications Framework Council, Adelaide, South Australia, 2nd ed 2013, 47–52, 59–62. Retrieved 28 September 2014, from www.aqf.edu.au/.

Australian Research Council, 2010 Selection Report and Funding Outcomes for 2011, Discovery Program. Retrieved 24 April 2014, from www.arc.gov.au/ncgp/lp/LP11_rd1_selrpt.htm.

Avis, James, 'Re-Thinking Trust in a Performative Culture: The Case of Education' (2003) 18(3) *Journal of Education Policy* 315–32.

Bacon, Francis, *The Tvvoo Bookes of Francis Bacon. Of the Proficience and Advancement of Learning, Divine and Humane*, London, 1605, reprinted in Thomas Case (ed.), *The Advancement of Learning and New Atlantis*, Oxford University Press, London, 1951 [1906].

Baird, Bruce, *Stronger, Simpler, Smarter: Supporting International Students: Review of the Education Services for Overseas Students (ESOS) ACT 2000: Final Report*, Canberra, 2010 (*Baird Report*).

Bakker, Irene, *The Strategic Silence: Gender and Economic Policy*, Zed Books/North-South Institute, London, 1994.

Baldwin, Gabrielle, and Richard James, 'The Market in Australian Higher Education and the Concept of Student as Informed Consumer' (2000) 22(2) *Journal of Higher Education Policy and Management* 139–48.

Balfour, Danny and Joseph Grubbs, 'Character, Corrosion and the Civil Servant: The Human Consequences of Globalization and the New Public Management' (2000) 22(3) *Administrative Theory & Praxis* 570–84.

Ball, Stephen, 'Performativities and Fabrications in the Education Economy: Towards the Performative Society?' (2000) 27(2) *The Australian Educational Researcher* 1–23.

Bamber, Greg, Jodie Hoffer Gittell, Thomas Kochan, and Andrew Von Nordenflycht, (eds), *Up in the Air: How the Airlines Can Improve Performance by Engaging Their Employees*, Cornell University Press, Ithaca, 2009.

Bansel, Peter and Bronwyn Davies, 'Through a Love of what Neoliberalism puts at Risk' in Jill Blackmore, Marie Brennan and Lew Zipin (eds), *Re-Positioning University Governance and Academic Work*, Sense Publishers, Rotterdam, 2010.

Bansel, Peter, Bronwyn Davies, Susanne Gannon and Lynn Sheridan, 'Technologies of Audit at Work on the Writing Subject: A Discursive Analysis' (2008) 33(6) *Studies in Higher Education* 673–83.

Barnett, Ronald, *Beyond all Reason: Living with Ideology in the University*, Society for Research into Higher Education and Open University Press, Buckingham, 2003.

—— *Reading the University in an Age of Super Complexity*, Open University Press, Buckingham, 2000.

Baron, Paula, 'Borderlines: Socio-legality as the Abject' in Kerry Petersen (ed.), *Socio-Legality: An Odyssey of Ideas and Context*, Federation Press, Annandale NSW, 2013.

Barr, Robert B and John Tagg, 'From Teaching to Learning: A New Paradigm for Undergraduate Education' (1995) 27(6) *Change* 12–25.

Bauman, Zygmunt, *Work, Consumerism and the New Poor*, Open University Press, Maidenhead, Birks, 2nd ed, 2005.

—— 'Tourists and Vagabonds' in Peter Beilharz (ed.), *The Bauman Reader*, Blackwell, Oxford, 2001.

—— *Liquid Modernity*, Polity, Oxford, 2000.

—— *Postmodernity and its Discontents*, Polity, Oxford, 1997.

—— *Modernity and Ambivalence*, Polity, Oxford, 1991.

—— *Modernity and the Holocaust*, Polity, Oxford, 1989.

Baume, Senator Michael, 'Australian Research Grants Scheme: Report on Grants Approved for 1987' (Hansard: Senate), 18 March 1987.

*Bayley-Jones v University of Newcastle* (1990) 22 NSWLR 424.

Beck, Ulrich, *Risk Society: Towards a New Modernity*, trans Mark Ritter, Sage, London, 1992 [1986].

Beilharz, Peter, 'Modernity and Motion', in Ghassan Hage and Emma Kowal (eds), *Force, Movement, Intensity*, Melbourne University Press, Melbourne, 2011.

—— (ed.), *The Bauman Reader*, Blackwell, Oxford, 2001.

—— *Transforming Labor: Labour Tradition and the Labor Decade in Australia*, *Cambridge University Press*, Cambridge University Press, Melbourne, 1994.

Beilharz, Peter and Robert Manne (eds), *Reflected Light: La Trobe Essays*, Black Inc, Melbourne, 2006.

*Bell v Victoria University of Wellington* [2010] NZHC 2200.

Bell, Sharon, 'Women in Science: The Persistence of Gender in Australia' (2010) 22(1) *Higher Education Management and Policy* 47–65.

—— *Women in Science and Technology in Australia: Maximising Productivity, Diversity and Innovation*, FASTS, Canberra, 2009.

Bell, Sharon and Ronda Bentley, *Women in Research Discussion Paper*, Prepared for the Australian Vice Chancellors Committee National Colloquium of Senior Women Executives, Griffith University, Brisbane, 2005.

Benson, Simon, 'Abbott vows to cut futile research', *Daily Telegraph*, 5 September 2013. Retrieved 23 September 2014, from www.dailytelegraph.com.au/news/nsw/abbott-vows-to-cut-futile-research/story-fni0cx12-1226710934260/.

Bento, Fabio C, 'A Complex Perspective Towards Leadership in Academic Departments: Investigating Organisational Changes in a Norwegian Research-Intensive University' (2013) 1(2) *International Journal of Complexity in Leadership and Management* 116–32.

Berkovic, Nicola, 'Fewer law graduates are choosing practice as a career', *The Australian* [online]. 1 July 2011. Available from www.theaustralian.com.au/business/legal-affairs/fewer-law-graduates-are-choosing-practice-as-a-career/story-e6frg97x-1226085138499 at 11 September 2013.

Bernays, Edward L, *Propaganda*, Ig Publishing, New York, 1928.

Bertolin, Julio Cesar G, 'The Quasi-Markets in Higher Education: From the Improbable Perfectly Competitive Markets to the Unavoidable State Regulation' (2011) 37(2) *Educação e Pesquisa* 237–48.

Besley, Tina (ed.), *Assessing Quality in Educational Research*, Sense Publishers, Rotterdam, 2010.

Bessant, Bob, 'Robert Gordon Menzies and Education in Australia' in Stephen Murray-Smith (ed.), *Melbourne Studies in Education*, Melbourne University Press, Melbourne, 1977, 163–87.

Bexley, Emmaline, Richard James and Sophie Arkoudis, *The Australian Academic Profession in Transition: Addressing the Challenge of Reconceptualising Academic Work and Regenerating the Academic Workforce*, Centre for the Study of Higher Education, University of Melbourne, for Department of Education, Employment and Workplace Relations, Melbourne, 2011. Retrieved 24 April 2014, from www.cshe.unimelb.edu.au/people/bexley_docs/The_Academic_Profession_in_Transition_Sept2011.pdf.

Biggins, David, 'The Politics of Knowledge' (1984) 3(10) *Australian Society* 6–9.

Bishop, Glenys, 'Seeing the Trends in the Data' in Katrina Hutchison and Fiona Jenkins (eds), *Women in Philosophy: What Needs to Change?* Oxford University Press, Oxford, 2013.

Blackmore, Jillian, 'Anticipating Policy and the Logics of Practice: Australian Institutional and Academic Responses to the Globalising "Quality Research" Agenda' (2009a) 27(1 & 2) *Access: Critical Perspectives on Communication, Cultural & Policy Studies* 97–113.

—— 'Academic Pedagogies, Quality Logics and Performative Universities: Evaluating Teaching and What Students Want' (2009b) 34(8) *Studies in Higher Education*, 857–72.

—— '"The Emperor Has No Clothes": Professionalism, Performativity and Educational Leadership in High-Risk Modern Times' in J Collard and C Reynolds (eds), *Leadership, Gender and Culture in Education: Male and Female Perspectives*, Open University Press, Berkshire, 2005, 173–94.

—— 'Tracking the Nomadic Life of the Educational Researcher: What Future for Feminist Public Intellectuals and the Performative University?' (2003) 30(3) *Australian Educational Researcher* 1-24.

—— 'Globalisation and the Restructuring of Higher Education for New Knowledge Economies: New Dangers or Old Habits Troubling Gender Equity Work in Universities?' (2002) 56(4) *Higher Education Quarterly* 419–41.

Blackmore, Jill and Judyth Sachs, *Performing and Reforming Leaders: Gender, Educational Restructuring & Change*, SUNY Press, New York, 2007.

Blackmore, Jill, Marie Brennan and Lew Zipin (eds), *Re-positioning University Governance and Academic Work*, Sense Publishers, Netherlands, 2010.

Blackmore, Paul and Camille Candiko, *Strategic Curriculum Change: Global Trends in Universities, Routledge*, Abingdon, Oxon, 2012.

Blichner, Lars and Andres Molander, 'Mapping Juridification' (2008) 14 *European Law Journal* 36–54.

Bloom, Sandra L, 'Every Time History repeats itself the Price goes up: The Social Reenactment of Trauma' (1996) 3(3) *Sexual Addiction and Compulsivity* 161–94.

Bode, Katherine and Leigh Dale, 'Bullshit'? An Australian Perspective; Or, What can an Organisational Change Impact Statement Tell Us About Higher Education' (2012) 53 *Australian Journal of Humanities* Retrieved 11 April 2014, from www.australianhumanitiesreview.org/archive/Issue-November-2012/home.html.

Boden, Rebecca and Debbie Epstein, 'Managing the Research Imagination: Globalisation and Research in Higher Education' (2006) 4(2) *Globalisation, Societies and Education* 223–36.

Boden, Rebecca and Maria Nedeva, 'Employing Discourse: Universities and Graduate Employability' (2010) 25(1) *Journal of Education Policy* 37–54.

Boden, Rebecca, Penny Ciancanelli and Susan Wright, 'Trust Universities? Governing Post-Capitalist Futures (2012) 45(2) *Journal of Co-operative Studies* 16–24.

Boden, Rebecca, Rosemary Deem, Debbie Epstein, Fazal Rizvi and Susan Wright (eds), *World Year Book of Education: Geographies of Knowledge, Geometries of Power: Higher Education in the 21st Century*, Routledge, Abingdon, Oxon, 2008.

Böhme, Gernot, *Invasive Technification: Critical Essays in the Philosophy of Technology*, Bloomsbury, London, 2012.

Boltanski, Luc and Eve Chiapello, *The New Spirit of Capitalism*, Verso, London, 2005.

Boni, Alejandra and Melanie Walker (eds), *Human Development and Capabilities: Re-imagining the University of the Twenty-First Century*, Routledge, Abingdon, Oxon, 2013.

Bonnell, Andrew, 'Humanities & social science under attack' (2014) 21(1) *NTEU Advocate* 20–1.

Bourdieu, Pierre, *Logics of Practice*, Polity Press, Oxford, 1990.

—— *Homo Academicus*, Polity Press, Cambridge, 1988.

—— 'The Forms of Capital', in John Richardson (ed.), *Handbook of Theory and Research for the Sociology of Education*, Greenwood Press, New York, 1986.

Boutang, Yann Moulier, *Cognitive Capitalism*, Polity Press, Cambridge, 2008.

Bowden, Peter, 'A Practical Role for Philosophy' (2005) 52 *Philosophy Now* 34–5.

Brabazon, Tara, *The University of Google: Education in the (Post) Information Age*, Ashgate, London, 2007.

—— *Digital Hemlock: Internet Education and the Poisoning of Teaching*, UNSW Press, Sydney, 2002.

Bradley, Denise, Peter Noonan, Helen Nugent and Bill Scales, *Review of Australian Higher Education: Final Report*, Department of Education, Employment and Workplace Relations, Canberra, 2008 (*Bradley Report*).

Brady, Aron and Mike Konczal 'From Master Plan to No Plan: The Slow Death of Public Higher Education' (2012) 59(4) *Dissent* 10–6.

Braidotti, Rosie, *Nomadic Theory: The Portable Rosi Braidotti*, Columbia University Press, New York, 2011.

—— 'A Critical Cartography of Feminist Post-Postmodernism' (2005) 20(47) *Australian Feminist Studies* 169–80.

*Bray v University of Melbourne* [2001] VSC 391.

Bremer, John, 'Britain Facing an End to Enlightenment' *The Australian: Higher Education Supplement*, 17 February 1982.

Brennan, Geoffrey and Francis Teal, *ASSA Report of the 1991 Annual Meeting*, Academy of the Social Sciences in Australia, Canberra, 1991.

Brennan, Geoffrey and Philip Pettit, *The Economy of Esteem: An Essay on Civil and Political Society*, Oxford University Press, Oxford, 2004.

Brennan, John, 'Burton Clark's The Higher Education System: Academic Organization in Cross-National Perspective' (2010) 8(3) *London Review of Education* 229–37.

Brett, Judith, *Australian Liberals and the Moral Middle Class: From Alfred Deakin to John Howard*, Cambridge University Press, Cambridge, 2003.

Brewer, John D, *The Public Value of the Social Sciences: An Interpretative Essay*, Bloomsbury, London, 2013.

Briggs, Robert, 'Shameless! Reconceiving the Problem of Plagiarism' (2003) 46 *Australian Universities Review* 19–23.

Broadbent, Graeme and Pamela Sellman, 'Great Expectations? Law Schools, Websites and "the Student Experience"' (2013) 47(1) *The Law Teacher* 44–63.

Brooks, Ann and Alison Mackinnon (eds), *Gender and the Restructured University*, Open University Press, Buckingham, 2000.

Brown, Phillip, 'The Opportunity Trap: Education and Employment in a Global Economy' (2003) 2(1) *European Educational Research Journal* 141–79.

Brown, Roger, 'The March of the Market' in Mike Molesworth, Richard Scullion and Elizabeth Nixon (eds), *The Marketisation of Higher Education and the Student as Consumer*, Routledge, New York, 2011, 11–24.

Browne Report (UK Government Independent Review, *Securing a Sustainable Future for Higher Education: An Independent Review of Higher Education Funding and Student Finance*), UK Government, London, 2010.

Buchanan, James and Gordon Tullock, *The Calculus of Consent*, University of Michigan Press, Ann Arbor, 1962.

Buckley, Ken and Edward L Wheelwright, 'Commentary on the Murray Report' (1958) 1(1) *Vestes* 2–5.

Burgmann, Verity, 'The Seven Wonders of the Labour World' in Bobbie Oliver (ed.), *Labour History in the New Century*, Black Swan Press, Perth, 2009.

Bushby, David, *Friday Partner's Lunch Audio Webcast: UWA v Gray Round Table*, 2009. Retrieved 8 March 2014, from www.brr.com.au/event/60552/partner/theaustralian.

Butler, Judith, *Bodies that Matter: On the Discursive Limits of 'Sex'*, Routledge, London, 1993.

Cain, John and John Hewitt, *Off Course: From Public Place to Marketplace at Melbourne University*, Scribe, Carlton North, 2004.

Calhoun, Craig, 'The Public Mission of the Research University' in Diana Rhoten and Craig Calhoun (eds), *Knowledge Matters: The Public Mission of the Research University*, Columbia University Press, New York, 2011.

Candy, Philip, Gay Crebert and Jane O'Leary, *Developing Lifelong Learning Through Undergraduate Education*, National Board of Employment, Education and Training, Canberra, 1994.

Capano, G, 'Government Continues To Do Its Job: A Comparative Study of Governance Shifts in the Higher Education Sector' (2011) 89(4) *Public Administration* 1622–42.

Capano, G, J Rayner and AR Zito, 'Governance From The Bottom Up: Complexity And Divergence In Comparative Perspective' (2012) 90(1) *Public Administration* 56–73.

Casey, Catherine, 'A Knowledge Economy and a Learning Society: A comparative analysis of New Zealand and Australian Experiences' (2006) 36(3) *Compare* 343.

Casper, G, 'The Search to Know – What? Reflections on the Purposes of the University', Curriculum Workshop, the Van Leer Jerusalem Institute, Jerusalem, 2010.

Castells, Manuel, *Communication Power*, Oxford University Press, NY, 2009.

Castles, Frank, *The Working Class and Welfare*, Allen and Unwin, Sydney, 1985.

Castoriadis, Cornelius, *The Imaginary Institution of Society*, Polity, Oxford, 1985.

Cerny, Phil, *Rethinking World Politics: A Theory of Transnational Neopluralism*, Oxford University Press, Oxford, 2010.

Chalmers, Denise, *Indicators of University Teaching and Learning Quality*, Australian Learning and Teaching Council, Sydney, Australia, 2008.

Chan, Stephen and Hui Po-keung, 'For the Critical Uses of Cultural Research: Educational Reform as Cultural Process in the Integrated Humanities (S1-S3) Policy Implementation', Inter-Asia Cultural Studies Shanghai Conference, Shanghai University, China, 2007.

Chandrasoma, Ranamukalage, Celia Thompson, and Alastair Pennycook, 'Beyond Plagiarism: Transgressive and Nontransgressive Intertextuality' (2004) 3 *Journal of Language, Identity and Education* 171–93.

Chapleo, Chris, María Victoria Carrillo Durán and Ana Castillo Díaz, 'Do UK Universities communicate their Brands effectively through their Websites?' (2011) 21(1) *Journal of Marketing for Higher Education* 25–46.

Chesterman, Colleen, Ann Ross-Smith, and Margaret Peters, 'Changing the Landscape? Women in Academic Leadership in Australia' (2003) 38(3) *McGill Journal of Education* 421–36.

Chesterman, Simon, 'The Evolution of Legal Education: Internationalization, Transnationalization, Globalization' (2009) 10 *German Law Journal* 877–88.

Chomsky, Noam, *Everyday Anarchist: The Modern Success Interview*, 2013. Retrieved 13 April 2014, from www.modernsuccess.org/noam-chomsky-everyday-anarchist-the-modern-success-interview/.

Christensen, Clayton and Henry J Eyring, *The Innovative University: Changing the DNA of Higher Education from the Inside Out*, Jossey-Bass/Wiley & Sons, San Francisco, 2011.

Clark, Burton R, *The Higher Education System: Academic Organization in Cross-National Perspective*, University of California Press, Berkeley, CA, 1983.

*Clark v University of Lincolnshire and Humberside* (2000) 1 WLR 1988.

Clark, William, *Academic Charisma and the Origins of the Research University*, Chicago University Press, Chicago, 2006.

Clegg, Sue, 'Academic identities under threat?' (2008) 34(3) *British Educational Research Journal* 329–45.

Clunies Ross, Ian to AP Rowe, 1 February 1955, ICR Papers Universities Commission Personal File, NAA/A10651/ICR23/41, NAA, Canberra.

Coates, Hamish, Ian Dobson, Daniel Edwards, Tim Friedman, Leo Goedegebuure and Lynn Meek, 'The Attractiveness of the Australian Academic Profession: A Comparative Analysis', Centre for Higher Education, University of Melbourne, 2009.

Coates, Hamish, Ian Dobson, Leo Goedegebuure and Lynne Meek, 'Across the Great Divide: What Do Australian Academics Think of University Leadership?' (2010) 32(4) *Journal of Higher Education Policy and Management* 379–87.

—— 'Australia's Casual Approach to its Academic Teaching Workforce' (2009) 17 (4) *People and Place* 47–8.

Coates, Hamish and Leo Goedegebuure, *The Real Academic Revolution: Why We Need to Reconceptualise Australia's Future Academic Workforce and Eight Possible Strategies as to how to go about This*, Martin Institute, The University of Melbourne, Melbourne, 2010. Retrieved 16 September 2015, from http://www.lhmartininstitute.edu.au/documents/pubications/therealacademicrevolutio.pdf.

Cohen, Stanley, *States of Denial: Knowing About Atrocities and Suffering*, Oxford University Press, 2001.

Collier, Richard, 'Privatizing the University and the New Political Economy of Socio-Legal Studies: Remaking the (Legal) Academic Subject' (2013) 40(3) *Journal of Law and Society* 450–67.

—— '"Be Smart, Be Successful, Be Yourself..."?: Representations of the Training Contract and Trainee Solicitor in Advertising by Large Law Firms' (2005) 12 *International Journal of the Legal Profession* 51–92.

—— '"We're All Socio-Legal Now?" Legal Education, Scholarship and the "Global Knowledge Economy" — Reflections on the UK Experience' (2005) 26(4) *Sydney Law Review* 503–36.

Collini, Stefan, *What are Universities For?* Penguin, London, 2012.

—— 'From Robbins to McKinsey' (2011) 33(16) *London Review of Books* 9–14.

Collins, Airini, Lindsey Conner, Kathryn McPherson, Brenda Midson and Cheryl Wilson, 'Learning to Be Leaders in Higher Education: What Helps or Hinders Women's Advancement as Leaders in Universities' (2011) 39(1) *Educational Management, Administration & Leadership* 44–62.

Committee on Research Universities, *Research Universities and the Future of America: Ten Breakthrough Actions Vital to Our Nation's Prosperity and Security*, National Academies Press, Washington, 2012.

*Competition and Consumer Act 2010* (Cth).

*Competition Policy Reform Act 1995* (Cth).

Conant, James B, *Confidential Report to the Carnegie Corporation on the University Situation in Australia in the Year 1951*, CCNY Records, Butler Library, Columbia University, New York, 1951.

Connell, Raewyn, 'Feminist Scholarship and the Public Realm in Postcolonial Australia' (2014) 29 *Australian Feminist Studies* 215–30.

—— 'Love, Fear and Learning in the Market University', NTEU Public Lecture, 24 April 2013. Retrieved 7 May 2013, from https://soundcloud.com/nteunsw/nteu-public-lecture-raewyn.

—— 'Open Letter to the Vice Chancellor', NTEU at University of Sydney, 2013. Retrieved 11 February 2014 from www.nteu.org.au/sydney/article/Open-Letter-to-the-Vice-Chancellor---Raewyn-Connell.-14301.

—— 'Test-Rich, Justice-Poor: Australian Education in the New Era', *Theodore Fink Memorial Seminar in Australian Education Deans' Series*, 2013 (unpublished).

—— 'Peripheral Visions' in Jane Kenway and Johannah Fahey (eds), *Globalising the Research Imagination*, Routledge, London, 2009, 53–72.

—— *Southern Theory: The Global Dynamics of Knowledge in Social Science*, Allen & Unwin, Sydney, 2007.

—— 'Glass Ceilings or Gendered Institutions: Mapping the Gender Regimes of Public Sector Worksites' (2006) 66(6) *Public Administration Review*, 837–49.

Connell, Raewyn, Barbara Fawcett and Gabrielle Meagher, 'Neoliberalism, New Public Management and the human service professions: Introduction to the Special Issue' (2009) 48(4) *Journal of Sociology* 331–8.

Connell, WF, GE Sherington, BH Fletcher, Clifford Turney and Ursula Bygott, *Australia's First: A History of the University of Sydney* (Volume 2: 1940–1990), Hale & Ironmonger, Sydney, 1995.

Connor, Linda, 'Union Fight Was Necessary to Keep University Strong', *Sydney Morning Herald*, 12 August 2013. Retrieved 6 January 2013, from www.smh. com.au/comment/union-fight-was-necessary-to-keep-university-strong-20130812-2rrzz.html.

Coper, Michael, 'Law Schools and Legal Education: What is Really Important?' (Paper presented at Legal Education for a Global Community, Australasian Law Teachers Association Conference 2012, University of Sydney Law School, 1–4 July 2012).

Corden, Max, 'Australian Universities: Moscow on the Molonglo' (2005) 11 *Quadrant* 7–20.

Crawford, Robert, 'I Lived in Funeral' (2013) 35(3) *London Review of Books* 29–30.

Creed, Marcel, 'The Science of Compliance' *Campus Review*, 14 May 2013. Retrieved 6 January 2014, from http://www.campusreview.com.au/ blog/2013/05/the-science-of-compliance/.

Creyke, Robin, '"Soft Law" and Administrative Law: A New Challenge' (2010) 61 *Australian Institute of Administrative Law Forum* 15–22

Cripps-Day, Francis, 'Cambridge University Jurisdiction' (1894) 19(4) *Law Magazine and Law Review* 271–78.

Crook, Andrew, 'Marcia Langton defends non-disclosure on mining cash before Boyers', *Crikey*, 22 February 2013. Retrieved 9 September 2014, from www. crikey.com.au/2013/02/22/marcia-langton-defends-mining-money-for-boyer-lectures/.

Currie, Jan, Paula Harris and Bev Thiele, 'Sacrifices in Greedy Universities: Are They Gendered?' (2000) 12(3) *Gender and Education* 269–91.

Daly, Lowrie J, *The Medieval University*, Sheed & Ward, New York, 1961.

Davies, Bronwyn, 'The (Im)possibility of Intellectual Work in Neoliberal Regimes' (2005) 26(1) *Discourse: Studies in the Cultural Politics of Education* 1–14.

Davis, Glyn, 'The Australian Idea of a University' (2013) 72(3) *Meanjin* 32–48.

Davis, Kevin, Angelina Fisher, Benedict Kingsbury and Sally Engle Merry (eds), *Governance by Indicators: Global Power through Classification and Rankings*, OUP, Oxford, 2012.

Davis, Mark, 'The Hurried Life' (2013) 118 *Thesis Eleven* 7–18.

Davison, Graeme, *The Unforgiving Minute. How Australia Learned to Tell the Time*, OUP, Melbourne, 1993.

Dawkins, John, *Higher Education: A Policy Statement* (White Paper), Australian Government Publishing Service, Canberra, 1988.

——'Higher Education: A Policy Discussion Paper', Australian Government Publishing Service, Canberra, 1987a.

—— *Skills for Australia,* Australian Government Publishing Service, Canberra, 1987b.

Dawson, Christopher, 'Commercial Uni Ventures "Not a Threat to Scholarship"' *The Australian Higher Education Supplement*, 22 August 1984.

De Angelis, Massimo, 'Value(s), Measure(s), and Disciplinary Markets' (2005) 10 *The Commoner* 66–86.

De Angelis, Massimo and David Harvey, '"Cognitive Capitalism" and the Rat-Race: How Capital Measures Immaterial Labour in British Universities' (2009) 17 *Historical Materialism* 3–30.

De Lambert, Kelly, Nicky Ellen and Louise Taylor, 'Chalkface Challenges: A Study of Academic Dishonesty Amongst Students in New Zealand Tertiary Institutions' (2006) 31(5) *Assessment and Evaluation in Higher Education* 485–503.

De Ridder-Symoens, H (ed.), *Universities in the Middle Ages*, Cambridge University Press, Cambridge, 2003.

Deakin University Student Academic Misconduct Procedure, 14 November 2011. Retrieved 24 April 2014, from www.deakin.edu.au/health/current-students/files/Student-academic-misconduct-procedure-2012.pdf/.

Deech, Ruth, 'The Student Contract' (2009) 43(1) *The Law Teacher* 3–13.

Deem, Rosemary, '"New Managerialism" and Higher Education: The Management of Performances and Cultures in Universities in the United Kingdom' (2003) 8(1) *International Studies in Sociology of Education* 47–70.

Deem, Rosemary and Kevin Brehony, 'Management as Ideology: The Case of "New Managerialism" in Higher Education' (2005) 31(2) *Oxford Review of Education* 217–35.

Department of Business and Innovation (UK Government), *Higher Education: Students at the Heart of the System*, London, 2011.

Department of Education, Employment and Workplace Relations, *Student 2010 Full Year: Selected Higher Education Statistics*, Canberra, 2011.

Department of Education, Training and Youth Affairs (DETYA), *Time Series Report,* Australian Government Publishing Service, Canberra, 2000.

Dever, Maryanne, Warren Laffan, Paul Boreham, Karin Behrens, Michele Haynes Michele, Mark Western and Matthias Kubler, *Gender Differences in Early Post-PhD Employment in Australian Universities The influence of PhD Experience and Family Circumstances on Women's Academic Careers,* University of Queensland Social Research Centre, Brisbane, 2008.

Devlin, Marcia, Richard James and Gabrielle Grigg, 'Studying and Working: A National Study of Student Finances and Student Engagement' (2008) 14(2) *Tertiary Education and Management* 111–22.

Dewar, John, 'Vice-Chancellor: La Trobe Protestors Abused Freedom of Speech', *The Conversation*, 28 August 2012. Retrieved 6 January 2014, from http://theconversation.com/vice-chancellor-la-trobe-protestors-abused-freedom-of-speech-9104.

Diezmann, Carmel and Susan Grieshaber, *Understanding the Achievements and Aspirations of New Women Professors: A Report to Universities Australia,* Faculty of Education, Queensland University of Technology, Brisbane, 2009.

Dill, David D, 'Evaluating the "Evaluative State": Implications for Research in Higher Education' (1998) 33(3) *European Journal of Education* 361–77.

Dill, David D and Maarja Soo, 'Academic Quality, League Tables, and Public Policy: A Cross-National Analysis of University Ranking Systems' (2005) 4 *Higher Education* 495.

—— 'Transparency and Quality in Higher Education Markets' in Pedro Teixeira, Ben Jongbloed, David Dill and Alberto Amaral (eds), *Markets in Higher Education*, Springer, Netherlands, 2004.

Dillabough, Joanne and Sandra Acker, 'Gender, "Symbolic Domination" and Female Work: The Case of Teacher Education' (2005) 26(2) *Discourse* 127–48.

Donoghue, Frank, *The Last Professors: The Corporate University and the Fate of the Humanities*, Fordham University Press, 2008.

Douglass, John, *Higher Education's New Global Order: How and Why Governments Are Creating Structured Opportunity Markets*, Research & Occasional Paper

Series, Center for Studies in Higher Education, University of California, Berkeley, 2009. Retrieved 14 April 2014, from http://cshe.berkeley.edu/publications/docs/ROPS.Douglass.SOMarkets.12.18.09.pdf, 2009.

—— *The California Idea and American Higher Education 1850 to the 1960 Master Plan*, Stanford University Press, Stanford, 2000.

Doyle, Peter, *Marketing Management and Strategy*, Prentice Hall, Hemel Hempstead, UK, 2001.

Drever, James, 'Academic Freedom in British Universities' (1953) 9(3) *Journal of Social Issues* 17–24.

Dryden, Windy (ed.), *Cognitive Behavior Therapies*, Sage, London, 2012.

Eagleton, Terry, *Why Marx Was Right*, Yale University Press, New Haven, 2011.

*Education Services for Overseas Students Act 2000* (Cth).

Edwards, John, *Beyond the Boom*, Penguin Special, Melbourne, 2014.

Edwards, Julian, Darren Van Laar, Simon Easton and Gail Kinman, 'The Work-Related Quality of Life Scale for Higher Education Employees' (2009) 15(3) *Quality in Higher Education* 207–19.

Epstein, Debbie, Rebecca Boden, Rosemary Deem, Fazal Rizvi and Susan Wright (eds), *World Yearbook of Education 2008: Geographies of Knowledge, Geometries of Power – Framing the Future of Higher Education*, Routledge, Abingdon Oxon, 2008.

Evans, Alicia, 'Governing Student Assessment: Administrative Rules, Silenced Academics and Performing Students' (2011) 36(2) *Assessment and Evaluation in Higher Education* 213–23.

Evans, Mary, *Killing Thinking: The Death of the Universities*, Continuum, London, 2004.

Fearn, Hannah, 'Plymouth's "Enterprising" Spirit is Called Into Question' (2010) *Times Higher Education*, 21 January 2010.

Federici, Silvia and George Caffentzis, 'Notes on the Edu-Factory and Cognitive Capitalism' (2007) 12 *The Commoner* 63–70.

Ferguson, Michelle, 'More Scholar for the Dollar', *The Australian Higher Education Supplement*, 26 August 1981.

Feteris, Susan, *The Role of Women Academics in Australian Universities*, Deakin University, Geelong, 2013.

Fischman, Gustavo, Sarah Igo and Diane Rhoten, 'Are Public Research Universities in Crisis?' (2007) 50 *Reencuentro* 117–30.

Fitzclarence, Lindsay, 'New Generation Police Tactics' (2013) 121 *Arena* 5–7. Retrieved 11 February 2014, from http://arena.org.au/new-generation-police-tactics/.

Fitzgerald, Tanya, 'The Continuing Politics of Mistrust: Performance Management and the Erosion of Professional Work' in T Fitzgerald and H Gunter (eds), *Educational Administration and History: The State of the Field,* Routledge, London, 2009, 33–48.

Flexner, Abraham, *Universities: American English German,* OUP, London, 1930.

Folbre, Nancy, *The Invisible Heart: Economics and Family Values,* New Press, New York, 2001.

Forbes, JR, 'University Discipline: A New Province for Natural Justice?' (1970) 7 *University of Queensland Law Journal* 85–108.

Ford, Jane, 'Rebel Professor Attacks "Dead System" in NSW', *The Australian Higher Education Supplement*, 20 June 1984.

—— 'National Scheme to Improve University Links with Industry', *The Australian Higher Education Supplement*, 17 August 1983.

Forsyth, Hannah, *A History of the Modern Australian University,* NewSouth Publishing, Sydney, 2014.

Foskett, Nick, 'Markets, Government, Funding and the Marketisation of UK Higher Education' in Mike Molesworth, Richard Scullion and Elizabeth Nixon (eds), *The Marketisation of Higher Education and the Student as Consumer*, Routledge, New York, 2011.

Foster, Stephen Glynn and Margaret Varghese, *The Making of the Australian National University 1946–1996*, ANU E Press, Canberra, 2009.

Foucault, Michel, 'Governmentality' in Graham Burchell, Colin Gordon and Peter Miller (eds), *The Foucault Effect: Studies in Governmentality, with Two Lectures by and an Interview with Michel Foucault*, University of Chicago Press, Chicago, [1978] 1991.

—— *Discipline and Punish: The Birth of the Prison*, Vintage Books, New York, 1979.

—— *Power/Knowledge: Selected Interviews and Other Writings 1972–1977*, Pantheon Books, New York, 1972.

Frank, David and Jay Gabler, *Reconstructing the University: Worldwide Shifts in Academia in the 20th Century*, ILR Press/Cornell University Press, Ithaca, 2006.

Franklyn-Stokes, Arlene and Stephen Newstead, 'Undergraduate Cheating: Who Does What and Why' (1995) 20(2) *Studies in Higher Education* 159–72.

Franzway, Susan, *Sexual Politics and Greedy Institutions, Union Women, Commitments and Conflicts in Public and Private Life*, Pluto Press, Sydney, 2001.

Fraser, Nancy and Alex Honneth, *Redistribution or Recognition? A Political-Philosophical Exchange*, Verso, London, 1998.

Fredman, Nick and James Doughney, 'Academic Dissatisfaction, Managerial Change and Neo-Liberalism' (2012) 64 *Higher Education* 41–58.

Frey, Bruno, *Not Just for the Money*, Edward Elgar Publishing, Cheltenham, 1997.

Frey, Bruno S and Katja Rost, 'Do Rankings Reflect Research Quality?' Working Paper No. 2008–22, Centre for Research in Economics, Management and the Arts, Basel, 2008.

Friedman, Milton and Rose Friedman, *Free to Choose: A Personal Statement*, Harcourt Brace Jovanovich, New York, 1980.

Friedman, Milton, with the assistance of Rose D Friedman, *Capitalism and Freedom*, University of Chicago Press, Chicago, 1962.

Frijters, Paul, *Timothy Devinney on Overpaid Vice-Chancellors*, Core Economics, 15 May 2013. Retrieved 10 January 2014, from http://economics.com.au/?p=9716.

Fukuyama, Francis, *The End of History and the Last Man*, New York, Free Press, 1992.

Fuller, Steve, 'The Genealogy of Judgment: Towards a Deep History of Academic Freedom' (2009) 57(2) *British Journal of Educational Studies* 164–77.

Furedi, Frank, 'Introduction to the Marketisation of Higher Education and the Student as Consumer' in Mike Molesworth, Richard Scullion and Elizabeth Nixon (eds), *The Marketisation of Higher Education and the Student as Consumer*, Routledge, New York, 2011.

Furlong, John and Martin Lawn, *Disciplines of Education: Their Role in the Future of Educational Research*, Routledge, New York, 2011.

Gabbatt, Adam, 'UC Davis pepper spray police officer awarded $38,000 compensation', *The Guardian*, 24 October 2013. Retrieved 4 January 2014, from www.theguardian.com/world/2013/oct/23/pepper-spray-cop-uc-davis-compensation.

Gallagher, AP, *Coordinating Australian University Development: A Study of Australian Universities Commission 1959–1970*, University of Queensland Press, St Lucia Qld, 1982.

Gamble, Andrew, 'Two Faces of Neo-liberalism' in Richard Robison (ed.), *The Neoliberal Revolution: Forging the Market State*, Palgrave, Houndsmill, 2006.

Garnaut, Ross, *Dog Days: Australia after the Boom*, Redback, Collingwood, 2013.

Garrett, Geoff, and Graeme Davies, *Herding Cats: Being Advice to Aspiring Academic and Research Leaders*, Triachy Press, Axminster, 2010.

Gibson-Graham, JK, *A Postcapitalist Politics*, University of Minnesota Press, Minneapolis, 2006.

Gillies, Douglas, 'Quality and Equality: The Mask of Discursive Conflation in Education Policy Texts' (2008) 23(6) *Journal of Education Policy* 685–99.

Gilmore, Heath, 'Call for University of Sydney convocation to consider fee deregulation', *Sydney Morning Herald,* 8 July 2014. Retrieved 9 September 2014, from hwww.smh.com.au/nsw/call-for-university-of-sydney-convocation-to-consider-fee-deregulation-20140708-zt0jb.html.

Gilson, Lucy, 'Trust and the Development of Health Care as a Social Institution' (2003) 56 *Social Science & Medicine* 1453–68.

Ginsberg, Benjamin, *The Fall of the Faculty: The Rise of the All-Administrative University and Why it Matters*, Oxford University Press, New York, 2011.

Giroux, Henry, 'When Hope is Subversive' (2012) 19(6) *TIKKUN* 38–9.

—— 'Beyond the Swindle of the Corporate University: Higher Education in the Service of Democracy', *Truthout*, 18 January 2011. Retrieved 6 January 2014, from www.truth-out.org/opinion/item/69-beyond-the-swindle-of-the-corporate-university-higher-education-in-the-service-of-democracy.

—— 'Slouching Towards Bethlehem: The New Gilded Age and Neoliberalism's Theater of Cruelty', *Dissident Voice*, 11 March 2008. Retrieved 5 May 2013, from http://dissidentvoice.org/2008/03/slouching-towards-bethlehem/.

Giroux, Henry and Peter McLaren (eds), *Critical Pedagogy: The State and Cultural Struggle,* State University of New York Press, Albany, 1989.

*Glynn v Keele University* (1971) 1 WLR 487.

Go8 Australia, 'The Role and Importance of Research Intensive Universities in the Contemporary World', *Australian Policy Online,* 1 April 2013. Retrieved 14 April 2014, from http://apo.org.au/research/role-and-importance-research-intensive-universities-contemporary-world.

Gordon, George and Celia Whitchurch, *Academic and Professional Identities in Higher Education: The Challenges of a Diversifying Workforce,* Routledge, London, 2010.

Grafton, Anthony, 'Our Universities: Why Are They Failing?' *The New York Review of Books,* 24 November 2011. Retrieved 14 April 2014, from www. nybooks.com/articles/archives/2011/nov/24/our-universities-why-are-they-failing/?pagination=false.

Greenwood, Davydd, Susan Wright and Rebecca Boden 'Report on a field visit to Mondragón University: a cooperative experience/experiment' (2011) 4(3) *Learning and Teaching: The International Journal of Higher Education in the Social Sciences* 38–56.

Gross, E and JS Western, *The End of a Golden Age: Higher Education in a Steady State,* University of Queensland Press, St Lucia Qld, 1981.

Grove, Jack, 'Big pay rises for Russell Group chiefs in £9K fees era', *Times Higher Education,* 2 January 2014. Retrieved 4 January 2014, from www. timeshighereducation.co.uk/news/big-pay-rises-for-russell-group-chiefs-in-9k-fees-era/2010075.article.

—— 'University of London V-C steps into Student Protest' *Times Higher Education,* 11 December 2013. Retrieved 8 January 2014, from www. timeshighereducation.co.uk/news/university-of-london-v-c-steps-into-student-protests-row/2009858.article.

—— 'Senate House Occupation ends with Arrests' *Times Higher Education,* 5 December 2013. Retrieved 10 February 2014, from www. timeshighereducation.co.uk/news/senate-house-occupation-ends-with-arrests/2009671.article.

Guderley, Jacquelyn, 'Women in STEM: It's Time to Take Ownership of Being Female', *The Guardian,* 28 May 2013. Retrieved 14 April 2014, from www.theguardian.com/women-in-leadership/2013/may/28/women-stem-ownership-of-being-female.

Gunew, Sneja, *Moving Ideas: Mobile Policies, Researchers and Connections in the Social Sciences and Humanities — Australia in the Global Context, 2006–2010*, Interview conducted by Jane Kenway for ARC project, 27 June 2008.

—— *Haunted Nations: The Colonial Dimensions of Multiculturalisms*, Routledge, London, 2004.

—— 'The Home of Language: A Pedagogy of the Stammer' in Sarah Ahmed, Claudia Castaneda, Anne-Marie Fortier and M Sheller (eds), *Uprootings/Regroundings: Questions of Home and Migration*, Berg, Oxford, 2003, 41–58.

—— *Framing Marginality: Multicultural Literary Criticism*, Melbourne University Press, Melbourne, 1994.

Gunew, Sneja and Fazal Rizvi, *Culture, Difference and the Arts*, Allen & Unwin, Sydney, 1994.

Habermas, Jurgen. 'The Idea of the University: Learning Process' (1987) 41 *New German Critique* 3–22.

Hage, Ghassan, *Against Paranoid Nationalism: Searching for Hope in a Shrinking Society*, Pluto Press, Annandale NSW, 2003.

Halford, Susan and Pauline Leonard, *Gender, Power and Organisations*, Palgrave, Basingstoke, 2001.

Hamilton, William, 'The challenge is to do better with less', *The Australian Higher Education Supplement*, 2 April 1980.

Hare, Julie, 'List of vice-chancellor salaries', *The Australian Higher Education Supplement*, 6 June 2012.

Harman, Grant, 'Implementing Comprehensive National Higher Education Reforms: The Australian Reforms of Education Minister John Dawkins, 1987–90' (2005) 8 *Higher Education Dynamics* 160–85.

—— 'Australian Higher Education Administration and the Quality Assurance Movement' (1994) 16(1) *Journal of Tertiary Education Administration* 25–43.

Harpur, John, *Innovation, Profit and the Common Good in Higher Education: The New Alchemy*, Palgrave Macmillan, New York, 2010.

Harrington, Christine, and Umat Turem, 'Accounting for Accountability in Neoliberal Regulatory Regimes' in M Dowdle (ed.), *Public Accountability: Designs, Dilemma and Experiences*, Cambridge University Press, New York, 2006.

Harvey, David, *A Brief History of Neoliberalism*, Oxford University Press, Oxford, 2005.

—— 'Common and Communities in the University: Some Notes and Some Examples' (2004) 8 *The Commoner*. Retrieved 5 September 2014, from http://www.commoner.org.uk/08harvie.pdf.

—— *Spaces of Hope*, University of California Press, Berkeley, 2000.

Haskins, Charles H, *The Rise of Universities*, New York, Cornell University Press, 1957 (originally given as the Colver Lectures, 1923).

Haslanger, Sally, *Preliminary Report of the Survey on Publishing in Philosophy'*, *APA Committee on the Status of Women in the Profession*, MIT, 2009. Retrieved 9 September 2012, from www.mit.edu/~shaslang/papers/HaslangerPRSPP.pdf.

—— 'Changing the Ideology and Culture of Philosophy: Not by Reason (Alone)' (2008) 23(2) *Hypatia* 210–23.

Hayek, Friedrich A von, *The Road to Serfdom*, Routledge & Kegan Paul, London, 1976.

—— *The Constitution of Liberty*, Routledge & Kegan Paul, London, 1960.

Haywood, Rebecca Jenkins and Mike Molesworth, 'A Degree will make your Dreams come true: Higher Education as the Management of Consumer Desires' in Mike Molesworth, Richard Scullion and Elizabeth Nixon (eds), *The Marketisation of Higher Education and the Student as Consumer*, Routledge, New York, 2011, 183–95.

Hazelkorn, Ellen, 'The Effects of Rankings on Student Choices and Institutional Selection' in Ben WA Jongbloed and Hans Vossensteyn (eds), *Access and Expansion Post-Massification: Opportunities and Barriers to Further Growth in Higher Education Participation*, Routledge, 2015 (forthcoming).

—— *Rankings and the Reshaping of Higher Education: The Battle for World-Class Excellence*, Palgrave Macmillan, London, 2011.

—— 'The Impact of League Tables and Ranking Systems on Higher Education Decision Making' (2007) 19(2) *Higher Education Management and Policy* 81–105.

Hearn, Jeff, 'On the Complexity of Feminist Intervention in Organizations' (2000) 7(4) *Organisation* 269–84.

Hearn, Jeff and Wendy Parkin, *Gender, Sexuality and Violence in Organizations*, Thousand Oaks, London, 2001.

Hesse, Herman, *The Glass Bead Game*, Vintage, London, 1970.

Hiatt, Bethany, 'More Cheat at WA Universities', *The West Australian*, 19 April 2013.

*Higher Education Standards Framework (Threshold Standards) 2011* (Cth).

*Higher Education Support Act 2003* (Cth).

Hil, Richard, *Whackademia: An Insider's Account of the Troubled University*, NewSouth Publishing, Sydney, 2012.

*Hilmer Report* (Independent Committee of Inquiry into Competition Policy in Australia, *National Competition Policy*), Australian Government Publishing Service, Canberra, 1993.

Hirsch, Fred, *The Social Limits to Growth*, Harvard University Press, Cambridge, 1976.

Hobbins, Peter and Hannah Forsyth, 'Mobilising Medical Knowledge for the Nation, 1943-49' (2013) 15 *Health and History* 59–79.

Hobsbawm, Eric, 'Introduction: Inventing Traditions' in Eric Hobsbawm and Terence Ranger (eds), *The Invention of Tradition*, Cambridge University Press, Cambridge, 1983.

Hoffer Gittell, Jodie, *High Performance Healthcare: Using the Power of Relationships to Achieve Quality, Efficiency and Resilience*, McGraw Hill, New York, 2009.

Holt, Douglas B, 'Why Do Brands Cause Trouble? A Dialectical Theory of Consumer Culture and Branding' (2002) 29(1) *Journal of Consumer Research* 70–90.

Horne, Julia and Geoffrey Sherington, *Sydney: The Making of a Public University*, Miegunyah Press, Melbourne, 2012.

Howard, Jane, 'Reliance on Government Funding "Unhealthy"', *The Australian Higher Education Supplement*, 24 August 1983.

Hughes, Helen, 'Education as an Export Industry' in DR Jones and J Anwyl (eds), *Privatizing Higher Education: A New Australian Issue*, Centre for the Study of Higher Education, Melbourne, 1988, 217–46.

Hugo, Graeme, and Anama Morriss, *Investigating the Ageing Academic Workforce*, University of Adelaide for Universities Australia, Adelaide, 2010.

Hui, Po-keung, 'In Search of a Politics of Hope in the Context of Education Reform — From Cultural Critique to Critical Pragmatics', Departmental Seminar, Department of Cultural Studies, Hong Kong, February 2006.

Hull, Darryl and Vivienne Read, 'Simply the Best Workplaces in Australia', Working Paper No 88, Australian Centre for Industrial Relations Research and Training, University of Sydney, Sydney, 2003.

Humboldt, Wilhelm von, 'On the Spirit and the Organisational Framework of Intellectual Institutions in Berlin' in 'University Reform in Germany' (1970) 8(2) *Minerva* 242–67.

Huntington, Samuel, *The Clash of Civilisations and the Remaking of the World Order*, Simon and Schuster, New York, 1996.

Hutchison, Katrina and Fiona Jenkins (eds), *Women in Philosophy: What Needs to Change?* Oxford University Press, Oxford, 2013.

Illinois State Bar Association (ISBA), Special Committee on the Impact of Law School Debt on the Delivery of Legal Services: Final Report & Recommendations, ISBA, Springfield, Il, 2013.

IMF (International Monetary Fund), *Bank/Fund Expo 1998: The Knowledge Economy*, IMF, Washington DC. Retrieved 14 May 1014, from www.imf.org/external/am/1998/expo.htm.

Independent Commission Against Corruption, *Report on Investigation into the University of Newcastle's Handling of Plagiarism Allegations*, Sydney, June 2005.

International Education Advisory Council, *Australia Educating Globally: Advice from the International Education Advisory Council*, Australian Government, Canberra, 2013 (*Chaney Report*).

International Legal Services Advisory Council (ILSAC), *Internationalisation of the Australian Law Degree*, ILSAC, Canberra, 2004.

James, Nickolas J, 'Why has Vocationalism Propagated so Successfully within Australian Law Schools?' (2004) 6 *University of Notre Dame Australia Law Review* 41–62.

James, Richard H, Gabrielle Baldwin, and Craig McInnis, 'Which University?: The Factors Influencing the Choices of Prospective Undergraduates', Department of Education Training and Youth Affairs, Commonwealth of Australia, Canberra, Australia, 1999.

James, Richard, Tom Karmel and Emmaline Bexley, 'Participation' in Gwilym Croucher, Simon Marginson, Andrew Norton and Julie Wells (eds), *The Dawkins Revolution 25 Years On*, Melbourne University Press, Melbourne, 2013, 126–45.

Jayasuriya, Kanishka, "Building Citizens: Empire, Asia and the Australian Settlement" (2010a) 45(1) *Australian Journal of Political Science* 29–43.

—— 'Learning by the Market: Regulatory Regionalism, Bologna, and Accountability Communities' (2010b) 8(1) *Globalisation, Societies and Education* 7–22.

—— *Statecraft, Welfare and the Politics of Social Inclusion*, Palgrave, Houndsmill, 2006.

Jenkins, Fiona, 'Singing the Post-discrimination Blues: Notes for a Critique of Academic Meritocracy' in Katrina Hutchison and Fiona Jenkins (eds), *Women in Philosophy: What Needs to Change?* Oxford University Press, Oxford, 2013.

Johnson, Carol, *Governing Change: From Keating to Howard*, University of Queensland Press, St Lucia Qld, 2000.

Johnson, Stephen, 'Academics Far Too "Selfish"', *The Australian Higher Education Supplement*, 12 May 1982.

Johnstone, Richard and Sumitra Vigaendra, *Learning Outcomes and Curriculum Development in Law: A Report Commissioned by the Australian Universities Teaching Committee*, Commonwealth of Australia, Canberra, 2003.

Joint Committee on Quantitative Assessment of Research, *Citation Statistics: A Report from the International Mathematical Union (IMU) in Cooperation with the International Council of Industrial and Applied Mathematics (ICIAM) and the Institute of Mathematical Statistics* (IMS), 2008. Retrieved 14 April 2014, from www.mathunion.org/fileadmin/IMU/Report/CitationStatistics.pdf.

Jones, Todd Edwin, 'Budgetary Hemlock: Nevada Seeks to Eliminate Philosophy', *Boston Review*, 5 April 2011. Retrieved 10 October 2013, from www.bostonreview.net/todd-edwin-jones-nevada-philosophy.

Jongbloed, Ben, 'Marketisation in Higher Education, Clark's Triangle and the Essential Ingredients of Markets' (2003) 57(2) *Higher Education Quarterly* 110–35.

Jons, Heiki, 'Transnational Academic Mobility and Gender' (2011) 9(2) *Globalisation, Societies and Education* 183–209.

Junor, Ann, 'Casual University Work: Choice Risk and Equity and the Case for Regulation' (2004) 14(2) *The Economics and Labour Review* 276–304.

Kagan, Jerome, *The Three Cultures: Natural Sciences, Social Sciences, and the Humanities in the 21st Century*, Cambridge University Press, Cambridge, 2009.

Kelly, Paul, *The End of Certainty: The Story of the 1980s*, Allen and Unwin, St Leonards NSW, 1992.

Kelsey, Jane, *The New Zealand Experiment: A World Model of Structural Adjustment?* Bridgit Williams, Wellington, 1995.

Kendzior, Sarah, 'Academia's Indentured Servants', *Al Jazeera*, 11 April 2013. Retrieved 6 January 2014, from www.aljazeera.com/indepth/opinion/2013/04/20134119156459616.html.

Kennedy, Duncan, 'A Cultural Pluralist Case for Affirmative Action in Legal Academia' (1990) 39 *Duke Law Journal* 705–57.

Kenway, Jane, 'A Melancholic Melody' in Richard Tinning and Karen Sirna (eds), *Education, Social Justice and the Legacy of Deakin University: Reflections of the Deakin Diaspora*, Sense Publishing, Netherlands, 2011.

Kenway, Jane, Chris Bigum, Lindsay Fitzclarence, 'New Education in New Times' (1994) 9(4) *Journal of Education Policy* 317–33.

Kenway, Jane, Elizabeth Bullen and Johannah Fahey, with Simon Robb, *Haunting the Knowledge Economy*, Routledge, London, 2006.

Kenway, Jane and Johannah Fahey (eds), *Globalising the Research Imagination*, Routledge, London, 2009.

Kern, Stephen, *The Culture of Time and Space, 1880–1918*, Harvard University Press, Cambridge, 1983.

Kerr, Clark, *The Great Transformation in Higher Education: 1960–1980*, State University of New York Press, Albany NY, 1991.

—— *The Speed of Change* in R McCaig (ed.), *Policy and Planning in Higher Education*, University of Queensland Press, St Lucia Qld, 1972, 167–76.

Kickert, Walter, 'Steering at a Distance: A New Paradigm of Public Governance in Dutch Higher Education' (1995) 8(1) *Governance* 135–57.

Kift, Sally, 'Lawyering Skills Finding Their Place in Legal Education' (1997) 8 *Legal Education Review* 43–73.

Kimber, Megan, 'The Tenured 'Core' and the Tenuous 'Periphery': The Casualisation of Academic Work in Australian Universities' (2003) 25(1) *Journal of Higher Education Policy and Management* 41–50.

King, Roger, 'Analysing the Higher Education Regulatory State', Discussion Paper No 38, Centre for the Analysis of Risk and Regulation, London School of Economics, London, 2006.

Knight, Michael, *Strategic Review of the Student Visa Program*, Australian Government, Canberra, 2011.

Knorr-Cetina, Karen, *Epistemic Cultures: How the Sciences Make Knowledge*, Harvard University Press, London, 1999.

Kolowich, Steve, 'The Professors behind the MOOC Hype', *Chronicle of Higher Education*, 18 March 2013.

Kotter, John and Dan Cohen, *The Heart of Change: Real Life Stories of How People Change Their Organizations*, Harvard Business School Press, Boston, 2002.

KPMG, 'Evaluation of La Trobe University Faculty of Humanities and Social Sciences Change Process 2012', unpublished report submitted to the Vice-Chancellor and Council of La Trobe University, May 2013.

Kramer, Roderick M and Todd L Pittinsky, *Restoring Trust in Organizations and Leaders: Enduring Challenges and Emerging Answers*, Oxford University Press, Oxford, 2012.

Kramer, Roderick M and Tom R Tyler (eds), *Trust in Organizations: Frontiers of Theory and Research,* Sage Publications, London, 1996.

Krefting, Linda A, 'Intertwined Discourses of Merit and Gender: Evidence from Academic Employment in the USA' (2003) 10(2) *Gender, Work & Organization* 260–78.

Kuh, George D, 'The State of Learning Outcomes Assessment in the United States' (2010) 22(1) *Higher Education Management & Policy* 9–28.

Lambert, Cath, Andrew Parker and Michael Neary, 'Entrepreneurialism and Critical Pedagogy: Reinventing the Higher Education Curriculum' (2007) 12(4) *Teaching in Higher Education* 525–37.

La Trobe University, *Future Ready: Strategic Plan 2013–2017*, La Trobe University, Bundoora, Vic, 2012.

Lane, Bernard, 'Women falling foul of ERA', *The Australian Higher Education Supplement*, 12 December 2012.

—— 'UWA Fails to Appeal', *The Australian Higher Education Supplement*, 17 February 2010.

Larsen, Kurt, John Martin, and Rosemary Morris, 'Trade in Educational Services: Trends and Emerging Issues', OECD Working Paper, 2002.

Lattimore, Owen, *Ordeal By Scandal*, Carol & Graf Publishers, New York, 2004.

*Lawyers Weekly*, 'Universities Put on Notice over IP Rights', 7 September 2009. Retrieved 18 October 2011, from www.lawyersweekly.com.au/news/universities-put-on-notice-over-ip-rights.

Lazzarato, Maurizio, 'Immaterial Labour' in Paolo Virno and Michael Hardt (eds), *Radical Though in Italy: A Potential Politics*, University of Minnesota Press, Minneapolis, 1996.

Lee, Jane, 'Student protests at La Trobe must be officially approved', *The Age*, 21 August 2012. Retrieved 14 April 2014, from www.theage.com.au/victoria/student-protests-at-la-trobe-must-be-officially-approved-20120821-24k2b.html.

Lee Dow, Kwong, *Review of Student Income Support Reforms*, Australian Government, Canberra, 2011 (*Lee Dow Report*).

Lee Dow, Kwong and Valerie Braithwaite, 'Review of Higher Education Regulation Report', Department of Industry, Innovation, Climate Change, Science, Research and Tertiary Education, Canberra, 2013.

Le Grand, Julian, 'Quasi-markets and Social Policy' (1991) 101(408) *Economic Journal* 1256–67.

LERU (League of European Research Universities), *Women, Research and Universities: Excellence without Gender Bias Report*, 2012. Retrieved 23 September 2014, from http://www.gleichstellung.uzh.ch/politik/LERU_Paper_Women_universities_and_research.pdf.

Levinson, Paul, *Digital McLuhan: A Guide to the Information Millennium*, Routledge, London, 1999.

Lindsay, Bruce, 'Delivering In-House Justice? Practice and Procedure in University Hearings' (2012a) 17(2) *International Journal of Law and Education* 87–112.

—— 'The Future of University Tribunals' (2012b) 71 *Australian Institute of Administrative Law Forum* 71–83.

—— 'Rates of Student Disciplinary Action in Australian Universities' (2010) 52(2) *Australian Universities Review* 27–32.

—— 'Breaking University Rules: Discipline and Indiscipline Past and Present' (2008a) 50(1) *Australian Universities Review* 37–9.

—— 'Student Discipline Rules and Fair Procedures' (2008b) 15(3) *Australian Journal of Administrative Law* 146–68.

Lingard, Bob and Shaun Rawolle, 'New Scalar Politics: Implications for Education Policy' (2011) 47(4) *Comparative Education* 489–502.

Linke, Russel D (ed.), *Performance Indicators in Higher Education: Report of a Trial Evaluation Study Commissioned by the Commonwealth Department of Employment, Education and Training, Performance Indicators Research Group*, Department of Employment Education and Training, Canberra, 1991.

Lisbon Council, *University System Rankings*, Lisbon Council, Brussels, 2008.

Lo, Vai Io, 'Before Competition and beyond Complacency: The Internationalisation of Legal Education in Australia' (2012) 22 Legal Education Review 3–49.

Lomax-Smith Report (Commonwealth of Australia, *Higher Education Base Funding Review: Final Report*), Department of Education, Employment and Workplace Relations, Canberra, 2011.

Lorenz, Chris, 'If You're So Smart, Why Are You Under Surveillance? Universities, Neoliberalism, and New Public Management' (2012) 38 *Critical Inquiry* 599–629.

Lowenthal, David, *The Past is a Foreign Country*, Cambridge University Press, Cambridge, 1985.

Lowrie, Anthony and Jane Hemsley-Brown, 'This Thing Called Marketisation' (2011) 27 *Journal of Marketing Management* 1081–6.

Lubienski, Christopher, *Do Quasi-Markets Foster Innovation in Education? A Comparative Perspective*, OECD, Paris, 2009.

Lyotard, Jean-Francois, *The Postmodern Condition: A Report on Knowledge*, Manchester University Press, Manchester, 1984.

Macfarlane, Bruce, 'Professors as Intellectual Leaders: Formation, Identity and Role' (2011) 36(1) *Studies in Higher Education* 57–73.

Macintyre, Stuart, *The Poor Relation: A History of the Social Sciences in Australia*, Melbourne University Press, Melbourne, 2010.

—— 'Academic Freedom' in Eva Baker, Penelope Peterson and Barry McGaw (eds), *The International Encyclopedia of Education*, Elsevier, Oxford, 3rd edn 2010, vol 4, 328–33.

Macintyre, Stuart, Gwilym Croucher, Glyn Davis and Simon Marginson, 'Making the Unified National System' in Gwilym Croucher, Simon Marginson, Andrew Norton and Julie Wells (eds), *The Dawkins Revolution 25 Years On*, Melbourne University Press, Melbourne, 2013, 9–55.

Maher, JaneMaree, Jennifer Mitchell, and Kate Brown, 'Student/Worker/Carer: The Intersecting Priorities of Arts Students' (2009) 51(2) *Australian Universities Review* 19–26.

Marceau, Jane, *Steering From a Distance: International Trends in the Financing and Governance of Higher Education*, Evaluations and Investigations Program, Department of Employment, Education and Training, Canberra, 1993.

Marginson, Simon 'On the Impossibility of Markets in Higher Education' (2013) 28(3) *Journal of Education Policy* 353–70.

—— 'The Impossibility of Capitalist Markets in Higher Education' (2012) 28(3) *Journal of Education Policy* 353–70.

—— 'Higher Education and Public Good' (2011) 65(4) *Higher Education Quarterly* 411–33.

—— 'How Universities Have Been Positioned as Teams in a Knowledge Economy World Cup' in Jill A Blackmore, Marie Brennan, and Lew D Zipin (eds), *Re-Positioning University Governance and Academic Work*, Netherlands Sense Publishers, 2010, 17–34.

—— 'Dynamics of National and Global Competition in Higher Education' (2006) 52(1) *Higher Education* 1–39.

—— *Markets in Education*, Allen and Unwin, Sydney, 1997a.

—— 'Investment in the Self: The Government of Student Financing in Australia' (1997b) 22(2) *Studies in Higher Education* 119–31.

—— *Educating Australia: Government, Economy, and Citizen since 1960*, Cambridge University Press, Cambridge, 1997c.

—— 'Steering from a Distance: Power Relations in Australian Higher Education' (1997d) 34(1) *Higher Education* 63–80.

—— *Education and Public Policy in Australia*, Cambridge University Press, Cambridge, 1993.

Marginson, Simon and Marijk van der Wende, 'To Rank or To Be Ranked: The Impact of Global Ranking in Higher Education' (2007) 11(3/4) *Journal of Studies in International Education* 306–29.

Marginson, Simon and Mark Considine, *The Enterprise University: Power, Governance and Reinvention in Australia*, Cambridge University Press, Cambridge, 2000.

Marope, Mmantsetsa, Peter Wells, and Ellen Hazelkorn, *Rankings and Accountability in Higher Education: Uses and Misuses*, UNESCO, Paris, 2013.

Marsden, Helen, Marie Carroll, and James Neill, 'Who Cheats at University? A Self-Report Study of Dishonest Academic Behaviours in a Sample of Australian University Students' (2005) 57(1) *Australian Journal of Psychology* 1–10.

Marsh, James (dir), *Man on the Wire: There's a Fine Line Between Genius and Madness* (DVD), Magnolia Home Entertainment, New York, 2008.

Martin, AW and Patsy Hardy, *Robert Menzies: A Life* (Vol 2: 1944–1978), Melbourne University Press, Melbourne, 1999.

Martin Report (Committee on the Future of Tertiary Education in Australia, *Tertiary Education in Australia: Report to the Australian Universities Commission*), Government Printer, Melbourne, 1964, (Vol II).

Marx, Karl, *Grundrisse*, Penguin, London, 1973.

Mason, Mark, 'Complexity Theory and the Philosophy of Education' (2008) 40(1) *Educational Philosophy and Theory* 4–18.

Mason, Mary Ann, Marc Goulden, Karie Frasch, and Sharon Page-Medrich, *Doctoral Student Career and Life Survey Findings, 2006–2007*, University of California Press, San Francisco, 2008.

Matthews, David, 'University student marketing spend up 22%', *Times Higher Education* (London), 10 February 2013: www.timeshighereducation.co.uk/story.asp?storycode=422601 at 3 March 2013.

—— 'Gender Equity and Rankings', *Times Higher Education*, 6 December 2012.

McCabe, Darren, *Power at Work: How Employees Reproduce the Corporate Machine*, Routledge, Abingdon, 2007.

McCracken, Grant, *Culture and Consumption: New Approaches to the Symbolic Character of Consumer Goods and Activities*, Indiana University Press, Bloomington, 1988.

McCulloch, A, 'The Student as Co-Producer: Learning From Public Administration About the Student–University Relationship' (2009) 34(2) *Studies in Higher Education* 171–83.

McCulloch, Grahame, 'Casualisation: "The Dirty Little Secret of University Expansion", Union to Tell Public Parliamentary Hearings into Insecure Employment Bill' (2013), National Tertiary Education Union, 24 May 2013. Retrieved 14 April 2014, from www.nteu.org.au/women/ article/Casualisation-%E2%80%9Cthe-dirty-little-secret-of-university-expansion%E2%80%9D,-union-to-tell-public-parliamentary-hearings-into-insecure-employment-bill--14739.

McGettigan, Andrew, *The Great University Gamble: Money, Markets and the Future of Higher Education*, Pluto, London, 2013.

McInnis, Craig, 'From Marginal to Mainstream Strategies: Responding to Student Diversity in Australian Universities' (2003) 38(4) *European Journal of Education* 387–400.

—— 'Signs of Disengagement? The Changing Undergraduate Experience in Australian Universities – Inaugural Professorial Lecture', Centre for the Study of Higher Education, University of Melbourne, Melbourne, 2001.

McKeough, Jillian and Andrew J Stewart, *Intellectual Property in Australia*, Butterworths, Chatswood, 3rd edn, 2004.

McKernan, Jim, 'The Idea of a University: Grey Philistines Taking Over Our Universities' (2011) 14(2) *College Quarterly* 6. Retrieved 24 April 2014, from www.collegequarterly.ca/2011-vol14-num02-spring/mckernan.html.

McLelland, Charles, *State, Society and University in Germany 1700–1914*, Cambridge University Press, Cambridge, 1980.

McNeillage, Amy, 'Uni bosses earn 10 times more than staff', *Sydney Morning Herald*, 25 August 2013. Retrieved 14 April 2014, from www.smh.com. au/national/tertiary-education/uni-bosses-earn-10-times-more-than-staff-20130824-2sihh.html.

McPhee, Peter, 'Evidence Free Policy: The Pyne Reforms to Higher Education', *Inside Story: Current Affairs and Culture from Australia and Beyond*, 1 September 2014. Retrieved 3 September 2014, from http://inside.org.au/policy-without-evidence-the-pyne-reforms-to-higher-education/.

McSherry, Corynne, *Who owns Academic Work? Battling for Control of Intellectual Property*, Harvard University Press, Cambridge Mass, 2001.

McWilliam, Erica and Paul Taylor, 'Teacher Im/material: Challenging the New Pedagogies of Instructional Design' (1998) 27(8) *Educational Researcher* 29–35.

Menzies, Heather and Janet Newson, 'Time, Stress and Intellectual Engagement in Academic Work: Exploring Gender Difference' (2008) 15(5) *Gender, Work and Organization* 504–22.

Menzies, Robert Gordon, Confidential Cabinet Notes, Australian Universities Commission – Legislation NAA/A463/1959/4214 National Archives of Australia, Canberra.

Merritt, Chris, 'Bathurst rethinks "drone" attack', *The Australian* (Sydney), 11 May 2012, 33.

Metcalfe, Amy and Sheila Slaughter 'The Differential Effects of Academic Capitalism on Women in the Academy' in Judith Glazer-Raymo (ed.), *Unfinished Agendas: New and Continuing Gender Challenges in Higher Education*, Johns Hopkins University Press, Baltimore, 2008.

Mewburn, Inger and P Thomson, 'Why do Academics Blog? An Analysis of Audiences, Purposes and Challenges' (2013) 38(8) *Studies in Higher Education* 1105–19.

Meyer, Katrina A, 'The "Virtual Face" of Institutions: Why Legislators and Other Outsiders View Higher Education as Aloof' (2008) 11 *The Internet and Higher Education* 178–85.

*Migration Regulations* 1994 (Cth).

Mitchell, Katharyne (ed), *Practising Public Scholarship: Experiences and Possibilities beyond the Academy*, Wiley-Blackwell, Chichester, 2008.

Molesworth, Mike, Richard Scullion, and Elizabeth Nixon (eds), *The Marketisation of Higher Education and the Student as Consumer*, Routledge, New York, 2011.

Monotti, Ann L and Sam Ricketson, *Universities and Intellectual Property: Ownership and Exploitation*, Oxford University Press, Oxford, 2003.

Moran, Michael, *The British Regulatory State*, Oxford University Press, Oxford, 2003.

*Moran v University College Salford (No 2)* [1994] ELR 187.

Morin, Edgar, *Seven Complex Lessons in Education for the Future*, (translated by Nidra Poller), UNESCO Paris, France, 1999.

Morley, Louise, 'The Micropolitics of Gender in the Learning Society' (2013a) 25(2) *Higher Education in Europe* 229–35.

—— 'The Rules of the Game: Women and the Leaderist Turn in Higher Education' (2013b) 25(1) *Gender and Education* 116–31.

—— *Quality and Power in Higher Education*, Society for Research into Higher Education & Open University Press, Philadelphia, 2003.

Morris, Katelin, 'Centre Helps Inventors Develop Products and Avoid Duplication', *The Australian Higher Education Supplement*, 11 January 1984.

Morris, Meaghan, Keynote Address at Moving Ideas and Research Policies: Australian Intellectuals in the Global Context Conference, Monash University, 22–23 July 2008; also published in J Fahey (ed.) (2009) 5(1) Special Section, *Around the Globe* 41–7.

Mowery, David and Bhaven Sampat, 'Universities in National Innovation Systems,' in Jan Fagerberg, David C Mowery and Richard R Nelson (eds), *The Oxford Handbook of Innovation*, OUP, Oxford, 2005, 209–39.

Mowles, Charles, 'Keeping Means and Ends in View: Linking Practical Judgement, Ethics and Emergence' (2012) 24 (5) *Journal of International Development* 544–55.

Murphy, Peter, 'The Rise and Fall of Our Bureaucratic Universities' (2013) 57(5) *Quadrant* 48–52.

Murray, KAH, I Clunies Ross et al., *Report of the Committee on Australian Universities,* Committee on Australian Universities, Commonwealth Offices, Melbourne, 1957.

Murray Report (Committee on Australian Universities, *Report of the Committee on Australian Universities*), Canberra, 1957.

Naidoo, Ravindah, 'Fields and Institutional Strategy: Bourdieu on the Relationship between Higher Education, Inequality and Society' (2004) 25(4) *British Journal of Sociology of Education* 457–71.

*National Code for of Practice for Registration Authorities and Providers of Education and Training to Overseas Students 2007* (Cth).

*National Tertiary Education Union and Bessant v Royal Melbourne Institute of Technology* [2013] FCA 451.

Newman, John HC, *The Idea of a University Defined and Illustrated in Nine Discourses Delivered to the Catholics of Dublin in Occasional Lectures and Essays Addressed to the Members of the Catholic University*, Holt, Rinehart and Winston, New York, 1966 [1852].

Niemelä-Nyrhinen, Jenni, 'Baby Boom Consumers and Technology: Shooting Down Stereotypes' (2007) 24(5) *Journal of Consumer Marketing* 305–12.

Niklasson, Lars, 'Quasi-Markets in Higher Education: A Comparative Analysis' (1996) 18(1) *Journal of Higher Education Policy and Management* 7–22.

Nixon, Elizabeth, Richard Scullin and Mike Molesworth, 'How Choice in Higher Education can create Conservative Learners' in Mike Molesworth, Richard Scullion, and Elizabeth Nixon (eds), *The Marketisation of Higher Education and the Student as Consumer*, Routledge, New York, 2011, 196–208.

Noonan, Peter, 'VET Funding in Australia and the Role of TAFE', Paper presented at TAFE Directors Association Conference, Sydney, 2 September 2014.

Nooteboom, Bart and Frédrique Six (eds), *The Trust Process in Organizations: Empirical Studies of the Determinants and the Process of Trust Development*, Edward Elgar, Cheltenham, 2003.

Norton, Andrew, *The Unbundling and Re-bundling of Higher Education*, Grattan Institute, Melbourne, 2013.

Norton, Lin, Alice Tilley, Stephen Newstead, and Arlene Frankly-Stokes, 'The Pressures of Assessment in Undergraduate Courses and their Effect on Student Behaviours' (2001) 26(3) *Assessment and Evaluation in Higher Education* 269–84.

NSW University of Technology Developmental Council Minutes, 11 December 1947, UNSW Archives, Sydney.

Nüssbaum, Martha, *Political Emotions: Why Love Matters For Justice*, University of Chicago Press, Chicago, 2013.

—— *Not for Profit: Why Democracy Needs the Humanities*, Princeton University Press, Princeton, 2010.

Obama, Barack, *The Audacity of Hope: Thoughts on Reclaiming the American Dream*, Barnes & Noble, New York, 2006.

O'Connor, James, *Fiscal Crisis of the State*, Transaction Publishers, New York, 1979.

OECD (Organisation for Economic Co-operation and Development), *Main Economic Indicators*, OECD, Paris, 2014.

—— *Education at a Glance*, OECD, Paris, 2013.

—— *Tertiary Education for the Knowledge Society* (Volume 1: Special Features: Governance, Funding, Quality and Volume 2: Special Features: Equity, Innovation, Labour Market, Internationalisation), OECD, Paris, 2008.

—— *The Knowledge-based Economy*, OECD, Paris, 1996.

—— *Policies for Higher Education in the 1980s*, Proceedings of the Intergovernmental Conference of the OECD, October 1981, OECD, Paris, 1983.

Office for Learning and Teaching, Department of Industry, Innovation, Science, Research and Tertiary Education (Australian Government), Internationalising the Australian Law Curriculum for Enhanced Global Legal Practice, Australian Government Office for Learning and Teaching, Canberra, 2012. Retrieved 28 September 2014, from www.olt.gov.au/resource-internationalising-australian-law-curriculum-enhanced-global-legal-practice-2012.

Öhrn, Elisabeth, Petra Angervall, Jan Gustafsson, Lisbeth Lundahl and Eva Nyström, 'Gender and Careeer in Academia', Paper presented at the Nordic Educational Research Congress in Trondheim Norway, 5–7 March, 2009.

Olssen, Mark, and Michael Peters, 'Neoliberalism, Higher Education and the Knowledge Economy: From the Free Market to Knowledge Capitalism' (2005) 20(3) *Journal of Education Policy* 313–45.

Opoku, Robert, Russell Abratt and Leyland Pitt, 'Communicating Brand Personality: Are the Websites Doing the Talking for the top South African Business Schools?' (2006) 14 *Brand Management* 20–39.

Page, Libby. 'Students and unions criticise wage hikes for vice-chancellors', *The Guardian*, 3 January 2014. Retrieved 8 January 2014, from www.theguardian.com/education/2014/jan/02/vice-chancellor-wage-increase-angers-students-unions.

Palmer, Nigel, 'Scope, Transparency and Style: System-Level Quality Strategies and the Student Experience in Australia' in Mahsood Shah and Sid Nair (eds), *External Quality Audit: Has it Improved Quality Assurance in Universities?* Woodhead Publishing, Oxford, 2013.

—— 'Development of the University Experience Survey: Report on Findings From Secondary Sources of Information' in Ali Radloff, Hamish Coates, Richard James and Kerri-Lee Krause (eds), *Report on the Development of the University Experience Survey*, Department of Education, Employment and Workplace Relations, Canberra, 2011.

Partridge, Perce H, 'Comment on the Social Role of Higher Education by S Encel' in Edward L Wheelwright (ed.), *Higher Education in Australia*, F W Cheshire, Melbourne, 1965.

Pearce, Dennis, Enid Campbell and Don Harding, *Australian Law Schools: A Discipline Assessment for the Commonwealth Tertiary Education Commission*, Australian Government Publishing Service, Canberra, 1987 (*Pearce Report*).

Pearson, Christine M and Christine Porath, 'On the Nature, Causes and Remedies of Workplace Incivility: No Time for "Nice"? Think Again' (2005) 19(1) *Academy of Management Executive* 7–18.

Percy, Alisa, Michele Scoufis, Sharon Parry, Allan Goody, Margaret Hicks, Ian Macdonald, Kay Martinez, Nick Szorenyi-Reischl, Yoni Ryan, Sandra Wills and Lynn Sheridan, *The RED Report – Recognition, Enhancement, Development – The Contribution of Sessional Teachers to Higher Education*, 2008. Retrieved 11 October 2013, from www.olt.gov.au/resource-red-report-sessional-teachers-unsw-2008.

Peters, Michael, 'The University in the Knowledge Economy' (2002) 17 *Arena* 137–52.

Peters, Michael and Ergin Bulut (eds), *Cognitive Capitalism, Education and Digital Labour*, Peter Lang, New York, 2011.

Petersen, Eva B and Bronwyn Davies, 'In/Difference in the Neoliberalised University' (2010) 3(2) *Learning and Teaching: The International Journal of Higher Education in the Social Sciences* 93–109.

Pillay, Soma, Rom Kluvers, Subhash Abhayawansa and Vranic Vedran, 'An Exploratory Study into Work/Family Balance within the Australian Higher Education Sector' (2013) 32(2) *Higher Education Research and Development* 228–43.

Pitman, Tim, 'Is Student Activism Dying in Australia's Universities?', *The Conversation*, 9 January 2014. Retrieved 11 February 2014, from https://theconversation.com/is-student-activism-dying-in-australias-universities-20970.

Plato, 'Apology' in *The Trial and Death of Socrates* (trans FJ Church), Macmillan, London, 1956, 33–78.

Pocock, Barbara, *The Work/Life Collision: What Work is Doing to Australians and What to do about It*, The Federation Press, Annandale, 2003.

Polanyi, Michael, *The Logic of Liberty: Reflections and Rejoinders*, Routledge, London, 1951.

Pomeroy, John, 'Morale on the Home Front in Australia during the Second World War', PhD thesis, University of Sydney, Sydney, 1995.

Preiss, Benjamin, 'La Trobe Cuts 45 Jobs in Humanities', *The Age*, 20 June 2012. Retrieved 11 February 2013, from www.theage.com.au/national/education/la-trobe-cuts-45-jobs-in-humanities-20120620-20o5s.html.

Pringle, Rosemary, *Secretaries: Sexuality, Power and Work*, Allen and Unwin, Sydney, 1988.

QS Top Universities. Retrieved 28 September 2014, from www.topuniversities.com/university-rankings/world-university-rankings.

*R v Aston University Senate; ex parte Roffey* (1969) 2 WLR 1418.

Ramsden, P, 'A Better Student Experience', Paper presented at Group Student Experience Conference, British Library, London, 17 November 2009.

Rankin, Sara, 'Tired of Talking: A Call for Clear Strategies for Legal Education Reform: Moving Beyond the Discussion of Good Ideas to the Real Transformation of Law Schools' (2012) 10 *Seattle Journal of Social Justice* 11–47.

Raue, Tom, 'My Wonderful Day', *Honi Soit*, 15 May 2013. Retrieved 6 January 2014, from www.honisoit.com/2013/05/my-wonderful-day/.

Readings, Bill, *The University in Ruins*, Harvard University Press, Cambridge Mass, 1996.

Reay, Diana, '"Dim Dross": Marginalized Women both Inside and Outside the Academy' (2000) 23(1) *Women's Studies International Forum* 13–21.

Redden, Guy, 'Publish and Flourish, or Perish: RAE, ERA, RQF, and Other Acronyms for Infinite Human Resourcefulness' (2008) 11(4) *M/C (Media & Culture) Journal*. Retrieved 24 April 2014, from http://journal.media-culture. org.au/index.php/mcjournal/article/view/44.

Reid, Janice, 'Menzies, Whitlam and Social Justice: A View From the Academy', *Sir Robert Menzies Oration on Higher Education,* 2012. Retrieved 14 April 2014, from http://www.unimelb.edu.au/speeches/Docs/menzies-oration-2012.pdf.

Reiger, Kerreen, 'The Gender Dynamics of Organizations: A Historical Account', in Jill Blackmore and Jane Kenway (eds), *Gender Matters in Educational Administration and Policy: A Feminist Introduction*, Falmouth Press, London, 1993.

Reiger, Kerreen, Toni Schofield and Margaret Peters, 'Innovating Universities: Technocratic Reform and Beyond' in Renu Agarwal, Willem Selen, Goran Roos and Roy Green, *The Handbook of Service Innovation*, Springer-Verlag, London, 2015.

Rhee, Robert J, 'On Legal Education and Reform: One View Formed from Diverse Perspectives', 2011. Retrieved 25 March 2014, from http://ssrn.com/abstract=1724398.

Richardson, Paul, 'Introductory Textbooks and Plagiarism in Higher Education: A Case Study from Economics', paper presented at the Annual Meeting of the American Educational Research Association, New Orleans LA, 1–5 April 2002.

Rini, Adriene, 'Models and Values: Why did New Zealand Philosophy Departments Stop Hiring Women Philosophers?' in Katrina Hutchison and Fiona Jenkins (eds), *Women in Philosophy: What Needs to Change?* OUP, Oxford, 2013.

Ritzer, George, McDonaldization: The Reader, Pine Forge Press, Thousand Oaks, CA, 2010.

—— 'Enchanting McUniversity: Toward a Spectacularly Irrational University Quotidian' in Dennis Hayes and Robin Wynyard (eds), *The McDonaldization of Higher Education*, Bergin & Garvey, Westport, CT, 2002, 19–41.

—— *The McDonaldization of Society: New Century Edition*, Pine Forge Press, Thousand Oaks, CA, 2nd edn 2000.

Roberts, Peter, 'Rereading Lyotard: Knowledge, Commodification and Higher Education' (1998) Electronic Journal of Sociology. Retrieved 15 September 2014, from www.sociology.org/content/vol003.003/roberts.html.

Robertson, Susan, 'Globalisation, Rescaling of National Education System and Citizenship Regimes' in K Roth and N Burbules (eds), *Changing Notions of Citizenship Education in Contemporary National States*, Sense Publishers, Rotterdam, 2007.

Robins, Kevin and Frank Webster, *Times of the Technoculture*, Routledge, London, 1998.

Robinson, Richard and Gary Rodan, 'Economic Restructuring and the Reform of the Higher Education System' (1990) 25(1) *Australian Journal of Political Science* 21–36.

Rochford, Francine, 'The Relationship Between the Student and University' (1998) 3(1) *Australian and New Zealand Journal of Law and Education* 28–48.

Rosa, Hartmut, *Social Acceleration: A New Theory of Modernity*, Columbia University Press, Columbia, 2013.

Rose, Nikolas, *Powers of Freedom: Reframing Political Thought*, Cambridge UP, Cambridge, 1999.

—— 'The Death of the Social? Refiguring the Territory of Government' (1996) 25 *Economy and Society* 327–56.

—— *Governing the Soul: The Shaping of the Private Self*, Routledge, New York, 1990.

Ross-Smith, Anne, Colleen Chesterman, and Margaret Peters, '"Not Doable Jobs!" Exploring Senior Women's Attitudes to Academic Leadership Roles' (2005) 28 *Women's Studies International Forum* 163–80.

Rowe, AP, *If the Gown Fits*, Melbourne University Press, Melbourne, 1960.

Rowe, Mary, 'Saturn's Rings: A Study of the Minutiae of Sexism Which Maintain Discrimination and Inhibit Affirmative Action Results in Corporations and Non-Profit Institutions', Graduate and Professional Education of Women, American Association of University Women, Washington DC, 1974, 1–9.

Rowlands, Julie, 'Academic Boards: Less Intellectual and more Academic Capital in Higher Education Governance? (2013) 38(9) *Studies in Higher Education* 1274–89.

Russell, Conrad, *Academic Freedom*, Routledge, London, 1993.

Ryan, Allen, *On Politics* (Vol 2), Liverwright, New York, 2012.

Salazar, Jose, and Peodair Leihy, 'Keeping Up with Coordination: From Clark's Triangle to Microcosmographia' (2011) 38(1) *Studies in Higher Education* 53–70.

Sappey, Jenny and Greg Bamber, 'Change in Universities and Some Consequences for Academics', Proceedings of the 21st Australia and New Zealand Academy of Management (ANZAM) Conference – Managing Our Intellectual and Social Capital, 4–7 December 2007, Promaco Conventions, Canning Bridge WA, 1–15.

Sattler, Sebastian, Peter Graeff and Sebastian Willen, 'Explaining the Decision to Plagiarise: An Empirical Test of the Interplay between Rationality, Norms, and Opportunity' (2013) 34 *Deviant Behaviour* 444–63.

Sauntson, Helen, and Liz Morrish, 'Vision, Values and International Excellence: The "Products" that University Mission Statements Sell to Students' in Mike Molesworth, Richard Scullion and Elizabeth Nixon (eds), *The Marketisation of Higher Education and the Student as Consumer*, Routledge, New York, 2011, 73–85.

Sawer, Marian, 'Populism and Public Choice in Australia and Canada: Turning Equality-seekers into "Special Interests"' in Marian Sawer and Barry Hindess (eds), *Us and Them: Anti-elitism in Australia*, Academy of Social Sciences in Australia & Curtin University of Technology, Perth, 2004.

Sawer, Marian and Barry Hindess (eds), *Us and Them: Anti-elitism in Australia*, Academy of Social Sciences in Australia & Curtin University of Technology, Perth, 2004.

Schiebinger, Londa and Martina Schraudner, 'Interdisciplinary Approaches to Achieving Gendered Innovations in Science, Medicine, and Engineering' (2011) 36(2) *Interdisciplinary Science Reviews* 154–67.

Schivelbusch, Wolfgang, *The Railway Journey: The Industrialization of Time and Space in the Nineteenth Century*, Berg, London, 1986.

Schon, D, *The Reflective Practitioner: How Professionals Think in Action*, Basic Books, New York, 1983.

Schrecker, Ellen W, *No Ivory Tower: McCarthyism and the Universities*, Oxford University Press, Oxford, 1986.

Scott, G, *Accessing the Student Voice: Using CEQuery to Identify what Retains Students and Promotes Engagement in Productive Learning in Australian Higher Education*, Final Report, Department of Education, Science and Training, Commonwealth of Australia, Canberra, 2006.

Scott, Geoff, Hamish Coates and Michelle Anderson, *Learning Leaders: Academic Leadership Capabilities for Australian Higher Education*, ACER, Melbourne, 2011.

——'Learning Leaders in Times of Change: Academic Leadership Capabilities for Australian Higher Education', Australian Council for Educational Research, May 2008. Retrieved 14 April 2014, from http://research.acer.edu.au/higher_education/3.

Scott, Joan Wallach, 'Knowledge, Power and Academic Freedom' (2009) 76(2) *Social Research* 451–80.

Scullion, Richard, Mike Molesworth and Elizabeth Nixon, 'Arguments, Responsibility and What is to be Done about Marketisation' in Mike Molesworth, Richard Scullion and Elizabeth Nixon (eds), *The Marketisation of Higher Education and the Student as Consumer*, Routledge, New York, 2011, 227–36.

Seddon, Terri, *Educators, Professionalism and Politics: Global Transitions, National Spaces and Professional Projects, World Yearbook of Education 2013*, Routledge, Abingdon Oxon, 2013.

Seddon, Terri, Dawn Bennett, Janette Bobis, Sude Bennett, Neil Harrison, Sue Shore, Erica Smith and Philip Chan, *Living in a 2.2 World: ERA, Capacity Building and the Topography of Australian Educational Research*, ACDE, Deakin ACT, 2012. Retrieved 24 April 2014, from www.aare.edu.au/data/AARE_ACDE_Report_Final_130313.pdf.

Segal, David, 'What They Don't Teach Law Students: Lawyering', *The New York Times*, 9 November 2011. Retrieved 25 March 2014, from www.nytimes.com/2011/11/20/business/after-law-school-associates-learn-to-be-lawyers.html?pagewanted=all&_r=0.

Sennett, Richard, *The Corrosion of Character The Personal Consequences of Work in the New Capitalism,* Norton, New York, 1998.

Serle, Geoffrey, *The Golden Age: A History of the Colony of Victoria 1851–1861*, Melbourne University Press, Melbourne, 1963.

Shah, Mahsood, Ione Lewis and Robert Fitzgerald, 'The Renewal of Quality Assurance in Australian Higher Education: The Challenge of Balancing Academic Rigour, Equity and Quality Outcomes' (2011) 17(3) *Quality in Higher Education* 265–78.

Shapper, J and S Mayson. 'Managerialism, Internationalisation, Taylorisation and the Deskilling of Academic Work: Evidence from an Australian University' in Peter Ninnes and Meeri Hellstén (eds), *Internationalising Higher Education*, Springer-Verlag, New York, 2005.

Sharrock, Geoff, 'Four Management Agendas for Australian Universities' (2012) 34(3) *Journal of Higher Education Policy and Management* 323–37.

Shattock, Michael, *The UGC and the Management of British Universities*, Society for Research into Higher Education and Open University Press, Bristol, 1994.

Sherington, Geoffrey and Hannah Forsyth, 'Ideas of Liberal Education: An Essay on Elite and Mass Higher Education' in Luciano Boschiero, *On the Purpose of a University Education*, Australian Scholarly Publishing, Melbourne, 2012.

Shirky, Clay, 'Clay Shirky's Internet Writings: Napster, Udacity, and the Academy', 2012. Retrieved 17 December 2013, from www.shirky.com/weblog/2012/11/napster-udacity-and-the-academy/.

Shore, Cris and Laura McLauchlan, '"Third Mission" Activities, Commercialisation and Academic Entrepreneurs' (2012) 20 *Social Anthropology* 267–86.

Shore, Cris and Susan Wright, 'Audit Culture and Anthropology: Neo-Liberalism in British Higher Education' (1999) 5(4) *The Journal of the Royal Anthropological Institute* 557–75.

*Simjanoski v La Trobe University* [2004] VSC 180.

Simmel, Georg, 'The Metropolis' in KH Wolff (ed.), *The Sociology of Georg Simmel*, Free Press, New York, 1950.

Simmonds, Carol, 'WA College Wants to Set up Specialised Research Park', *The Australian Higher Education Supplement*, 11 December 1985.

Simmons, Geoffrey J, '"i-Branding": Developing the Internet as a Branding Tool' (2007) 25 *Marketing Intelligence and Planning* 544–62.

Sitkin, Sim and Darryl Stickel, 'The Road to Hell: The Dynamics of Distrust in an Era of Quality' in Roderick Kramer and Tom Tyler (eds), *Trust in Organizations: Frontiers of the Theory and Research*, Thousand Oaks, California, 1996.

Skolnik, Michael L, 'Quality Assurance in Higher Education as a Political Process', (2010) 22(1) *Higher Education Management and Policy* 1–19.

Slater, Don, *Consumer Culture and Modernity*, Polity Press, Cambridge Massachusetts, 1997.

Slaughter, Sheila and Jim Leslie, *Academic Capitalism: Politics, Policies, and the Entrepreneurial University*, Johns Hopkins University Press, Baltimore, 1997.

Slaughter, Sheila and Gary Rhoades, *Academic Capitalism and the New Economy: Markets, State, and Higher Education*, Baltimore, Johns Hopkins University Press, 2004.

Small, Helen, *The Value of the Humanities*, Oxford University Press, Oxford, 2013.

Smart, Barry, '(Dis)Interring Postmodernism or a Critique on the Political Economy of Consumer Choice' in Jason L Powell and Tim Owen (eds), *Reconstructing Postmodernism: Critical Debates,* Nova Science Publishers, 2007, 167–86.

Smith, Adam, *An Inquiry into the Nature and Causes of the Wealth of Nations*, 1776. (Reprinted in RH Campbell, AS Skinner, and WB Todd (eds), *Adam Smith: An Inquiry into the Nature and Causes of the Wealth of Nations* (Glasgow Edition of *The Works and Correspondence of Adam Smith*), Clarendon, Oxford, 1976.

Snow, CP, *The Two Cultures: And a Second Look*, Cambridge University Press, Cambridge, 1964.

Song, Ji Hee and George M Zinkhan, 'Determinants of Perceived Web Site Interactivity' (2008) 72 *Journal of Marketing* 99–113.

Soyfer, Valery N, 'New Light on the Lysenko Era' (1989) 339 *Nature* 415–20.

Spence, Alex, 'Asia the prize as City lawyer seals deal', *The Times* (London), 29 June 2012, 39.

Stacey, Ralph, *Complexity and Organizational Reality: Uncertainty and the Needs to Rethink Management after the Collapse of Investment Capitalism*, Routledge, London, 2010.

Stacey, Ralph and David Griffin (eds), *A Complexity Perspective on Researching Organizations: Taking Experience Seriously*, Routledge, London, 2005.

Stanford, Jon, 'International Trade in Education' in Roselyn R Gillespie and Colin B Collins (eds), *Education as an International Commodity,* Australia and New Zealand Comparative and International Education Society, St Lucia, 1986, Vol 1, 39–49.

Stanton, John, 'Research Takes Commercial Turn at University', *The Australian Higher Education Supplement*, 24 October 1984.

Stolz, Ingo, Darwin Hendel and Aaron S Horn, 'Ranking of Rankings: Benchmarking Twenty-Five Higher Education Ranking Systems in Europe' (2010) 60 *European Higher Education: The International Journal of Higher Education and Educational Planning* 507–28.

Strum, Philippa, 'Leadership and Equality: A Social Scientist at Work' in Michael Beschloss and Thomas Cronin (eds), *Essays in Honor of James McGregor Burns*, N J Prentice Hall, Englewood Cliffs, 1989, 181–205.

Sugarman, David, 'Legal Theory, the Common Law Mind and the Making of the Textbook Tradition' in William Twining (ed.), *Legal Theory and Common Law*, Blackwell, Oxford, 1986, 26–62.

Sunstein, Cass, *Infotopia*, Basic Books, New York, 2006.

Symes, Colin, 'Selling Futures: A New Image for Australian Universities?' (1996) 21 *Studies in Higher Education* 133–47.

Tamboukou, Maria, 'Truth telling in Foucault and Arendt: Parrhesia, the Pariah and Academics in Dark times' (2012) 27(6) *Journal of Education Policy* 849–65.

Tannock, Peter D, *The Government of Education in Australia: The Origins of Federal Policy*, University of Western Australia Press, Nedlands, WA, 1975.

Teixeira, Pedro Nuno and David D Dill, *Public Vices, Private Virtues? Assessing the Effects of Marketization in Higher Education*, Sense Publishers, Rotterdam, 2011.

Teixeira, Pedro, Ben Jongbloed, David Dill and Alberto Amaral (eds), *Markets in Higher Education: Rhetoric or Reality?* Kluwer, Dordrecht, 2004.

Temple, Paul, 'University Branding' (2011) 15(4) *Perspectives: Policy and Practice in Higher Education* 113–6.

*TEQSA Higher Education Standards Framework (Threshold Standards) 2011* (Cth).

*TEQSA Regulatory Risk Framework* (Cth).

*Tertiary Education Quality and Standards Agency Act 2011* (Cth).

Thornton, Margaret, *Privatising the Public University: The Case of Law*, Routledge, Abingdon Oxon, 2012.

—— 'An Inconstant Affair: Feminism and the Legal Academy' in Martha Albertson Fineman (ed.), *Transcending the Boundaries of Law: Generations of Feminism and Legal Theory*, Cavendish-Routledge, London, 2011, 25–39.

—— *Academic Un-Freedom in the New Knowledge Economy* in Angela Brew and Lisa Lucas (eds), *Academic Research and Researcher*, Open University Press, London, 2009, 19–34.

—— 'The Retreat from the Critical: Social Science Research in the Corporatised University' (2008) 50(1) *Australian Universities Review* 5–10.

—— 'The Dissolution of the Social in the Legal Academy' (2006) 25 *Australian Feminist Law Journal* 3–18.

—— 'The Demise of Diversity in Legal Education: Globalisation and the New Knowledge Economy' (2001) *International Journal of the Legal Profession* 37–56.

Thornton, Margaret and Trish Luker, 'Age Discrimination in Turbulent Times' (2010) 19(2) *Griffith Law Review* 141–71.

Tierney, William, *The Impact of Culture on Organizational Decision-Making: Theory and Practice in Higher Education*, Stylus Publishing, Sterling, 2008.

—— *Trust and the Public Good*, Peter Lang, New York, 2006.

Times Higher Education World University Rankings. Retrieved 28 September 2014, from www.timeshighereducation.co.uk/world-university-rankings/.

Tombs, Steve and Dave Whyte (eds), *Unmasking the Crimes of the Powerful: Scrutinizing States and Corporations*, Peter Long, New York, 2003.

Torlakovic, Alma, 'Strikers Defy Management to Shut Down Sydney University' *Socialist Alternative Magazine*, 8 March 2013. Retrieved 6 January 2014, from www.sa.org.au/index.php?option=com_k2&view=item&id=7680:strikers-defy-management-to-shut-down-sydney-university&Itemid=392.

Torr, Rachel, 'What's Wrong with Aspiring to what Really Happened in Academic Feminism's Recent Past? A Response to Clare Hemmings' "Telling Feminist Stories"' (2006) 8(1) *Feminist Theory* 59–67.

Tosey, Paul, 'Teaching on the Edge of Chaos: Complexity Theory, Learning Systems and Enhancement', Working Paper, School of Education Studies, University of Surrey, Guilford, 2002.

Trinca, Helen 'Professor Finds an Entrepreneurial Approach Pays Off', *The Australian Higher Education Supplement*, 11 January 1984.

Trounson, Andrew, 'La Trobe spares Indonesian but 37 jobs to go in Humanities and Social Sciences', *The Australian*, 11 August 2012.

Trowler, Paul, *Cultures and Change in Higher Education: Theories and Practices*, Palgrave MacMillan, Basingstoke, 2008.

Tsui, Amy, 'Transforming Student Learning: Undergraduate Curriculum Reform at the University of Hong Kong' in Paul Blackmore, Camille B Kandiko, *Strategic Curriculum Change: Global Trends in Universities*, Routledge, Abingdon Oxon, 2012.

Twining, William, 'Pericles and the Plumber' (1967) 83 *Law Quarterly Review* 396–426.

UNESCO Institute for Statistics, *UNESCO Global Education Digest: Comparing Education Statistics Across the World*, UNESCO, Montreal, 2009.

Universitas 21, *Ranking of Higher Education Systems*, Melbourne Institute, Melbourne, 2012.

Universities Australia, *A Smarter Australia: An Agenda for Australia 2013–2016*, Universities Australia, Canberra, 2012.

—— *Submission to the Review of Australian Higher Education*, Universities Australia, Canberra, 2008a.

—— 'Submission to the Review of the Australian Broadcasting Corporation and the Special Broadcasting Service', Universities Australia, Canberra, 2008b.

—— *Student to Teacher Ratio for Academic Staff with a Teaching Function*, 2006. Retrieved 16 May 2013, from www.universitiesaustralia.edu.au/resources/404/388.

Universities Commission, 'Minutes of Conference with the Vice-Chancellors of Australia held at 119 Phillip Street Sydney 4–6 September 1946' in Universities Commission NAA/SP36/21, National Archives of Australia, Canberra, 1946.

*Universities in the Knowledge Economy*, 8 April 2014. Retrieved 14 April 2014, from http://unike.au.dk.

'Universities put on notice over IP rights', *Lawyers Weekly*, 9 July 2009. Retrieved 18 October 2011, from www.lawyersweekly.com.au/blogs/top_stories/archive/2009/09/07/universities-put-on-notice-over-ip-rights.aspx.

*University of Ceylon v Fernando* (1960) 1 All ER 631.

University of Melbourne, *Academic Performance Policy*, 3 July 2009. Retrieved 14 April 2014, from https://policy.unimelb.edu.au/MPF1024.

—— *Academic Progress Review Procedure*, 3 July 2009. Retrieved 14 April 2014, from https://policy.unimelb.edu.au/MPF1025.

*University of Western Australia v Gray* [2008] FCA 498.

University World News, *Special Report: Women in Higher Education,* Issue 0098. Retrieved 14 April 2014, from www.universityworldnews.com/publications/ archives.php?mode=archive&pub=1&issueno=98&format=html.

Urciuoli, Bonnie, 'Neoliberal Education: Preparing Students for the New Workplace', in Carol J Greenhouse (ed.), *Ethnographies of Neoliberalism,* University of Pennsylvania Press, Philadelphia, 2010, 162–176.

Van der Kolk, Bessel A, 'The Compulsion to repeat the Trauma: Reenactment, Revictimization, and Masochism' (1989) 12(2) *Psychiatric Clinics of North America* 389–411.

Van Witteloostuijn, Arjen and Gjalt de Jong, 'The Evolution of Higher Education Rules: Evidence for an Ecology of Law' (2007) 73 *International Review of Administrative Sciences* 235–55.

Varnham, Sally and Patty Kamvounias, 'Getting What They Paid For: Consumer Rights of Students in Higher Education' (2006) 15 *Griffith Law Review* 306–32.

Veblen, Thorstein, *The Higher Learning in America: A Memorandum on the Conduct of Universities by Business Men*, Sagamore Press, New York, 1957 [1918].

Veness, Kirsten, 'Vice-Chancellor flees Uni mob via underground tunnels',*ABC News,* 27 Aug 27 2012. Retrieved 6 January 2014, from www.abc.net. au/news/2012-08-26/vice-chancellor-escapes-uni-mob-through-tunnel-network/4223688.

Vercellone, Carlo, 'From Formal Subsumption to General Intellect: Elements of a Marxist Reading of the Thesis of Cognitive Capitalism' (2007) 15 *Historical Materialism* 13–36.

Victorian Ombudsman, *Investigation into how Universities deal with International Students*, Melbourne, 2011.

—— *Investigation into an Allegation of Improper Conduct within RMIT's School of Engineering (TAFE) – Aerospace*, Melbourne, 2010.

Vidovich, Lesley, 'Quality Assurance in Australian Higher Education: Globalisation and "Steering at a Distance"' (2002) 43(3) *Higher Education* 391–408.

Vidovich, Lesley and Jan Currie, 'Governance and Trust in Higher Education' (2010) 36(1) *Studies in Higher Education* 43–56.

Vidovich, Lesley and Roger Slee, 'Bringing Universities to Account? Exploring Some Global and Local Tensions' (2010) 16 (5) *Journal of Education Policy* 431–53.

Virno, Paolo, 'The Ambivalence of Disenchantment' in Paolo Virno and Michael Hardt (eds), *Radical Thought in Italy: A Potential Politics*, University of Minnesota Press, Minneapolis, 1996.

VPSEC (Victorian Post-Secondary Education Commission), *Report of Review of Legal Education in Victoria*, Melbourne, 1991.

Wade, HWR, 'Judicial Control of Universities' (1969) 85 *Law Quarterly Review* 468–70.

Wajcman, Judith, *Managing Like a Man: Women and Men in Corporate Management*, Allen & Unwin, Sydney, 1999.

Wall, Howard J, 'Don't Get Skewed Over by Journal Rankings' (2009) 9(1) *BE (Berkeley Electronic) Journal of Economic Analysis & Policy* 1–10.

Waring, Marilyn, *Counting for Nothing: What Men Value and What Women are Worth*, Allen & Unwin, Sydney, 1988.

Watts, Don, 'The Private Potential of Australian Higher Education' in David R Jones and John Anwyl (eds), *Privatizing Higher Education: A New Australian Issue*, Melbourne Centre for the Study of Higher Education, Melbourne, 1987.

Weick, Karl, *Sensemaking in Organizations*, Sage, London, 1995.

Welch, Anthony, 'Academic Salaries Massification, and the Rise of an Underclass in Australia' in Phillip Altbach, Liz Reisberg, Maria Yudkevich, Gregory Androushchak, and Ivan Pacheco (eds), *Paying the Professoriate: A Global Comparison of Compensation and Contracts,* Routledge, London, 2012.

Weller, M, 'A Pedagogy of Abundance' (2011) *Spanish Journal of Pedagogy* 223–36.

Wentworth, WC, 'New South Wales Constitution Bill' in *Speeches in the Legislative Council*, Parliament of New South Wales, Sydney, 16 August 1853.

Whitchurch, Celia, *Reconstructing Identities in Higher Education: The Rise of Third Space Professionals*, Routledge, London, 2013.

Wildavski, Ben, Andrew Kelly and Kevin Carey (eds), *Reinventing Higher Education: The Promise of Innovation*, Harvard Education Press, Cambridge Massachusetts, 2011.

Wilks, Vicky, *Survey Reveals Hidden High Stress Levels and Long-Hours Culture at Universities*, University and College Union, 4 October 2012. Retrieved 8 January 2014, from www.ucu.org.uk/index.cfm?articleid=6344.

Williams, Joanna, 'Constructing Consumption: What Media Representations reveal about Today's Students' in Mike Molesworth, Richard Scullion, and Elizabeth Nixon (eds), *The Marketisation of Higher Education and the Student as Consumer*, Routledge, New York, 2011, 170–82.

Williams, Raymond, *Marxism and Literature*, OUP, Oxford, 1977.

Williams, Raymond and Robin Gable (eds), *Resources of Hope: Culture, Democracy, Socialism*, Verso, London, 1989.

Wimshurst, Kerry, Richard Wortley, Merrelyn Bates, and Troy Allard, 'The Impact of Institutional Factors on Student Academic Results: Implications for 'Quality' in Universities' (2006) 25(2) *Higher Education Research and Development* 131–45.

Withers, Glenn, 'Deregulation is De Rigueur', *Campus Review*, 21 October 2013, 16.

—— 'Knowledge Production in Australia', *Campus Review*, 3 August 2009, 11.

Witteloostuijn, Arjen van and Gjalt de Jong 'The Evolution of Higher Education Rules: Evidence for an Ecology of Law' (2007) 73 *International Review of Administrative Sciences* 235–55.

Woolf, Harry, 'An Enquiry into LSE's links with Libya and Lessons to be Learned', October 2011. Retrieved 14 April 2014, from http://woolflse.com/dl/woolf-lse-report.pdf (*The Woolf Inquiry*).

Woolf, Sue, 'Open Letter to the Vice Chancellor and University', 3 May 2013, National Tertiary Education Union. Retrieved 11 February 2014, from www.nteu.org.au/sydney/article/Open-Letter-to-the-Vice-Chancellor-and-University---Sue-Woolf-14576.

World Bank, *World Development Reports*, The World Bank, Washington DC, 1998-99. Retrieved 14 April 2014, from http://web.worldbank.org/WBSITE/EXTERNAL/EXTDEC/EXTRESEARCH/EXTWDRS/0,,contentMDK:22293493~pagePK:478093~piPK:477627~theSitePK:477624,00.html.

Wylie, Alison, 'Feminist Philosophy of Science: Standpoint Matters,' APA Presidential Address (2012) 86(2) *Proceedings and Addresses of the APA* 46–76.

*X v University of Western Sydney (No. 3)* [2013] NSWSC 1329.

Yellen, David, 'The Impact of Rankings and Rules on Legal Education Reform' (2013) 45 *Connecticut Law Review* 1389–407.

Zabrodska, Katerina, Sheridan Linnell, Cath Laws, and Bronwyn Davies, 'Bullying as Intra-Active Process in Neoliberal Universities' (2011) 17 *Qualitative Inquiry* 709–19.

Zimbardo, Philip, *RSA Animate: The Secret Powers of Time*, 2010. Retrieved 23 May 2013, from http://comment.rsablogs.org.uk/2010/05/24.

Zimbardo, Philip and John Boyd, *The Time Paradox: The New Psychology of Time*, Rider, London, 2008.

Zipin, Lew, 'Situating University Governance in the Ethico-Emotive Ground Tone of Post/late Times' in Jill Blackmore, Marie Brennan and Lew Zipin (eds), *Repositioning University Governance and Academic Work*, Sense Publishers, Netherlands, 2010.

Zobel, Joel and Margaret Hamilton, 'Managing Student Plagiarism in Large Academic Departments' (2002) 45(2) *Australian Universities Review* 23–30.

Zwagerman, Sean, 'The Scarlet P: Plagiarism, Panopticism, and the Rhetoric of Academic Integrity' (2008) 59(4) *College Composition and Communication,* 676–710.

www.ingramcontent.com/pod-product-compliance
Lightning Source LLC
Chambersburg PA
CBHW061241270326
41928CB00041B/3360